GREAT EVENTS OF BIBLE TIMES

GREAT EVENTS OF BIBLE TIMES

NEW PERSPECTIVES ON THE PEOPLE, PLACES AND HISTORY OF THE BIBLICAL WORLD

Doubleday & Company, Inc.
Garden City, New York

Great Events of Bible Times
was conceived, edited and designed by
Marshall Editions Limited
170 Piccadilly
London W1V 9DD

First published in the United States of America in
1987
by Doubleday & Co Inc.
New York, Toronto, London, Paris

Doubleday
666 Fifth Avenue
New York, NY 10103

Published by The Reader's Digest Association,
Inc., with permission of Doubleday, a Division of
the Bantam Doubleday Dell Publishing Group
Inc., and Marshall Editions Limited.

Library of Congress Cataloging-in-Publication
Data

Great events of Bible times.

    Bibliography: p.
    Includes indexes.
    1. Bible—History of Biblical events. 2. Bible—
History of contemporary events.
BS635.2.G68 1987   220.9′5   86–24155
ISBN 0–385–23678–6

Originated by Reprocolor Llovet SA,
Barcelona, Spain
Typeset by Servis Filmsetting Limited,
Manchester, UK

In the preparation of *Great Events of Bible Times*,
the publishers and authors used quotations from
The New Jerusalem Bible, © 1985 by Darton,
Longman & Todd Ltd and Doubleday &
Company, Inc.

The publishers and authors acknowledge the help
of Tony Livesey and Amélie Kuhrt in the making
of this book.

Editor	**James Harpur**
Assistant Editor	**Jazz Wilson**
Managing Editor	**Ruth Binney**
Art Director	**Paul Wilkinson**
Art Assistant	**Richard McAndrew**
Picture Research	**Sarah Wergan**
Production	**Janice Storr**
Chief Illustrator	**Harry Clow**

Contributors

Great Events of Bible Times

Consultant

Professor B.M. Metzger, George L. Collord
Professor of New Testament Language and
Literature, Emeritus, at Princeton
Theological Seminary, Princeton, New
Jersey.

One of the world's best known scholars on
the text of the New Testament, Professor
Metzger is the author or editor of 25 books,
several of which have been translated into
foreign languages.

Old Testament

Consultant

Dr David Goldstein, Curator of Hebrew
Books and Manuscripts at the British
Library.

Dr Goldstein was formerly the President
of the Jewish Historical Society of England
and was founding editor, and co-editor,
of the Littman Library of Jewish Civilisation.
His books include: *Jewish Poets of Spain*
(1971), *The Religion of the Jews* (1978), *Jewish
Folklore and Legend* (1980) and *The Ashkenazi
Haggadah* (1985).

Writers

Nicole Douek, BA, Tutor in Egyptology
and Ancient Near Eastern history at
University College, London.

Peter James, BA, postgraduate researcher in
Philistine history at University College,
London.

Margaret Oliphant, BA, Visiting Lecturer on
Near Eastern archaeology at the British
Museum.

Sue Rollin, MA, Tutor in Ancient Near
Eastern history at University College,
London.

New Testament

Consultant and writer

John Ferguson, MA, BD, FIAL, formerly
President of Selly Oak Colleges,
Birmingham, England.

John Ferguson is a New Testament and
Classics scholar with over 50 books to his
name. He was first Dean of Arts at Britain's
Open University and has held Chairs in
various universities including, in the USA,
those of Florida and Minnesota. Among his
writings are the well-known *Religions of the
Roman Empire* (1971) and *Jesus in the Tide of
Time* (1980).

Writers

The Rev Dr William S. Campbell, Head of
Religious Studies at Westhill College, Selly
Oak, Birmingham, England, and a minister
of the United Reformed Church.

The Right Rev Patrick Kalilombe, Third
World Lecturer at Selly Oak Colleges,
Birmingham, England, and a Roman
Catholic bishop.

Professor Frances Young, MA London, PhD
Cantab, Edward Cadbury Professor of
Theology at Birmingham University,
England, and a Methodist minister.

Foreword

The Old Testament is the backbone of Western civilisation. It is the foundation of the Judaeo-Christian heritage, and as such it has provided the moral and spiritual basis for the lives of countless millions of people in Europe, the Americas and wherever the Bible has been cherished. The great figures of Biblical history, such as Abraham, Moses, David and the prophets have impressed themselves on human consciousness, and the events described in its pages, from the Flood and the building of the Tower of Babel, which are shrouded in mystery, to the conflicts between empires, which affected Judah and Israel so crucially, are an integral part of our own literary and religious traditions.

Great Events of Bible Times takes a fresh look at the Old Testament, putting the stories and their background into the context of their own times. It does this by the painstaking use of all the tools of modern scholarship and technology. The latest archaeological discoveries are used to the full, and the pictorial element is enhanced by computer graphics and satellite photography, so that the readers can feel personally involved in the events described. They will be treading the same terrain as the men and women of bygone days. Of the many books on Bible themes this one really does offer something entirely new.

David Goldstein

The New Testament is the story of Jesus of Nazareth, the central figure in one of the world's great religions, and acknowledged as a prophet or divinely inspired person in other faiths; it goes on to tell of the beginnings of the community he inspired. The story is sometimes beautiful, sometimes terrible and shocking, often dramatic, always fascinating.

To tell the story, we brought together a small group of writers of high calibre, both as scholars and communicators; they include Catholic and Protestant, black and white, female and male. We asked them to write according to their own consciences, and to respect the consciences of others.

The illustrations, visually exciting, make use of satellite photographs, three-dimensional computer graphics, artists' reconstructions, archaeological photographs, and the traditions (especially the early ones) of Christian painting and sculpture.

The whole takes the reader back, accurately and adventurously, into the great events of New Testament Times.

John Ferguson

Contents

The books of the Hebrew Bible

The Hebrew Bible comprises 24 books which chronicle the relationship between the Lord (whose name may have been pronounced Yahweh), and his people Israel. It is not only the cornerstone of Judaism but also a record of Israel's religious aspirations and development. It tells, for example, of the Israelites' bondage in Egypt, their conquest of the Promised Land and their exile in Babylon. There are also reflections on man's character and destiny, plus prayers of lament and thanksgiving. And there are the oracles of prophets from Amos, in the eighth century BC, down, at least, to Malachi, in the fifth.

The books of the Old Testament almost all stem from a compiler rather than a single author. The reason is that the Old Testament began as a body of oral traditions and brief documents handed down from generation to generation. At certain periods, when conditions were suitable, they were then collected together and painstakingly written down into one coherent body of work by scribes. The reigns of David and his son Solomon (tenth century BC) probably provided the earliest period of compilation and, with the time during and after the Jews' exile in Babylon (sixth century BC), the most fruitful.

Evidence for different traditions behind the Old Testament stories can be detected through variations and duplications. For example, in Genesis, there are two accounts of the creation of the world. Genesis 2:4–3:24 tells the well-known story of God shaping man – Adam – from the soil of the ground, and settling him in the garden of Eden. There, Adam is free to eat of all the trees in the garden 'except the tree of knowledge of good and evil'. God then creates for him animals and birds, and also a woman – Eve – from one of Adam's ribs. The story tells of the snake seducing Eve into eating the forbidden fruit and Adam and Eve's consequent expulsion from Eden.

But before the Adam and Eve story, there is another account of the creation – probably set down at a later date – in Genesis 1–2:4a. Here, God creates the world in seven days, and then man *after* the animals, not before, as implied in the Genesis 2:4–3:24 account. Why and when the two accounts were placed side by side is a matter of scholarly debate, but examples of similar anomalies can be found elsewhere.

Jewish tradition arranges the books of the Old Testament in descending order of authority, rather than chronologically. First, there are the five books of Moses (Genesis–Deuteronomy). These contain the divine laws; in Hebrew they are collectively called the *torah* (meaning 'teaching' rather than 'law') and are also known as the 'Pentateuch', derived from the Greek 'book in five volumes'. Second, there are histories ascribed to prophets (Joshua–Kings) and the books of the prophets themselves, for example Isaiah and Jeremiah; and third, the other writings. For Jews, all this constitutes not the Old Testament, (which term implies replacement by the New) but the entire Bible.

Christians, however, prefer chronological arrangement of the Old Testament: history (Genesis–Esther), prayers and speculation about the present (Job–Solomon's Song), and finally the prophecies. The last tell how God would visit Israel in judgement and salvation – and are fulfilled, Christians believe, in the events described in the New Testament.

The books of the Old Testament would almost all have been written down in Hebrew. The earliest complete manuscripts extant date to the ninth century AD. But the Dead Sea scrolls preserve a complete text of Isaiah, and fragments of every other book except Esther. Further evidence of the original Hebrew comes from ancient translations, which often indicate the lost Hebrew text that lay before the translator.

The earliest translation (third to second century BC) is the Greek Septuagint, so called because it was imagined to have been translated by 70 people. There are also later translations in Greek, and in Syriac, Latin and Aramaic. The Aramaic version has been preserved by the Jews, the rest by the Church. Scholars choose between alternative readings by considering which best fits the language and content and which best explains the origin of its rivals. Occasionally, the true text seems lost through corruption, and can only be guessed at.

Outside the Old Testament itself, little survives of the Hebrew of the Biblical period. About 1,000 words appear in the Bible just once and cannot be checked in any other Biblical passage. Jewish tradition and the ancient translations are invaluable, but occasionally inadequate, guides to the sense.

Consequently, there is a growing tendency among scholars to compare Biblical Hebrew with related languages, such as Aramaic and Arabic, and languages recovered through archaeology to shed light on Biblical Hebrew. This has revealed, for example, that the Hebrew verb *ydʿ*, 'know', had a forgotten homonym meaning 'subdue' – as in the description of God's martyred Servant (whom Christianity identifies with Jesus) in Isaiah 53:3, where the context requires the sense of a man 'humbled' with suffering (New English Bible) and not merely 'acquainted' (Authorised Version).

1 עַד כִּי־יָבֹא שִׁילֹה

2 ἕως ἂν ἔλθῃ τὰ ἀποκείμενα αὐτῷ,

3 עַד דְּיֵיתֵי מְשִׁיחָא דְּדִילֵיהּ הִיא מַלְכוּתָא

4 עדמא דנאתא דידלה הי מלכותא ... מ,

Biblical scholars use ancient translations to guide them on passages where the sense is not clear. For example, in the Hebrew text, 1, of Genesis 49:10, it says that kingship shall not depart from Judah until 'Shiloh' comes. But, for the obscure word 'Shiloh', the Greek, 2, has 'what is in store for him'; the Aramaic, 3, reads 'the Messiah, to whom kingship belongs'; the Syriac, 4, has 'he to whom it belongs'; all three translations read the Hebrew as *shelo*, 'his', which they interpreted in different ways.

5 וַיִּקְרָא אַרְיֵה עַל־מִצְפֶּה אֲדֹנָי אָנֹכִי עֹמֵד תָּמִיד
יוֹמָם וְעַל־מִשְׁמַרְתִּי אָנֹכִי נִצָּב כָּל־הַלֵּילוֹת

6 ויקרא הראה על מצפה ... על מעמד
אורן אנוכי עומד יומם ולמ... ומם ואל משמרתי א...א ... על
משמרתי...

The discovery of the Dead Sea scrolls (see pp.186–7) has shed new light onto the Hebrew Bible. For example, the traditional Hebrew, 5, of Isaiah 21:8, mentions a 'lion', *aryeh* (boxed), – 'And he cried [as] a lion'. The Dead Sea scroll, 6, has 'seer', *ha-roeh* (boxed), which fits the context better – 'And the seer cried'.

An illumination from the Kennicott Bible, a 15th-century Hebrew manuscript from Spain. It faces the Book of Psalms.

The geography of ancient Palestine

Ancient Israel was a small land, traditionally extending 'from Dan to Beersheba' (Judges 20:1), a distance of only 150mls/240km. But it occupied a unique geographical situation: it was the only landbridge between Africa and Asia. As such, it was often the focus of the political aspirations of Egypt on the one side, and of the Mesopotamian empires on the other. Its main international highway, the Via Maris, was used both by traders and invading armies.

This small country depended on the climate for its fertility. Unlike Egypt and much of Mesopotamia, where the economy was based on irrigation agriculture, the farmers and pastoralists of ancient Palestine relied on the annual winter rainfall and heavy spring dews. If these failed, there could be disastrous droughts and famine.

In Deuteronomy 11:10–11, Moses describes to the Israelites the contrast between Egypt and the 'Promised Land', which 'is not like the country of Egypt . . . where, having done your sowing, you had to water the seed by foot, as though in a vegetable garden. No, the country which you are about to enter is a country of hills and valleys watered by the rain of heaven. . . .'

The varied topography is remarkable for such a small land. The most densely populated area was the fertile coastal plain and its eastern continuation, the valley of Jezreel. Despite the long coastline, however, the lack of good harbours meant that seafaring was never important.

The central mountain range, a limestone ridge running from Galilee to the eastern Negeb desert, forms the backbone of the country. In antiquity, much of this region was wooded but, as the land was settled, most of the forests were cut down and overgrazing has prevented forest renewal and contributed to soil erosion.

To the east, the great Rift valley, through which the River Jordan flows, is the land's most dramatic feature. The lowest point on the earth's surface, over 1200ft/365m below sea level, is near the Dead Sea. Throughout the Jordan rift, the climate is tropical and humid and rainfall is scanty south of the Sea of Galilee. The western part of the valley is rather desolate except for oases such as Jericho and En-gedi, the latter, with 'henna flowers among the vines' (Song of Songs 1:14), famed for its beauty and fertility. Rising steeply from the eastern valley bottom is the Transjordanian plateau, from where rivers and streams flow down into the Jordan.

Unlike Palestine proper, the Transjordanian highlands have a continental climate, hot and dry in summer and cold and wet in winter. In antiquity, the western plateau was a rich, grain-producing area. As well as cereals, the farmers of Palestine cultivated a variety of fruits. Theirs was 'a fine country . . . a land of wheat and barley, of vines, of figs, of pomegranates, a land of olives, of oil, of honey' (Deuteronomy 8:7–8). Dates were grown in the Dead Sea area and the Jordan valley. Pastoralists with their sheep and goats were also important for the ancient economy, producing meat and dairy products.

Palestine was also a country 'where the stones are iron and the hills may be quarried for copper' (Deuteronomy 8:9). There are a few iron mines in Transjordan and copper in the Arabah, but Palestine is not rich in raw materials. Many of these were obtained from elsewhere, in exchange for products such as grain, wine, oil and honey as well as perfumes and unguents.

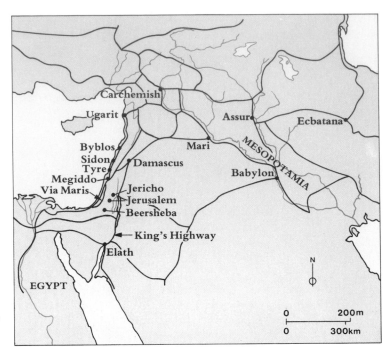

The coastal plain, with its alluvial soil, was the richest area of Palestine. South of forested Mount Carmel, oak trees grew on the red sand, several miles wide, along the shoreline. The plain broadens farther south and rainfall decreases, but cereals were cultivated as far south as Gaza.

The Shephelah, a low range of hills between the coast and the central plateau, was densely settled in antiquity. A fertile area, it was famous for its olives and sycamore trees.

The Judaean hill country produced fruit trees and vines on its terraced hillsides. The eastern wilderness provided only grazing for animals.

The fertile Jezreel valley connects the coast with the Transjordan.

The Arabah, south of the Dead Sea, is part of the Rift valley. Hot and desolate, it was nevertheless important for its copper mines.

Edom and Moab were situated on the southern part of the Transjordanian plateau, the western edge of which had moderate winter rainfall. This part of Edom was called Mount Seir, 'the hairy mountain', because of its thick shrub forests. The economy of Moab was largely pastoral.

Both the history and culture of the land of Palestine have always been influenced by its position at the crossroads between civilisations and continents. Armies, merchants and their caravans, and messengers constantly passed along the Via Maris, one branch of which went to Phoenicia, while another crossed over to Damascus.

The great Trans-jordanian road, 'The King's Highway', also terminated at Damascus, a major meeting point of ancient caravan routes. The major roads of the region are shown by the black lines on the map, *left*.

Mt Carmel

GALILEE

Dan

BASHAN

Valley of Jezreel

River Jordan

Coastal plain

GILEAD

Shephelah

Jerusalem

Judaean country

Jericho

JUDAH

En-Gedi

MOAB

EDOM

Galilee, a region of wooded mountains and fertile valleys, produced olives and fruit trees. Fish abounded in the lake.

Gilead and Bashan were rich cereal producing areas. Gilead also grew olives, vines, oak and pine; Bashan was famous for its cattle.

The River Jordan flows strongly along its winding course through the Rift valley. Deep-lying currents make it unnavigable and it has tended to divide rather than unite the peoples living on either side. In Biblical times, lions still roamed through the dense vegetation on the high banks. The west bank was mostly desolate but the east was fertile, 'irrigated everywhere . . . like the Garden of Yahweh or the land of Egypt' (Genesis 13:10) and supported a chain of cities from Galilee to the Dead Sea.

The Flood: Noah's ark

'Every living thing on the face of the earth was wiped out, people, animals, creeping things and birds; they were wiped off the earth and only Noah was left, and those with him in the ark' (Genesis 7:23).

Next to the Creation itself, the Flood is undoubtedly the most controversial episode in the Old Testament, and the two themes are intimately related in the Biblical narrative. Genesis treats the creation of life as an experiment on God's part but one which failed. After Adam and Eve's fall from grace and their expulsion from the Paradise of Eden, the human race continued its downward spiral into degeneracy and sin. Yahweh eventually decided to exterminate all life: 'I shall rid the surface of the earth of the human beings whom I created . . . for I regret having made them' (Genesis 6:7–8).

What precisely displeased Yahweh is not specified. Adam's son Cain had already 'invented' murder by killing his brother Abel. Otherwise the Bible explains in very general terms that 'the earth was corrupt and full of lawlessness' (Genesis 6:11).

A vague picture of the mysterious antediluvian world of the Bible can be reconstructed. Already 'people were numerous on the earth'. It was a technological society, metallurgy having been invented by one Tubal-Cain, 'forger of all tools made of copper and iron' (4:22). The earth was also visited by angels called the 'sons of God', who mated with women and produced a race of semi-divine beings. It was a remarkable time on earth and Genesis records fantastic ages for its inhabitants. Noah, the only person of his time who found Yahweh's favour, was supposedly 600 years old when the Flood came.

Noah was warned by Yahweh of the impending cataclysm and given precise instructions for the building of a boat. The ark was duly built by Noah and his family, then provisioned and boarded. Not every kind of creature they took with them went in 'two by two'. Ritually clean (kosher) animals and birds were represented by seven pairs of each kind; only unclean animals were to be taken as one pair.

Seven days after Noah had completed his preparations, the Flood began. On the seventeenth day of the second month, 'that very day all the springs of the great deep burst through, and the sluices of heaven opened. And heavy rain fell on earth for forty days and forty nights' (Genesis 7:11–12). The combined force of subterranean waters and heavenly downpours rapidly scoured the earth of all airbreathing life, 'everything on dry land' – except, of course, Noah and his companions.

Three months after the beginning of the Flood, the water level had fallen sufficiently for the ark to come to rest on the mountains of Ararat. To ascertain whether any land was visible, Noah sent birds out to scout. A raven returned, as did a dove on its first release. On its second excursion, the dove returned with an olive leaf in its beak. On the third occasion it did not return at all. Then 'Noah lifted back the hatch of the ark and looked out. The surface of the ground was dry!' (Genesis 8:13).

Thus the human experiment could begin again. Noah repopulated the Earth with the creatures he had saved and became the ancestor of all the world's races through his sons Ham, Shem and Japheth. There is a curious pendant to the story. Noah planted the first vine, made wine and became inebriated. As he lay, drunk and uncovered, in his tent, his son Ham entered and saw him naked. For this sin the Canaanites, descendants of Ham, were to be forever cursed.

Building the ark

Noah's ark is described in the Bible as being an enormous rectangular structure but its true dimensions and design have been the subject of considerable speculation. The Bible gives the ark's length as 'three hundred cubits, its breadth fifty cubits, and its height thirty cubits' (Genesis 6:15). The roof may have added an extra cubit in height. Allowing the maximum estimate for the cubit, this gives an ark 513ft/157.5m long, 84ft/26.25m wide and 54ft/16.28m high.

As far as can be ascertained the ark seems to have been a simple construction. It had three storeys – which perhaps were intended to symbolise heaven, earth and the underworld – with an entrance on one side. The material which Noah used to construct the ark was, according to the Biblical narrative, 'gofer', usually thought to be some kind of resinous wood such as pine, while the entire vessel was waterproofed, inside and out, with a layer of pitch.

Teba, the word translated as 'ark', is rare in the Bible, the only other reference being to the reed boat in which the infant Moses was abandoned on the Nile (Exodus 2:3). *Teba* seems to be related to an Egyptian word meaning 'chest' or 'coffin'. This prompts a connection with Osiris, the Egyptian god of death and resurrection. He, like Noah, was set afloat in a wooden chest on the seventeenth of the month. This in turn suggests that there was a sacred element to the Noah story, beyond the straightforward tale of a catastrophic flood.

The 'solar boat' of King Cheops, dating from about 2600 BC, is the world's oldest surviving ship. In 1954, excavations around the Great Pyramid (Cheops' tomb) revealed the boat, lying in an enormous pit. It is now displayed in a special museum next to the pyramid.

More than 138ft/43m long and nearly 21ft/6m wide, it was made from more than 1,200 pieces of timber, mainly cedarwood from the Lebanon. The planks were held together with ropes and wooden pegs, around a central frame. Twelve enormous oars were used for steering and propulsion.

Analysis of its water content showed that it was used at least once on the Nile, probably for some ceremonial purpose. Then, presumably at the time of the king's burial, the ship was carefully dismantled and laid in the pit. It was covered with stone blocks, up to 18 tons each, and plastered over, thereby preserving the boat for some 4,500 years.

Owing to the lack of inscriptions, the precise purpose of the boat is unknown but it was probably intended to carry the Pharaoh to the Afterlife.

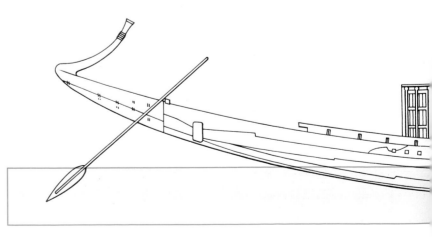

זה עץ כתוך היוׁיבה והיונה עליו נחה ׃

The wild beasts of ancient Palestine

Although it is impractical to compare the animals which existed before the Flood with those that survived, there have been great changes in the fauna and flora of Biblical lands within comparatively recent times. For most of the Old Testament period, the climate and fauna of Palestine were of a more African cast than exists now. Elephants were common in Syria and were a major source of ivory, used to decorate palaces. Hunting Syrian elephants was a favoured sport of Egyptian and Assyrian kings until the tenth century BC. The Asian lion, now confined to a single game reserve in India, was still common in some areas of Syria and Palestine, as the feats of some Biblical heroes show.

Samson was a particularly ferocious lion killer. 'Samson went down to Timnah and, as he reached the vineyards of Timnah, he saw a young lion coming roaring towards him. The spirit of Yahweh seized on him and he tore the lion to pieces with his bare hands as though it were a kid . . .' (Judges 14:5–6). David, too, was a slayer of lions. 'David said to Saul, "Your servant used to look after the sheep for his father and whenever a lion or a bear came and took a sheep from the flock, I used to follow it up, lay into it and snatch it out of its jaws. If it turned on me, I would seize it . . . and batter it to death"' (1 Samuel 17:35).

Other creatures of ancient Palestine include the hippopotamus, bones of which, dating from around 2000 BC, have been found in the Jordan valley, and giraffe, of which rock-carvings have been found in Sinai. The Sinai giraffe seem to be mentioned by classical writers when they call them 'camel-leopards'. Definite evidence of the rhinoceros surviving in Palestine into Biblical times is lacking but it has been suggested as the prototype for the 'unicorn', although wild aurochs (bison) seem to fit the Biblical description better.

Medieval legend has it that most 'unicorns' were exterminated by the Deluge. Whatever the case – and Noah's Flood seems to have played no part – the fauna of Palestine has dramatically, though gradually, changed. The elephants, lions, hippopotami, aurochs, giraffes and other animals which once roamed Palestine have all, for one reason or another, departed or become extinct.

'After waiting seven days more, he again released the dove from the ark. In the evening, the dove came back to him and there in its beak was a freshly-picked olive leaf!' (GENESIS 8:10–11).

This stylised representation of Noah and his ark is from a late 13th-century Hebrew Bible and Prayer book in the British Library.

The Flood: fact or fiction?

There have been many attempts to elucidate the Biblical story of the Flood. Some take the idea of a global deluge almost at face value and invoke past physical catastrophes on a grand scale, such as melting ice caps or the impact of a giant comet. There are also more mundane interpretations, which argue that legends of a universal Flood are exaggerated memories of purely local events.

The most popular explanation of the Flood legend claims that the Biblical story was borrowed from ancient Babylonia. Early archaeological work discovered tablets with a Babylonian version of the deluge legend and some excavators went further in claiming to have found physical evidence of the Flood. However, such 'deluge deposits' are clearly the result of localised flooding which had little impact, even on Mesopotamian civilization.

The theory that the Biblical story is 'based' on a Babylonian tradition misunderstands the evidence. Extraordinary similarities exist, to the point that they are certainly related stories. But they both probably descend from a common legend, rather than one version being 'older' than the other.

The attempts to locate Noah's ark at its traditional resting-place on Mount Ararat have been equally futile. Expeditions undertaken to find it in recent times have been led by Biblical fundamentalists; none has been sponsored by a recognised scientific institution or even been legal (Ararat is in the military zone between Turkey and the USSR). Boat-shaped objects have been detected and many fragments of wood have been recovered by these expeditions, but such finds are not surprising. Mount Ararat was a cult centre for medieval monks, who could have positioned wooden crosses and even boats to commemorate the site of Noah's landing. Hence the radiocarbon dates of all the wood recovered from the 'ark sites' are well within the AD period.

The study of Flood legends is not simply a question of identifying one local tradition, such as the Babylonian, as the 'original'. This can only be done at the expense of ignoring the other tales of a universal deluge from widely separated parts of the globe. Analysis of the world's Flood myths shows that they often have deeper mythological meanings, other than the obvious message about a watery catastrophe.

Some find Noah suspiciously like a demi-god: he was the 'father of all mankind', the guardian of animals, the inventor of viniculture and the builder of a huge rectangular 'boat', which sounds as much like a symbolic model of the cosmos as a seaworthy vessel. There is also a series of striking parallels between Noah and some ancient fertility gods.

Perhaps a key to understanding the Biblical Flood story lies more in understanding the curious figure of Noah than hunting for the ark or seeking flood deposits in Iraq. If there ever was a widespread deluge which provided the inspiration for the Babylonian and Biblical Flood stories, the most reasonable view is that it took place in remote prehistoric times, perhaps during the climatic upheavals which accompanied the end of the last Ice Age some 10,000 years ago. Even so, the story has been heavily overlaid with a layer of myth about a culture hero or demi-god who fathered the human race, protected animals and was associated with wine. The truth is that the Biblical Flood story cannot yet be properly understood in historical, geological, theological, or mythological terms.

The Babylonian 'Flood'

'Aboard the ship take thou the seed of all living things!' So reads a line from the Babylonian version of the Flood, the major source for which is a cuneiform tablet, part of which is shown *above*. It was found in ancient Nineveh and published in 1872. The account provides striking parallels to all the major elements of the Biblical Flood story: the destructive rains, the warning given to one person (in this case a man called Utnapishtim), the construction of an enormous vessel to protect both people and animals, and the release of birds to test conditions.

The discovery was hailed by devout Victorians as proof of the Biblical story – particularly welcome to them at a time when the Old Testament's authority was being challenged by Darwinism.

The Babylonian text was written in the seventh century BC, but earlier fragments and versions suggest that it may go back to a Sumerian version, dating from about 2000 BC. Because of its antiquity, the Babylonian story is thought by some to provide evidence that the Biblical story is true. However, while the cuneiform versions are the closest known deluge stories to the legend of Noah's Flood, they are, equally, mythological accounts and probably derive from a common oral tradition.

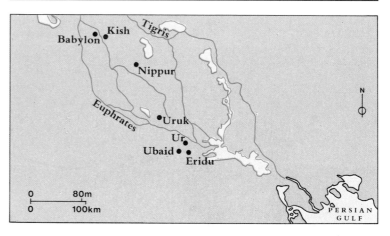

Ur was the ancient Sumerian city where the British archaeologist Sir Leonard Woolley claimed to have found evidence of the Flood. Excavating the earliest levels of the site in 1928, he unexpectedly struck 'virgin soil'. After digging through 8ft/2.5m of clean soil, he again discovered pottery and flints. His wife 'solved' the mystery. As Woolley wrote, 'She turned away remarking casually, "Well, of course, it's the Flood." That was the right answer.'

The mud was indeed a flood deposit, but hardly that of the universal Flood of legend. The layer of river-laid mud was found at Ur but nowhere else, not even at Ubaid, a mere 20mls/33km distant. Ancient Mesopotamian cities often suffered disastrous but highly localised floods from the Euphrates and Tigris.

This Greek vase, *below*, of 530 BC, depicts 'Dionysus at sea', a common theme in Greek art and myth.

Mount Ararat, *above*, the highest peak in the Ararat Mountains in eastern Turkey, rises to almost 17,000 feet above sea level. The tradition that it was here Noah's ark came to rest when the Flood began to subside possibly arose from a misreading of Genesis 8:4, which properly reads, 'on the mountains of Ararat'. For this reason, other mountains in the range farther north have also been suggested as possible sites.

Despite many searches and aerial photography, no authenticated remains of the ark have yet been found.

Noah, Dionysus and Osiris

In Greek myths, the gods flooded the world and destroyed the human race because of its wickedness. However, Deucalion and his wife built and provisioned an enormous wooden chest and were spared, after which they repopulated the world by throwing over their shoulders stones, which were magically transformed into people.

Deucalion was also strongly associated with the vine – as indeed, was Dionysus (Bacchus), god of wine and vegetation in general. A common theme in Greek art and myth was that of 'Dionysus at sea', sailing in a boat with grapes hanging from the rigging. Also, Greek hymns describe the boat crowded with wild animals.

In Egypt, Osiris was a god with almost identical attributes to Dionysus. He was murdered by his brother and his body, locked in a wooden chest, was set afloat on the sea on the seventeenth of the month, the same day as that given for the beginning of the Biblical Flood.

While firm conclusions are difficult to draw in this matter, some assume that these figures – Dionysus, Osiris and Noah – drew on a common archetype, a hero who was remembered for his connections with the vine and agriculture and a fateful journey in an enormous boat.

Babel: the building of the tower

After the Flood, according to the Bible, all men lived together and spoke the same language. During their nomadic wanderings in the east, they came across a plain in southern Mesopotamia where they decided to settle. There they began preparations for building. 'For stone they used bricks and for mortar they used bitumen' (Genesis 11:3). Their ambition was to build 'a city and a tower with its top reaching to heaven', as a permanent monument to themselves and a symbol of their cooperation so they would 'not get scattered all over the world' (11:4).

But their god Yahweh had other plans for them. Displeased by their arrogance, he decided to confuse their language so they could no longer understand one another. Then he 'scattered them thence all over the world and they stopped building the city' (Genesis 11:8). The city and tower were left deserted and in ruins. The city was called Babel 'since there Yahweh confused the language of the whole world'.

The story illustrates the futility of mankind's attempt to challenge Yahweh's supremacy. The city is clearly Babylon – 'Babel', a Hebrew word, means 'Gate of God', which the writer cleverly links with the word *bālal* meaning 'confuse'. Behind the story is an attempt to explain both the existence of different languages and the strange temple towers or ziggurats which dominated the flat plains of Babylonia.

The Sumerians built the first ziggurats in the third millennium BC. These monumental stepped towers surmounted by a shrine represented sacred mountains where men could make contact with the gods. The best preserved Mesopotamian ziggurat, at Ur, was dedicated to the moon-god.

The great ziggurat at Babylon, called Etemenanki, was part of the temple complex Esagila and could well have inspired the story of the 'tower of Babel'. It probably dates back to the early second millennium BC, when Hammurabi raised Babylon and its god Marduk to supremacy.

The Babel story finds echoes in the Babylonian creation epic in which Marduk vanquishes the forces of chaos and the grateful gods undertake for him the construction of Babylon and Esagila. In accordance with tradition they first prepared the sacred bricks: 'For one year they moulded bricks. When the second year arrived they raised high the head of Esagila.'

The Babel legend accurately reflects Babylonian building techniques. As there was no stone, mud was used to make baked or sun-dried bricks. Bitumen, which seeped through the ground in some places, served as mortar. One of a king's duties was to mould the first brick for a temple symbolising royal responsibility for the housing and care of the gods.

The tower of Babel story perhaps became part of Hebrew lore towards the end of the second millennium BC, after the fall of Hammurabi's dynasty, when the ziggurat of Babylon may indeed have been in ruins for a time. Later, some of the Jewish exiles in Babylon would have seen the great edifice as restored by Nebuchadnezzar.

The Greek historian Herodotus has his own story of the mysterious ziggurat. He says that it had a temple on its topmost tower with a couch in it. He also reports the Chaldaeans' (i.e. the Babylonians') claim that 'the god enters the temple in person and takes his rest upon the bed.' Today, only the foundations remain of the 'tower of Babel', the fabled monument of a people's attempt to come closer to heaven.

Temple storehouse
Royal palace
High priestess's residence

The ziggurat at Ur formed the core of a sacred precinct, *left*, dedicated to the moon-god Nanna. The precinct also enclosed a temple storehouse, the residence of the high priestess of the moon-god, and a royal palace.

Ur-nammu built in many cities. His restoration of the temples at Nippur, the traditional Sumerian cult centre, helped earn him the title 'King of Sumer and Akkad'.

The king and his court paid occasional visits to the city. During religious festivals, animals were slain on the sacrificial tables in front of the ziggurat steps. The king and his entourage then probably made a ceremonial ascent to the shrine. Huge horns, cast in shining bronze, projected from the temple walls, decorated with gold, silver and ochre mosaic.

This ziggurat was built by King Ur-nammu (2112-2095 BC), the first ruler of the last great Sumerian dynasty. The story of the tower of Babel was probably inspired by a ziggurat such as this. From his capital Ur, in southern Mesopotamia, Ur-nammu ruled over a powerful, well-organised empire. The chief deity of Ur was Nanna, the moon-god, to whom the king dedicated his eldest daughter as high priestess.

The buildings in the sacred precinct were constructed at vast expense. The ziggurat stood on a high terrace from where it dominated the city. Its corners were oriented to the points of the compass. Originally, it probably had three stages but today only the first stage survives. Three stairways led up to the first stage. They converged at a gatehouse, **1**, from where the central stair, **2**, continued up to the summit of the ziggurat.

The imposing structure, which measures 190 × 130ft/58 × 40m at its base, was cased with baked brick. The outer face was decorated with buttresses, **4**.

The centre of the tower was a mass of brickwork, with layers of reed matting for cohesion. The alluvial plains of Babylonia provided an infinite supply of mud for brick making.

The northwest side of the ziggurat housed the god's kitchen, where his meals were prepared. Little is known about the shrine on the summit, **3**. It was later rebuilt by Nebuchadnezzar in blue glazed brick.

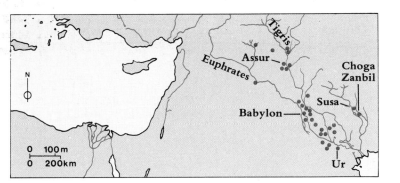

Ziggurats: the great stepped towers

The custom of building ziggurats spread outside Babylonia to Assyria in the north and Elam in the east. This map shows the distribution of ziggurats in the ancient Near East. The best preserved ziggurat is at Choga Zanbil, near the Elamite capital of Susa. It was part of a new religious centre, the brilliant conception of the 13th-century Elamite monarch Untash-napirisha. The ziggurat, surrounded by a wall with seven gates, had four storeys, surmounted by a temple to Inshushinak, the chief god of Susa.

Babel: peoples and languages

'Come, let us go down and confuse their language there, so that they cannot understand one another' (Genesis 11:7). Thus says Yahweh in the Babel story which seeks to explain why the peoples of the world, although originally from one family, spoke different languages.

In fact, during the second millennium BC, the period which probably provides the setting for the story, the Near East was the home of many different peoples. It was an age of political change and international commerce. Akkadian, the language of Babylonia, became the diplomatic lingua franca.

The Assyrians to the north of Babylonia spoke a different dialect of Akkadian. Assur, their capital, was a flourishing commercial centre. Family firms organised a profitable trade with the Anatolian states far away to the northwest. There they established colonies which traded tin and textiles, brought across the mountains from Assur by donkey caravans, in exchange for silver and gold.

Towards the end of the nineteenth century BC, a new dynasty arose in Assyria. Its first king, Shamshi-Adad, conquered as far west as the key trading centre of Mari on the middle Euphrates, where a splendid palace with more than 260 rooms and courts was excavated. The study of the correspondence of the rulers of Mari has brought to life many personalities of the day, including Shamsi-Adad and his contemporary Hammurabi of Babylon. By the end of his reign, Hammurabi in his turn controlled Mari and also Assyria.

The centuries after Hammurabi's death saw great political change in western Asia. Groups of non-Semitic peoples, the Kassites, Hittites and Hurrians, began to exert pressure on Babylonia. Eventually, the Kassites, a mountain people from the east, took power in Babylon. Little is known about the language the Kassites spoke, because they wrote in Akkadian. The Kassites ruled Babylonia for four centuries, longer than any other dynasty. They fell at last under attack from the Elamites, whose kingdom in southwest Iran had a long history of rivalry with Mesopotamia.

The fourteenth century BC was a time of grand international diplomacy. The archives of the Egyptian pharaoh Amenophis IV (Akhenaten) from El-Amarna on the River Nile contained not only letters from the petty princes of Syro-Palestine but also correspondence with the 'great kings' of western Asia. The Egyptian and Kassite royal houses were linked by marriage and gifts were exchanged. Babylon sent horses, chariots and lapis lazuli in return for Egyptian gold.

In northern Mesopotamia there was the kingdom of Mitanni whose ruler wrote to the pharaoh in Akkadian and also in his own language, Hurrian. The Mitanni empire was a confederation of Hurrian states whose rulers were answerable to the central regime. Since its capital, Washukanni, has not been located, much of the history of Mitanni remains a mystery and the Hurrian language still poses problems of decipherment. Mitanni came into conflict with the Egyptians and the Hittites over control of north Syria.

The Hittite empire, which fell around 1200 BC, was the main political force in Anatolia for most of the second millennium BC. The Hittites spoke an Indo–European language, the earliest example of the language group which includes Greek and Latin, and some Hittite words are easily recognisable, for example *wātar*, 'water' and *kwis*, the same as the Latin *quis*, 'who'.

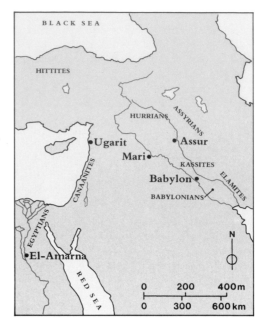

A map of the Near East in the 2nd millennium BC shows the distribution of the different peoples. During this period, Egypt expanded into the Levant and established control over the Canaanite states of Palestine. Mitanni, Egypt and the Hittites fought over the domination of Syria. Farther east, the Kassites, Assyrians and Elamites disputed their respective spheres of influence.

This Assyrian nobleman, with the customary long hair and curled beard, wears a tasselled robe with a belt.

A typical Babylonian wore, in contrast, a round, brimmed cap, possibly made of wool, and a long robe.

Early writing and its development

Writing was invented in Mesopotamia for administrative purposes. The earliest texts, from the city of Uruk (Biblical Erech) in the south, are lists of animals and agricultural equipment. They date from around 3100 BC and were written on clay, like most later Mesopotamian documents. This early writing was pictographic, each sign being a drawing of a particular object scratched into the clay. The first tablets were probably written in the Sumerian language; this is, however, not certain because although the meaning of each 'word sign' is clear there is no clue as to its spoken sound. The Sumerians soon simplified the signs and used them not only to represent whole words but also individual syllables.

The writing gradually lost its pictographic character and signs were turned on their sides and formed of wedge-shaped ('cuneiform') strokes impressed into the wet clay with a reed stylus. The Akkadian-speaking peoples took over the cuneiform script from the Sumerians and used it to write their own language. Over the centuries the signs were modified. The table, *below*, shows the development of five signs. They are, from top to bottom: **1**, the earliest pictographic signs; **2**, Sumerian signs of *c*.2500 BC; **3**, Old Babylonian signs of *c*.1800 BC; **4**, Neo-Assyrian signs of *c*.700 BC and, **5**, Neo-Babylonian signs of *c*.600 BC.

The cuneiform writing system was one of the greatest gifts of Mesopotamian civilisation to the surrounding world. Many different peoples adopted it. It was used early in Elam and Syria and later by Hurrians and Hittites, among others. As the script represented either entire words or syllables, there were hundreds of different signs. However, alphabets imitating cuneiform were invented to write Ugaritic and Old Persian. Cuneiform was used for about 3,000 years, eventually disappearing at around the beginning of the Christian era.

This clay tablet, *left*, from Sumer, written *c*.2800 BC, is a record of fields and crops. The archaic signs are clearly derived from the early pictographic script.

A tablet from Nineveh, *left*, written *c*.645 BC, records how Kakkulani, a high military official, exchanged a slave girl of his for a male slave belonging to three men, two of them brothers.

	Ox	Mountain	Man	Grain	Fish	Bird
1						
2						
3						
4						
5						

This survey tablet, *left*, dated *c*.1980 BC, records the area and dimension of five fields. Since the fields are irregular, the area is calculated by regarding them as forming rectangles or regular shapes, and then adding or subtracting from the area the parts of the field that lie outside or inside these lines.

Abraham's migration

Abram, later called 'Abraham', migrated from his birthplace, Ur of the Chaldaeans, with his father Terah, his wife and half-sister Sarai and his nephew Lot. They settled in Haran in Upper Mesopotamia, where Terah died.

In Haran, the 75-year-old Abram received a divine command to journey to Canaan. 'Leave your country, your kindred and your father's house for a country which I shall show you; and I shall make you a great nation . . .' (Genesis 12:1). Accordingly, Abram, together with Sarai and Lot, set out for the unknown land. This was the first of Abram's unquestioning acts of faith which led to the formation of the religious people Israel.

As he travelled through Canaan, Abram built altars to Yahweh at Shechem and east of Bethel. By degrees he made his way to the Negeb. Driven by famine, he moved down to Egypt, the traditional haven in times of hardship. After returning to Canaan, shortage of land owing to the increase in their livestock forced Abram and Lot to separate. Lot settled in the fertile Jordan valley, while Abram stayed in the Negeb. For his unselfish act in leaving the choice of land to Lot, Yahweh renewed his promise to Abram: 'All the land within sight I shall give to you and your descendants for ever' (Genesis 13:15).

The story of the patriarch Abram as told in the Bible is a series of consecutive episodes from his life, whose aim is to show the origins of Israel. It is, moreover, not simply the story of Abram and his family, but an account of the beginnings of a new religion and society seeking its identity. The principal themes are the making and fulfilment of the promise, made several times by Yahweh, that Abram would be the ancestor of a great nation. This was despite the fact that he and his wife were old, and she beyond the age of child-bearing.

In Genesis 17:1–27, Yahweh gives Abram details of the covenant that confirms his promise to the patriarch. Abram must change his name to Abraham, meaning 'father of many nations', while circumcision is to be a sign of the covenant: 'The uncircumcised male . . . must be cut off from his people: he has broken my covenant.' Furthermore, Sarai's name must be changed to Sarah (both forms meaning 'princess'). She is to be the mother of kings and, elsewhere in the Old Testament, she is depicted as the mother of the nation (Isaiah 51:2). Portrayed as Abraham's faithful companion, Sarah nevertheless, through jealousy, drove away Hagar (the maid she had given to Abraham) and Ishmael, Hagar's son by Abraham.

Although the traditions relating to Abraham refer to certain sacred localities in Canaan, they provide no clear evidence for determining when these events took place. The wanderings of the patriarchs seem to have been part of a general nomadic movement which extended over several centuries during the Early and Middle Bronze Ages. Increasingly, however, scholars relate them to the time of the Israelite occupation of Canaan (c. 1200 BC). Anachronisms in the Biblical account, such as the presence of Aramaeans and camels, neither of which is attested before the first millennium, make the second millennium an uncertain dating; nor does archaeological evidence in Canaan accord well with such a hypothesis.

Either way, the stories of Abraham cannot be corroborated on strict historical evidence, nor can the patriarchal narratives be taken as a whole. Rather they should be regarded as a saga of collective traditions showing the workings of Yahweh in calling and establishing his people Israel.

Negeb Desert

Abraham had left his birthplace, Ur of the Chaldaeans, and was living in Haran, an important town on the River Balikh, when he received Yahweh's divine command to leave for Canaan. His journey to Egypt is shown in red on the maps, *above* and *right*.

He passed through Canaan to Shechem, where he built an altar to Yahweh, and from there to Bethel, where he built another.

Then Abraham made his way, stage by stage, to the Negeb. Famine in that area induced him to reside in Egypt for a time, after which he returned to Bethel. Finally he settled at Hebron, west of the Dead Sea.

Excavations at Nuzi, Ebla and elsewhere tell much about the life of the patriarchs. Nuzi was a centre of Hurrian culture and shows many parallels with the social and judicial conditions of Biblical Haran. Excavated material helps to explain patriarchal marriage, adoption, inheritance and land tenure systems.

Ebla, a flourishing city in patriarchal times, was excavated by the Italians in the 1970s and a large archive was discovered. One of the Eblaite kings was called Ebrium, the name resembling Eber, an ancestor of Abraham.

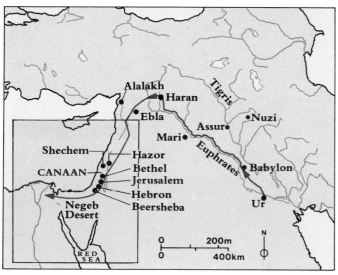

Life among the nomads

As the stories of the patriarchs show, Israel's beginnings were nomadic or semi-nomadic. Even when permanently settled, the Israelites retained institutional and linguistic features of this earlier life. What has been termed the 'nomadic ideal' is evident in the later prophets' condemnation of contemporary luxurious urban life, which they compared unfavourably with Israel's time in the desert, when life, they supposed, was simple and unsophisticated – a golden age.

Nomadism of various forms has existed throughout the long history of the Near East, as it still does today. Studies of early and contemporary nomadic societies in the region can, to a limited extent, provide a picture of this early phase of Israelite life. Nomads obviously leave few remains to shed light on their history and customs and so it is not surprising that what we know of them in earlier times comes from the records of the settled peoples with whom they came in contact.

A Sumerian text, which displays the scorn of the settled town-dwellers for the nomad, relates how 'they do not know houses', nor do they 'know grain', and they 'dig up truffles in the desert', a practice that continues to this day.

Long-range nomadism, such as is carried on today by the Bedouin Arabs, is a relatively recent occurrence, for it depends on the camel, which does not appear to have been domesticated before the first millennium. The patriarchs more closely resemble semi-nomadic shepherds who practised seasonal travelling in search of pasture for their flocks, using the donkey as their beast of burden. They did not inhabit the desert but migrated along routes where water was accessible – hence the disputes that related to rights over waterholes: 'But when Isaac's servants, digging in the valley, found a well of spring-water there, the herdsmen of Gerar disputed it with Isaac's herdsmen, saying, "That water is ours!" So Isaac named the well Esek, because they had disputed it with him. They dug another well, and there was a dispute over that one too . . .' (Genesis 26:19–21).

Nomadic society needs to be compact but it must also be strong enough to defend itself. Thus today, as in antiquity, descendants of a common ancestor are grouped into tribes, which are further divided into clans or family groups. Such a division took place when Abraham and Lot separated because the area was becoming too crowded. Each tribe has authority within its own defined area, encompassing such matters as rights over waterholes. Features of contemporary nomadic society, such as blood vengeance and the laws of hospitality and asylum, can be observed in the patriarchal world.

The home of the nomad is traditionally a black, goat-hair tent, made of cloth from his own flocks. The hair, spun by the women, is woven into a fabric which is waterproof and absorbs the sun's rays, rendering it cooler than European, white canvas tents. It is shaped in the form of a parallelogram, supported by poles of various sizes and held by ropes and pegs.

The imagery of the tent is a powerful one in the Bible and the term was for long used to denote a house. After Solomon's death, on the division of the kingdom, 'every man to his own tent' (1 Kings 12:16) expressed rebellion: each man for himself, that is to his own house.

The binding of Isaac

Isaac, the son promised by Yahweh to Abraham and Sarah, was born when they were both very old. By divine command he was named Isaac, meaning 'laughter', because Sarah had laughed at the idea that she would bear a child at the age of 90.

The ultimate trial of Abraham's faith came when Isaac had grown to boyhood: Abraham was called on by God to make a sacrifice of this his only son: 'Take your son . . . your beloved Isaac . . . offer him as a burnt offering' (Genesis 22:2). Abraham unquestioningly did as he was bidden. The next day, he saddled his donkey, chopped the wood for the burnt offering and, accompanied by Isaac and two servants, set out as instructed for the land of Moriah. On reaching the appointed place, Abraham built an altar. 'Then he bound his son and put him on the altar on top of the wood. Abraham stretched out his hand and took the knife to kill his son' (Genesis 22:9–10).

Satisfied by this proof of Abraham's readiness to sacrifice what he valued most, Yahweh, through his angel, intervened at the last moment. 'Do not raise your hand against the boy . . . for now I know you fear God.' Abraham offered a ram caught by its horns in a nearby bush instead, and he and Isaac returned home.

This testing of Abraham forms the climax in the account of the development of his faith. As well as showing the steadfastness of Abraham's faith, the story also conveys the degree of Isaac's obedience and submission to the will of God. Some scholars regard it as evidence for the existence of child sacrifice at this time; the story, they argue, is aetiological, that is, it is designed to explain the origin of something – in this case the replacement of human sacrifice by that of animals.

It is possible that, though in general the practice of child sacrifice had died out among the Israelites, its memory lingered on: in times of trouble, the Israelites may have sometimes been tempted to resume it, as a prophetic text from the time of King Hezekiah (early seventh century BC) indicates: 'Shall I offer my eldest son for my wrongdoing, the child of my own body for my sin?' (Micah 6:7).

Alternatively, the ancient account of the foundation of a sanctuary may lie behind the story. From its very beginnings, only animals were sacrificed at the sanctuary, in contrast to the Canaanite sanctuaries where humans were the sacrificial victims. In fact, after the conquest of Canaan, the Israelite prophets protested against Canaanite human sacrifice. The story of Isaac, which was probably written down at about this time, may have been intended to show that, unlike the Canaanites, Yahweh's people did not offer him their children.

The Bible shows men from earliest times bringing offerings in worship, as Genesis 4:3–4 indicates: '[Cain] brought some of the produce of his soil as an offering for Yahweh, while Abel brought the first born of his flock'. Certainly the story of Isaac shows the boy's familiarity with the sacrificial ritual.

Sacrifice was man's gift to God. The most complete offering was that in which a whole animal was sacrificed to God by burning, the 'burnt offering' or 'holocaust'. Other offerings included bread and oil, pure wheat bread or incense. Sacrifice could be offered to accompany a request, in fulfilment of a vow, to give thanks or to expiate sin and guilt. Here, the sacrifice is linked with the blood of the animal, which was its life. It was believed that this blood could be used to save man from the consequences of his sin (Leviticus 17:11).

'Take your son . . . your beloved Isaac . . . offer him as a burnt offering' (GENESIS 22:2). This mosaic, from the Capella Palatina, Palermo, in Sicily, depicts the story of the binding of Isaac. God first orders Abraham to sacrifice his only son; unquestioningly, Abraham sets out with his donkey and his obedient son to the appointed place of sacrifice in the land of Moriah. At the very moment of raising his hand to strike down his son, Abraham's hand is arrested by an angel sent by God: Abraham had proved his devotion and Isaac was spared. In his place, a ram, caught by its horns in a nearby thicket, was sacrificed.

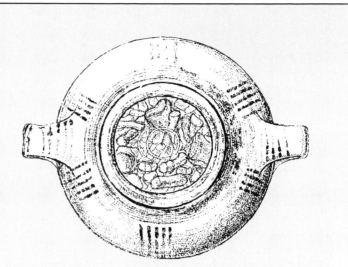

Child sacrifice

This urn from Carthage containing a burnt child's bones is is powerful evidence of child sacrifice, and of human sacrifice in general. Though the practice has been recorded, it does not appear to have been widespread in the ancient Near East. In Mesopotamia, large numbers of skeletons have been found accompanying the early dynastic royal burials at Ur, but this does not definitely mean that people were sacrificed, though such is usually inferred. Apart from the Phoenician world, there is little evidence that the ritual was practised generally.

The story of Iphigeneia, who was sacrificed by her father Agamemnon so that Greek ships could set sail for the Trojan War, is atypical of both Bronze Age and historic ancient Greece. In the Old Testament, too, the rare instances are related as being extraordinary, such as the story of Jepthah's daughter. Jepthah had vowed that should he return victorious from battle, he would give as a burnt offering the first thing to come out of his house. In the event it was his only daughter, but he kept his vow and sacrificed her (Judges 11:30–40).

Similarly infamous but unusual is the story of the king of Moab sacrificing his son upon the ramparts of his capital when it was being besieged by the Israelites (2 Kings 3:27). Some scholars regard the story of Isaac as evidence for the existence of child sacrifice in Israel's distant past. It is more probable that the practice was adopted from the Canaanites and some suggest that it was introduced from Phoenicia late in Israel's history.

Child sacrifice was expressly forbidden by Israelite law – the penalty was stoning to death (Leviticus 18:21; 20:2). It is recorded, however, that King Manasseh sacrificed his son (2 Kings 21:6). To prevent the practice, Josiah desecrated the place of Moloch worship at Hinnom (2 Kings 23:10).

The present understanding of the term 'moloch' is imprecise. In the Bible, it is always used in connection with the sacrifice of a child, who was said to 'pass through fire': this took place in the *topheth* or 'roaster'. Canaanite culture extended to sites in North Africa, including Carthage, and elsewhere in the western Mediterranean, where it is known as Punic.

In the sanctuary of Tanit at Carthage, urns have been found containing the burnt bones of lambs and goats, but many more of children. According to Diodorus, the Sicilian historian (d. after 21 BC), when disaster was threatening Carthage in 310 BC, the city's inhabitants concluded that it was because they had begun to offer sickly children or children they had bought, so that the god was angry with them; they then sacrificed 200 children from the noblest families.

In Mesopotamian religion, man was created for the service of the gods, who themselves prescribed the rites, ceremonies and services which were due from man. One of these services was the provision of food and drink for the deity and early cylinder seals often show worshippers bringing offerings of animals to the god.

This inlay, *left*, in ivory and mother-of-pearl of the third millennium BC, is from Mari, a city on the Euphrates, and shows a ram being sacrificed by priests.

There are a number of cuneiform texts that provide information about sacrifice. These include the killing of animals, the term for which was *niqu* ('pouring') because the blood was poured out before the deity. The victim, usually a sheep, was carefully chosen according to certain specific conditions, including its colour and age.

In the Old Testament, there are also similar regulations to be observed (Exodus 12:5). The *nash-patri*, the sword bearer, cut the animal's throat while reciting an incantation. The blood formed a libation. To the accompaniment of another incantation, the head was then placed near an incense burner and sprinkled with holy water. A *shangu* priest offered the sacrifices on special altars or on the temple roof.

The destruction of Sodom and Gomorrah

The story of Sodom and Gomorrah (Genesis 13–14; 18–19) is set at the time when Abram (i.e. 'Abraham') and his nephew Lot were travelling together with their flocks in southern Palestine. During their wanderings, the tribes had become rich, but this led to conflict over grazing grounds and 'dispute broke out between the herdsmen of Abram's livestock and those of Lot' (13:7). The obvious solution was to separate and Abram offered Lot first choice of land. Lot chose the fertile Jordan-Dead Sea valley and 'settled among the cities of the plain, pitching his tents on the outskirts of Sodom'.

When four kings from the north swept down to attack the area where Lot had settled, the allied forces of Sodom, Gomorrah, Admah, Zeboiim and Zoar – the five cities of the plain – were routed. They either fell into the 'bitumen wells in the Valley of Siddim' or fled into the hills. Lot was taken prisoner, but when Abram heard the news, he immediately set off in pursuit and recaptured him.

A worse calamity was soon to descend on the lands where Lot was living. 'The people of Sodom were vicious and great sinners' (13:13) so Yahweh determined their destruction. Lot was urged by two angels to flee with his wife and daughters, without stopping or looking behind.

Heeding their advice, Lot and his family were entering Zoar when catastrophe struck: 'Yahweh rained down on Sodom and Gomorrah brimstone and fire. . . . He overthrew those cities and the whole plain, with all the people living in the cities and everything that grew there' (19:24–5). Lot and his daughters were saved, but his wife was not so fortunate: she 'looked back and was turned into a pillar of salt'.

Lot left Zoar and settled in a cave in the mountains. Since they seemed to be the last people on earth, his daughters were worried about not perpetuating the race, so they devised a plan to get their father drunk and then sleep with him. Both became pregnant and gave birth to sons whom they named Moab and Ben-Ammi. Thus the Bible explains the origins of the Moabite and Ammonite peoples.

The story of Sodom and Gomorrah poses several problems of historical interpretation. Most scholars believe that the account of the invasion of the four kings has no historical foundation. The search for the cities of the plain has concentrated on the area south of the Dead Sea, and ancient and modern writers record bitumen in the Dead Sea region.

The destruction of Sodom and Gomorrah may preserve the memory of an earthquake, a not uncommon phenomenon in the Rift valley, perhaps causing the bitumen to ignite. As for Lot's unfortunate wife, travellers have always found some pinnacle among the strange, crystalline salt formations of Jebel Usdum, 'the mountain of Sodom', with which to identify her.

Recent archaeological investigations have produced interesting results. Early Bronze Age pottery was discovered at five sites, including es-Safi (identified with Zoar since Byzantine times), all on wadis leading to the southern basin of the Dead Sea. They were all deserted around 2350 BC, on current chronology, and Numeira, Feifeh and Bab edh-Dhra', the latter a religious centre and burial ground, show signs of destruction by fire. This area could have been more fertile in antiquity with careful water conservation and is a likely site for the cities of the plain. However Zoar was supposedly spared destruction and most scholars would date Abram and Lot several centuries later.

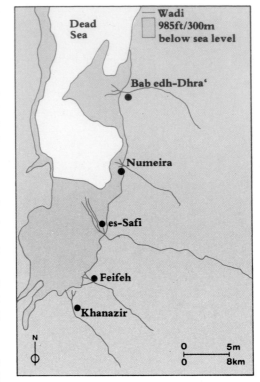

Five sites were discovered in the southern Dead Sea area, but it is doubtful whether all belong to the 'cities of the plain' – Sodom, Gomorrah, Admah, Zeboiim and Zoar. Conversely, more sites may still await discovery; the remains of yet others could now be under water.

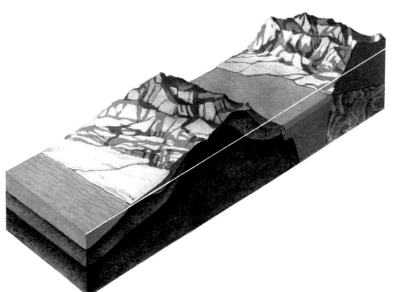

This section across southern Palestine to the southern basin of the Dead Sea shows how shallow this part of the lake is.

In antiquity, the southern basin may have been a plain, later submerged due to earth movements and the natural rise in the water level. Submerged trees are today visible around the shoreline, and there is evidence that in Roman times a road ran across the sea's narrow neck to the western shore.

In Lot's time, the Dead Sea region looked 'like the garden of Yahweh' (Genesis 13:10). Today it appears a wasteland. Nothing lives in the salt waters of the lake and the climate is oppressively hot. Salt-encrusted cliffs rise from the desolate shores. Nevertheless, where there is fresh water, the land can be fertile; in antiquity irrigation may have allowed luxuriant gardens and orchards to be cultivated.

Lot, while living in Sodom, was forewarned by Yahweh of its forthcoming destruction. He fled the city with his family; his wife, disobeying Yahweh's orders, looked back — and was turned into a pillar of salt.

The Dead Sea, on whose shores Sodom was situated, cannot support marine life because of its high salt content. Deposits of salt form over the years into solid blocks, often in pillar shapes.

Moab and Ben-Ammi

According to tradition, Lot's son by his eldest daughter was the ancestor of the Moabites. The Moabites probably settled on the high tableland east of the Dead Sea during the thirteenth century BC. They were neighbours of Israel throughout her ancient history, and northern Moab was an area of frequent territorial dispute.

The best known Moabite king is the ninth-century ruler Mesha. A stela from his capital, Dibon, records his victories over Israel. The Bible says: 'Mesha king of Moab was a sheep-breeder' (2 Kings 3:4), reflecting the pastoral basis of the Moabite economy.

Ben-Ammi, the son of Lot's younger daughter, became traditionally the ancestor of the Ammonites, who probably settled east of the Jordan north of Moab during the thirteenth or twelfth century BC. Amman, the capital of modern Jordan, has retained part of the name of the ancient Ammonite capital Rabbath-Ammon. This city was strategically situated at the junction of several ancient roads, including the important King's Highway which ran the length of Transjordan. There were frequent conflicts between the Israelites and the Ammonites, and at times Israel controlled the small Ammonite state.

Jacob steals Esau's birthright

According to Genesis 25:23, the rivalry between Jacob and Esau, Isaac's twin sons, was foretold before they were born. During her difficult pregnancy, Rebekah, their mother, went to a holy place to consult Yahweh and was told: 'There are two nations in your womb, your issue will be two rival peoples. One nation will have the mastery of the other and the elder will serve the younger.'

At birth, Esau, who emerged first, was 'red, altogether like a hairy cloak' (Genesis 25:25). Then came Jacob, holding on to his brother's heel. As they grew up, Esau became a skilled hunter, while Jacob opted for a quieter life at home: 'Isaac preferred Esau, for he had a taste for wild game; but Rebekah preferred Jacob' (25:28).

One day Esau returned exhausted after a hard day's hunting and asked his brother for some stew. Jacob cleverly saw how he could benefit from the situation and demanded his brother's birthright in return for the food. Esau was too hungry to be concerned about anything but his stomach so 'he gave him his oath and sold his birthright to Jacob' (25:33).

Some years later, when Isaac was old and blind, and felt he was nearing the end of his life, he wished to give Esau his blessing. He told his son to hunt some game and make an appetising dish which he would eat before blessing him. Rebekah, however, overhearing Isaac's words, determined that Jacob would get the paternal blessing. With two young kids that Jacob brought her, she prepared a delicious stew. Then she dressed Jacob in Esau's clothes, put the kidskins on his arms to imitate his brother's hairy skin and sent him to Isaac. The blind old man was fooled into believing he was Esau and consequently blessed Jacob in his brother's stead.

Just then, Esau, having returned from hunting, brought the food he had prepared for his father. When he realised he had been duped, Isaac trembled with rage but the blessing he had given Jacob was irrevocable. Esau was distraught and cried out: 'Now he has supplanted me twice. First he took my birthright and look, now he has gone and taken my blessing!' (Genesis 27:36) and planned that after his father's death he would kill Jacob in revenge. So Rebekah sent Jacob to her brother Laban in Haran, far away to the north. Jacob was safe but paid for his deceit by being forced into exile.

Twenty years later, Jacob returned to Canaan. He was still afraid of his brother and sent messengers ahead to Edom, where Esau was living. The elder brother's resentment had long since disappeared and he came to meet Jacob. There was an affectionate reunion as Esau took Jacob in his arms and 'wept as he kissed him' (Genesis 33:4).

The Jacob and Esau story reflects family customs among the Israelites. The eldest son enjoyed certain privileges. During his father's lifetime, he took precedence over his brothers, and on his father's death received a double share of the inheritance and became head of the family. With twins, the first to see light was considered the elder. The eldest son could lose his due rights for a serious offence, as Jacob's son Reuben did by his incest (Genesis 49:3–4). In Esau's case, he lost his birthright and his father's blessing although the relative significance of birthright and blessing is not clear from the story.

The displacing of the elder son by a younger one occurs elsewhere in the Old Testament. Isaac inherits, not Ishmael; Joseph is Jacob's favourite and David leaves his kingdom to Solomon, his youngest son. The Bible emphasises, however, that divine purpose, which always takes precedence over human customs, lies behind each of these exceptional instances.

The story of Jacob's treachery towards his brother Esau has been a popular subject with many artists. In this page from the illustrated Nuremberg Bible (1493), Jacob and his mother Rebekah are depicted in the act of deceiving Isaac.

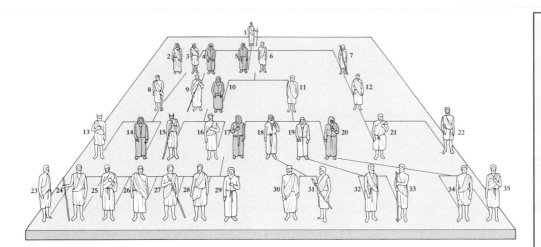

Edom: at the crossroads of trade
According to Biblical tradition, Esau was the ancestor of the Edomites. The land of Edom, which comprised the high mountains of southern Transjordan, was also known as Mount Seir. By describing Esau as 'red' (Hebrew *'admoni*) and 'hairy' (Hebrew *sa'ir*), the Biblical author alludes to Edom and Seir.

The prominence given to Esau in the patriarchal tradition reflects the significant role played by Edom in the early history of Israel. Evidence suggests that the Edomites settled in Transjordan during the thirteenth century BC. Traditionally, Edom had kings before Israel, and by the time of David in the tenth century they seem to have been hereditary.

Edom had two capitals, Teman in the south and Bozrah in the north. The King's Highway passed through Edom to the important Red Sea port of Elath. The Arabah Road, which crossed the Negeb, met the King's Highway at Bozrah. These routes brought the south Arabian and east African trade through Edom and were its main source of wealth. The land also had rich copper deposits.

The family tree shows the descendants of Terah, **1**, the father of Abraham, **3**, down to Jacob, **16**, and his 12 sons.

Marriages between first cousins were common, as that between Isaac and Rebekah. A man might have several wives and a wife (blue tint) might provide a concubine (light blue tint) for her husband.

Terah's descendants, their spouses and concubines, are as follows: Hagar, **2**; Sarai, **4**; Nahor, **5**; Bethuel, **6**; Haran, **7**; Ishmael, **8**; Isaac, **9**; Rebekah, **10**; Laban, **11**; Lot, **12**; Nebaioth, **13**; Mahalath, **14**; Esau, **15**; Jacob, **16**; Leah, **17**; Zilpah, **18**; Bilhah, **19**; Rachel, **20**; Moab, **21**, and Ben-Ammi, **22**.

Jacob had 12 sons, the ancestors of the 12 tribes of Israel, and a daughter, Dinah, **29**. The sons were: Reuben, **23**; Simeon, **24**; Levi, **25**; Judah, **26**; Issachar, **27**; Zebulun, **28**; Gad, **30**; Asher, **31**; Dan, **32**; Naphtali, **33**; Joseph, **34**, and Benjamin, **35**.

On his way to exile in Haran, Jacob stopped one night in the Judaean hill country north of Jerusalem. He lay down to sleep, using a stone as a pillow. He had a strange, symbolic dream, during which Yahweh promised him that the ground where he was lying would be given to him and his descendants.

When Jacob awoke he realised he was in a holy place, so he 'took the stone he had used for his pillow, and set it up as a pillar, pouring oil over the top of it' (Genesis 28:18). He renamed the place Bethel, or, 'house of God'.

Like other sacred sites associated with the patriarchs, Bethel was originally a Canaanite sanctuary. The Bible refers to such open-air sanctuaries as *bamot*, usually translated as 'high places'. They were often in the shade, 'under any spreading tree' (Deuteronomy 12:2). Characteristic of these sanctuaries were *matsevot* or 'standing stones'. As cult objects, these stones commemorated a divine manifestation, as at Bethel, and were generally regarded as symbols of the divinity. They could also be memorials to the dead.

One of the most impressive of the 'high places' is at Gezer, *left*, where a row of ten massive stones, dating from the mid-second millennium BC, bears witness to this ancient form of worship.

Joseph's rise to power

The story of Joseph in Genesis 37-48 brings to a close the age of the patriarchs and provides a link to the events in the book of Exodus. According to the Bible, Joseph was the eleventh son of Jacob by his beloved wife Rachel. The family led a semi-nomadic life in Canaan, tending their flocks and cultivating small fields. Joseph was his father's favourite son and Jacob 'had a decorated tunic made for him' (37:3).

Joseph's older brothers resented this and they became increasingly jealous of him, especially when Joseph told them of his dreams which seemed to foretell his future greatness. Finally, in a fit of rage, the brothers seized an opportunity to sell Joseph into slavery to Ishmaelite caravaners travelling to Egypt.

From then onward, through a series of adventures, Joseph's fortunes rose steadily. He was sold in Egypt to Potiphar, a commander of Pharaoh's guards and, because of his honesty and diligence, he quickly took charge of his master's estates.

But it was Joseph's ability to interpret dreams which was ultimately responsible for his extraordinary career. Pharaoh had dreamed of seven fat cows, followed by seven lean cows, and Joseph was able to prophesy that Egypt would go through seven years of prosperity and plenty, followed by seven years of misery and famine. As a result, Pharaoh ordered reserves of grain to be built up during the years of abundance. When the lean years duly arrived, famine and disease were avoided. In gratitude, Pharaoh appointed Joseph vizier – the highest position in the land after the king.

Because the lands adjoining Egypt were also affected by famine, neighbouring peoples went to Egypt searching for food and pasture for their animals. Among them were Joseph's brothers. They did not realise that the Egyptian high official in charge of distributing rations was their brother, but Joseph recognised them immediately. Attempts at punishing them for their wickedness to him did not last long: Joseph made himself known to them and got Pharaoh's permission to settle them in the land of Goshen, a region east of the Nile Delta. The brothers came with children and grandchildren, led by Jacob. They lived and prospered and, when Jacob died, Joseph had him buried in Canaan, alongside his ancestors.

The story of Joseph is one of the most popular in the Bible. But it is difficult to trace it back to a historical past. The pharaoh of the story is not named; there are no Egyptian records mentioning a Semitic vizier by the name of Joseph; archaeology does not provide any information.

Some scholars place Joseph's life during the reign of the Hyksos, when Semitic kings had conquered Egypt and governed the country from their Delta capital at Avaris (1650–1550 BC). More controversial is the view that the story took place as late as the seventh century, closer in time to the compilation of the Biblical account.

Whatever the origins of the story, the presence of Semitic people in the Delta area is well attested throughout Egyptian history. The motifs of the magician and the interpreter of dreams are standard in Israelite prophecy and in Egyptian tradition. Although famines are rarely mentioned in Egyptian accounts, inscriptions and reliefs describe such occurrences.

So, even if no known historical figure has been traced and no firm dating is possible, the story of Joseph embodies many cultural, political and social elements present in the Near East between the second and first millennium BC.

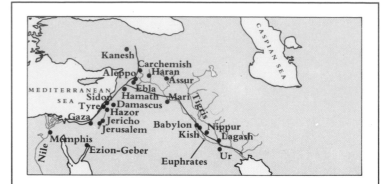

The Ishmaelites and trade

'They [Joseph's brothers] saw a group of Ishmaelites, their camels laden with gum tragacanth, balsam and resin, which they were taking to Egypt' (Genesis 37:25). Trade between Egypt and western Asia is attested from earliest times. On the map, *above*, the trade routes are shown in red.

The products transported by the Ishmaelites were aromatic substances used in large quantities in Egypt for medicinal purposes, for the manufacture of perfumes and in temple ritual They were specially important in the process of mummification, when the body, having been emptied of viscera and dehydrated with natron salt, was treated with ointments, resins and spices before being wrapped in mummy bandages. Joseph himself was embalmed, as recorded in Genesis 50:26. 'Joseph died at the age of a hundred and ten; he was embalmed and laid in a coffin in Egypt.'

While Egypt was rich in most mineral and agricultural resources, and largely self-sufficient, it had to import timber – particularly the famous cedars of Lebanon – suitable for large-scale carpentry and boat-building. Other products brought in from Asia included wine, olive oil, silver, tin, and semi-precious stones, such as lapis-lazuli from Afghanistan and turquoise from the Sinai region.

Exotic commodities such as incense, sandalwood, ebony, leopard skins, monkeys, leopards and giraffes, ostrich feathers and ivory were imported from the land of Punt, situated somewhere along the coast of Somalia.

In exchange, Egypt exported a variety of produce such as fine linen fabric, papyrus rolls, salted fish and grain. But the main export was gold, of which she was the biggest producer in the ancient Near East. Gold acted as a powerful diplomatic weapon in Egypt's relationship with her neighbours, and the possession of gold mines, more than any military power, gave Egypt complete superiority over other Asiatic nations.

This is clearly seen in the Amarna letters, the diplomatic correspondence between the pharaohs Amenophis III and Akhenaten (1391–1335 BC) and contemporary kings and rulers. Egypt had then reached the summit of her power, and gold was requested again and again by Mitanni, Assyria and Babylon. Tushratta, king of Mitanni, wrote to Amenophis III: 'My brother, pray send gold, in very great quantities such as cannot be counted; and may my brother send me more gold than my father got. In the land of my brother, is not gold as dust upon the ground?'

'*Joseph collected all the food of the seven years while there was abundance in Egypt*' (GENESIS 41:48). Wooden model granaries, *left*, were placed in tombs to ensure abundance of food for the deceased in the afterlife. This model shows a scribe recording the amount of grain, before it is stored in three large bins with the hatches above. In the foreground, a woman is shown grinding barley.

The Greek historian Herodotus states that during the 26th Dynasty (664–525 BC), the priests of Egypt were exempt from taxation. Parallels have been drawn with the agrarian reforms carried out by Joseph, whereby one fifth of all the land and the produce of Egypt went to the pharaoh, except the land belonging to priests.

'*Pharaoh said to Joseph: "I hereby make you governor of the whole of Egypt"*' (GENESIS 41:41). The painting, *above*, from the tomb of the vizier Reckhmire in Thebes, shows him, accompanied by his mother, before a table piled with food, with jars of beer below it and containers of ointment above.

He is shown wearing the garb of office, similar to that which Joseph may have worn, and holding the ceremonial staff.

On the walls of his tomb are listed the numerous duties of the vizier. He was the chief magistrate in the land, in charge of all legal judgements; he was also foreign minister and the head of the treasury, with the duty of assessing and collecting taxes. He was responsible for mobilising troops in times of war; for appointing mayors and district governors, for maintaining state archives and for monitoring natural phenomena affecting the life of the country, such as the level of the Nile inundation and the state of the crops.

Building for the pharaoh

'Then a king ascended the throne of Egypt, one who knew nothing of Joseph' (Exodus 1:8). The events which led to the Exodus of the Israelites from Egypt to the Promised Land took place against a political background very different from that behind the story of Joseph (see pp.28–9).

After the defeat of the Hyksos – the Semitic kings who had been ruling Egypt – and their expulsion from Egypt (c.1550 BC), the pharaohs of the Eighteenth Dynasty began a series of vigorous military campaigns in Palestine and Syria. Within the space of a hundred years, Egypt conquered and ruled over an empire which extended from the River Euphrates in northern Syria to the Fourth Cataract of the Nile in Nubia.

Egypt exploited the natural resources of the Near East to the full and controlled the main trade routes to and from Anatolia and Mesopotamia. This meant that vast amounts of goods and tribute poured into the treasuries of its capitals, Thebes, in the south, and Memphis, in the north. With luxury goods, precious stones, wood and metals, horses and cattle, came large numbers of captives and prisoners of war, Hurrians and Semitic peoples such as Canaanites and Amorites, who were deported to Egypt to work in fields and mines, and on the huge building projects of the pharaohs.

It is at this time that the figure of Moses emerges, the great legislator and prophet, one of the few people to have had a profound impact on the history and thought of mankind. The Bible tells us many things about Moses, yet the reality of his birth is still obscured by legend.

In fear that their numbers would constitute a danger to Egypt, Exodus relates, Pharaoh had decreed that all the Israelites' male children should be put to death. Moses, however, was saved from the waters of the Nile by Pharaoh's daughter, who discovered the child in a reed basket and entrusted him to his mother until the time when he could be brought to court to further his education.

The miracle of Moses' rescue resembles a myth well known in the ancient Near East. For example, the birth of Sargon of Agade, the king of Sumer who founded the first empire in Mesopotamia, is told in similar terms: 'My mother . . . she set me in a basket of rushes, with bitumen she sealed my lid. She cast me in the river which rose not over me. Akki, the drawer of water lifted me out, he took me as his son and reared me.'

In Egypt, during the period of the New Kingdom (c.1550–1200 BC), it was not unusual for foreign boys, many of whom were the sons of Egypt's vassals in Palestine, to be brought up at the court of Pharaoh together with the royal children. Moses itself is a common Egyptian name. The Egyptian word *ms*, meaning 'to be born', is usually associated with the name of a god (e.g. Ra*meses* means 'son of Ra' and Thut*mosis* means 'son of Thoth').

The exact date of the events described in Exodus is unknown. However, scholars generally believe that the Biblical description of the living and working conditions of the Israelites best fits the reign of Pharaoh Rameses II (1290–1224 BC).

Egyptian sources are of no help with regard to the events of the Exodus narrative. Only one record mentions Israel as a settled people and it comes from the reign of Merneptah, the son and successor of Rameses II, who commemorates his victories in battle: 'Canaan is captive with all woe, Ashkelon is conquered, Gezer seized, Israel is wasted, bare of seed. . . .'

The sophisticated tools of Egypt
Many Egyptian objects made of wood and metal have survived because of the extreme dryness of Egypt's climate. A selection of tools used by stonemasons, sculptors and carpenters, *above*, include an axe, **1**; a bronze saw blade, **2**; a large adze, **3**; a handsaw, **4**; an oil flask, **5**; a slate hone for sharpening tools, **6**; an adze with a bronze blade, **7**; a bronze chisel, **8**; a bronze bradawl, **9**; a wooden bow-drill, **10**; with two drilling bits, **11** and **12**. The Egyptians' belief that the afterlife was a mirror image of life on earth was the main reason why they employed stone for their funerary monuments, since these had to last forever.

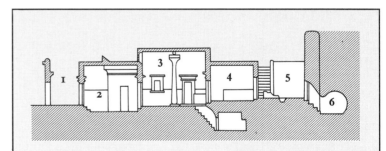

A village for the craftsmen
Although there are no traces of the Israelites' settlements, it is possible that they lived in villages not dissimilar to that of the workmen of Deir el Medineh, who were employed in the construction of the royal tombs in the Valley of the Kings. The village, purpose-built by the pharaohs of the Eighteenth Dynasty (c.1550 BC) and occupied for several centuries, was located in the desert not far from the necropolis.

The dwellings were built along two parallel roads, **1**, and were originally surrounded by a thick mud-brick enclosure. At its peak, the settlement comprised 70 terraced back-to-back houses, one storey high, each consisting of an outer hall, **2**, a main living area, **3**, a bedroom, **4**, and a back kitchen, **5**, with a cellar for storage, **6**, and a flat roof where household activities took place.

Because these workmen were literate, they have left a vast amount of information about their daily lives. They were divided into two work gangs, each living along one of the narrow streets, and each with its foreman, his deputy and one or more scribes, together with quarrymen, carpenters, sculptors and painters.

31

Building for the pharaoh: the temple of Karnak

Exodus 1:11 relates how harshly the Egyptians treated the Israelites as they made bricks to build Pharaoh's store cities, Pithom and Rameses. Pithom, the Egyptian Per-Atum, has now been identified as the great mound of Tell el Maskuteh, in the eastern Delta. Rameses had built it as a border fortress. Recent discoveries suggest that it may also be the location of the Biblical Succoth, the Israelites' first stop on their later flight from Egypt to Sinai.

Rameses, the new residence of the kings of the Nineteenth Dynasty, was the royal city of Per-Rameses, built upon the ruins of ancient Avaris, which had been abandoned since the days of the Hyksos three centuries earlier. Both Pithom and Rameses were in the vicinity of the land of Goshen and the Semitic settlers who inhabited the area were most probably part of the workforce employed in their construction.

Unfortunately, conditions in the Delta are such that very little archaeological excavation has been possible. A high water table, as well as the presence of modern towns and villages above ancient sites, make them virtually inaccessible. To this must be added the problem of the 'sebbakhin' – peasants who for centuries have used ancient brick fragments made of Nile silt as fertiliser for their fields. Enough remains, however, as a reminder of the splendour and wealth of Per-Rameses, which an ancient Egyptian writer described in lyrical terms as a city 'dazzling with halls of lapis lazuli and turquoise'.

In an address to his workmen, Rameses II boasts of the care he lavished upon them: 'I am your constant provider; the supplies assigned to you are weightier than the work. The granaries groan with grain; I have filled the stores for you with everything, bread, meat, cakes to sustain you; sandals, clothing, unguents for anointing your heads. . . .'

Not so for the slave workers of the Bible, whose life could not have been harder or more brutal. Moses was a witness to the plight of his kinsmen, and rose to their defence. He struck down an Egyptian whom he had seen beating an Israelite and, in fear of being discovered, fled to the desert. There he was welcomed into the tribe of the Midianite priest Jethro, whose daughter he married and where he learnt to survive in the harsh conditions of the desert.

Recent excavations in the Negeb desert have thrown some light on these formative years in the life of Moses and have helped to illuminate possible links between Israel and the people who lived around the time when the Exodus took place. Archaeologists have uncovered evidence of Midianite settlements in the Timnah valley. Here, the Egyptians maintained large-scale copper-smelting facilities and built a sanctuary to the goddess Hathor, the 'Lady of the Turquoise'.

After the twelfth century BC, the Midianites took over the exploitation of the mines from the Egyptians and put up their own tented shrine over the ruins of the Hathor temple. In its Holy of Holies, excavators discovered a copper snake with a gilded head, suggestive of the metal serpent fashioned by Moses (Numbers 21:9).

It was while he was in the desert that Moses had his first vision of God and was told his destiny. God, 'the God of his ancestors, the God of Abraham, the God of Isaac, the God of Jacob', appeared to him, told him that his people would be delivered from slavery in Egypt and commanded Moses to lead them to freedom, to the land flowing with milk and honey.

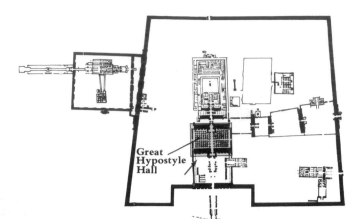

Great Hypostyle Hall

Egyptian temples were usually built to the same plan, each element symbolising a part of the mythical Island of Creation from which life first began. The pylon, or main gateway, led into one or two courtyards then hypostyle halls. These gave access to the sacred roofed area of the temple, at the far end of which was sited the Holy of Holies, housing the statue of the god. Behind it was a series of administrative rooms.

Apart from its functions as the home of the deity and the focus of the state cult, the temple also played an important role in the economic, administrative and social life of Egypt. The temple owned vast estates, employing large numbers of personnel – administrators, scribes, craftsmen, farmers and gardeners, as well as the clergy, musicians and singers. Temples were also the repositories of all the knowledge accumulated over the centuries and were centres of learning for scribes, artists and doctors.

The great Hypostyle Hall of the temple of Karnak at Thebes was built by Seti I, and completed by his son Rameses II, thought to be the pharaoh from whom Moses freed the Israelites. The roof, **1**, was supported by 134 columns, **2**, in the shape of plant forms, representing the vegetation surrounding the mythical Island of Creation.

A double row of central columns, 3, along each side of the processional way was higher than the others; light filtered through clerestory windows, **4**, situated just below the roof. All the walls and columns were carved and painted with scenes illustrating cultic acts and heroic deeds of the pharaoh.

In the New Kingdom, the temple of Amun at Karnak became the main treasury of the state, to which the pharaoh dedicated booty from victorious campaigns abroad. To this was added tribute from foreign provinces and revenue from taxation, making it the most powerful economic entity in the country.

This head is from a colossal statue of Rameses II, wearing the royal crowns of Egypt: the Red Crown of Lower Egypt, the White Crown of Upper Egypt and the 'Nemes' headcloth. On the front of the headdress is the ureus, symbol of kingship.

The temple: centre of Egyptian religion

There are few archaeological remains of the cities of Pithom and Per-Rameses in the Delta, but much more has survived in Upper Egypt. Buildings from the time of Rameses II include some of the most grandiose architectural schemes in ancient Egypt. The temple, the centre of Egyptian religion and the regular observance of religious rituals, ensured the survival and the well-being of the country.

Rituals are recorded and preserved in reliefs and inscriptions in various parts of the temple. There were two types of ceremony. The daily ritual took place three times a day, morning, noon and evening, when the statue of the god was purified, adorned with fresh clothing, anointed and presented with offerings of food and drink. At certain times of the year, the great festivals of the gods took place, when the statue of the god was carried in procession by priests outside the temple precincts, to be seen and worshipped by the whole population of Egypt, which otherwise took no part in the daily cult ceremonies.

The ten plagues

Commanded by God to go back to his people and to set them free, Moses returned to Egypt from the desert. God had warned him that his people would go free only when Egypt had been struck with wonders and signs that would demonstrate the power of the God of Israel over the gods of Egypt and the will of Pharaoh.

In an attempt to impress Pharaoh by magic, Moses transformed his staff into a serpent – but the deed failed to have impact because Pharaoh's magicians were able to repeat the performance. Moses, together with his brother Aaron, returned to Pharaoh to plead his case for his people's liberation, but in vain. Pharaoh's obstinacy caused God to bring about ten plagues to make him change his mind.

First, the Nile turned to blood, the fish died and the Egyptians were unable to drink the water. Pharaoh's magicians were able to copy this miracle and still Pharaoh hardened his heart against Moses' request. Then frogs swarmed over Egypt, a plague which Pharaoh's magicians could again conjure up. The third plague was an invasion of mosquitoes throughout the land, but this time Pharaoh's magicians failed. Still Pharaoh did not relent. So God sent a plague of flies.

This was followed by the death of the Egyptians' livestock. Pharaoh remained unmoved. The sixth plague was an epidemic of boils that afflicted men and animals alike. Then severe hail fell over the country accompanied by thunder and lightning, so that flax and barley crops were ruined and trees uprooted. The eighth plague was an infestation of locusts.

Then darkness fell over Egypt and for three days nobody could see or move about. Even then Pharaoh did not change his mind. And so God inflicted the most devastating blow on the Egyptians: at midnight, all the first-born males in Egypt died, Pharaoh's son among them. Pharaoh finally relented and Moses, having instructed his people on what preparations to make for their journey, led the Israelites out of Egypt.

In the Biblical account of the plagues, there is a big difference between the first nine and the last one, the death of the first-born. The former can be explained as natural phenomena, occurring as a result of an abnormally high Nile inundation between July and the following March, but the last plague belongs entirely to the realm of the supernatural.

The Nile turning to blood could reflect the fact that its waters were filled with red earth carried in suspension from the highlands of Ethiopia. As a result, the river would then become polluted and frogs would infest the shores in search of shelter. Mosquitoes and flies would find ideal breeding grounds in the brackish ponds left behind by the receding floodwaters.

The death of Egypt's livestock could be due to an anthrax epidemic spread by the insects, with men and animals breaking out into sores. Hail ruining the crops of flax and barley could have happened in January, when such a climatic phenomenon, though rare, is most likely to occur. Swarms of locusts could have been blown into the Nile valley by winds from the Sudan and Ethiopia and the three days of darkness are typical of a severe *khamsin,* a sandstorm of unusual proportions.

The death of the first-born is what makes Pharaoh relent and give his consent. To the Israelites, it was the affirmation of God's supreme power, his intervention on the side of the humble and the oppressed against Pharaoh, who was the greatest ruler of the ancient world of the time.

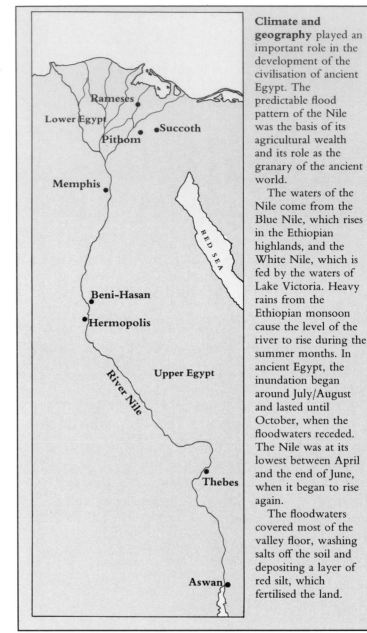

Climate and geography played an important role in the development of the civilisation of ancient Egypt. The predictable flood pattern of the Nile was the basis of its agricultural wealth and its role as the granary of the ancient world.

The waters of the Nile come from the Blue Nile, which rises in the Ethiopian highlands, and the White Nile, which is fed by the waters of Lake Victoria. Heavy rains from the Ethiopian monsoon cause the level of the river to rise during the summer months. In ancient Egypt, the inundation began around July/August and lasted until October, when the floodwaters receded. The Nile was at its lowest between April and the end of June, when it began to rise again.

The floodwaters covered most of the valley floor, washing salts off the soil and depositing a layer of red silt, which fertilised the land.

Slavery in ancient Egypt

'Accordingly, they [the Egyptians] put taskmasters over the Israelites to wear them down by forced labour' (Exodus 1:11). The traditional view that Egypt was a society based on slavery is not borne out by evidence. It was not until the New Kingdom, when Egypt's empire comprised Syria, Palestine and Nubia, that captives and prisoners of war were used as slave labourers.

During the months of inundation, it was impossible to work in the fields. After the floodwaters subsided, dykes and canals had to be repaired. So a system of conscription ('corvée') appears to have been instituted fairly early in Egypt by which men were put to work on building projects, mining and quarrying, or on land reclamation schemes and other fieldwork. The precise way by which individuals were called up is not known, but it seems that a conscripted person could appoint a substitute. Penalties for desertion were harsh and only certain categories of persons, such as priests and scribes, appear to have been exempt from conscription.

Magic: an everyday part of Egyptian life

'Pharaoh called for the sages and sorcerers, and by their spells, the magicians of Egypt did the same' (Exodus 7:11). In ancient Egypt, magic was an integral part of all aspects of life, and was believed to have powers even after death. Evidence for this is found in magical and medical texts, folk literature, funerary practices, religious rituals, in buildings and in sacred objects.

The use of magic was based upon the belief that spirit and substance were essentially one and the same, and that it was possible, by formulating the appropriate spells, to change the course of destiny and to ward off evil influences. The Egyptians believed in the power of the word, both written and spoken, and to this purpose hieroglyphic inscriptions on temple walls, in tombs, on other inanimate objects, and in magical treatises were written and recited to bring about the desired outcome. Thus, the daily ritual in the temples was designed to ensure that the natural good order of the universe, Ma'at, was upheld.

Magic was also used as a system of defence, both to protect the individual from everyday dangers through the wearing of the correct amulets, and to protect the state from its enemies. An example of this is the 'Execration texts' which involve inscribing figurines and ostraca with the names of Egypt's enemies and of ceremonially mutilating and smashing them.

Disease could be cured not only with the use of the correct potions, but by reciting incantations over the patient. After death, magical ceremonies, performed on the mummified body, made the dead person come alive again in the next world. Special funerary texts contain spells providing magical protection for the deceased in his passage into the next world. Reliefs and paintings on tomb walls of agricultural scenes and moments of leisure were intended to ensure that the persons depicted did not suffer a second death if their relatives neglected to bring offerings regularly to their tombs. Model figurines, *shabtis*, were supposed to act as substitutes for the dead person in performing the annual conscription duty.

Small stelae, called Cippi of Horus, show the figure of the god Horus standing on crocodiles, holding in his hands snakes, scorpions and gazelles – all creatures thought to possess a special malevolence. Protection against their evil could be obtained by touching water which had previously been poured on to the stela, thereby taking over the magical powers of the inscription.

'Moses threw [his staff] on the ground, the staff turned into a snake' (EXODUS 4:3). The wand illustrated, *above left*, is probably similar to the 'magic staff' of Moses. Made of ivory, it is covered with fine incisions representing both real and mythical animals, and magical signs: a frog, a dragon-like creature, a serpent, and the hippopotamus-headed goddess Thoeris biting a serpent.

Prince Khaemwaset, son of Rameses II, was reputed to be a great magician as well as being the first Egyptologist. A number of folktales were written about his magical powers, but he was merely one of many attributed with these gifts. Other famous magicians included Imhotep, the vizier and architect of King Djoser (2630 BC), and Djedi who, in the tale of Cheops and the Magicians, entertained the king by performing feats of magic and predicting future events.

These hieroglyphs are from a spell inscribed on one of the 'Cippi of Horus'. Part of the spell reads: 'Go away serpent, take back your poison which is in the body of the one who has been bitten. Behold, the magic power of Horus is stronger than yours. Go and hide, rebel! Go back on your steps, poison.'

The Exodus

The devastating plague of the death of the first-born sons of Egypt persuaded Pharaoh to allow the Israelites to leave Egypt. So they departed hurriedly with their flocks and herds. They travelled to Succoth, then 'God did not let them take the road to the Philistine territory, although it was the shortest' (Exodus 13:17). Instead they took a longer route, through the wilderness of the Sea of Reeds, via Etam to Pi-Hahiroth between Migdol and the sea, opposite Baal-Zephon.

It is here that Pharaoh's army, sent in pursuit, caught up with them. The terrified Israelites watched as Moses 'stretched out his hand over the sea, and Yahweh drove the sea back with a strong easterly wind all night and made the sea into dry land' (14:21). The Israelites passed through but as the Egyptians tried to follow them, the waters flowed back and they all drowned. The Israelites were then able to continue their journey towards the Promised Land.

It is difficult to reconstruct the route of the Exodus and the Israelites' wandering in the desert. Unfortunately, Egyptian records do not help. Accounts of Egyptian officials are usually full of the success of their expeditions and they invariably conclude that 'the army returned in safety, everyone being accounted for'. The escape of a number of slaves would therefore be unlikely to have been documented.

Archaeological surveys of Sinai have not produced any trace of the Israelites' passage. However, people living in tents and carrying few material possessions would not leave very much behind. Only the first part of the itinerary can be reconstructed with any degree of certainty, since the geographical names are known from Egyptian sources and are located east of the Delta.

The fleeing Israelites probably did not take the coastal route, the later route of the Philistines, because it was well guarded by a network of Egyptian forts. Succoth is most likely the Egyptian fortress of Tkw, near Pithom. Both Migdol and Baal-Zephon have been identified – the former is the Egyptian fortress northeast of Sileh, while the latter is located on a narrow stretch of land separating the Gulf of Serbonis from the Mediterranean.

The location of the Israelites' miraculous escape from Pharaoh's armies is the crucial point in the reconstruction of their journey. The conventional rendering, 'Red Sea', is in fact a mistranslation. The Hebrew words *yam suph* mean the 'Reed Sea' or the 'Sea of Marshes'. It probably refers to sweetwater lagoons and papyrus swamps near Per-Rameses and along the coast of the Mediterranean.

This may help explain the escape of the Israelites, since it would have been possible for people moving on foot to get across shallow waters, whereas fastmoving chariots, horses and riders would quickly get bogged down and sink in the mud.

The Bible tells us that there were about 'six hundred thousand men on the march, men, that is, not counting their families' (Exodus 12:37). Such a large number, however, could not have travelled undetected and it would have been impossible for all of them to survive in the desert. The figure probably represents a national census of the population of Israel at the time of David (tenth century BC), which was projected back to the time of the Exodus.

The miracle of the parting of the Sea of Reeds ends with a song of victory, a hymn of gratitude to God: 'Yahweh, who is like you, majestic in sanctity, who like you among the holy ones, fearsome of deed, worker of wonders?' (Exodus 15:11).

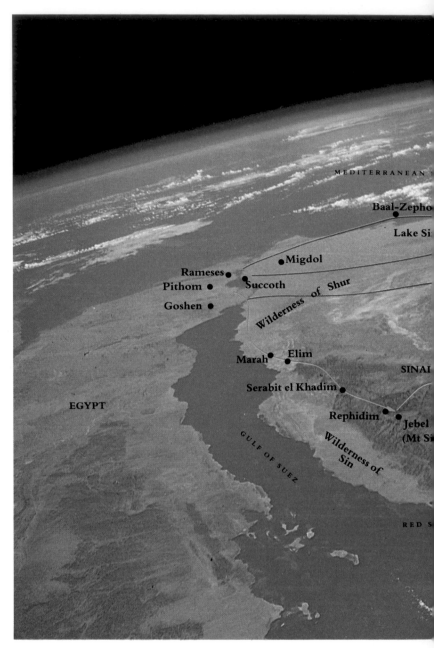

'Three months to the day after leaving Egypt, the Israelites reached the desert of Sinai . . . There, facing the mountain, Israel pitched camp' (EXODUS 19:1–2). Identifying the route of the Exodus across Sinai is difficult, since it is impossible to identify many of the locations named in the Bible. There are four main routes across Sinai.

The first, along the coast from Migdol towards Gaza, is referred to in the Bible as the Way of the Philistines, though they did not settle there until much later. It was not the route taken by the fugitives, probably because it was strongly guarded by a network of Egyptian forts. The report of a frontier official stationed at Tkw (the Biblical town Succoth) shows the care with which the Egyptians recorded the comings and goings of nomads through their borders. He wrote: 'We have just finished passing the tribes of Shasu of Edom through the fortress of Merneptah-Hotephirma in Tkw, to the pools of Pithom, in order to sustain them and their herds in the domain of the pharaoh.'

The second route, through the wilderness of Shur, led directly across the desert to Beersheba and Hebron, bypassing Kadesh-Barnea where the Israelites pitched their camp before entering the Promised Land.

The third route is the direct way across the desert to Ezion-Geber, a way often

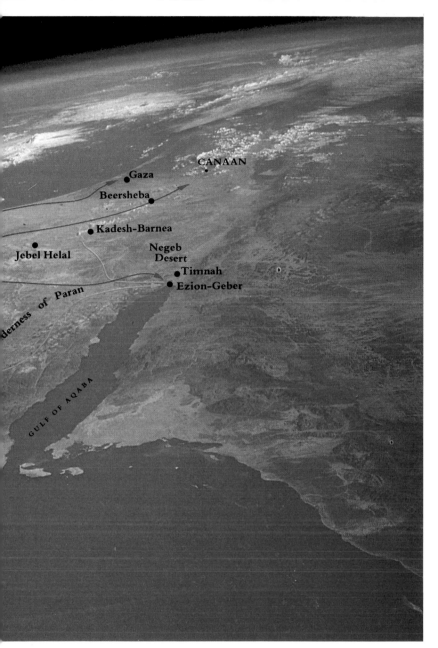

'So Pharaoh took 600 of his best chariots . . . with officers in each' (EXODUS 14:7). The New Kingdom witnessed a rapid expansion in the art of warfare, with the introduction of new weapons, the organisation of a professional standing army, the use of new battle tactics and a consummate strategy. The most important innovation was that of the two-wheeled horse-drawn chariot, which appeared in Egypt from Western Asia during the Hyksos period (c.1650 BC). It was a light vehicle, made of wood with some leather and metal parts. It was manned by two soldiers – a charioteer and a chariot warrior armed with a bow and spear and carrying a shield. It was the speed and mobility of the chariotry that introduced a daunting element of surprise on the battlefield.

The chariots were not armoured and so were unsuitable for direct attack. However, they were the ideal weapon for pursuing and harassing infantry. The prominence of the chariot corps and their officers, who were given special titles, suggests that they were an élite group within the Egyptian army. The same appears to be the case among other contemporary Near Eastern peoples, such as the Hurrians. On the lists of captives from the great battle of Megiddo of Thutmosis III and the battle of Kadesh of Rameses II, the 'Mariannu', the chariot warriors, are always mentioned separately.

taken by Egyptian merchants but which is harsh, waterless and unsuitable for slow-moving nomads.

The most favoured route (shown in blue) is the traditional way leading to the Egyptian turquoise mines at Serabit el Khadim, going south through the wilderness of Shur towards the wilderness of Sin. From there, the route continued into the highland area of southern Sinai, to Jebel Musa, the mountain usually identified as Mount Sinai. From there, a year later, the Israelites moved north into the wilderness of Paran, towards the oasis of Kadesh-Barnea. The tradition identifying the Biblical Mount Sinai with the present-day Mount Sinai is relatively late, dating to the emperor Constantine's mother, who had a chapel built at the foot of the mountain (4th century AD).

In the 6th century AD, the emperor Justinian built the monastery of St Catherine, which survives to this day. Attempts to identify Mount Sinai with Jebel Helal, not far from Kadesh-Barnea, do not carry conviction. It was from Kadesh-Barnea that Moses sent one man from each tribe to reconnoitre the best way to enter the Promised Land.

The Feast of the Passover

'Why is this night different from every other night?' These are among the first words of the Seder, the Passover meal celebrated by Jews the world over, in memory of the Exodus, the Israelites' deliverance from Egypt. 'Passover' refers to the angel of death's 'passing over' the Israelite homes. As a result, their first-born were saved from the last plague sent by God to persuade Pharaoh to release the Israelites from bondage. By answering the question and repeating the story with prayers and songs, the miracles of the past are called to mind, when God's promise was fulfilled and Israel returned to its ancient land.

The origins of the Passover festival are complex and the Biblical account differs from the Passover ritual as it has been practised since it evolved in the last days of the second Temple, more than a thousand years after the Exodus. It is suggested that the sacrifice of the lamb at springtime was connected with an ancient wilderness festival and that the eating of unleavened bread for seven days was a harvest festival, celebrated with the arrival of new crops. Both festivals subsequently merged into a single celebration of the Exodus.

Life in the wilderness

Once safe from the pursuing army of the Egyptians, Moses led the Israelites deeper and deeper into Sinai. They walked for three days in the desert of Shur, without finding any water. Finally, they reached the oasis of Marah, where the bitter water was undrinkable. So they began to complain about their condition – a complaint which recurs throughout their journey – and Moses, with the help of God, made the water sweet so that the Israelites could drink.

They continued their march to the oasis of Elim, where they rested under the shade of its palm trees. From there they went on into the desert of Sin. As they progressed into the desolate and barren wasteland, their years of slavery were forgotten and they started reminiscing about the good things of Egypt - the plentiful food, the abundant water, the shade of the trees, and they bemoaned their hunger and thirst: 'Why did we not die at Yahweh's hand in Egypt, where we used to sit round the flesh pots and could eat to our hearts' content!' (Exodus 16:3).

Moses once again had to appeal to God and the following morning 'manna', a fine edible substance, had fallen on the ground. That evening, quails flew over the desert, which the Israelites were able to catch.

They next pitched camp at Rephidim, where Moses miraculously made water gush out of the rocks. But they were not yet out of danger. A group of Amalekites, a fierce desert tribe, attacked them. The battle was won and the journey continued until the Israelites reached Mount Sinai, where they pitched their tents facing the awesome granite mountain.

Survival in the desert could not have been easy for a people used to a sedentary life in the fertile valley of the Nile. The desert is a forbidding place with great mountains, deep ravines and an almost total lack of vegetation. However, some form of existence is possible even in such hostile conditions.

From as early as the Third Dynasty onward (2600 BC), the Egyptians sent regular expeditions to Sinai, to mine turquoise at Wadi Meghara and Serabit el Khadim, in the vicinity of the Biblical Rephidim. Well-trodden caravan routes cross Sinai at many points, along wadis, and the caravans could have made use of caves for shelter. Nomads have always travelled within long-established patterns, from oasis to oasis, using waterholes, of which there are many under the porous limestone rocks of the desert.

Ancient travellers often describe the miraculous appearance of water when everything seemed lost. This happened to the commander of a mining expedition in the Wadi Hammamat, where Egyptian soldiers had been sent to quarry stone for the sarcophagus of King Mentuhotep (c.2060 BC). The inscription tells how, when the rays of the sun were beating inexorably and thirst was unbearable, a gazelle appeared and led the men towards an outcrop of rocks, where water began to sprout.

Desert nomads tend their goats, gather dates, figs and wild grasses; they supplement their diet by catching migrating birds such as quails, many of which fall exhausted in the desert after their long flight across the sea. They also gather the honey-sweet substance produced by insects feeding on the sap of the tamarisk trees, thought to be the 'manna' of the Bible.

In the days of the Exodus, donkeys, not camels, were used as beasts of burden, carrying the travellers' tents and their few utensils. Life was hard, but the Israelites survived, eventually to reach Canaan, the land promised to them by God.

This detail from the tomb of prince Khnumhotep at Beni Hassan illustrates a desert hunt, a popular pastime among the nobility of Egypt. They hunted wild animals such as gazelles, hare, ibexes, ostriches and antelopes, creatures which are now rare or extinct in the desert.

Lion and wild bull hunts were a royal sport, symbolising both the supreme power of the king over the most dangerous adversaries of the animal kingdom and his role as protector of his people. Hunting expeditions were accompanied by

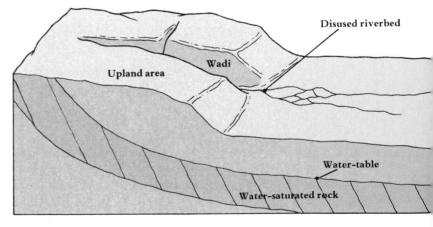

A cross-section of a desert valley shows the possible sources of water in such a barren environment. Although some historical and archaeological evidence suggests otherwise, the climate of the Near East was largely the same in Biblical times as it is now. There are naturally runs of good and bad years, and human activity, e.g. dam-building and deforestation, has changed the proportion of water infiltrating into the ground or evaporating. Recent

greyhounds, trained to detect the prey.

Other favourite sports of the ancient Egyptians were fowling and fishing in the marshes found at the edge of the desert, where floodwaters were trapped by the annual inundation. Scenes on tomb walls often depict family parties among tall papyrus thickets, women accompanying their menfolk on their light boats.

The wild birds were caught with 'throwsticks', cats being used to flush them out. Fish were either harpooned or caught in nets, then hauled onto land to be dried in the sun. Hunting desert animals did not greatly contribute to the Egyptian economy, but was rather a pleasant pastime. Furthermore, it varied a diet consisting mainly of cereals and pulses.

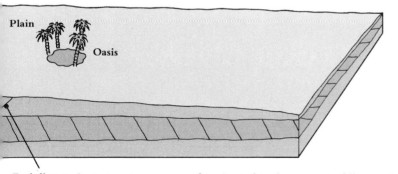

Plain

Oasis

Fault line Bedouin practices are a good guide to ancient survival techniques.

Water supplies were derived from wells; occasional, perennial or seasonal springs, often situated in the area where a fault comes to the surface; oases, found near a fault or where the water-table rises to ground level; flash floods, formed when rain falls on upland areas, collects in the wadis and flows in disused river channels.

These sources could be enhanced by quite modest works: springs could be led into tanks and walled in to reduce trampling by animals; wells could be lined and covered, and flash floods tamed by building small check dams to promote infiltration.

In the wilderness of Sinai, nomads follow the course of wadis – dry river valleys – on their journeys from one oasis to another. Occasional torrential downpours of rain cause flash floods which produce much of the water necessary for human and animal survival.

The Ten Commandments

Exodus 19 relates that three months after they had escaped from Egypt, Moses and the Israelites reached the desert of Sinai and pitched camp near Mount Sinai. Moses then ascended the mountain and Yahweh spoke to him, promising a covenant that would consecrate Israel and make the people God's sacred and 'personal possession': 'For me you shall be a kingdom of priests, a holy nation' (Exodus 19:6).

As instructed by Yahweh, Moses made the people purify themselves and two days later he led them out of the camp to meet God, 'and they took their stand at the bottom of the mountain' (19:17). Amid thunder and lightning, and with the sound of trumpets, Yahweh descended in the form of fire on the mountain, which was wrapped in smoke. He then proclaimed the words of the Law. The terrified people begged Moses to speak to them himself, but Moses said: 'Do not be afraid: God has come to test you so that your fear of him, being always in your mind, may keep you from sinning' (20:20).

The Ten Commandments or Decalogue are the core of Mosaic Law, and prescribe religious and moral rules of conduct. Also, the clauses forbidding the worship of nature and the making of images clearly established Israelite monotheism in marked contrast to the religions of neighbouring peoples. Although the Decalogue provided the religious and ethical basis of Israel's religion, it did not cover ritual duties. These were given to Moses by Yahweh in further revelations, which Moses in turn transmitted to the people. With the Decalogue, these became known as 'the Law'.

When Yahweh had finished giving the laws to Moses 'he gave him the two tablets of Testimony, tablets of stone inscribed by the finger of God' (31:18). These tablets, which Moses broke when he returned from Mount Sinai and saw the people worshipping a golden calf (32:19), were replaced by two new tablets on which God promised to rewrite the words of the first two; they were kept safe in the ark of the covenant.

The Law, known also as the 'Torah', is contained in the Book of the Covenant (Exodus 21–23), the code of Deuteronomy (Deuteronomy 12–24), the Holiness code (Leviticus 17–26), the Priestly code (Exodus 25:1–31;17:35–40), and most of Numbers and Leviticus. These collections possibly came from various sanctuaries after the conquest of Canaan. From the earliest times, the sanctuaries were the depositories of the Law, and their priests were Yahweh's spokesmen. Each of the collections has laws which originated at the time of Moses. But although Moses was reputedly the founder of the Torah, he did not create the finished code; the laws would have been transmitted orally from one generation of priests to another and committed to writing later.

While there are similarities with the laws of other peoples of the ancient Near East, Israelite law contains a considerably greater body of humanitarian precepts. Certain duties were enjoined, particularly to help the poor and the weak, whether friend or enemy. The Sabbath applied to animals. Restrictions were placed on the powerful, so that an employer was not to exploit his workmen or withold their wages when they were due.

Slaves, too, had rights; any injury would give a slave his freedom and if he ran away he was not to be returned to his master. The Law, first given by Yahweh to Israel through Moses, had then a threefold character, judicial, ceremonial and moral. It presented a new ethical challenge to the Israelites.

The Ten Commandments

'I am Yahweh your God who brought you out of Egypt where you lived as slaves.
You shall have no other gods to rival me.
You shall not make yourself a carved image or any likeness of anything in heaven above or on earth beneath. . . .
You shall not misuse the name of Yahweh your God for Yahweh will not leave unpunished anyone who misuses his name.
Remember the Sabbath day and keep it holy. . . .
Honour your father and mother. . . .
You shall not kill.
You shall not commit adultery.
You shall not steal.
You shall not give false evidence against your neighbour.
You shall not set your heart on your neighbour's house . . . spouse, or servant, man or woman, or ox, or donkey, or any of your neighbour's possessions' (Exodus 20:1–17).

The Ten Commandments or, more correctly, the Decalogue, the 'Ten Words', are the ethical code prefixed to the Sinaitic legislation. They are also called the Testimony (Exodus 25:21) and the Covenant (Deuteronomy 9:9). According to the Bible, this law was written by God himself, and so was regarded as sacred and binding. The Commandments are repeated in similar form in Deuteronomy 5. Originally, they were probably brief, for easy remembrance, and it is likely that the longer explanatory sections were later additions. Such collections of 'words' are known from elsewhere in the ancient world. Exodus 34:14–28 is such a collection, but there the concern is with ritual purity rather than morality.

Mount Sinai, on which Yahweh gave the Law to Israel, is also called Mount Horeb (Exodus 33:6). Its whereabouts are uncertain and there are three places which have been so far identified with it.

Early Christian tradition sited it at Jebel Musa, *above*, in the south of the Sinai peninsula. The setting of this mountain, 7,497ft/2,290m high, would seem an ideal place for the theophany but, if this tradition is accepted, it implies that the Israelites made an extended detour southwards.

Another possible site is Jebel Helal, 30mls/48km to the west of the oasis of Kadesh Barnea. This is feasible if the northerly route for the journey in the wilderness is accepted.

A 13th-century miniature from the manuscript of the treatise *La Somme Le Ray*, shows Moses on Mount Sinai, *top*, and Israelites worshipping the golden calf, *below*.

Moses destroys the golden calf

While Moses was communing with God on Mount Sinai, the people became impatient at his long absence and prevailed on Aaron, Moses' brother, to make a god 'to go at our head'. Aaron gathered the gold of the women's and children's earrings and 'melted it down in a mould and with it made the statue of a calf' (Exodus 32:4). He built an altar in front of the statue and proclaimed: 'Tomorrow will be a feast in Yahweh's honour.'

When Moses returned from Mount Sinai with the 'two tablets of the Testimony, tablets of stone inscribed by the finger of God', the sight of the calf and of the people dancing roused him to such anger that he threw down the tablets, and shattered them. He seized the calf, then burned and ground it 'into a powder which he scattered on the water and made the Israelites drink it' (Exodus 32:20).

With the people out of control, Moses rallied the Levites with the shout: 'Who is for Yahweh? to me!' He then gave them Yahweh's order to slaughter 'brother, friend and neighbour': about 3,000 men were killed. Later, after the Israelites had repented, the Covenant was renewed and new tablets were inscribed.

One of the purposes of the story of the golden calf was probably to give an account of the consecration of the tribe of Levi to the priesthood, for their fidelity to Yahweh and Moses. Another aim of the story, which was probably set down during the period of the division of the kingdom (see pp.94–5), was to condemn implicitly the practice of the bull cult in the northern kingdom of Israel.

In the late tenth century BC, on the division of the kingdom, King Jeroboam of Israel wished to lessen the attraction of the Temple at Jerusalem in southern Judah. So he set up golden calves at Dan and Bethel, the northern centres of Yahweh worship. These calves were probably intended to be regarded as visible figures on which the invisible god rode. It is doubtful, though, whether many worshippers made a distinction such as this. 'The sin of Jeroboam, son of Nebat', was idolatry, the linking of Yahweh with a nature deity and in turn the identifying of him with the Canaanite gods.

The golden calf itself can be linked, some scholars think, to either the Egyptian Apis bull of Memphis or the Heliopolitan Mnevis bull. However, the bull was a common symbol of power and fertility in the ancient Near East. In Mesopotamia, Sin, the moon-god, is called 'mighty young bull with strong horns, perfect limbs', and in the Babylonian Gilgamesh epic 'the bull of heaven' comes down to rampage on the earth. Protective, winged genie figures, with the bodies of bulls and the heads of men, guarded gateways. Later these were sometimes called 'kuribu', the cherubim of the Bible, and as such they were used as the seat of God's presence in the Temple.

Among the people of Canaan, into which Joshua, Moses' successor, would lead the Israelites, the bull or calf was the animal of Baal, the god of thunder and lightning. Baal was often depicted as wearing a helmet with horns; the latter, some scholars suggest, indicate that he once had the form of a bull. But horns were often a symbol of divinity and there is no explicit evidence for the figure of Baal deriving from that of a bull. Whatever its origins, the golden calf in Exodus 32 represents the reduction of Yahweh to the status of a nature god, like those of surrounding peoples.

The Code of Hammurabi
The Law Code of Hammurabi, king of Babylon in the eighteenth century BC, is inscribed in cuneiform on a diorite stela, $7\frac{1}{2}$ft/2.3m high. It is surmounted by a bas-relief showing Hammurabi, standing, receiving instructions to write the laws from the sun-god Shamash, the god of justice. The stela was discovered by French archaeologists in 1901–2. It had been taken from Babylon to Susa (the Shushan of Esther) by a raiding Elamite king in the twelfth century BC. For a long time it was regarded as the oldest known collection of laws and certain striking parallels between it and the Mosaic Law gave rise to the notion that the Biblical laws had been borrowed from this Mesopotamian collection.

It has now become clear that there was a common or generally recognised body of law in the ancient Near East. Substantial parts of collections older than the Hammurabi Code are now known, the earliest being the Sumerian laws of Ur-Nammu, c.2100 BC. In addition, material has been recovered from elsewhere, including Assyrian and Hittite laws.

Today it is thought that the parallels between Babylonian and Biblical laws should be seen as local modifications of the common tradition. The Mosaic laws show many similarities with the Hammurabi Code. For example, according to the Hammurabi Code 'If a citizen steals a citizen's child he shall be put to death', while the Bible states: 'Anyone who abducts a person will be put to death' (Exodus 21:16). Likewise, in the Hammurabi Code, 'If a son has struck his father, they shall cut off his hand', which the Bible expresses as, 'Anyone who strikes father or mother will be put to death' (Exodus 21:15).

There are, however, differences. For example, in Babylonian law, crimes connected with property and possessions carried similar penalties to crimes against people, whereas in the Bible there is a clear distinction, and only the latter call for physical penalties.

This bronze cult bull, *above*, was found at an open-air cult site and is dated to about 1200 BC. The site itself was at the centre of a small number of Iron Age settlements and lies on top of a ridge between Dothan and Tirzah. It is possible that these were Israelite settlements of the tribe of Manasseh.

The bull's deep eye sockets indicate that they might once have held precious stones. The figurine, possibly a votive offering, is 7in/18cm long and 5in/13cm high and stands on its hooves without support.

The Egyptians cast statues of their fertility god, the sacred bull Apis, in bronze, as in the example, *left*. Some scholars link Apis with the golden calf of the Israelites. The bull's back bears the distinguishing marks of an eagle's wing. At Memphis, the Egyptians also worshipped Apis in the form of a living bull; at his death, the bull was embalmed and buried, then replaced by another bull of similar appearance and characteristics.

The many names of God

YHWH is the name by which the earliest Israelites called God. Later, the name was regarded as being too sacred to be uttered and so Adonai, 'My Lord', was substituted. Although the original pronunciation is not certain, early Greek transcriptions indicate that it was probably 'Yahweh'.

Yahweh shares some characteristics of a sky god – a god of thunder and lightning (Exodus 19:16; 20:18). He was associated with mountains and was called by the enemies of Israel 'a god of the hills' (1 Kings 20:23). His manifestation was often as fire, as at Mount Sinai and in the burning bush.

A shorter form, 'Yah', was also used (Exodus 15:2) and some scholars believe that this is the older form, originating in an exclamation to God – 'Yah!' – which came to be accepted as the divine name. Others claim that it is a verb from the root 'hayah', 'to be' or 'to become', and that it meant 'I am that I am' or 'I will be that I will be' (Exodus 3:14). According to one tradition of the call of Moses, the divine name Yahweh was revealed to him in Egypt: 'To Abraham, Isaac and Jacob I appeared as El Shaddai, but I did not make the name Yahweh known to them' (Exodus 6:3).

As specifically the name of the Covenant God, it was thereafter used of the Israelite deity, often in contrast with the gods of other peoples. With the Covenant, Yahweh had adopted Israel as his people and, as a jealous god, demanded total allegiance from them. They were to worship no other god but Yahweh. Much later, the Jewish exiles in Babylon were given an explicit statement of Yahwistic monotheism: 'I am Yahweh, and there is no other, there is no other god but me' (Isaiah 45:5).

God, manifested as fire

In the Bible, fire often indicates the presence of God. At Horeb, Yahweh revealed himself to Moses 'in a flame blazing from the middle of a bush . . . God called to him from the middle of the bush . . .' (Exodus 3:2–4). When the Israelites left Egypt, Yahweh preceded them as a guide through the wilderness '. . . by day in a pillar of cloud to show them the way, and by night in a pillar of fire to give them light, so that they could march by day and by night. The pillar of cloud never left its place ahead of the people during the day, nor the pillar of fire during the night' (Exodus 13:21).

Again, he appeared as fire on Mount Sinai: 'Mount Sinai was entirely wrapped in smoke, because Yahweh had descended on it in the form of fire. The smoke rose like smoke from a furnace and the whole mountain shook violently' (Exodus 19:18). Fire was also a symbol of the holiness and justice of God: 'For Yahweh your God is a consuming fire, a jealous God' (Deuteronomy 4:24). Here jealousy is the extravagance of God's love for his people. Divine anger with humanity was considered as being like fire and the element was also associated with punishment.

When challenged to show his presence, Yahweh descended as fire at the contest between Elijah and the prophets of Baal. There, as a mark of his presence and approval, fire fell on the victim sacrificed to Yahweh (1 Kings 18:38).

Building the sanctuary

After the Book of the Covenant had been given by Yahweh (see pp.40–1), Moses spent 40 days and nights on Mount Sinai. During this time, Yahweh gave him instructions for the building of a sanctuary by the Israelites: 'Make me a Sanctuary so that I can reside among them. You will make it all according to the design for the Dwelling and the design for its furnishing I shall now show you' (Exodus 25:8). There follows an elaborate and lengthy description of the way in which the ark of the covenant, the tabernacle and the furnishings were to be made (Exodus 25:10–27).

The Israelites themselves were to contribute the precious metals and materials required for this undertaking. Bezalel of the tribe of Judah and Oholiab of the tribe of Dan were chosen by Yahweh to be the main craftsmen.

The tabernacle, as it is now known in Christian literature, through the Vulgate, the first Latin Bible, is called in Hebrew the *ohel mo'ed*, the Tent of Meeting, or the *mishkan*, the Dwelling or Abode. The latter term seems originally to have been used for the temporary dwelling of the nomad – namely, a tent.

It was here that Yahweh communed with Moses. Yahweh's presence was indicated by a cloud hanging over the entrance to the tent. Those wishing to consult him went to the tent, where Moses acted as intermediary: the desert sanctuary seems, therefore, to have also had a role as an oracle.

The Dwelling was made of wooden frames put together to make a building of 30 cubits (45ft/14m) long and 10 cubits (15ft/5m) wide and high. The east side was left open. The structure was covered with bands of fabric sewn together to make two big pieces; they were joined by hooks and clips and were embroidered with figures of cherubim. Goatskin bands, wider and longer than the first fabric, were stretched 'like a tent over the Dwelling'. Finally, all was covered with ramskins, dyed red, and then by fine leather hides.

At the entrance to the Dwelling was a finely woven linen curtain of red, violet and purple. As with other elements of the Dwelling, the description of the hangings is reminiscent of Solomon's Temple (see pp.86–9). The textiles of that period would have been dyed with the famous purple manufactured by the Phoenicians. The colour is secreted by a special gland of a marine mollusc, the murex trunculus. Purple was highly prized and was the characteristic colour of royalty and power. Fabrics made of this colour were expensive. Linen was made in Egypt; crimson colouring was obtained by crushing the tiny cochineal insect, the Kermocollus vermilio, which is a parasite of oak.

Over the ark, which contained the stone tablets inscribed with the Law, there was a lid of gold, called the *kapporeth*, on which there were two cherubim. It was from above the *kapporeth* that Yahweh met Moses and spoke to him. It would seem that the ark represented the footstool of the deity, who was seated on a throne formed by the cherubim. However, as Israelite religion forbade the representation of images, it is not clear how God's presence was envisioned.

It is possible that the *kapporeth* was a later tradition and that it subsequently took the role ascribed to the ark – that is, the sign of the divine presence – in the period after the Exile in Babylon. While the traditions about the sanctuary and the ark are ancient, going back to the period of the Jews' desert wanderings, the descriptions of them were probably written at the time of Solomon and were based on his Temple.

So that he might 'dwell in their midst', Yahweh gave the Israelites, through Moses, precise directions on how to build a portable sanctuary.

The heart of the sanctuary was the tabernacle, **1**, which was divided into two compartments by a veil called the *parokhet*. Made of finely woven linen, it was dyed 'violet-purple, red-purple and crimson and embroidered with great winged creatures'.

The first compartment was the Holy Place and contained an incense altar, a lampstand and the shewbread table. The incense burner was made of acacia wood and was covered with gold. It was 18in/0.4m square and 36in/0.8m high, it had horns projecting at the four corners and a gold moulding around the top.

The lampstand, or *menorah*, was in the form of a stylised tree and made of gold. From the base and central column stemmed six branches, rising to the same height as the centre. The seven lamps were placed one on the end of each of the branches and on the central shaft.

Outside the entrance to the tabernacle stood a bronze basin, **2**, where priests could wash during ceremonies, and an altar of sacrifice, **3**, for burnt offerings.

The open court surrounding the tabernacle was 150ft/46m by 75ft/23m. This was bounded, **4**, by bronze posts and silver rods, from which fell linen curtains.

The table was for the permanent offering of personal loaves (shewbread) to Yahweh. It was a wooden table, covered with gold and with rings attached to the legs for carrying. Also on it, according to tradition, were gold dishes, cups, jars and libation bowls.

Behind the veil in the tabernacle was the Holy of Holies, in which stood the ark of the covenant. At the entrance to the tabernacle there was a finely woven curtain of red, violet and purple.

The ark of the covenant

The tabernacle was designed to house the ark of the covenant or Testimony, so called because the stone tablets containing the Law and given to Moses by Yahweh were placed in the ark. As described in Exodus 25:10–22; 37:1–9, the ark, from the Latin 'arca' meaning chest, was made of acacia wood and was about 4ft/1.2m long and 2½ft/0.7m wide and high.

The ark of the covenant was covered within and without with pure gold. Rings were attached, through which poles for carrying it were passed. Over the ark there was a lid of gold, called the *kapporeth*, generally translated as 'mercy seat' or 'propitiatory', from the Hebrew *kapper* which means 'to cover' or 'to perform the expiation'. Two cherubim stood facing each other at each end of the *kapporeth* and covered it with their wings.

The death of Moses

Yahweh spoke to Moses . . . and said to him: "Climb this mountain of the Abarim, Mount Nebo, in the country of Moab, opposite Jericho, and view the Canaan which I am giving to the Israelites as their domain. Die on the mountain you have climbed, and be gathered to your people . . .'" (Deuteronomy 32:48–50). By this time Moses was reputedly 120 years old, yet with 'his eye undimmed, his vigour unimpaired' (Deuteronomy 34:8) – a description that stretches credulity but fits well with the Biblical picture of Moses as a man of remarkable energy and charisma.

Not only had Moses engineered the Israelites' exodus from Egypt, he also preserved their unity during the years of wandering in the Sinai desert. There he developed a new definition of Israel's traditional belief in the one God of Abraham. The Law that Moses received gave the people a new mode of worshipping Yahweh and provided them a code governing almost every aspect of life. As his final achievement, he led the people out of the desert to the threshold of Canaan.

Although Canaan, as strictly defined, lay to the west of the River Jordan, some areas to the east were also included in the 'Promised Land'. These were conquered under the leadership of Moses himself. After the destruction of the towns of Arad and Hormah in the south of Canaan, the Israelites turned northeastwards to the country of Moab. From here they needed to move north of the Dead Sea in order to cross the Jordan into Palestine.

They sent messengers to the Amorite king Sihon, asking permission to pass through his territory. He refused, so the Israelites attacked and seized his cities. The same treatment was meted out to Og, king of Bashan. The nomadic Midianites were also crushed. Then Moses allowed the tribes of Reuben, Gad and Manasseh to settle in the Transjordanian lands taken from the Amorites. The Israelites, after their long wanderings, now possessed the core of a homeland. His work almost complete, Moses now attempted to ensure that Israel would not stray from the guidelines he had laid down for them.

Almost the entire book of Deuteronomy is taken up with Moses' final teachings. He particularly stressed how Yahweh had protected the Israelites and given them victory over their foes: 'The peoples of the world, seeing that you bear Yahweh's name, will be afraid of you.' (Deuteronomy 28:10). To keep this special status the Israelites had to obey without question Moses' laws – the Ten Commandments (see pp.40–1), plus a host of religious, civil and dietary regulations.

Knowing that he was about to die, Moses confirmed Joshua as the new leader. Then Moses went to meet his fate on Mount Nebo, from where he could have a glimpse of the Promised Land across the Jordan. For a glimpse was all that he was allowed. Curiously, the Bible relates that God wanted to punish the prophet who had practically invented the cult of Yahweh: 'Because, with the other Israelites, you broke faith with me at the Waters of Meribah-Kadesh . . . because you did not make my holiness clear to the Israelites; you may only see the country from outside; you cannot enter it.' (Deuteronomy 32:51–2).

The account of the Meribah incident hardly suggests a sin on Moses' part. On that occasion, only his followers doubted Yahweh – yet still Moses was punished, by being deprived of his ultimate goal. Still, his epitaph ran as follows: 'since then, there has never been such a prophet in Israel as Moses, the man who knew Yahweh face to face' (Deuteronomy 34:10).

The area shown here is the 'Promised Land' of Canaan, as defined in the Bible; also shown are the likely routes taken by the Israelites approaching from Sinai. From their desert camp at Kadesh-Barnea, Moses sent out spies, one from each tribe, to 'reconnoitre the land of Canaan' (Numbers 13:2).

The map, *left*, shows how the spies went north (black line) as far as Hebron, though one verse (Numbers 13:21) claims that they reached Rehob at the very limits of Canaan.

Moses then announced to the people that only Joshua and Caleb, of all those who had left Egypt, would be allowed to enter the Promised Land. The rest would die in the desert, but their children would inherit the land. Inflamed by this, the Israelites tried a direct assault on Canaan by the route of the spies, but they were soundly defeated

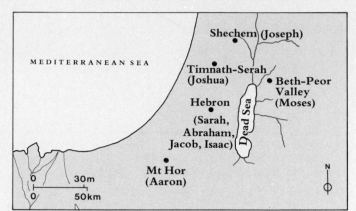

The patriarchs' graves

The map shows the burial sites of the patriarchs. Moses was buried in a valley near Mount Nebo, but the exact spot is unknown (Deuteronomy 34:6). His brother, Aaron, died on Mount Hor and was presumably buried there (Numbers 20:28). The burial place of Abraham was always known, for he had bought as a family plot the field and cave of Mamre from the Hittites of Hebron. Here he buried his chief wife, Sarah (Genesis 23:19). After his death, Abraham was buried by his sons Isaac and Ishmael in the same grave at Mamre (Genesis 25:9–10).

Isaac was also buried there (Genesis 35:27–29), as was his son Jacob (Genesis 50:1–14). Jacob's son Joseph died in Egypt, but his body was taken by the Israelites and placed in a family plot at Shechem (Joshua 24:32). Joshua was buried at a new site, Timnath-Serah in Ephraim (Joshua 24:30).

Moses: prince, prophet and miracle-worker

Moses is a well documented but elusive character. The Old Testament casts him in a bewildering number of roles. First he is seen as an Egyptian prince, then as a refugee and desert wanderer; next he appears as a rebel leader in Egypt, then as the archetypal Old Testament prophet and miracle-worker. Finally, he is described as a giver of laws and a military commander. It is a remarkable achievment for Moses to have performed all these deeds in one single, albeit long, lifetime.

Moses is the towering figure of the Hebrew Bible. It is he that moulded a rabble of slaves into a nation, Israel, committed to fulfil the divine purpose, and he never ceased to remind them of their origin: 'Love the stranger then, for you were once strangers in Egypt' (Deuteronomy 10:19). No other individual in the Old Testament has such a constant and deep relationship with God. He is the divine spokesman *par excellence*, but also flesh and blood, with human failings. He is passionate in his eagerness to convey God's teachings to Israel, but also irascible and short-tempered when they fall short of what is demanded of them: in the Bible, Moses' imperfections are not obscured.

Careful assessment of the material suggests that Moses was a historical figure – the Mosaic law-code, for instance, arguably bears the stamp of a single, original genius. Yet like any great religious teacher, his personal history is overlaid with a number of extra images, as important to the developing faith of Judaism as was Moses himself. It is only necessary to compare the elaborations which surround the other great religious teachers of the past, such as Jesus, Buddha and Mohammed. Because they succeeded in passing on their teachings, they became figures around whom various traditions and legends have gathered.

by the Amalekites and Canaanites at Hormah. After a visit to Mount Hor, where Moses' brother Aaron died, the Israelites moved to the east of the Dead Sea.

According to Numbers 20 and 21, they arrived there by going around the kingdom of Edom, which refused them passage. They travelled southeast to the Sea of Suph (Red Sea), then north up to Iye-Abarim (blue line).

Then they skirted the kingdom of Moab, marching in a northwesterly direction. After conquering the Amorite kingdom at Heshbon, they struck at Bashan, defeating its king, Og, at Edrei. Then they returned to camp in the plains of Moab, near the Jordan.

The account in Numbers 33 gives a very different route (broken line). Instead of going south to avoid Edom, the Israelites are said to have gone east to Zalmonah before arriving at Iye-Abarim. They then appear to have gone due north, passing Dibon to reach the plains of Moab. Here Moses gave his final instructions and blessings to the people, before climbing Mount Nebo to meet his fate.

The invasion according to Joshua and Judges

After Moses' death, according to the Bible, the Israelites entered and conquered the 'Promised Land'. The best known version of the conquest (Joshua 1–12) begins with Yahweh's instructions to Joshua, Moses' successor: '. . . go now and cross the Jordan, you and this whole people, into the country which I am giving to them [the Israelites]. Every place you tread with the soles of your feet I shall give to you' (Joshua 1:2–3). There is then a description of how the unified tribes, under Joshua's leadership, systematically conquered within a few years the land west of the River Jordan. The narrative ends with a list of conquered kings.

A more fragmentary version of the conquest, supposedly relating to the time immediately after Joshua's death, appears in Judges 1–2:5. Apparently contradicting the Joshua account, it describes the Israelites as only just beginning to gain a foothold in Canaan. The conquest is described in terms of sporadic military operations by individual tribal groups. Judges 1 concludes with a list of important cities whose inhabitants the various tribes did not drive out, including several which Joshua is supposed already to have conquered.

The discrepancies between the two accounts have led to widely differing ideas on the nature of the conquest. Early scholars tried to harmonise the two versions by explaining that, although Joshua conquered the land, the tribes delayed taking possession of it. Many scholars still hold a modified form of this view. They maintain that Joshua's initial conquest involved certain key cities which weakened the Canaanite city-state system. This made possible a second stage of conquest, when the tribes gradually gained complete possession of the land.

Other scholars think there was a gradual movement of the nomadic or semi-nomadic tribes into the Palestinian hill country. These tribes initially coexisted peacefully with the Canaanite cities. Later, the Israelites became sedentary farmers and moved into the arable lands of the city-states. There they came into conflict with the Canaanites and sometimes resorted to military conquest. This view rejects a sweeping, unified conquest under Joshua. It is based more on the Judges account, and on other selected passages, which are generally agreed to belong to a more reliable and older tradition.

A third approach maintains that there was no conquest from outside but an internal revolt against the Canaanite authorities by exploited elements of the rural population. The Hebrews are equated with the *habiru* – the term *habiru* seeming to denote individuals or groups who were in some way outside the social system.

There is not yet any definite solution to the problem. Certainly, examples within the context of Near Eastern history show that such a 'conquest' usually occurs as a result of the gradual infiltration of new groups rather than a sudden violent invasion. If the Joshua version is ignored, the other Biblical sources more or less support this interpretation of events.

Though Joshua implies otherwise, many scholars are convinced that the tribes came into being after the settlement in Canaan. Some tribal names apparently came from the names of regions where the people settled, such as 'mountain of Naphthali', and 'desert of Judah'. The Joshua account, which in fact refers almost exclusively to the small territory of the tribe of Benjamin, was probably used by the later writers as the basis of an idealised, rather than an actual, pan-Israelite conquest.

The inscription on the Merneptah stela, which dates to the late 13th century BC, probably refers to a small scale Palestinian campaign by the Egyptian pharaoh. It is the earliest text which explicitly mentions Israel.

Israel seems to be located in Canaan, perhaps in the Judaean hill country. The way the name is written indicates a 'people', so it seems that at this period Israel existed as a people but not yet as a nation.

Archaeology and Biblical scholarship

Most scholars date the 'conquest' of Canaan to the end of the Late Bronze Age and the beginning of the Iron Age (thirteenth to twelfth centuries BC) and see the process of settlement continuing until the time of David. In view of the conflicting nature of the Biblical sources, archaeological evidence is of prime importance in any attempt to reach the truth.

Attempts to correlate the archaeological and literary evidence in relation to particular cities mentioned in the Biblical account have not on the whole been successful. Of the three cities specifically said to have been destroyed by Joshua – that is, Jericho, Ai and Hazor – the first two were abandoned at this period or had only an insignificant population. Some other places mentioned in the conquest account were also uninhabited. Hazor, however, was destroyed at about this time. The Israelites may have been responsible, but the destruction could equally well be attributed to other factors. The same holds true for other cities which show evidence of destruction, such as Bethel and Lachish.

In the more densely populated areas of Syro-Palestine, there is no marked break in continuity between the Bronze and Iron Ages. There is, however, a significant change in the pattern of settlement. With the beginning of the Iron Age, numerous unfortified villages appear in hitherto unsettled areas, particularly the central and southern hill country and parts of Galilee. There are a few villages on abandoned mounds such as Arad and Ai, and villages supersede the Bronze Age cities of Hazor and Megiddo. These villages had an economy based on agriculture and stock breeding. It is tempting to equate this new settlement with the Israelites, but so far nothing definite can be said of the origin of these settlers.

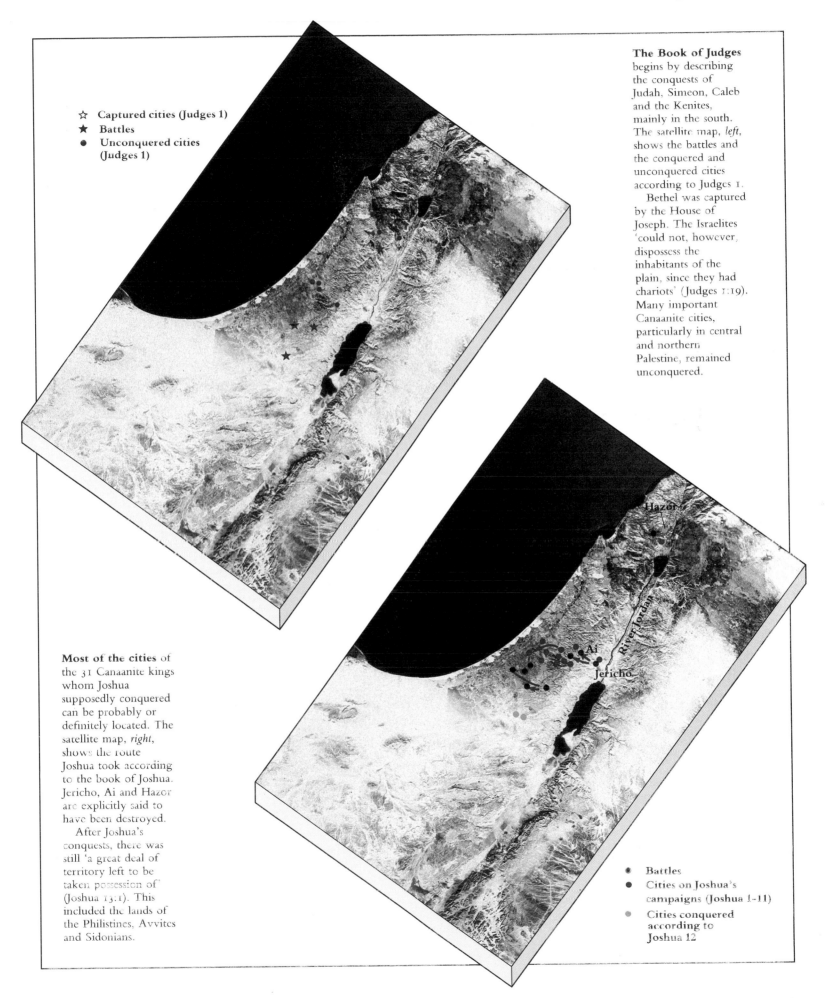

☆ Captured cities (Judges 1)
★ Battles
● Unconquered cities (Judges 1)

The Book of Judges begins by describing the conquests of Judah, Simeon, Caleb and the Kenites, mainly in the south. The satellite map, *left*, shows the battles and the conquered and unconquered cities according to Judges 1.

Bethel was captured by the House of Joseph. The Israelites 'could not, however, dispossess the inhabitants of the plain, since they had chariots' (Judges 1:19). Many important Canaanite cities, particularly in central and northern Palestine, remained unconquered.

Most of the cities of the 31 Canaanite kings whom Joshua supposedly conquered can be probably or definitely located. The satellite map, *right*, shows the route Joshua took according to the book of Joshua. Jericho, Ai and Hazor are explicitly said to have been destroyed.

After Joshua's conquests, there was still 'a great deal of territory left to be taken possession of' (Joshua 13:1). This included the lands of the Philistines, Avvites and Sidonians.

Hazor

Ai
Jericho
River Jordan

● Battles
● Cities on Joshua's campaigns (Joshua 1-11)
● Cities conquered according to Joshua 12

Canaanite culture

The 'Promised Land' was, as the Israelites had hoped, reasonably blessed with natural resources. But their new home offered spiritual as well as material temptations. Yahweh warned: '. . . if you go astray, serve other gods . . . Yahweh's anger will be kindled against you, he will shut the heavens, there will be no more rain, the soil will not yield its produce and, in the fine country given you by Yahweh, you will quickly perish' (Deuteronomy 11:16). Indeed, if the Israelites had not struggled so hard to preserve their identity, they might well have been overwhelmed by Canaan – as much by its seductive culture as by its powerful chariotry.

Occupying the hill country of central Palestine would not have posed insurmountable problems for the Israelites, since much of it seems to have lain empty. However, Galilee, the Jezreel valley and the coastlands were highly urbanised and well guarded by a vigorous Canaanite population.

The accounts in Joshua and Judges paint a picture of numerous independent city-states. Ruled by 'kings', such states were based on a fortified capital – cities such as Hazor, Ai and Jericho – dominating a satellite region of villages and farmland. The population was racially mixed, including Semites, Hurrians, Indo-Europeans and others of indeterminate origin such as the Philistines. Despite this apparent disunity there are enough common factors to describe, in general terms, a Canaanite civilisation.

The Israelites were impressed by Canaanite culture, particularly by its wealth and technology. The Bible records with some wonder such things as the king of Hazor's iron chariots (Judges 4:3) and the splendid scale armour of Goliath (1 Samuel 17:5). Apart from metalwork, the Canaanites excelled at ivory carving and textile manufacture – the name Canaanite may even come from the word for the purple dye (*kinahhu*), famous in the coastal region.

Though their economy was largely based on agriculture, the Canaanites also profited from their manufactured goods and their excellent position at the crossroads of the trade routes between Asia, Africa and the Mediterranean. In Egypt, Canaan was well known for its produce (notably oil, wine, grain, timber and cattle), luxury goods (inlaid chariots and ornate silver and gold vessels), and skilled musicians.

Canaanite gods mirrored Canaanite society. While Yahweh was a desert god, whose shrine was a tent carried about by nomadic followers, the Canaanite gods had established temples which were an important focal point of city life. As varied as its devotees, Canaanite religion had room for foreign gods, including Egyptian deities such as Ptah and Amun. Most popular, however, were Canaan's native gods and goddesses, the *baalim* and *ashtaroth*, so detested in the Bible.

Canaan's pantheon of deities personified, broadly speaking, natural forces. This was anathema to the official cult of Yahweh, but attractive to some of his more wayward followers. For it is unlikely that all the ancient Israelites worshipped the male god of the Old Testament – there is some evidence that he was often worshipped in company with a female deity. Otherwise he was worshipped alongside Baal and the other gods as people saw fit. Indeed, the major theme of the Old Testament after the conquest is the constant struggle to preserve the integrity of monotheistic Yahwism within a people who were constantly backsliding into the abominations of Canaan.

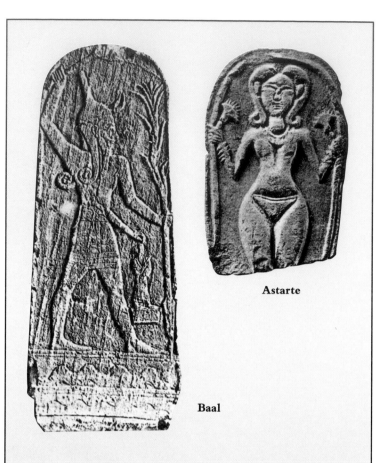

Astarte

Baal

The gods of Canaan

Judging from the myths recorded at Ugarit, the pantheon of gods and goddesses worshipped by the ancient Canaanites was like that of the Greek Olympian deities – a quarrelsome family of individuals with larger-than-life personalities. El, reminiscent of the Biblical Elohim, was the oldest deity and considered to be 'creator of creatures' and 'father of mankind'. Despite his senior role, he played a minor part in cult and legend. The younger deity, Baal, was chief of the gods and personification of the Storm. Many Ugaritic poems relate Baal's adventures, such as his incestuous affair with his sister Anath, both in the guise of buffaloes. Another saga concerns Baal's ambition, as a junior god acquiring new status, for more magnificent accommodation, and his struggles against Yam ('Sea') and Mot ('Death'), rivals for the favours of El.

The gods were balanced by a complex of great goddesses, with interweaving personalities sometimes hard to distinguish. Thus Astarte shared her warlike character with Anath; but while Anath was generally described as a 'maiden', Astarte was a voluptuous figure, often depicted as a naked fertility goddess. The similarly named Asherah was called the 'Lady of the Sea', whose cult was favoured in the Phoenician ports of Tyre and Sidon. There was also a supporting cast of lesser deities, such as Shapash the sun-goddess and Kothar, god of craftsmanship. In addition, many towns had their local variants of Baal ('the Lord') or Baalat ('the Lady'), such as the Baal-Zebub ('Lord of the Flies') who had an oracle at Ekron (2 Kings 1:2). It is against this background that we must see the Israelite struggle to impose the monotheistic cult of Yahweh.

The excavation of Ugarit

Modern knowledge of Canaanite civilisation was revolutionised by the discovery of the ancient city of Ugarit in 1929. Before then, archaeologists were largely dependent for information on scraps of data preserved by classical authors and the Old Testament's polemical diatribes against the 'sinful' Canaanites. With the excavation of Ugarit's massive libraries, the ancient Canaanites were at last able to speak for themselves.

The rich strata of Ugarit (modern Ras Shamra) have also provided an almost complete picture of the development of a Canaanite town over some 6,000 years. Ugarit, on the north

Syrian coast, began as a small fishing and farming community during the seventh millennium BC. Over the centuries it developed into a substantial urban settlement which, despite several major catastrophes (probably due to earthquake), was always rebuilt. In the fourteenth century BC, Ugarit reached its 'golden age'. Its dynasty of kings ruled as respected merchant princes, dealing with the great kings of the Hittites, Egypt and Babylonia. Cyprus was an established trading partner, linking Ugarit with the Mycenaean world of the Aegean. The city was finally destroyed by an earthquake in about 1200 BC.

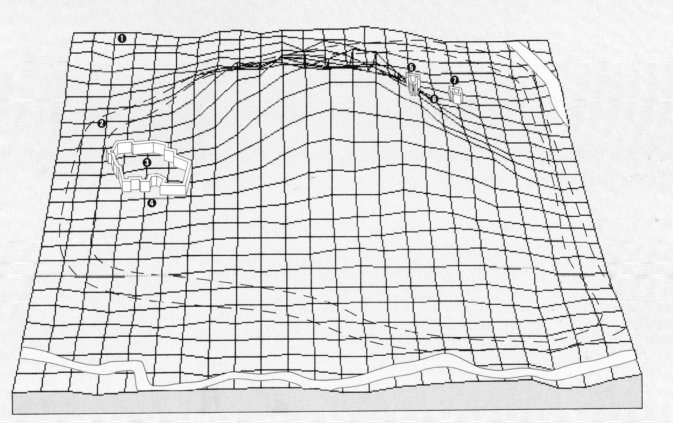

Considered the supreme example of a Canaanite city, Ugarit actually lay outside the strict Biblical limits of Canaan, being on the north Syrian coast. By the 14th century, Ugarit controlled some 30mls/48km of coastland, including four ports, and was thus well placed for sea trade. The main port was the nearby harbour of Minet el Beida, **1**. Commerce brought great

prosperity. At its largest extent during the 14th century, the massive defensive rampart, **2**, enclosed an area of some 50 acres (20.2 hectares). Inside was the extensive palace complex, **3**, comprising 67 rooms and five courtyards on the ground floor over some 10,000 square yards/9,145 square metres, plus an extensive upper storey. It was probably the largest

palace in Syro-Palestine at this period. Lavish wood and ivory panelling once decorated the walls of the state rooms.

The palace served both as a royal residence, including the royal burial vaults and the centre of administration. Enormous libraries, **4**, stored thousands of cuneiform tablets – legal documents, treaties and royal correspondence. There

were two major temples in the Upper City for the storm-god Baal, **5**, and his father Dagon, the corn-god, **7**. Nearby was a priest's library, **6**, containing a large and invaluable archive of ritual and mythological texts, the main source for the religion of the Canaanites.

'The heavens rained oil, the valleys flowed with honey.' The imagery in these

Ugaritic verses is inescapably the same as that used by Moses in describing Canaan: 'a country flowing with milk and honey' (Exodus 3:8).

Most exciting of all the finds from Ugarit are the many texts with similar parallels to the Old Testament language. An early discovery was that Ugarit's scribes had simplified the cuneiform script for writing on clay an alphabet of 30 letters,

practically identical to the Hebrew. Many of the texts written in this script reveal striking parallels with Biblical style, vocabulary and grammar. The way in which Baal is characterised as a god who rules the storm, rain, snow and lightning, and defeats the old 'dragon' of the sea, is markedly similar to the poetic descriptions of Yahweh in the Psalms.

The fall of Jericho

When the people heard the sound of the trumpet, they raised a mighty war cry and the wall collapsed then and there' (Joshua 6:20). As the walls of Jericho crumbled, Joshua led the Israelites into the city, which they utterly destroyed. The capture of Jericho was the Israelites' first major success in the Promised Land. Prior to the attack on Jericho, the Israelites had achieved victories only on the east side of the River Jordan – the land of Canaan proper remained untouched. The next phase of the conquest depended on establishing a foothold to the west of the Jordan.

Also known as the 'City of Palms', Jericho was situated in a lush part of the Jordan valley, commanding some important trade routes. It must have been considerably wealthy. The account in Joshua refers to booty of silver, gold, bronze and iron, and to rich vestments imported from Babylonia – all seized by the Israelites for Yahweh's treasury.

Carefully planning his attack, Joshua sent two spies across the Jordan to explore the country and Jericho. The spies entered Jericho and took lodgings with Rahab, a prostitute, who concealed them and then helped them to slip away safely the next day back to the Israelite camp: their news was that Jericho's morale was low – Canaan was terrified by Israel's military reputation and imminent approach.

As the Israelite army crossed the Jordan, the river miraculously stopped flowing. On the other side, they interrupted their march at Gilgal for all the men to be circumcised. After a necessary period of rest, they marched on Jericho. Joshua's instructions were clear. Protected by troops to the front and rear, seven priests were to march around the city, carrying ram's horn trumpets and leading the holy ark of the covenant. Though the priests were to blow their trumpets, the war cry was not to be raised until Joshua gave the order.

Marching to the sound of the trumpets, the army circled the walls of Jericho for six days. On the seventh day, the trumpets sounded, the war cry was raised and the walls collapsed. As Joshua ordered, the city was burnt to the ground while the citizens were put to the sword. Only Rahab the prostitute and her family were spared.

Geological evidence suggests a possible explanation for the miraculous elements in the Jericho story. The tumbling of the city's walls was preceded, a few days earlier, by the crossing of the Jordan on dry land. A comparable phenomenon has been witnessed in modern times. The Jordan valley lies on a major geological rift, subject to frequent earthquakes. Quake-induced mudslips have been known to dam the river on a number of occasions, most recently in 1927. Some scholars have speculated that the same phase of earthquake activity dammed the Jordan and destroyed Jericho's walls.

Yet it is often stated that there is no archaeological evidence of the tumbled walls of Jericho. The conventional dating of the conquest places the event around 1200 BC, when Jericho was an insignificant settlement with no trace of walls.

However, a recent reassessment of the conquest, following traditional Biblical dates, places it around 1400 BC, arguing that Joshua confronted an earlier settlement. At this time, Jericho had walls, perhaps, and shows signs of earthquake and burning. But further excavations have not confirmed the dating, and it remains controversial; still, it is true that the Biblical story of Jericho's fall has not yet been ruled out by archaeology.

This sculptured head, one of the best preserved of those found from Neolithic Jericho, is 9in/23cm high; the whole statue, when intact, would have been roughly natural size. It is made of unbaked clay with pale orange sea-shells for eyes and probably dates from the end of the fourth millennium.

Some human skulls from Jericho, dating to about 7000 BC, have their features restored in plaster. They are painted with a flesh-coloured tint and also have shells for eyes. Many burial sites have been found beneath the floors of Jericho's Neolithic houses; the corpses often have no heads. These were probably removed to be prepared in this manner. Perhaps the people of Jericho hoped to preserve the wisdom of their ancestors in this way.

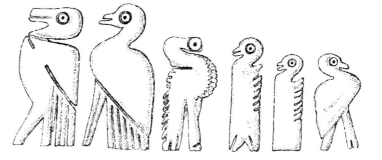

Bone carvings of birds, used as inlay decoration on wooden boxes, have been found in the Middle Bronze Age (c.1850–1550 BC) tombs of Jericho, contemporary with the city's last period of greatness. The tombs contain mass burials, perhaps the result of a plague that struck the city shortly before its destruction.

Found carefully placed next to the bodies were weapons, wooden stools, tables laden with offerings of food, and baskets and pots containing personal effects – combs, wigs, boxes for cosmetics and trinkets. These finds attest not only to a prosperous community but also to a strong belief in the afterlife.

Outside the city, an extremely valuable group of Middle Bronze Age tombs was found. They contained organic material (including baskets and wooden furniture) in a remarkable state of preservation, considering they were buried some 3,500 years ago.

Scientific analysis suggests that subterranean gases had seeped into the tombs shortly after the burials, killing all the bacteria and preventing decay. This further suggests that there was some earthquake activity at about the same time as the city fell.

The first Jericho was a city of small, round, mudbrick houses, surrounded by a stone defensive wall – including an impressive tower, **1** – enclosing some eight acres.

In the later Neolithic Age, the city seems to have declined, but recovered during the Early Bronze Age (*c*.3000 BC), when huge mudbrick walls were built for the city's defence.

Jericho's greatest period was during the Middle Bronze Age (*c*.1850–1550 BC). Imposing double defences were built (see cross-section, *below left*) around a greatly expanded city.

Leading up from the outside walls, 2, was a defensive slope, **3**, crowned with another wall, **4**. Inside, a number of closely-packed houses of this period have been excavated, **5**.

Whether earthquake or invasion was responsible, the thriving Middle Bronze Age city was completely gutted by fire.

Little evidence has been found of settlement from later periods, and Jericho only became important again in the time of the Maccabees.

This cross-section and reconstruction, *below*, shows Jericho's Middle Bronze Age defences, the last known to have been built before the arrival of the Israelites. Over an existing mound of earlier walls and debris was built an enormous bank of earth, in some places as much as 66ft/20.75m wide and 46ft/14.5m high. It was protected at its base by a strong stone wall and crowned with another wall of mudbrick.

The outside slope of the defence was covered with a layer of plaster to make a steep, slippery surface, a feature thought to have been developed in response to the threat of battering-rams.

Jericho may be the oldest city in the world, for radiocarbon dating suggests that it was first built as early as 8000 BC in a phase of the New Stone Age.

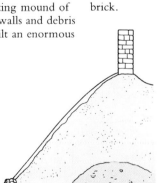

The curse of Jericho

After the burning of Jericho, Joshua made the Israelites swear a solemn oath over its ruins: 'Accursed before Yahweh be the man who rises up and rebuilds this city [Jericho]! On his first-born will he lay its foundations, on his youngest son set up its gates!' (Joshua 6:26).

To lift this curse, the next builder would have to kill his eldest son and bury him under the foundations, then his youngest to bury under the gates. So Jericho lay abandoned for several centuries, until the time of King Ahab when Hiel, a man of Bethel, rebuilt Jericho and sacrificed his sons Abiram and Segub, 'just as Yahweh had foretold through Joshua son of Nun' (1 Kings 16:34).

The battle of Ai

With Jericho captured, according to the Biblical account, Joshua sent scouts into the Judaean hill country to the west to reconnoitre the territory around the city of Ai. They returned with an optimistic report and advised Joshua that a token force of some two or three thousand should be ample to capture the town. Their optimism was ill-founded. The 3,000 men who were sent out 'broke before the people of Ai, who killed some thirty-six of them and pursued them from the town gate as far as Shebarim, and on the slope cut them to pieces' (Joshua 7:4–5).

At this the Israelites lost heart. In desperation, Joshua and the elders of Israel went to the ark of Yahweh to seek an oracle. They were told that one of their number had brought bad luck upon them by stealing something from the accursed city of Jericho, thus violating the rules of 'holy war' whereby all booty belonged to Yahweh.

By a process of elimination, the culprit was discovered. He was a certain Achan of the tribe of Judah, who had stolen a fine robe, 200 shekels of silver and a gold ingot weighing 50 shekels. The unfortunate man was led away from the camp and stoned to death.

Their confidence now restored, the Israelites decided to renew the attack on Ai. Joshua devised a simple stratagem, designed to draw the city's inhabitants away from the fortifications so the Israelites could then enter the town.

He picked 30,000 of his best men and carefully explained to them his plan and their part in it: 'You must take up a concealed position by the town, at the rear, not very far from the town, and be sure you all keep alert! I and the whole people with me, shall advance on the town, and when the people of Ai come out to engage us as they did the first time, we shall run away from them. They will then give chase and we shall draw them away from the town. . . . You will then burst out of your concealed position and seize the town. . . . When you have captured the town, set fire to it' (Joshua 8:4–8).

The select force left under cover of night for their place of ambush west of Ai on the way to Bethel. The following morning Joshua reviewed his main body of troops and then marched towards Ai at their head. They 'pitched camp north of Ai with the valley between them and the town' (8:11).

That night, Joshua made a conspicuous sally into the plain to make sure that the people of Ai were aware of the Israelite presence. At daybreak the forces of Ai duly came out to engage the Israelites in battle. All went according to plan. The Israelites retreated eastward along the road to Jericho with the enemy in hot pursuit, leaving Ai undefended.

The time had come for Joshua to give the pre-arranged signal. He raised his sword, pointing it in the direction of Ai and 'no sooner had he stretched out his hand than the men in ambush burst from their position, ran forward, entered the town, captured it and quickly set it on fire' (Joshua 8:19). As the men of Ai helplessly watched their city burning, the retreating Israelites turned around and attacked their pursuers. At the same time, the troops who had captured Ai came upon them from the rear. The men of Ai were trapped and 'the Israelites struck them down until not one was left alive and none to flee' (Joshua 8:22).

The Israelites then returned to the town and ruthlessly slaughtered the remaining inhabitants. 'The number of those who fell that day, men and women together, was twelve

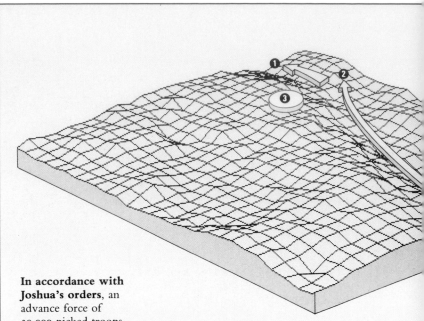

In accordance with Joshua's orders, an advance force of 30,000 picked troops made their way secretly, under cover of night, to a concealed position west of Ai, **1**, on the road to Bethel. There they set up an ambush and waited for the signal to attack the city. The following day, the main army, led by Joshua, marched on Ai, **3**. They pitched their camp to the north of the city, across a valley, **2**.

At daybreak, the men of Ai, **4**, left the city to attack the Israelite forces. The Israelites, **5**, feigned retreat down the road to Jericho and drew the Canaanites after them. Joshua raised his sword as a signal to the ambushing force, **6**, who emerged from their hideout and captured the city.

The retreating Israelites, **7**, turned to face the pursuing Canaanites, **8**, who were in disarray as they saw the smoke rising from their city. The troops who had captured Ai moved to attack them simultaneously from the rear, **9**, and the Canaanites were routed. The Israelites

Based on a 13th-century ivory carving from Megiddo, this reconstruction shows infantrymen carrying shields and sickle swords. Canaanite chariots had a bow case and quiver fitted to the body. They were heavy vehicles and difficult to manoeuvre because of their centre axle.

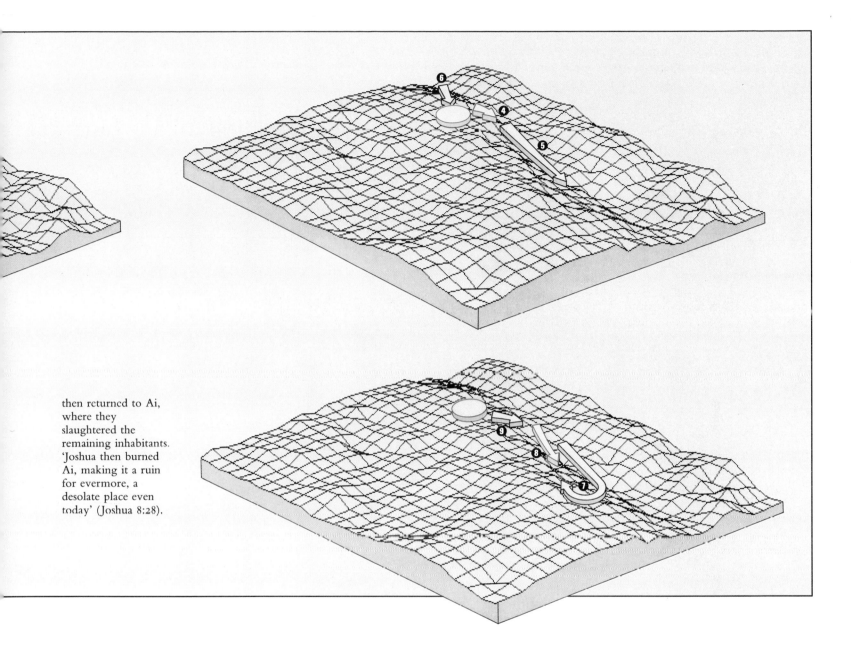

then returned to Ai, where they slaughtered the remaining inhabitants. 'Joshua then burned Ai, making it a ruin for evermore, a desolate place even today' (Joshua 8:28).

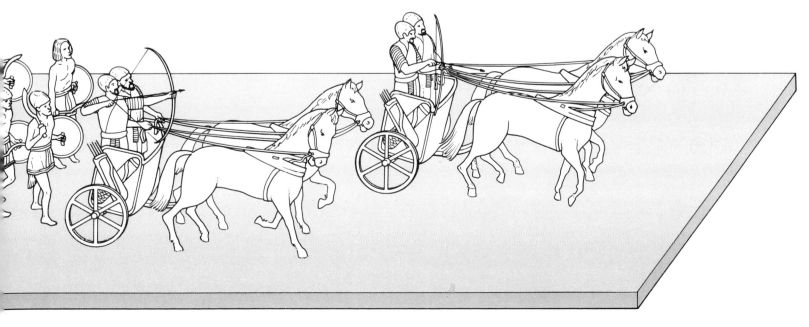

The battle of Ai *(continued)*

thousand, all people of Ai' (Joshua 8:25). The city was plundered and razed to the ground. The king of Ai, who had been captured alive, was hanged from a tree, but before nightfall his corpse was taken down. 'It was then thrown down at the entrance to the town gate and on top of it was raised a great mound of stones, which is still there today' (8:29).

The story of the conquest of Ai, so vividly described in the Bible, has not found support from archaeology. The imposing remains of Ai (identified with modern Et Tell) lie on a hill some ten miles north of Jerusalem. The great Early Bronze Age city was destroyed towards the end of the third millennium BC, about 1,000 years before Joshua, and the site seems to have been completely abandoned at the time of the conquest.

The Joshua narrative as a whole contains many legendary features and presents the conquest as a unitary, pan-Israelite enterprise which is almost certainly an expression of the ideals of the later authors. Many scholars see the Ai story as a typical folk myth, created to explain the presence of the impressive earlier ruins. It may reflect the period of the Judges when unfortified villages were built, probably by the Israelites, on ancient mounds. Other scholars believe that the Biblical account has transposed events from a neighbouring site with a different name, perhaps Bethel.

Although the story of Ai cannot, it seems, be backed up historically, it nevertheless presents several interesting features. The poorly-trained and ill-equipped Israelites were obviously no match for the experienced and well-armed Canaanite forces. Whenever the capture of a city is described, the victory is secured by espionage, treachery or clever strategy.

At Jericho the Israelite spies were helped by the prostitute Rahab, while at Bethel a traitor showed the scouts how the Israelites could gain entry to the town. The classic ruse employed by Joshua at Ai was used on another occasion at Gibeah, when the Israelites defeated the Benjaminites (Judges 20:29–41). Jehoram of Israel suspected the same trick when the Aramaeans raised the siege of Samaria (2 Kings 7:12).

The book of Joshua presents the conquest of Canaan as the 'holy war' *par excellence*. Yahweh was fighting for the life of his people and the people accordingly were commanded to have faith and conform to definite rules. Anyone who broke the rules, like Achan, was thought to bring down the 'curse of destruction' upon the entire people. The guilty person had to be executed to release everyone from the effect of the curse. The heap of stones piled up to mark the grave of the king of Ai reflects local custom. A similar cairn was built over the tomb of Absalom (2 Samuel 18:17) and the grave of Achan.

A final point of interest concerns the weapon which Joshua wielded when he gave the signal for the ambushing force to attack Ai. The weapon is described in Hebrew as a *kidon*. The Philistine Goliath also carried a *kidon* of bronze slung across his shoulders. The word has often been translated 'javelin' but a document from the caves of Qumran (see pp.186–7), which probably dates to the first century BC, seems to describe the *kidon* as a sword, one and a half cubits long (about 27in/67.5cm) and four finger-breadths wide.

Another possibility is that the *kidon* was a type of scimitar. Whatever its precise form, the *kidon* rarely occurs in the Biblical texts, and except when it is held up by Joshua at the Battle of Ai, it is never found in the hands of an Israelite.

The men of Ai, 3, fooled by Joshua's clever tactics, had pursued the retreating Israelites some distance down 'the road to the desert' before Joshua gave the signal for the Israelite ambushing force to attack the city. 'When the men of Ai looked back, they saw smoke rising from the town into the sky' (Joshua 8:20).

Joshua then turned his troops, 4, round to face the Canaanites. Before they had time to recover from the surprise attack, the other Israelites, **2,** came out from the town, **1,** to 'engage them too and the men of Ai were thus surrounded by Israelites, some on this side and some on that' (Joshua 8:22).

The result was a resounding victory for the Israelites. The enemy was routed and not a single man escaped alive from the dreadful massacre, except the king of Ai, who was captured and later hanged from a tree.

The victory at Merom Waters

After the conquests of Jericho and Ai, and the subjugation of other parts of the Judaean hill country, the Bible tells of Joshua's campaign in northern Canaan. His route took him from Gilgal, where the Israelite camp was, to Upper Galilee. The Israelites would have had to pass either through the central hill country or along the Jordan valley west of the river.

The kings of the north formed a formidable coalition. The alliance was headed by Jabin, king of the important Canaanite city of Hazor, and included the kings of Merom, Achshaph and Shimron. The Canaanites advanced to meet Joshua 'with all their troops, a people as numerous as the sands of the sea, with a huge number of horses and chariots' (Joshua 11:4).

At the 'Waters of Merom', presumably the water source of nearby Merom city, the Canaanites assembled and set up camp. Clearly the Israelites would be no match for the Canaanites in open battle. The Canaanites were not only better trained and equipped but had the advantage of a large chariot force which could attack with devastating effect. Accordingly, Joshua had to resort to non-conventional tactics. While the Canaanites were still preparing for battle, the Israelites advanced secretly and made a surprise attack on the enemy camp.

The Canaanites were caught completely unawares. Joshua's forces 'hamstrung their horses and burned their chariots' (Joshua 11:9), thus destroying the most effective arm of the Canaanite army. The confounded enemy troops scattered and were pursued by the Israelites, who cut them down 'until not one of them was left alive' (Joshua 11:8).

Joshua then turned his attention towards Hazor. The Israelites captured the city, slaughtered its king and the entire population and 'Hazor was burnt to the ground' (Joshua 11:11). In a mopping-up operation the other cities of the area were systematically plundered and their inhabitants massacred, 'yet of all these towns standing on their mounds, Israel burned none, apart from Hazor' (Joshua 11:13).

There are doubts about the historicity of the Biblical account of Joshua's northern campaign. One problem is that Jabin, king of Hazor, supposedly killed by Joshua, makes his appearance again at a later period, during the time of Deborah (see pp. 62–3).

Since it is unlikely that there were two kings of the same name, some scholars believe that Jabin, who plays no specific role in Deborah's battle, did not belong originally to the Deborah story. Others prefer to see the battle of Merom Waters and the destruction of Hazor as having taken place later than Joshua, when the northern tribes were consolidating their hold on Galilee, perhaps after Deborah's war.

The city of Merom, near which the Israelite victory took place, has not yet been definitely located, but can probably be identified with Tell el-Khirbeh, some eight miles from Hazor. At Hazor, so archaeology has shown, there was a great destruction in the later thirteenth century BC, at the end of the Bronze Age, the period usually associated with the Israelite conquest.

Although no exact date can be fixed for the destruction, nor definite conclusions drawn about who or what was responsible, the evidence conforms well to the Biblical tradition that the city was destroyed by the Israelites. Whether Joshua was at the head of the expedition or whether in fact a later conquest was subsequently associated with the figure of this charismatic leader still remains an open question.

Hazor (modern Tell el-Kedeh), near which the battle of Merom Waters was probably fought, is one of the most impressive archaeological sites in Syro-Palestine. It was first settled in the third millennium BC and by the second millennium was a large, flourishing city with a citadel and lower town. It is mentioned in Egyptian records and 18th-century letters from Mari, which show that it was an active centre of the important tin trade.

During the 14th century, its ruler, though a vassal of the Egyptian pharaoh, was called 'king'. At this period Hazor was particularly prosperous, with temples and fortifications like other great Canaanite cities. An interesting discovery was a small shrine, cut into the rampart of the lower town. It contained a statue of a seated man and ten stone stelae, one carved with two arms raised to a disc and crescent, suggesting the shrine was dedicated to a moon-god. Buildings adjacent to the shrine included a potter's workshop with his wheel.

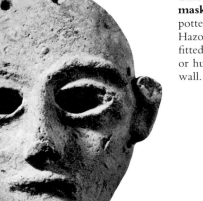

This small clay mask found in the potter's workshop at Hazor, may have been fitted to a statue's face or hung on a temple wall.

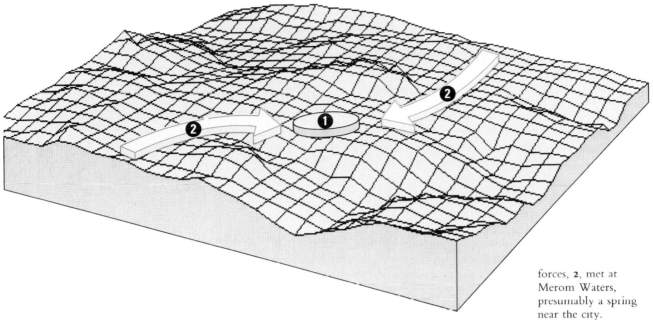

The decisive battle of Joshua's northern campaign was near Merom, **I**, probably Tell el-Khirbeh, some 8mls/13km from Hazor. The Canaanite forces, **2**, met at Merom Waters, presumably a spring near the city.

The allied troops, led by the king of Hazor, included contingents from Merom, from Shimron in the Jezreel valley and from Achshaph on the coastal plain. By a surprise attack on their unprepared forces, Joshua succeeded in routing the Canaanites. He immobilised the chariotry by burning the vehicles and hamstringing the horses. The Israelites then pursued and slaughtered the defeated Canaanites, who fled northwestwards to the coast and northeastwards to the Valley of Mizpeh.

At the battle of Merom Waters, the Israelites apparently had to contend for the first time with the war chariots of the Canaanites. The Canaanites had had chariots since the 16th century and probably introduced them into Egypt. From about 1500 BC, chariotry became one of the main arms in the military forces of the Near East. The Israelites, however, did not have a strong chariot force until Solomon's time and chariots were unknown in the tribal army of the early settlers.

The Canaanite chariots of the 'conquest' period were heavier than earlier models and had six-spoked wheels. The axle rod was under the centre of the body to avoid putting excessive strain on the horses. Consequently, however, this meant that the chariots were not easy to manoeuvre on the fast turn.

Chariots were made of wood, covered with leather or some other light material and drawn by two horses. In battle, they carried a charioteer and an archer, whose bow case and quiver were fitted to the chariot body.

The 12 tribes of Israel

The 12 tribes of Israel were traditionally descended from the 12 sons of Jacob, known also as 'Israel'. On his deathbed, Jacob blessed each of his sons in turn and foretold the different destinies of their descendants (Genesis 49). According to the book of Joshua, the 12 tribes together under Joshua's leadership invaded the 'Promised Land' (see pp. 48–9).

After the conquest, Reuben, Gad and the half-tribe of Manasseh returned to the Transjordan where they had already been allotted territory by Moses. Joshua divided the land west of the Jordan among the remaining nine and a half tribes and the individual groups went their separate ways. By this time the sons of Joseph had become two tribes, Ephraim and Manasseh.

Galilee was occupied by Asher, Zebulun, Issachar and Naphtali. Dan, after failing to take its assigned territory on the coastal plain, migrated to the far north of the Jordan valley. Ephraim and the other half-tribe of Manasseh settled in the central hill country and Benjamin took over the small area between Bethel and Jerusalem. Judah and Simeon occupied the southern hill country. Levi did not receive a tribal territory, but instead was given 48 towns which were dispersed throughout the country.

The concept of 12 distinct tribes in this early period is an oversimplification by the later writers. The process of settlement was complex and the tribes which eventually regarded themselves as 'Israelite' had various origins and occupied their respective territories under different circumstances. Most scholars believe that the consolidation of the tribal framework took place largely after the settlement and continued until the time of the monarchy.

The basic tribal unit was the family, several families constituted a clan and a group of clans formed a tribe. Authority was in the hands of the elders, the heads of the families of each clan.

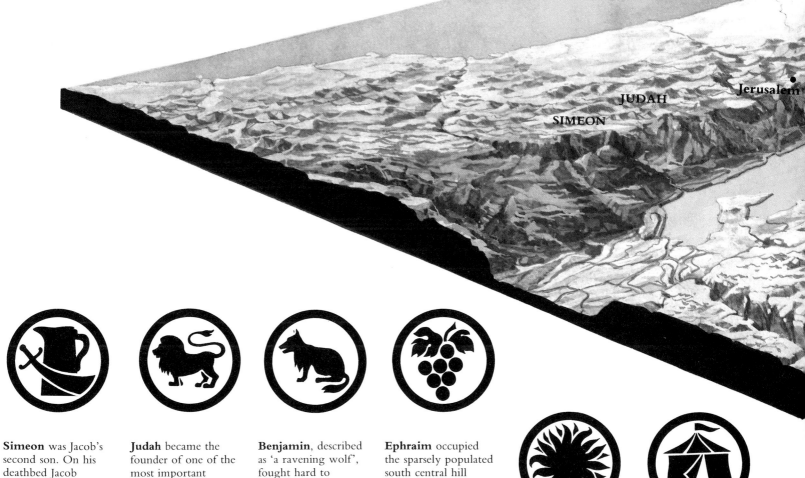

Simeon was Jacob's second son. On his deathbed Jacob reproved Simeon and Levi for their violent tempers and foretold they would be scattered throughout Israel. After the conquest of Canaan, Simeon received several towns 'within the heritage of the sons of Judah'.

Judah became the founder of one of the most important Israelite tribes. Judah settled in the southern hill country and eventually absorbed the tribe of Simeon. Other tribes which were in the area in the conquest period – Caleb, Kenaz, Jerachmeel and the Kenites – also became attached to Judah.

Benjamin, described as 'a ravening wolf', fought hard to establish itself in the area north of Jerusalem. The name Benjamin, 'son of the south', was probably adopted after the settlement.

Ephraim occupied the sparsely populated south central hill country. Ephraim is a typical geographical name, probably given to the tribe after the settlement.

Reuben settled in the Transjordan. The tribe remained partly nomadic and slowly declined in importance.

Gad occupied the forested lands of Gilead. The names of Gad and Gilead became almost synonymous.

Laish

DAN

ASHER NAPHTALI

ZEBULUN

ISSACHAR

MANASSEH

MANASSEH

EPHRAIM

JAMIN

GAD

REUBEN

Manasseh settled east and west of the Jordan. Several Canaanite cities were described as sons and daughters of Manasseh.

Issachar, described as 'a strong donkey' who 'became a slave to forced labour' had probably settled in Galilee by the 14th century.

Asher, who was said to 'furnish food fit for kings', is mentioned in Egyptian inscriptions of the end of the 14th century. At that time the tribe had apparently already settled in Galilee as neighbours to the Phoenician coastal towns. Like Issachar, Asher at this early period must have been subservient to the powerful Canaanite cities in the area.

'**Zebulun** will live by the seashore and be a sailor on board the ships, with Sidon on his flank.' Jacob's prophecy suggests that at least some of those who came to make up the tribe of Zebulun were orginally settled along the sea coast. Perhaps other peoples forced them inland, for after the conquest they occupied part of southern Galilee.

Naphtali is described by Jacob as 'a swift hind'. The tribal inheritance of Naphtali covered a wide area in eastern and central Galilee. It is not certain exactly when either Naphtali or Zebulun first moved into the area. Since both tribes participated in the wars of Deborah, they were certainly well established in the period of the Judges.

Dan was called 'a snake on the road, a viper on the path'. When the Danites attempted to occupy their allotted territory in the Shephelah region they met with strong opposition. They therefore migrated to the upper reaches of the Jordan valley. There they successfully attacked and occupied the Canaanite city of Laish, which was renamed Dan.

Deborah defeats Sisera

Deborah the prophetess lived during the period of the Judges, the time between the Israelite conquest and settlement of Canaan and the rise of the monarchy. Israelite society was still tribal, with no capital and no central government. The book of Judges depicts this period as one of local struggles between some of the Israelite tribes and the Canaanite city-states and neighbouring peoples.

The Israelites lapsed from their allegiance to Yahweh – 'they followed other gods; they served them and bowed down before them and would not give up the practices and stubborn ways of their ancestors at all' (Judges 2:19). As punishment, Yahweh 'delivered them to the enemies surrounding them' (2:14).

In particular crises, when tribal life was threatened, leaders were appointed who rescued the Israelites from oppression. These leaders were called 'Judges', although most of them do not seem to have had anything to do with the law. The one exception is Deborah, who 'used to sit under Deborah's Palm between Ramah and Bethel in the highlands of Ephraim, and the Israelites would come to her for justice' (Judges 4:5). Alongside these heroic leaders, also known as 'deliverers', there were other 'minor' Judges, about whom little is known.

Deborah bears the distinction of being the only woman who 'judged Israel'. Her deeds are narrated both in prose (Judges 4) and in a poem known as the Song of Deborah (Judges 5). There are some discrepancies between the two accounts. At that time 'Jabin, king of Canaan, who reigned at Hazor . . . had cruelly oppressed the Israelites for twenty years' (Judges 4:2–3). According to Judges 5:6 'there were no more caravans; those who went forth on their travels took their way along by-paths'.

The implication appears to be that communications between the tribes in Galilee and those in the central hill country, which passed through the territories of the Canaanite city states, had been broken. This created an emergency for the northern tribes who felt helpless, however, in the face of Jabin's great army, which included 900 iron chariots.

Accordingly, Deborah sent for Barak, son of Abinoam, of the tribe of Naphtali, and delivered an oracle from Yahweh. Barak was told to take 10,000 men from the tribes of Naphtali and Zebulun and march to Mount Tabor in Lower Galilee. Then, said Yahweh, 'I shall entice Sisera, the commander of Jabin's army, to encounter you at the Torrent of Kishon with his chariots and troops; and I shall put him in your power' (Judges 4:7). Not surprisingly, Barak was hesitant, and felt particularly unsure about his ability to get the timing of the operation right, so he asked Deborah to accompany him. She agreed, but warned him that the glory of victory would then be hers.

Everything went according to plan, and Deborah and Barak encamped on Mount Tabor with the 10,000 Israelites. Their position on the hilly ground gave them more security against a Canaanite chariot attack. Whereas Judges 4 mentions only Zebulun and Naphtali, the Song of Deborah says that Ephraim, Benjamin, Machir (perhaps Manasseh) and Issachar also took part. When Sisera was informed about the assembled Israelites he mustered his entire army, including the 900-strong chariot force, and marched to the Torrent of Kishon which flowed across the plain south of Tabor.

The time had come for action. At Deborah's signal, 'Barak charged down from Mount Tabor' (Judges 4:14) with 10,000 men at his back. The surprise Israelite attack coincided with a

---

The Song of Deborah
'That the warriors in Israel unbound their hair,
that the people came forward with a will,
bless Yahweh!' (Judges 5:2)

'Awake, awake, Deborah!
Awake, awake, declaim a song!
Take heart, to your feet, Barak,
capture your captors, son of Abinoam!' (Verse 12)

'Then Israel marched down to the gates;
like champions, Yahweh's people marched down
to fight for him!' (Verse 13)

'Most blessed of women be Jael
(the wife of Heber the Kenite);
of tent-dwelling women may she be most blessed!' (Verse 24)

'She hammered Sisera, she crushed his head,
she pierced his temple and shattered it.
Between her feet, he crumpled, he fell, he lay;
at her feet, he crumpled, he fell.
Where he crumpled there he fell, destroyed.' (Verse 27)

'At the window, she leans and watches,
Sisera's mother, through the lattice,
"Why is his chariot so long coming?
Why so delayed the hoof beats from his chariot?"' (Verse 28)

'So perish all your enemies, Yahweh!
And let those who love you be like the sun
when he emerges in all his strength!' (Verse 31)

The Song of Deborah is often quoted as one of the earliest examples of Hebrew poetry. Many scholars assume that it was composed at about the same time as the events it describes. Others, however, date it no earlier than the ninth century BC. The song consists of three parts: a long introduction (verses 2–11), the main poem (verses 12–30) and a brief conclusion (verse 31). The introduction and conclusion seem to be later additions, as does verse 18, which has a different form from the others.

The main body of the poem is a song of victory. It begins with the call to war, then lists the tribes which responded and reproaches those which chose to stand aside. The description of the battle, when even the stars themselves fought on Yahweh's side, is followed by a blessing for Jael and a dramatic account of her heroic deeds. The poem ends with Sisera's mother waiting in vain for the return of her son and the spoils of battle.

The introduction to Deborah's Song, a hymn to Yahweh's greatness and a summons to praise him, and the short concluding prayer, give the poem the style of a psalm. It has been compared with Psalm 68, which is also thought to be an early composition. Scholars have suggested that the song in its final form was originally sung at a festival of covenant renewal, and it may have been used as a psalm of praise in the Jerusalem Temple. It is a song of holy war, thought of as a sacred action. Yahweh fought for Israel, the fighting men were Yahweh's champions and Yahweh's enemies were annihilated. In fact, there are several other poems, like the Blessing of Jacob (Genesis 49) and the Song of Miriam (Exodus 15), believed by some scholars to belong to an early period of Israel's history. They have been compared with fourteenth-century Canaanite texts found at Ugarit.

Before the battle, Barak assembled the Israelite troops at his home base of Kedesh in Naphtali. The town can probably be identified with modern Khırbet Qedesh, a large site of this period on the slopes leading down to the Sea of Galilee, east of the valley of Jabneel. From there, the Israelites marched to Mount Tabor, a sacred mountain, 'where the people come to pray' and 'offer sacrifices' (Deuteronomy 33:19). The Canaanite coalition, commanded by Sisera, took up position nearby, at the Torrent of Kishon in the northern Jezreel valley.

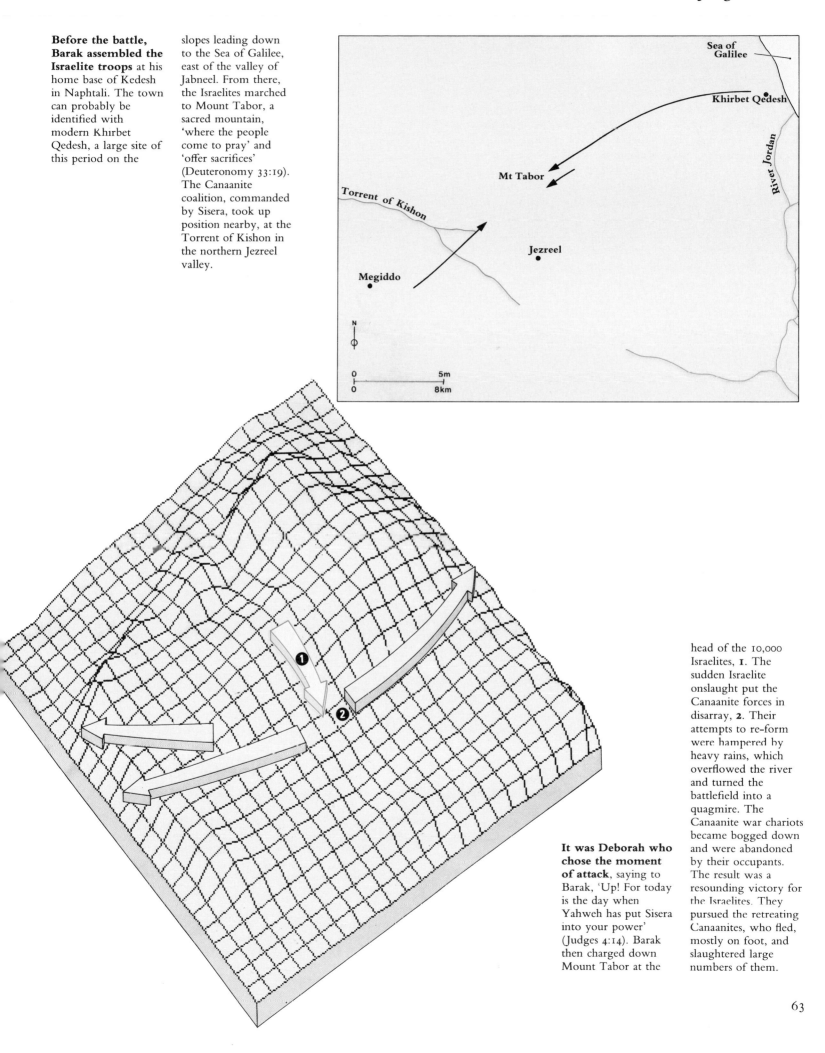

It was Deborah who chose the moment of attack, saying to Barak, 'Up! For today is the day when Yahweh has put Sisera into your power' (Judges 4:14). Barak then charged down Mount Tabor at the head of the 10,000 Israelites, **1**. The sudden Israelite onslaught put the Canaanite forces in disarray, **2**. Their attempts to re-form were hampered by heavy rains, which overflowed the river and turned the battlefield into a quagmire. The Canaanite war chariots became bogged down and were abandoned by their occupants. The result was a resounding victory for the Israelites. They pursued the retreating Canaanites, who fled, mostly on foot, and slaughtered large numbers of them.

Deborah defeats Sisera *(continued)*

heavy downpour, unusual in the region, which caused the river to rise and overflow its banks, and turned the battlefield into sticky mud. The chariots, bogged down and deprived of all power of manoeuvre, were easy prey for the Israelites. Even Sisera, the army commander, 'leapt down from his chariot and fled on foot' (Judges 4:15). Barak pursued the retreating Canaanites and 'Sisera's whole army fell by the edge of the sword; not one man was spared' (4:16).

Meanwhile, Sisera himself had fled eastwards towards Lake Galilee. He reached the camp of Heber the Kenite, whose family were at peace with Jabin, king of Hazor. Jael, Heber's wife, came out to meet him and offered him her hospitality. She took him into her tent, gave him some milk to drink and covered him with a rug. Fearful of Israelite pursuit, Sisera asked Jael to keep watch by the tent door and deny there was anyone inside if she was questioned. Then Sisera fell asleep, thinking he was safe. 'But Jael the wife of Heber took a tent-peg and picked up a mallet; she crept softly up to him and drove the peg into his temple right through to the ground ... and so he died' (4:21).

The battle by Mount Tabor was the first time the Israelites dared to confront the powerful Canaanite war chariots. The Israelite troops were still poorly equipped and their usual weapons were swords and slings. There was not 'one shield, one spear to be found among the forty thousand men in Israel' (5:8). Their great victory naturally made a deep impression, and Deborah and Jael became honoured as heroines.

There are, however, some problems as to the location of the battle. The Song of Deborah says that the Canaanite kings fought 'at Taanach, near the waters of Megiddo' (5:19), some 30 miles southwest of Mount Tabor, but all other evidence points to the vicinity of Mount Tabor as the location of the engagement. The reference to Taanach and Megiddo may reflect the fact that they were two of the most important Canaanite cities in the north and probably participated in the coalition. The Israelite success was not followed up by the conquest of the Canaanite cities, but communications between Galilee and the central hill country seem to have been restored.

The date of the battle is uncertain and suggestions have ranged from the late thirteenth century to the late eleventh century. A late date is probably preferable, towards the end of the period of the Judges. The confrontation clearly took place at a time when the tribes were well enough established to begin moving from the hill country into the plains.

Also the first event which can be seen as a repercussion of the Israelite success is the battle between the Israelites and the Philistines at Aphek, usually dated towards the end of the eleventh century. It has been suggested that the battle commander, Sisera, was a Philistine, because his name is of non-Semitic origin, and that there was some kind of alliance between the Canaanites and Philistines, which is not mentioned in the Biblical account.

The alliance between the different Israelite tribes is significant. Judges 4 names only Naphtali and Zebulun, but the Song of Deborah lists six groups involved in the battle. Reuben, Gilead (probably Gad), Dan and Asher are also mentioned, and the poet criticises the fact that they did not participate in the battle. This gives a total of ten tribes and presupposes an idea of a united people over a wide area. The southern tribes are notably absent, as is the tribe of Levi.

When Deborah gave the signal, Barak and the 10,000 Israelites, **1**, made a sudden charge down Mount Tabor, **3**, using typical Israelite surprise tactics. The unexpected attack 'struck terror into Sisera, all his chariots and his entire army' (Judges 4:15).

Until this time, the Israelites had avoided direct confrontation with the powerful Canaanite chariotry. Their tribal army was composed of contingents from the various clans, who were free to decide whether or not to respond to the call to war. They fought with swords and slings and had neither spears, shields nor chariots.

Chariots could only be used effectively in battle on the open plain. They would have been impractical for the hill-dwelling Israelites, even if they had possessed the resources to build up a force of chariots. For the Canaanites, however, chariot squadrons were the principal weapon and Sisera's force comprised 900.

Barak's daring onslaught was helped from an unexpected quarter, enabling him to follow up his initial success. Sudden heavy rains turned the ground into mud and the Torrent of Kishon overflowed its banks. To the Israelites it must have seemed a miracle. The Canaanite horses, **2**, floundered in the mud and the chariots lost all manoeuvrability. Some were swept away by the river. The chariot crews abandoned their vehicles and the disorganised Canaanite army was routed.

The strategic city of Megiddo

Megiddo was the most important city in the Jezreel valley owing to its strategic position at the entrance to the narrow pass of Wadi Ara, which connects the valley with the coastal plain. This was the route of the Via Maris, the great international highway which linked Egypt with Syria and Mesopotamia. Deborah's battle against Sisera is one of many that were fought between Megiddo and Mount Tabor and control of the Jezreel valley was always a major objective of rival powers.

The mound at Megiddo is immense: at its summit it covers 13 acres/6 hectares. It was first settled in the fourth millennium BC and throughout the Bronze Age, from the third millennium onwards, it was a large and flourishing city. Though often destroyed, it was always rebuilt. The Late Bronze Age city, probably contemporary with the early Israelite settlers, had massive fortification walls, a great gateway, a palace and a traditional Canaanite temple. A splendid collection of carved ivories was found in the ruins of the palace. The Bible does not mention when Megiddo became part of Israel but it is among the unconquered Canaanite cities listed in Judges 1. It was definitely in Israelite hands by the time of Solomon.

The Philistines: Israel's great foe

It is easy to gain the impression from the Old Testament that the most detested of Israel's enemies were the Philistines. Through the influence of the Bible, the word 'Philistine' has become a byword in the English language for anyone conspicuously uncivilised.

Yet the Philistines were not a race of barbarians. Their material culture was generally as high, if not higher, than that of the Israelites. Their decorated pottery, for example, is considered to be the finest locally made ware known from the whole of ancient Palestine.

The Philistines were renowned as warriors, and were almost certainly employed by the Egyptians as vassal troops in Palestine. They were ruled by the 'seranim', local lords of their five major states (Gath, Ashdod, Ashkelon, Ekron and Gaza). This coalition formed the heartland of Philistia, a fertile strip of maritime plain. From here the Philistines could strike at the hill country between the coast and the mountains of Judaea. They dominated southern and central Palestine for at least 200 years.

After the Philistines had faded as a major political entity they bequeathed their name to the area. The Greeks, who frequented the coasts of southern Israel from about 700 BC onwards, heard their name ('Pelishtim' in Hebrew) and dubbed the country, as a whole, 'Palestine'.

The influence of the Philistines on the ancient Israelites is indicated by the fact that their pottery was widely used as a luxury product in Israel. In the eleventh century, the future king David served for many years as the vassal of the Philistine king of Gath and later employed a band of 600 Philistines as a bodyguard.

Why then were the Philistines so hated by the Israelites? Above all, the Israelites considered them to be foreigners, uncircumcised heathens who did not worship Yahweh. And unlike the indigenous peoples of Canaan, the Philistines, like the Israelites, were also relative newcomers. Amos 9:7 suggests that they arrived in Palestine at much the same time as the Israelites left Egypt, so that from the beginning both peoples were rival invaders of the same territory. For many years, the Israelites lost the struggle against the Philistines and grew resentful of their highly urbanised and organised enemies.

Where the Philistines came from, and when they arrived in Palestine, remain mysterious. Some think they arrived around 1200 BC, when detailed reliefs of Rameses III depict an attempted invasion of Egypt by the Philistines and a motley crew of allies, usually referred to as the 'Sea Peoples'. The distinctive style of pottery which appeared in Philistia, showing strong influence from the Mycenaean style of the Greek world, was once thought to show that new people had arrived in Palestine at about the same time. Fresh evidence, however, shows that 'Philistine' ware was a local product, developed from a mixture of styles around 1140 BC.

Recent studies suggest that the Philistines did not arrive in a sudden mass migration around 1200 BC. Most of their 'Sea Peoples' allies had arrived much earlier, and the Philistines were probably already settled in Palestine when they made their famous attack on Egypt under Rameses III. They failed to penetrate Egypt and then seem to have turned their attention again on Canaan. By the time of Samson onwards, the Philistines are found in the role of 'oppressors', who had invaded and garrisoned the Israelite hill country.

The origin of the Philistines

Where the Philistines came from originally is still uncertain. In Genesis 10, they are called the descendants of Mizraim (Egypt), but this seems to reflect their cultural dependence on Egypt rather than that it was their original homeland. Other passages state that they had once lived on the island of Caphtor.

The traditional view holds that Caphtor was another name for Crete, and that the Philistines were refugees from the magnificent Minoan civilisation, arriving in Palestine in about 1200 BC. However, recent research suggests that Caphtor was in fact Cyprus, which had almost constant cultural contact with southern Palestine from about 1550 BC onwards.

Rather than arriving from the Aegean in about 1200 BC, the Philistines are more likely to have trickled in from Cyprus during the previous centuries. By the time there are detailed accounts of them, from Egyptian and Biblical records, they were already well adapted to the indigenous Canaanite culture.

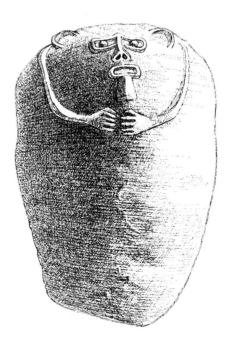

This distinctive 12th-century BC coffin lid was found at modern Tell Farah in southern Philistia. Such coffins are known as either 'anthropoid', because of their roughly human shape, or 'slipper' – owing to their appearance when the lid is removed. They were made of thick, baked clay and often decorated with grotesque faces. Examples have been found at a number of sites in southern and central Palestine and several within Philistia.

Considerably greater numbers have been found in Egypt and have sometimes been attributed to Philistine mercenaries who worked and died there. It seems, however, that the Egyptian examples were really those of poor people who could not afford expensive wooden coffins. Likewise, the examples from Palestine are simply copies of Egyptian sarcophagi and were certainly used by people other than the Philistines.

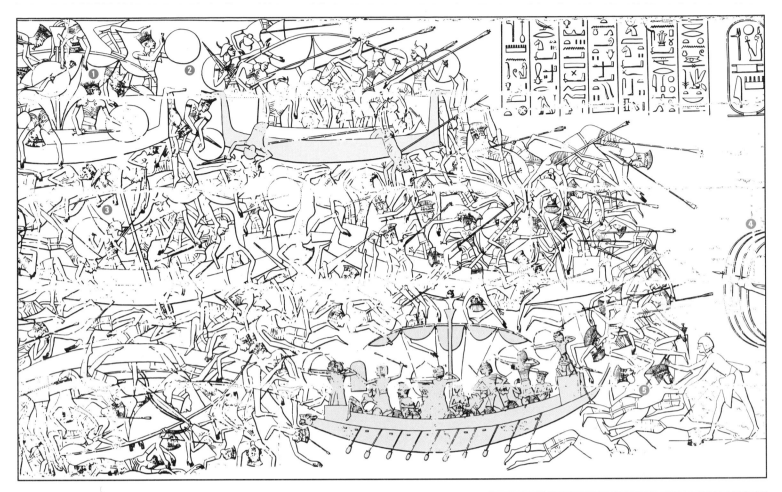

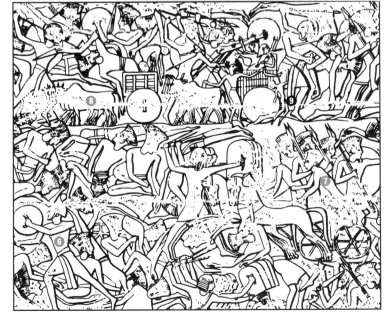

The reliefs left by Pharaoh Rameses III are the richest source of information on the costumes and weaponry of the Philistine warriors. In the eighth year of his reign (*c*.1200 BC), the Philistines and their allies launched a two-pronged attack on Egypt, by sea and by land. The Philistines and their most closely related allies (the Tjekker and Danuna peoples) are shown, in the relief, *above*, wearing helmets with crests, **1**, probably made of leather strips or horsehair. Their bodies are protected by corslets (similar to the 'lorica' later worn by Roman legionaries) and they wear short kilts with tassels.

Typical weapons are a long sword and round shield, **2**. Although it is often claimed that this equipment was derived from the Aegean, all the elements were present in the Levant long before 1200 BC. Another allied group with similar armour but horned helmets, **3**, are most likely the Shardana, whose ship is tinted blue, known as mercenaries and pirates, who had been operating along the coasts of Egypt, Libya and the Levant for more than two centuries.

In the inscriptions accompanying the reliefs, Rameses III described how the enemy dared to penetrate the mouth of the Nile, which he had well defended. Out of the picture to the right, towering over the whole scene, is an enormous figure of the pharaoh, standing on prostrate enemy soldiers. He and his archers, **4**, cut down the enemy with showers of arrows. 'His arrow pierces whoever he wishes, while the fugitive is become one fallen into the water. . . . Their weapons are scattered in the sea,' boasted Rameses. Enemy warriors, **5**, are shown tumbling into the water near the Egyptian ship, tinted grey, to be dragged out by Egyptians.

At about the same time, the Egyptian army, with their own Shardana auxiliaries, **6**, confronted the enemy land forces, *right*. Philistine charioteers and infantrymen with spears, **7**, are shown succumbing to another onslaught of the victorious pharaoh. Carts drawn by hump-backed cattle (zebu), **8**, carry the invaders' families, suggesting that they had intended to settle in Egypt. In the heat of the battle, Philistine women sacrifice their children, **9**, to the gods, to avert disaster, a common Canaanite custom.

Samson's life and death

Samson of the tribe of Dan was said by the Bible to have been a 'Judge' over Israel for 20 years. However, the Bible says nothing of him as a lawgiver and concentrates on his womanising, feasting and brawling. Today, the name of Samson is associated with the feats of superhuman strength he performed during his single-handed battles with the Philistines.

From birth, Samson was a special protégé of Yahweh. An angel told Samson's mother that her son would be a *nazir* – one chosen to spend his life in Yahweh's service. As such, Samson was strictly to avoid alcohol and certain foods and, as the condition which would preserve his great strength, his hair was never to be cut.

The young Samson grew up near the city of Zorah where 'the spirit of Yahweh began to stir him'. When he fell in love with a Philistine girl from nearby Timnah, his parents objected to the match but they 'did not know that all this came from Yahweh, who was seeking grounds for a quarrel with the Philistines' (Judges 14:4).

Once, on his way to Timnah, Samson encountered a young lion and 'the spirit of Yahweh seized upon him and he tore the lion to pieces with his bare hands as though it were a kid' (14:6). Soon after this, when returning to Timnah to marry the Philistine girl, he found a colony of bees in the lion's carcass and took some of their honey.

The incident inspired Samson to set a riddle for the Philistine guests at his wedding feast. As a wager he offered them 30 suits of fine clothes if they could explain the following conundrum: 'Out of the eater came what is eaten, and out of the strong came what is sweet.' Unable to answer, the Philistines threatened Samson's wife, who wheedled the solution from him. On the seventh day, they proclaimed to Samson: 'What is sweeter than honey, and what is stronger than the lion?' (Judges 14:18).

Realising he had been cheated, Samson went on a rampage in Ashkelon, where he killed 30 Philistines – enough to provide the clothing he owed on the wager. His debt was paid. However, on his next visit to Timnah, he found that his wife had been given away to another man, her father thinking that Samson was now displeased with her. Instead, Samson was enraged with the Philistines, who had forced her into deceiving him. He burnt down their corn fields by tying firebrands to the tails of 300 foxes and letting them loose at harvest time.

The Philistines retaliated by burning Samson's wife and in-laws. Samson struck at the Philistines again, then took refuge in a cave. However, the Israelites, who were terrified of the Philistines, bound Samson and handed him over. Yet 'the spirit of Yahweh was on him; the ropes on his arms became like burnt strands of flax and the cords round his hands came untied' (Judges 15:14). Seizing the jawbone of a donkey he attacked the Philistines and slew a thousand of them.

Samson continued his one-man war against the oppressors, until he was eventually betrayed by Delilah, his next lover. Whether she was a Philistine herself is not stated, but the Philistine chiefs persuaded her to discover the source of Samson's great strength. As Samson slept she cut off his seven locks of hair, in return for 1,100 silver shekels. With his hair cut, Samson's strength deserted him and the Philistines carried him off to Gaza where he was blinded, shackled and put to work grinding corn.

Before long, Samson's hair grew again. While he was being used as an amusement by the Philistines during a festival in the temple of Dagon, he seized his chance for revenge. The blind hero asked the boy guiding him to show him the pillars which supported the building. With a prayer to Yahweh Samson grasped the pillars, pulled and destroyed the whole building, killing many Philistines.

The stories of Samson, based around feats of fantastic strength counterbalanced by a weakness for women, have a distinctly folkloric flavour. The tales are of great historical interest, however, in that they might reflect real conditions from a misty period in Israel's past. The Samson stories are set against a background of border feuding between the Philistines and Danites but also, surprisingly, of occasional mixing and inter-marriage between the two groups.

One interpretation of the story, popular earlier this century, argued that Samson's adventures were merely allegories of the sun's behaviour, since his name is formed from the Hebrew word for sun – *shemesh*. Thus the burning of the fields could reflect the scorching heat of the summer, and the shearing of his locks (i.e. 'rays of sunlight') by Delilah, the eclipse of the sun's strength by the fall of night. This theory is now seen as rather fanciful. Samson was a common enough Hebrew name, while tricks such as the one using burning foxes' tails are known in ancient warfare.

Still, many consider it unlikely that Samson was a historical figure as such. Perhaps someone from the tribe of Dan named Samson distinguished himself as a guerrilla leader against the Philistines; the memory of his exploits might then have been exaggerated over generations of oral transmission.

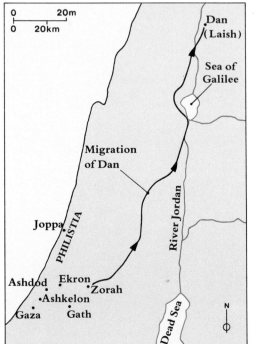

Originally, the Danites settled near Philistia and Joppa. They later moved north and seized Laish, renaming it 'Dan'.

The people of Dan were preoccupied with their work as sailors and sea merchants and they were blamed for not helping in a war against the Canaanites (Judges 5:17). They seem to have been distrusted as an 'improper' tribe in many respects. It has been suggested that they were not even a Hebrew tribe at all, but an affiliated 'Sea People' or Philistine group called the 'Danuna'.

Yet the indications are that Dan was originally counted as a Hebrew tribe. Dan's story is of a tribe breaking away from the fold.

The tale of Samson shows that the Danites sometimes had friendly relations with the Philistines. This could explain how they appear as allies of the Philistines in the Egyptian texts. Many were probably 'Philistinised' and absorbed. The rest moved north to form a somewhat isolated settlement, where they worked and mingled with the Phoenicians on the coast.

This reconstruction is of the Philistine temple from Tell Qasile, 11th century BC. No remains survive of the temple of Dagon in Gaza which Samson destroyed. Indeed, the only excavated Philistine temple is the one from Tell Qasile in northern Philistia, the area once claimed by the tribe of Dan.

The Bible says that the Gaza temple could house an enormous number of people, including 3,000 on the roof, so it is necessary to imagine a much larger version of the Tell Qasile building.

The temple complex included courtyards, **1,9**, leading to the street, **10**, and a small extra shrine, **5**.

Access to the main temple was through an entrance room, **2**, with wooden doors and a stone doorstep, **8**. Anyone entering Dagon's temple avoided treading on the doorstep (1 Samuel 5:5). The entrance room led to the main hall, **3**, with wallseats made of plastered brick.

The 'Holy of Holies', where the idol of the deity stood, was a raised platform with steps, **7**. Many offering vessels were found around it. Behind a partition wall was a room, **6**, where surplus offerings were removed for storage. The roof incorporated wooden beams, supported by two pillars of cedarwood on chalk bases, **4**. Such would have been the pillars grasped by Samson.

The Tell Qasile pillars are 7ft/2.20m apart, a possible span for someone of Samson's physique. The Philistines would have probably made sport of him in a courtyard of the temple (where he could be seen from the roof), then led him inside – where he sacrificed his life in a last feat of heroism.

The story of Ruth

During the time of the Judges, when there was famine in Judah, a certain Elimelech, his wife Naomi and their two sons left Bethlehem and settled in neighbouring Moab. After Elimelech's death his sons married Moabite girls, Orpah and Ruth. Within ten years the sons also died and Naomi decided to return home. She urged her daughters-in-law to remain in Moab and remarry. Orpah stayed behind, but Ruth insisted on accompanying Naomi.

Naomi and Ruth arrived in Bethlehem at the beginning of the barley harvest, and Ruth immediately went off to glean in the fields. She found herself on land belonging to Boaz, a wealthy relative of Naomi's, of Elimelech's clan. When Boaz discovered who she was, he urged her to continue gleaning in his field and, if thirsty, to help herself to water from the pitchers. When it was time to eat he invited her to share in the communal meal. In secret he told his workers to drop some extra grain for her to glean.

When Ruth returned home, Naomi was astonished at the amount of barley she had collected. On finding out that Boaz was responsible, she was delighted, 'for he is one of those who have the right of redemption over us' (Ruth 2:20). She advised Ruth to stay with Boaz's workwomen until the end of the harvest.

When winnowing time arrived, Naomi unfolded her plan for Ruth's future. She instructed her to beautify herself and go to the threshing floor where Boaz was winnowing the barley. 'Don't let him recognise you while he is still eating and drinking. But when he lies down, then go and turn back the covering at his feet and lie down yourself' (Ruth 3:3–4).

Ruth followed Naomi's instructions and during the night Boaz woke up to discover with a shock that there was a woman next to him. Ruth quickly made herself known. 'Spread the skirt of your cloak over your servant for you have the right of redemption over me' (3:9), she said, thereby asking Boaz to take her within his household. Boaz praised Ruth as 'a woman of great worth', but explained that there was a closer relative who had priority over her. If this other man renounced his rights, Boaz assured Ruth he would take her in. Before dawn he sent her back to Naomi, with a large amount of barley.

Later, Boaz assembled a group of the town's elders, including Naomi's close relative. He told them that Naomi was selling some land belonging to Elimelech and offered the relative his chance to redeem it. The man gladly accepted, but, when told he must also take Ruth he changed his mind, because, according to custom, a male child born to Ruth would be her first husband's heir, and the land would revert to him. Boaz then declared publicly that he would be Naomi's redeemer and marry Ruth. Ruth soon bore a son, named Obed. 'This was the father of Jesse, the father of David', and so Ruth became the ancestress of Israel's most venerated king.

The story of Ruth describes life in a provincial Israelite town and illustrates aspects of kinship, marriage and local customs, among them the institution of redemption. The members of a clan had a duty to help one another and the *go'el*, or redeemer, protected the group's interests. If an individual had to sell himself into slavery to repay a debt, one of his relations would redeem him. Likewise, if he had to sell land, the *go'el* had the right and duty to buy it, to prevent the alienation of family property. In his capacity as *go'el* Boaz redeemed Naomi's land; also, he married Ruth to perpetuate the name of her deceased husband.

The 'Gezer calendar', written on a limestone fragment, matches the periods of the agricultural year with the 12 lunar months. It is in an early form of Hebrew, dated to about 925 BC. The inscription reads: 'Two months: ingathering; Two months: seedtime; Two months: late seedtime; One month: flax gathering; One month: barley harvest; One month: harvest (of wheat) and accounting (?); Two months: pruning; One month: summer fruits.'

Ruth gleaned until the end of the wheat harvest.

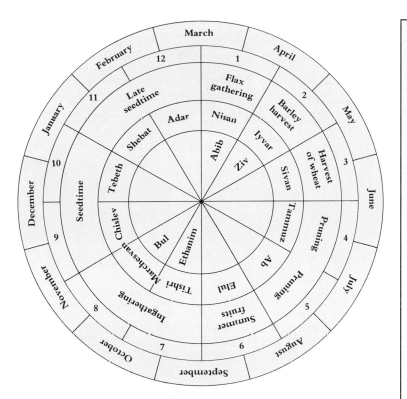

Marriage in ancient Israel

Marriage was a civil not a religious contract but was naturally an occasion for festivities. The bridegroom, accompanied by friends and music, first went to the bride's house. Then the bride, richly dressed and wearing a veil, was escorted to her new house and love songs were sung for the newly-weds. The marriage was consummated on the first night and there was a feast in the bridegroom's house, which normally lasted seven days.

According to Deuteronomy 25:5–10, if a married man died childless, one of his brothers should marry his widow and their first-born would become the heir of the deceased. This institution is called the levirate, from the Latin *levir*, 'brother-in-law'. To decline this was considered dishonourable – the woman was expected to remove her brother-in-law's sandal and spit in his face. The levirate occurs in societies where marriage is a contract between corporate groups, not simply a union of individuals. The lineage that has acquired rights over a woman maintains these rights, especially to future children, by substituting a new husband for the deceased one.

The story of Ruth illustrates the levirate, or at least something similar. Ruth had no brothers-in-law but apparently a close relative had some obligation to marry her, 'to perpetuate the dead man's name in his inheritance' (Ruth 4:10). The unnamed relative removed his sandal and gave it to Boaz when he renounced his claim on Ruth. The gesture is explained as confirming 'a transaction in matters of redemption or inheritance' (Ruth 4:7). The case of Naomi and Ruth seems to have been a matter for the whole clan and not just for the family, as Deuteronomy suggests.

The different ways in which the Israelites reckoned the year are shown in the diagram, *above*. At some time the Canaanite month names, *centre*, of which only four are known, were replaced in the official calendar by the ordinal

numerals. The months were then counted from the first to the twelfth, and this system continued until the Babylonian calendar was adopted after the Exile.

The Babylonian year began in the spring, in Nisan

(March–April). Farmers doubtless continued using the 'agricultural calendar' as on the Gezer tablet.

These drawings, based on 15th-century paintings from the tomb of an Egyptian official at Thebes, show the agricultural activities described in the book of Ruth.

Reapers in the harvest scene, *left*, cut off the tops of the corn with sickles. With them is a girl gleaning corn, like Ruth. She picks up the fallen ears and puts them in a basket.

The untied sheaves are heaped up in a wicker basket, *centre*. One man holds a staff across the sheaves, and his companion, by jumping up and hanging his weight on

the other end of the staff, crams the sheaves into the basket. He then ties the basket securely.

On a round floor of hard earth, girls winnow the corn, *right*. A pair of winnowing scoops form a shovel to lift the grain. When the scoops are parted, the

grain falls down between them and the breeze carries the chaff aside.

The anointing of Saul

For the Israelites, the institution of the monarchy marked a major turning point in their history. The background to this event centred on the danger from the Philistines who threatened all the tribes of Israel, so that unified action became imperative. The Book of Samuel contains two parallel accounts of the founding of the monarchy, one of which is favourable towards it, while the other is hostile.

According to the former, Saul was chosen by Yahweh to liberate his people from the Philistines. Saul, a Benjaminite, was sent by his father Kish to search for the family's donkeys which had strayed. After three days of fruitless endeavour, Saul, on the point of coming home, was persuaded by his servant to consult a man of God – Samuel – living in a nearby city. Saul consented. So, having entered the city, they asked for the seer, whom they met on his way to the High Place. The meeting was not accidental, for Yahweh had given a revelation to Samuel: 'I shall send you a man from the territory of Benjamin; you are to anoint him . . . and he will save my people from the power of the Philistines' (1 Samuel 9:16).

After recognising Saul, Samuel shared a sacrificial meal with him, and the next day he anointed Saul and informed him of his divine mission to deliver Israel from its oppressors. He then gave Saul three signs by which he might know that Yahweh had anointed him as 'prince of his heritage', and told him to do as occasion demanded when these signs had been fulfilled.

The signs were fulfilled and Saul returned home. Shortly afterwards, the occasion foretold by Samuel presented itself with the siege of Jabesh-Gilead by the Ammonites. Saul's prompt action and victory aroused the people's enthusiasm and they acclaimed him and crowned him at Gilgal (1 Samuel 11:15). Thus the charismatic leader, the Lord's appointed saviour, now became the king chosen by popular consent. With the emergence of kingship under Saul, the beginnings of the Israelite nation state can be discerned.

In the second account, it is the people themselves who demand a king. In this tradition, Samuel had grown old and his sons, whom he had appointed as Judges to follow him, were abusing their power. For this reason and because they wished to be 'like the other nations' (1 Samuel 8:5), the people demanded that a king should be set over them. Samuel opposed this request, regarding it as an act of rebellion against Yahweh, and he warned the people of the iniquitous ways of kings (8:11–18).

The people, however, persisted. Again Samuel summoned them to Mizpah, and having pointed out their ingratitude, instructed that lots be cast for the king. The choice fell on Saul. In choosing a king from among themselves, and in making this political act, the Israelites were rejecting Yahweh as king; in religious terms, they were overlooking the fact that as Yahweh's chosen people, they were indeed not 'like the other nations'.

Up to this time, they had existed as a tribal league which expressed the religious spirit of their covenant with Yahweh. Leadership had been 'charismatic' in the form of divinely inspired appointees, who emerged as circumstances dictated. Hereditary kingship, which was to emerge with the Davidic line, remained a permanent anathema to the northern tribes, for whom the charismatic element was to remain a feature. Under David (see pp.82–5), the monarchy came closest to its ideal. Then the political and religious elements were almost – but never fully – reconciled.

Wo samuel nam eyn
vaß des öls. vñ goß auff sein haubt.

Samuel: Judge, priest and prophet

Samuel the Ephraimite from Ramah lived from about 1070 to 1000 BC. In creating the kingship, he played an important role during the period when the Israelites were passing from tribalism to nationhood. Samuel was dedicated to Yahweh and sent as a child to serve under the priest Eli in the sanctuary at Shiloh. Here he was called on by Yahweh to be a prophet when he was entrusted with the divine message of judgement on Eli and his sons, for the latter's corruption. When Shiloh fell, Samuel returned home and became famous as a holy man and giver of oracles.

Though he was much more than a holy man or seer, he is portrayed in a variety of situations that illustrate his prophetic and priestly capabilities. On one occasion, he led a group of ecstatic prophets (1 Samuel 19:18–24). In his first meeting with Saul, he is described as a seer who is consulted in return for payment (1 Samuel 9:6–20). Sacrifice was one of his concerns, even though he was not a Levite (1 Samuel 13:8–14; 16:1–5).

Samuel was also a Judge of Israel (1 Samuel 7:15–16). Elsewhere he appears as a leader in the wars against the Philistines. Samuel's attitude towards the kingship was ambivalent – viewing it both as a rejection of Yahweh's authority, but also as a necessity if Israel were to withstand the Philistines. In essence, Samuel's stance was that the king was not an entirely independent monarch but subject to Yahweh's law and authority.

Samuel anointing Saul, from the Nuremberg Bible, 1493.

The dating of the kings of Judah and Israel		
Saul (1020–1000)		
David (1000–960)		
Solomon (960–930)		
JUDAH	ISRAEL	MESOPOTAMIA/ EGYPT
Rehoboam (930–913)	Jeroboam I (930–910)	
	Omri (881–874)	
Jehosaphat (871–849)	Ahab (874–853)	Shalmaneser III (858–824)
	Jehu (841–813)	
Ahaz (743–727)	Menahem (747–736)	
	Hoshea (732–723)	
Hezekiah (727–698)	Fall of Samaria (722)	Sargon II (722–705)
Manasseh (698–642)		Sennacherib (705–681)
Josiah (639–609)		Nabopolassar (625–605)
Jehoiakim (609–597)		Necho (610–595)
Zedekiah (597–587)		Nebuchadnezzar (605–562)

In Judah and Israel, as elsewhere in the ancient Near East, events were dated according to the regnal years of the kings. In the two Books of Kings there are references to the 'Chronicles of the Kings of Judah' and 'Chronicles of the Kings of Israel'. These would have been summaries of chronological material, providing the length of a king's reign, his father's name and sometimes his age at accession. Following the division of the kingdom, these details were supplemented by synchronisms which related the accession year of one king to the regnal year of the other. For example, 'Ahab son of Omri became king of Israel in the thirty-eighth year of Asa king of Judah and reigned over Israel for twenty two years in Samaria' (1 Kings 16:29).

The study of Biblical chronology is complex and, since antiquity, scholars have tried to reconcile the various dating contradictions in the Books of Kings. There are a number of reasons for these discrepancies. During the exile in Babylon, extensive chronographic works were composed. The compiler of the Books of Kings, using these as well as other, older chronicles and lists of kings, would also from time to time have added his own calculations where there were gaps or confusions.

Another problem is the uncertainty as to the way in which the regnal year was calculated. Was it from the time of the king's accession or was it according to the calendar year? To add to the confusion, each system may have been used at different times.

Nor is there any certainty as to which type of calendar was used in the Biblical period; it was probably a lunar-solar calendar, but unlike the Mesopotamian and Egyptian systems, which are understood, it is not known how the 365-day solar year and the 354-day lunar years were harmonised.

In establishing absolute dates, modern scholars use synchronisms from sources elsewhere, in general from Mesopotamia. Here the chronologies for the first millennium BC are based on continuous lists of years down to the Hellenistic period and these can be verified by astronomical reckoning. For example, from the evidence of the Bible and the Babylonian Chronicle it is possible to date Nebuchadnezzar's capture of Jerusalem to the eighth year of Nebuchadnezzar; that is 597 BC. But many dates, like those of Saul's reign, are not known original oral methods of transmitting dates and other information adds further difficulty to reaching a reliable chronology.

The figure of Saul who, for the Israelites, marked the beginning of kingship, resembles, in his charismatic element, Gilgamesh of Mesopotamian legend. This Akkadian cylinder seal, *c.*2300 BC, shows a struggle between bulls and male figures, sometimes thought to represent Gilgamesh and his friend – the 'wild man' Enkidu, though there is no evidence for such an interpretation.

Gilgamesh, hero of the Sumerian epics, was the king of Erech. The origins of kingship in Mesopotamia are not certain, but it has been suggested that at times of danger the assembly of elders elected a king to whom power was temporarily delegated. Ultimately, kingship became a permanent institution. Gilgamesh represents a stage in the evolution of kingship where the ruler was charismatic, martial and heroic.

The battle of Michmash

Saul's appointment as the first king over all Israel would have remained a hollow gesture had the people not chosen to follow him. His leadership, however, was fully established by a victory over the Philistine oppressors at Michmash. Israel's spirit revived, the scattered Hebrews rallied around their king, and the country's unification began in earnest.

Before the victory at Michmash, the authority of 'King Saul' was largely restricted to the area of his own kinsmen, the small but warlike tribe of Benjamin. Despite the efforts of the prophet Samuel, Israel still remained a divided people. Samuel had achieved some notable military successes against the Philistines. Yet not long afterwards it seems they were firmly established in the very heartland of Israel – the central hill country.

By the time Saul was anointed as king, the Philistines were controlling the hill country through garrisons which jealously guarded arms supplies to prevent any insurrection. One such garrison was at Gibeah of God, where Saul was sent by Samuel immediately after his anointing; it was not only deep in Benjaminite territory, but may also have been another name for Saul's family town.

It is significant that Saul's first act as king was not to fight the Philistines – popular support was still not strong enough for him to tackle such a major enemy. Instead, he scored a victory against a less formidable foe by striking across the River Jordan at the Ammonites, who had been besieging Jabesh-Gilead. The siege raised, Saul celebrated at the traditional meeting place of Gilgal, where the people 'proclaimed Saul king before Yahweh' (Samuel 11:15).

The real test for Saul, however, lay in the battle against the Philistines. While Saul mustered 2,000 volunteers at Michmash in Benjamin, his son Jonathan gathered another 1,000 at Geba and attacked the Philistine garrison occupying Gibeah. War was thereby declared: 'Saul had the trumpet sounded through the country, and all Israel heard the news, "Saul has killed the Philistine governor, and Israel has antagonised the Philistines". So all the people rallied behind Saul . . .' (1 Samuel 13:3)

The Philistine response seems to have been swift. A punitive force invaded and forced Saul to retreat from his strategic position at Michmash: 1 Samuel 13:5 says that the Philistines mustered 30,000 chariots and 6,000 horsemen and 'came up and pitched at Michmash'. Saul withdrew eastwards to Gilgal in the hope of attracting more support. He was disappointed. When the Israelites saw that their plight was desperate, 'the people hid in caves, crevices, in vaults, in wells' (13:6).

Saul was expecting Samuel to arrive at Gilgal to offer sacrifice before the battle and raise morale. However, the prophet arrived late, while the Israelite forces had been steadily deserting. When Saul reviewed his forces he counted a meagre 600 men prepared to face the mighty Philistine host. Nevertheless, he led his forces off to make camp at Geba, opposite the Philistine positions at Michmash to the northwest.

Mercifully for Saul and his small band, the Philistines continued their campaign by sending out raiding parties rather than descending on Geba to attack the main rebel force immediately. This enabled Jonathan to undertake a daring stratagem and turn the tide against them. Accompanied, so the story says, only by his armour-bearer, he took by surprise a Philistine guardpost on one of the rocky spurs near Michmash and succeeded in wiping it out. *(Continued on page 76)*

Iron: a Philistine monopoly?

A fine example of a Philistine bronze sword was found at Beth-Dagon, near Jaffa in northern Philistia. Dating from the eleventh century BC, it may well have been typical of the kind used by Saul's Philistine enemies. Saul's army, the Bible says, was not so well armed: 'There was not a single blacksmith throughout the territory of Israel, the Philistines' reasoning being, "We do not want the Hebrews making swords and spears"' (1 Samuel 13:19). So the Israelites had to take their farming implements to be sharpened, at great expense, by Philistine smiths.

The ban on Israelite smiths therefore meant that their army was equipped only with such implements as axes and mattocks: 'So it was on the day of the battle, no one in the army with Saul and Jonathan was equipped with either sword or spear; only Saul and his son Jonathan were so equipped' (1 Samuel 13:22).

This passage has frequently been read as meaning that the Philistines had a monopoly of iron, an interpretation which fitted well with the old-fashioned idea that the 'Iron Age' began with the invasion of new peoples who brought with them the secrets of iron working. However, a survey of the quantities of iron and bronze found at Philistine and Israelite sites shows no noticeable difference. In fact, at this period, iron was still rarely used in Palestine. The Bible suggests only that the Philistines were trying to control arms supplies. In any case, the measures they imposed could only have been temporary.

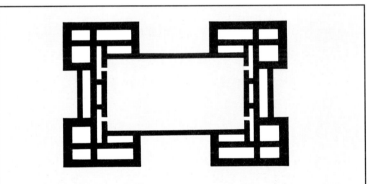

The 'Gibeah of Saul'

This reconstructed plan is of the building discovered at Tell el-Ful, thought to be Saul's 'palace'. Tell el-Ful was one of the first sites to be excavated in Palestine (by C. Warren in 1868) and its identification as the Biblical 'Gibeah of Saul' (1 Samuel 15:34) is reasonably certain. The first phase of the building found there dates from the eleventh century and could, therefore, be the remains of Saul's headquarters. A rectangular structure, about 170 × 115ft/52 × 35m, with at least two storeys, it was built of stone with a double wall and towers at each corner. Finds from the interior include cooking equipment, household tools, bronze arrowheads and slingstones. Everything suggests a simple, rather spartan, lifestyle. More a fortress than a 'palace', the Tell el-Ful building well suits what is known of Saul, who above all was a soldier. The Israelite kingship was nowhere near established enough to allow for the luxuries of later Solomonic times.

The decisive battle of Michmash

The strategic importance of Michmash, a small village in the land of Benjamin, lay in the fact that it guarded a major route from the Philistine coastland across the hill country to the River Jordan. By occupying it, the Philistines were also driving a wedge between the Israelite settlements. It seems that Saul initially held the pass (1 Samuel 13:2), but then, after the opening of hostilities, fled eastwards to rally more forces.

The Philistines arrived and seized Michmash. Saul, Jonathan and their comparatively small army took up positions to the southeast at Geba. Here they were somewhat protected from the Philistines at Michmash, as most of the area between them was occupied by a rocky gorge. Its steep sides would have made it impossible for the Philistine chariotry and cavalry to cross. Doubtless aware of the weakening of Saul's army by continued desertions, the Philistines decided to reduce Israel's resolve further by sending out raiding parties.

The Philistine army seized Michmash, **1**, while Saul's much smaller force took up position at Geba, **2**. This site afforded them considerable protection, since the area between the two armies mostly consisted of the Wadi Suweinit, **3**, a gorge strewn with rocks.

As desertions continued to weaken Saul's already numerically inferior army, the Philistines sent out raiding parties to harry the country. One of these marched in the direction of Beth-Horon, **4**, back along the route they had taken to Michmash. A second force moved north towards Ophrah, **5**, and a third made for the Valley of the Hyenas, **6**.

Saul, meanwhile, moved slightly northwards to Migron, **7**, on the higher ground between Geba and Michmash, presumably to block any enemy move farther south. The Philistines sent a unit to face his position and defend the Pass of Michmash, **8**.

The battle of Michmash *(continued)*

After Jonathan's daring, two-man commando raid on the Philistine guardpost, the enemy were suddenly thrown into disorder: 'There was panic in the camp, in the field and throughout the army; outpost and raiding party too were panic-striken; the earth quaked; it was a panic from Yahweh' (1 Samuel 14:15).

Jonathan's unexpected sortie, resulting in 20 enemy casualties, may have had a profound shock effect on the rest of the Philistine army. They were also terrified by an earth tremor, which the Israelites perceived as Yahweh helping them at a moment of crisis with a timely natural phenomenon. Whatever the reasons, the Philistine chiefs seem to have fallen out at this point and their camp broke up in turmoil. Saul, after a delay to consult the omens, advanced with his small force and routed the enemy.

Strangely, the outcome at Michmash seems to have been due mostly to chance, an element stressed by Jonathan himself, though he did consider 'chance' to be a sign of Yahweh's favour. Encouraging his armour-bearer to join him in the raid on the guardpost, he said: 'Perhaps Yahweh will do something for us, for Yahweh is free to grant deliverance through a few men, just as much as through many' (1 Samuel 14:6).

Both sides in the struggle seem to have been in a chaotic state. The Philistine army was a loose coalition from a number of independent states whose joint enterprises ran the risk of foundering through disagreements between the leaders. Their expeditionary force also included a large number of Hebrews who were liable to, and in the event did, desert on the very battlefield as fortunes favoured Saul.

The Israelites, meanwhile, were experiencing their first problems of kingship – for them, a new style of leadership invested with secular duties, but still unavoidably under the shadow of Yahweh. Saul had already fallen out with the prophet Samuel. Frustrated by Samuel's delay in arriving at the rallying point of Gilgal, Saul had gone ahead with the sacrifices that were a necessary preliminary to the battle. Samuel, however, was supposed to have officiated and he cursed Saul for his impatience and disobedience.

For this, his first transgression, Saul was informed by Samuel that the crown would be given to another. Such was the fragile status of Saul's 'kingship'. From his theoretical domain of 'all Israel' he had only been able to lead 600 men into battle. There is even the possibility that there were actually more Hebrews fighting on the Philistine side than there were on the side of Yahweh's anointed deputy.

The presence of these other Hebrews was probably the most important factor in the battle. When Saul advanced towards Michmash there was already 'fighting going on: and there they all were, drawing their swords on one another in wild confusion' (1 Samuel 14:20). The dissension in the Philistine ranks must have been largely due to the rebellion of their Hebrew mercenaries who now 'defected to the Israelites who were with Saul and Jonathan . . .' (14:21).

The fighting continued as the combined Israelite forces pursued the Philistines to Aijalon, almost to the borders of Philistia. Other Israelites, who had been hiding from the conflict, joined to harry the fleeing enemy. So it was that Israelites with widely differing loyalties began to rally behind a new leader. Through the fortunes of war, and largely the outcome of a single battle, the Hebrew kingship was established under Saul.

Unknown to Saul and the other Israelites, Jonathan, **1**, and his armour-bearer, **2**, decided to take out the Philistine unit, **3**, guarding the Pass of Michmash by a daring commando raid. They approached the unit the difficult way, by clambering down the steep slope of the gorge, known as Seneh, and then up the other side, called Bozez.

As they were in the gorge, they were seen by the Philistine guards who assumed them to be some of the fugitive Israelites coming out of hiding from the many caves lining the sides of the Wadi Suweinit. They mockingly invited Jonathan to come and speak to them, yet they evidently did not expect him to climb the steep face protecting them and launch a sudden assault.

Using the power of surprise to full effect, the heroes rapidly dispatched their enemies: 'the Philistines fell at Jonathan's onslaught, and his armour-bearer, coming behind, finished them off' (1 Samuel 14:13).

The Philistine army was thrown into complete panic by Jonathan's surprise attack on their guardpost at the Pass of Michmash, **1**. This probably began the rout, with those who escaped his onslaught spreading alarm among the rest of the army. An earth tremor increased their apprehension.

Fighting then broke out between the Philistines and their Hebrew mercenaries, who began to desert. Saul and the main Israelite army had by then moved to the lower ground of Migron, **2**, between Geba, **3**, and Michmash. News reached him from his watchmen higher up at Geba that the enemy camp was breaking up: 'Saul's look-out men in Geba of Benjamin could see the camp scattering in all directions' (1 Samuel 14:16).

The end of the battle

Saul, puzzled as to why the Philistine camp was breaking up, ordered a roll-call to 'see who has left us' and only then noticed that Jonathan and his armour-bearer were absent. He began to have omens cast, but 'while Saul was speaking to the priest, the turmoil in the Philistine camp grew worse and worse; and Saul said to the priest, "Withdraw your hand"' (1 Samuel 14:19). He regrouped his forces, 'advanced to where the fighting was going on' and joined forces with the Hebrew mercenaries who had defected from the Philistine ranks.

Seeing the tide had turned, more Israelites came out of their hiding places in the hills: 'all those Israelites who had been hiding in the highlands of Ephraim, hearing that the Philistines were on the run, chased after them and joined in the fight' (14:22).

The Philistines fled in the direction of Beth-Horon, and were harried all the way. 'That day the Philistines were beaten from Michmash all the way to Aijalon until the people were utterly exhausted' (1 Samuel 14:31). The Israelites took as booty sheep and cattle and then ravenously devoured them without having first drained off the blood, a grave ritual sin.

David and Goliath

The future King David first rose to prominence, according to the Bible, through the extraordinary courage he displayed in tackling the huge Philistine Goliath. The bravery of the shepherd boy, who with a simple sling defeated the heavily-armed giant, is still proverbial. Their battle took place during renewed fighting with the Philistines, after Saul's victory at Michmash. Up to that point, the account of Saul's kingship in 1 Samuel largely focuses on Saul's grave acts of disobedience. Then the narrative introduces its real hero, David.

Supposedly, David was already chosen as Yahweh's 'anointed'. Having broken with Saul, the prophet Samuel travelled to Bethlehem in southern Judah, to select a new king from the sons of a nobleman called Jesse. Surprisingly, he passed over the seven eldest sons and selected David, described as a fresh-faced and keen-eyed youngster. David was duly anointed and the grace of Yahweh descended on him. He then distinguished himself through his battle with Goliath.

Apparently an impasse had been reached between the Philistine and Israelite forces, facing each other from adjacent hillsides across a valley. Then the Philistine champion Goliath, of enormous size – the Biblical 'six cubits and one span' is equivalent to more than nine feet or three metres – covered with heavy armour and bristling with weapons, issued a challenge of single combat. No one accepted until David heard the rumour that Saul might offer his daughter to whoever slew Goliath.

Appalled that the 'armies of the living God' were put to shame by a heathen, David volunteered to be Israel's champion. Refusing armour, which he found uncomfortable, he picked some stones from the river and, armed only with his sling and shepherd's staff, strode forward to fight the giant.

Goliath, insulted that someone of such boyish appearance and apparently feeble weapons should dare approach, said to David: 'Am I a dog for you to come after me with sticks?' (1 Samuel 17:43). Yet before Goliath could strike a blow, David felled him with a single slingshot, drew Goliath's sword and beheaded him. With their champion slain, the Philistines fled.

The story of the young shepherd lad who kills 'a monster' to win the hand of a king's daughter, is more the stuff of folklore than serious history. Goliath, as described, is an unlikely character. As well as being freakishly tall, he was supposed to be descended from the *Rephaim*, wraith-like beings who, according to mythology, had once populated the land. Furthermore, in a little-known passage of the Bible, the credit for killing Goliath is actually given to somebody completely different – David's champion Elhanan (2 Samuel 21:19).

The Goliath episode is also awkwardly inserted into the narrative. That David was only noticed by Saul at this point seems impossible. According to an earlier passage in the Bible, David had already entered Saul's service – as a harpist employed to soothe the king's troubled mind with music. The Goliath episode seems to have been inserted to contrast David's heroism with Saul's instability.

Whether the contest between David and Goliath ever took place remains doubtful. However, David obviously distinguished himself as a warrior. Acclaimed as a hero, he was initially well received at Saul's court, although his successful raids on the Philistines incurred Saul's jealousy and a rift developed. By the time of Saul's death, the famous 'giant killer' David had actually joined the Philistines (see pp. 80–1).

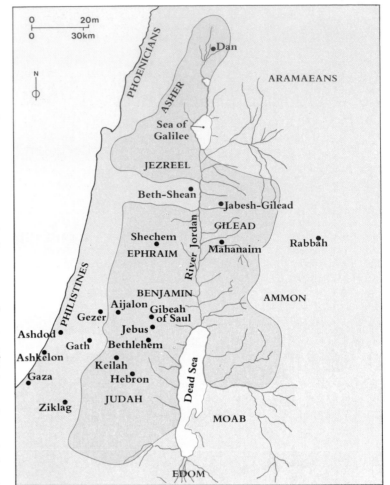

The boundaries of Saul's Israelite kingdom are not well defined in the Bible. It is known, however, that he ruled most of central Palestine, the nucleus of his kingdom being the tribal areas of Benjamin, Ephraim and Gilead, shaded blue on the map. He also had a measure of control over the remote northern tribes, and at least nominal control over the tribe of Judah, despite David's strong influence there.

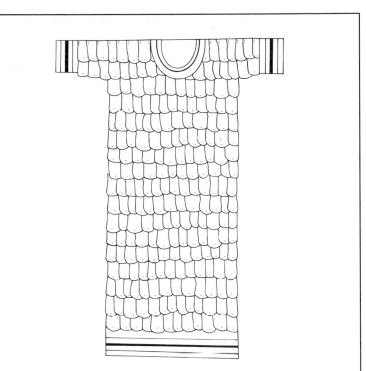

This 5th-century Greek vase depicts the contest between Achilles, *left*, and Hector, respective champions of the Greeks and Trojans. In the 'Heroic' ages of both Greece and Israel, the selection of champions to decide the outcome of a war or battle was an accepted alternative to full-scale battle.

Several instances are found in Homer's account of the Trojan war. In the Bible, Goliath threw down this challenge to any Israelite warrior: 'If he can fight it out with me and kill me, we will be your servants; but if I can beat him and kill him, you become our servants and serve us' (1 Samuel 17:9).

Slingstones, *left*, are of a kind often found at Israelite sites. Slings were used widely in the Near East, not only as rustic weapons for shepherds but also for deadly fire-power in battle. Some of King David's soldiers fired slings with both right and left hands (1 Chronicles 12:2).

The sling was a favourite weapon of the Israelites. Though just a leather or cloth pad with two attached cords, in skilled hands it was deadly. The slinger, based on an Egyptian relief, carried a bag of stones. After loading one into the pouch of the sling, he would have held up the pouch in one hand, using the other to pull the cords taut. He then swung the sling above his head, until the required momentum was reached. One of the cords was then released, hurling out the stone with terrific force.

Goliath: his weapons and armour

This tunic of scale-armour was drawn from an Egyptian painting of the fifteenth century BC. Scale armour of this sort was popular in Syria, Palestine and Mesopotamia for many centuries and would have been the kind worn by the heavily armoured Goliath: 'On his head was a bronze helmet and he wore a breastplate of scale-armour; the breastplate weighed five thousand shekels of bronze' (1 Samuel 17:5–6).

The weapons he carried included a heavy iron-headed spear, with a bronze scimitar slung across his back. A minion carried a large shield in front of him. Though Goliath's armaments have often been incorrectly described as Mycenaean, or Homeric Greek, they were typically Near Eastern. Only the bronze greaves were alien to Palestine, but since examples are known from nearby Cyprus from the twelfth century, Goliath cannot be imagined as wearing armour directly influenced by Greek styles.

Saul's death at Gilboa

When Saul saw the Philistine camp, he was afraid and his heart trembled violently' (1 Samuel 28:5). Throughout his reign, Saul had successfully challenged the Philistines, effectively replacing their authority over central and southern Palestine with a new force, the united kingdom of Israel. Now, however, after several unsuccessful attempts to crush the rebel king, the Philistines had mustered an army of such magnitude that victory for Saul was impossible.

Assembling at Aphek in the Sharon plain, 'the Philistine commanders marched past with their hundreds and their thousands' (1 Samuel 29:2). Even David, at this time a Philistine vassal, and his band of 600 followers were mustered for the decisive campaign against Saul. The appearance of these Hebrews in the vanguard of Achish, king of Gath, caused great consternation among the Philistine lords, who feared that David and his band might turn against them during the battle. After some debate, David and his men were dismissed from the army of the Philistine confederacy. Marching south with speed, David returned to his base at the Philistine city of Ziklag and to an unwelcome surprise – in his absence the town had been sacked by a band of Amalekite raiders.

Meanwhile the Philistines had completed their march to the Jezreel valley. Saul, terrified by the sight of the assembled enemy host, yearned for the advice of his old mentor, the late prophet

Samuel. Disguising himself, Saul skirted the Philistine lines in order to visit the famous medium who lived at Endor. Because Saul had previously banned all occult practitioners from the land, she was reluctant to help him but was eventually persuaded to raise the spirit of Samuel. But Saul's anxiety was not eased by Samuel's ghost, who warned him: 'Tomorrow you and your sons will be with me; and Yahweh will hand over the army of Israel into the power of the Philistines' (1 Samuel 28:19).

With a heavy heart Saul engaged his enemies in battle on the following day. Overpowered by enormous odds, Saul retreated from the plain to the heights of Mount Gilboa, pursued by chariotry. His sons Jonathan, Abinadab and Malchishua were killed, and Saul was severely injured by arrow wounds. Fearing capture and humiliation, Saul and his armour-bearer fell on their swords. Humiliation still followed: Saul's head and armour were sent around Philistia as tokens of Saul's defeat. What remained of the bodies of Saul and his sons was staked to the wall of Beth-Shean as an example for the Israelites. Those living in the Jezreel valley fled as the Philistines occupied their towns.

Conquest of the Jezreel valley would have given the Israelites control of the main trade route to the north and would also have removed the Canaanite wedge remaining between the tribes of central Palestine and the northerly tribes of Asher and Zebulun. This the Philistines could not allow and at Mount Gilboa they destroyed Saul and his army.

Having 'mustered all Israel', Saul led them northwards, entering the Jezreel valley through the pass of En-gannim. The Israelites camped at the 'spring of Jezreel' near modern Jenin (En-gannim). Meanwhile, the Philistines had mustered at the town of Aphek in the Sharon plain. They advanced on the Jezreel valley and pitched their camp at the town of Shunem. Saul then moved to the heights of Mount Gilboa, which gave a commanding view over the whole valley. He was terrified by the sight of the Philistine host.

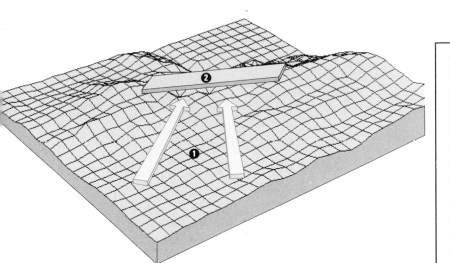

David's flight from Saul
Long before the Battle of Gilboa, an irreparable rift had developed between Saul and David. Despite his close links with Saul's family – his marriage to Saul's daughter Michal and his friendship with Saul's son Jonathan – David was mistrusted by Saul. The Bible attributes this to Saul's jealousy. After an attempt on his life, David fled the court to live in hiding. Efforts at reconciliation failed and David eventually sought the protection of Israel's arch-enemy, Achish, king of Philistine Gath.

David was given the town of Ziklag as his residence and lived there for 16 months, forming a personal army from Israelites opposed to Saul's regime. They survived by raiding and looting the non-Israelite tribes of the Negeb, particularly the Amalekites. They, however, took their revenge when David marched north to fight Saul at Gilboa. On his return to Ziklag he found that the unprotected town had been destroyed by the Amalekites and everyone living there, including his two wives, carried off. He pursued the Amalekite band and caught up with them when they were examining their booty and unprepared. Taking them by surprise, he massacred them and recovered his wives, the other captives and valuables, together with the flocks and herds of the Amalekites.

'The Philistines bore down on Saul and his sons . . .' (1 SAMUEL 31:2)
The Philistine chariots, **1**, would have profited from the gentle incline of Gilboa's southern slopes to launch a devastating attack on Saul and the Israelites, **2**.

Battle seems to have begun when the Philistines moved to dislodge Saul from his position on Mount Gilboa. Between Shunem and Gilboa there is a deep riverbed and the northern edge of the mountain is steep and rugged. So the Philistines must have attacked by way of the gentler southern slopes of the Gilboa range, **1**, on which they could manoeuvre their chariotry. 'The Israelites fleeing from the Philistines, fell and were slaughtered on Mount Gilboa' (1 Samuel 31:1). Saul's three sons were killed.

'When the Philistines came on the following day to strip the dead they found Saul and his three sons lying on Gilboa' (1 Samuel 31:8). The scene was later cursed by David: 'You mountains of Gilboa, no dew, no rain fall upon you, O treacherous fields!' (2 Samuel 1:21).

'The fighting grew fiercer around Saul', **2**, . . . 'the archers came upon him and he was severely wounded by the archers' (1 Samuel 31:3). To avoid capture, Saul committed suicide, together with his armour-bearer, as the Philistine chariots and cavalry bore down on them.

81

David captures Jerusalem

The king and his men then marched on Jerusalem, on the Jebusites living in the territory' (2 Samuel 5:6). During the siege, the Jebusites called out to David: 'You will not get in here. The blind and the lame will hold you off.' Cursing the disabled people of Jebus who had been employed to mock him, David stormed the city. He did, however, spare most of the inhabitants who were allowed to coexist with the Israelites.

After capturing the city, David set about making it the political and religious capital of Israel. It became Jerusalem, the special city of Israel's God. Psalm 132:13–14, inspired by David's achievement, remembers the event: 'For Yahweh has chosen Zion, he has desired it as a home. "Here I shall rest for evermore, here shall I make my home as I have wished."'

When David conquered Jerusalem around 1005 BC, he was a minor king subject to the Philistines. Israel, with its leader Saul, had been crushed at Gilboa by the Philistines, who resumed their customary dominance over the country. Yet they seem to have invaded and occupied only northern Israel, the area around the Jezreel valley. Rather than directly garrisoning the Hebrew lands, a strategy which had failed on previous occasions, they now preferred a policy of 'divide and rule'.

It suited the Philistines that, after Saul's death, the once united Israelite tribes should split into two groups. Saul's son Ish-Baal was set up by General Abner as the 'king of all Israel' on the east of the Jordan. David, meanwhile, took control of the south. He moved his centre of operations from Ziklag on the borders of Philistia to the traditional Hebrew centre of Hebron. 'The men of Judah came, and there they anointed David as king of the House of Judah' (2 Samuel 2:4).

At this point, David was still nominally a retainer of the Philistine king of Gath. David proved, however, far too ambitious and capable to remain anyone's vassal. War broke out with Saul's son Ish-Baal, during which 'David grew steadily stronger and the House of Saul steadily weaker' (2 Samuel 3:1). Eventually, Ish-Baal's right-hand man Abner switched his allegiance to David and came south to negotiate. He was slain by David's men as he left Hebron. Shortly afterwards, the unfortunate Ish-Baal was murdered by some old enemies and his head was presented to David.

David professed horror at both these murders while reaping the advantages. He was now left as the main, and only obvious, claimant to the throne of Israel: 'All the tribes of Israel then came to David at Hebron and said, "Look, we are your own flesh and bone. In days past when Saul was our king, it was you who led Israel on its campaigns. . . ." So all the elders of Israel came to the king at Hebron, and they anointed David as king of Israel' (2 Samuel 5:1–3).

David ruled at Hebron for seven and a half years until he decided to move his capital to the city of Jebus – the future Jerusalem. This ancient city was a Canaanite enclave which had somehow survived for centuries amid the Israelite settlements. Its citadel was strong but, since it was totally surrounded, it was almost inevitable that one day it would succumb to Hebrew conquest.

Jerusalem, during David's reign, played a unifying role within Israel. David chose it as his capital because of its position, almost on the very border of his own tribe of Judah and Saul's tribe of Benjamin. Well placed and belonging to no tribe in particular, Jerusalem was an ideal capital for the whole realm.

'Behold the King has set his name upon the land of Jerusalem for ever; so he cannot abandon the lands of Jerusalem!'

The early history of Jerusalem

So wrote Abdi-Hiba, king of Jerusalem, in a desperate plea to his overlord, the king of Egypt. His letter, part of which is reproduced *above* with a translation, comes from the famous archive of cuneiform tablets found at Tell el-Amarna in Egypt, dating from the reigns of the fourteenth-century BC pharaohs Amenophis III and Amenophis IV (better known as Akhenaten).

Abdi-Hiba was urgently requesting Egyptian troops to protect the city-state of Jerusalem, which was being threatened by several enemies but principally by the enigmatic group known as the 'Habiru'. Abdi-Hiba wrote: 'The land of the king has fallen away to the Habiru.' It was once thought that these Habiru were Hebrews in the process of conquering Canaan, but this is now doubted. Their exact relationship to the Israelites, if any, still awaits clarification.

The history of Jerusalem before the el-Amarna period is obscure, but it is known that it was an important and extremely ancient city. It is mentioned in the Egyptian inscriptions from the eighteenth century BC known as the 'Execration Texts'. These were bowls or figurines inscribed with the names of Egypt's enemies, then ritually smashed to bring them bad luck. One bowl fragment mentions the ruler of Jerusalem and his retainers.

Tradition holds that the city of Shalem ('Peace'), visited by the wandering patriarch Abraham, was Jerusalem. Shalem was ruled by the noble Melchizedek, a 'priest of the most high God', who welcomed Abraham and blessed him (Genesis 14:18) Jerusalem is next found in the hands of the hostile Jebusites. Joshua defeated their king, Adoni-Zedek, in battle, but it seems that the Israelites were unable to seize Jerusalem at the time of the conquest of Canaan. It was still in Jebusite hands when David conquered it.

The fate of the last, unnamed, ruler of Jebus is unknown – presumably he was killed after David captured the city. Most of the Jebusites, however, were spared: 'the Jebusites still live in Jerusalem today, side by side with the sons of Judah' (Joshua 15:63). Their rights seem to have been fully respected by the conquerors, as evidenced by the story of Araunah, the Jebusite nobleman who owned the land to the north of the citadel. David, ordered by Yahweh to build an altar, bought as a site Araunah's threshing-floor and some oxen for sacrifice, paying their full market price of 50 shekels of silver (2 Samuel 24:24). Araunah's threshing-floor eventually became the site of Solomon's Temple (see pp.86–9).

Why King David made Jerusalem his capital

Jerusalem was carefully selected by David as his new capital. Nominally within the area allotted to the tribe of Benjamin and slightly north of Judah, Jerusalem had never been captured by the Hebrews from the Jebusites. Thus its elevation to the status of capital would arouse little jealousy among the tribes. It was also strategically placed on a major north-south route; there was the further advantage of its being easily defendable, standing as it does among rugged hills. Refounded as David's capital, Jerusalem served three purposes: as the seat of the royal house of David; as the centre of government for all Israel; and as a new religious capital, the site of Yahweh's future Temple.

To establish its importance as the national cult centre, David transferred the ark of the covenant (see pp.44–5) there. This holy relic not only contained the tablets on which the Law was inscribed but was considered, in a mysterious way, to be Yahweh's 'seat', replete with immense powers.

Normally kept at Shiloh, the ark had been housed for some years at Kiriath-Jearim. David moved it to Jerusalem in a triumphal procession – '. . . with war cries and blasts on the horn, David and the entire house of Israel brought up the ark of Yahweh' (2 Samuel 6:15). The ark meant that Yahweh himself was now in Jerusalem, consecrating it as a holy city.

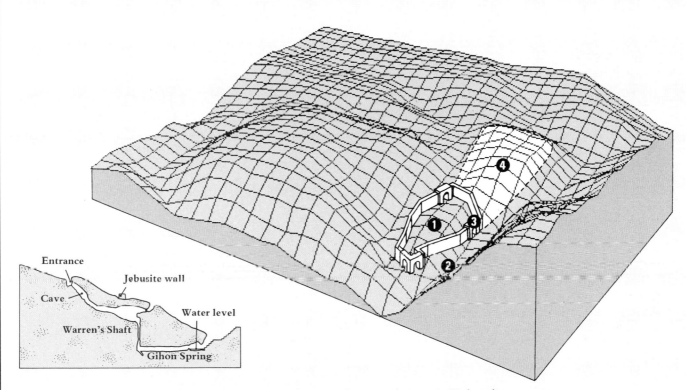

Entrance
Jebusite wall
Cave
Water level
Warren's Shaft
Gihon Spring

The Jebusite city seized by David in about 1005 BC was a small fortified area on the southern spur of a hill. 'David went to live in the citadel, **1**, and called it the city of David' (2 Samuel 5:9).

Little remains of the pre-Davidic city. However, tombs from the 14th century BC found in the Kidron valley, **2**, reveal the rich, cosmopolitan life-style of the Jebusites.

David promised great rewards to the first of his army to enter the city: 'The first man to kill a Jebusite will be made army chief and commander' (1 Chronicles 11:6). Joab was the first to do so and was made Israel's general.

An interesting variant is found in 2 Samuel 5:8: 'Whoever gets up the tunnel and kills a Jebusite. . . .' The tunnel in question is thought to be a water tunnel, through which the Israelites could have made a surprise attack. It may have been Warren's Shaft, **3**, (see also cross-section, *above left*), dug straight through the rock to allow water to be drawn up into the city from the Gihon Spring outside. This was certainly in use by the 10th century BC.

Possible traces of David's buildings have been found in a few areas. He built a new city wall and some kind of supporting structure called the Millo ('filling'), as well as a palace of cedar wood (2 Samuel 5:10–11). He bought the hill north of the citadel from a Jebusite noble and erected an altar there on the future site of Jerusalem's Temple, **4** (2 Samuel 24:25).

The expansion of the empire

Under King David's leadership, Israel flourished briefly as a major military power. Its rapid growth, from the shattered kingdom left by Saul into an empire dominating almost the whole of Syro-Palestine, was remarkable.

Quite early in his reign, David managed to best the Philistines. After the murder of Saul's son Ish-Baal, David had himself proclaimed as 'king of Israel'. The Philistines, aware that their erstwhile vassal was becoming too powerful, attacked in force, occupying the Valley of Rephaim which leads up to Jerusalem. Yet David drove them out so rapidly that they abandoned their idols as they fled. Again they invaded and were thrown back. They were now effectively neutralised.

Israel, rather than Philistia, became the dominant power in Palestine. It was probably at this time that Israel finally absorbed the rich Canaanite cities of the Jezreel valley, a prize awaited since the original settlement in Canaan. Next to feel the growing might of Israel were the Aramaeans. By the tenth century BC, this warlike people had settled over an extensive area of the Near East. Aramaean kings ruled northern Palestine, the whole of Syria and large areas of Mesopotamia beyond the Euphrates.

In David's time the leading Aramaean state was Zobah. As its king Hadadezer was mounting an expedition against Mesopotamia, David marched north and launched a successful surprise attack, destroying Hadadezer's chariotry and looting his towns. The Aramaeans of Damascus moved to help their ally Hadadezer but were themselves defeated. David seized Damascus and installed Israelite governors.

David also campaigned in the south, where the Edomites were ruthlessly dealt with. David's general Joab reputedly 'slaughtered the entire male population of Edom', except those who managed to flee to Egypt (1 Kings 11:15). The Israelites now ruled a virtual empire stretching from the borders of Egypt to the River Euphrates. How was this achieved by a people who, only a generation before, had been poorly-armed farmers rebelling against the Philistines?

David's early career provides the answer. During his years as a Philistine vassal at Ziklag and Hebron, he had built up a private army of malcontents and mercenaries drawn from both Philistia and Israel. This small, but professional, group, supplemented by David's 600-strong Philistine bodyguard, formed the core of a new Israelite army, able to train and command a much wider army of Israelite conscripts.

David's success was also due to his diplomacy. He married the daughter of the Aramaean king of Geshur, befriended Hiram the powerful Phoenician king of Tyre and formed an alliance with the king of Hamath in Syria. Each partner was carefully chosen for his strategic value in particular struggles – against Ish-Baal, the Philistines and the Aramaeans of Zobah.

The price of empire was almost continuous war. The Ammonites across the Jordan resisted control and invited in Hadadezer, beginning a second Aramaean war. Joab was sent to capture its capital Rabbah and enslave the Ammonites. Two rebellions within Israel also had to be quelled – one led by David's ambitious son Absalom, the other by Sheba the Benjaminite, who rallied the northern Israelites who disliked David's southern origin. Yet David and his generals succeeded in maintaining the hegemony which they had imposed on the Levant; and, at his death, David passed on to his son Solomon a valuable, though shaky, inheritance.

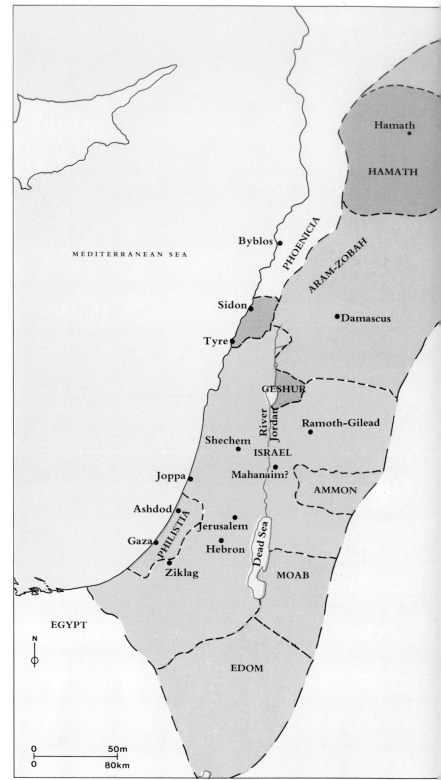

'Wherever David went, Yahweh gave him victory' (2 SAMUEL 8:14). During David's reign (c.1010–970 BC), Israel expanded to its greatest extent. His empire included most of the habitable territory between the Red Sea and the Euphrates. Many areas were subjugated to direct military force: the people of Edom were almost exterminated; its neighbour Moab was bludgeoned into paying tribute, while the Ammonites were used as forced labour.

Farther north in Transjordan lay the kingdom of Geshur, whose alliance with David was sealed by his marriage to its princess. After David's victory over Aram-Zobah, its rival Hamath allied itself

River Euphrates

iphsah

nor

Kingdom of Israel

Allied states

Subjugated areas

with David: 'Tou king of Hamath . . . sent his son Hadoram to King David to greet him and to congratulate him (2 Samuel 8:10). Damascus was also seized from the Aramaeans and garrisoned.

On the coast, David formed an alliance with Hiram, king of Tyre, overlord of the Phoenicians. The Philistines were at last cowed into submission and restricted to a small coastal area.

The darker side of King David

King David, seen in this illumination from the Kennicott Bible in the Bodleian Library, Oxford, was unquestionably an astute general and diplomat. He was also an accomplished musician and poet who, if he did not compose the Psalms personally, probably initiated their form and style. The Bible praises his achievements in politics, military affairs, religion, building and the arts. Yet there is a bias in the way in which his career is reported. The young David is represented as a picture of naïve faith, blended with flawless courage. For his victories over the Philistines, honours were bestowed upon him by King Saul. Their relationship was marred only by Saul's insane jealousy. The tragic rift between them grew as Saul declined into madness, induced by Yahweh because of his disobedience.

On two occasions, according to the Bible, David held King Saul completely at his mercy. Though David spared him, Saul continued to hate him. Yet David was still loyal to the king, expressing in song immense grief at his death. Later, when Saul's son Ish-Baal was murdered, David professed great anger and had the killers executed.

Despite its whitewashing of David's career, there is enough detail in the Bible to suggest the less attractive side of his character. His loyalty to the house of Saul is stressed, yet he was clearly Saul's rival. Leaving Saul, he became a vassal of Israel's most hated enemies, the Philistines. In this role he prospered, drawing into his service anyone who had lost favour with Saul's regime, and he even tried to join the expedition which crushed Saul at Mount Gilboa.

David, when king, 'looked after' Saul's surviving family. Saul had broken an old treaty between the Israelites and Gibeonites and when a famine occurred David blamed it on the breaking of the treaty. He gathered together Saul's remaining descendants and handed them over to the Gibeonites, 'who dismembered them before Yahweh on the hill' (2 Samuel 21:9). Only Meribbaal, the son of Saul's son Jonathan, was spared. Since he was lame in both feet, Meribbaal posed little threat to David's leadership, and he was kept safely at David's court as an example of the king's generosity.

The Biblical narratives greatly favour David because he was the founder of Israel's eternal dynasty in Jerusalem, truly believed to be God's city. Chroniclers working within this tradition had, therefore, to present its founder in a favourable light. By contrast, his enemy Saul had to be portrayed as a glorious failure.

Solomon builds the Temple

King David conquered Canaanite Jerusalem and made it his capital (see p.82), but it was Solomon who tranformed it into a true royal city. The Temple, which dominated Jerusalem, became the centre of the royal state cult and survived in changing circumstances for almost 1,000 years after the death of Solomon, its creator.

Solomon, younger son of David by his favourite wife Bathsheba, succeeded his father in an atmosphere of palace intrigue. Bathsheba was ambitious for her son. When a coup by Solomon's elder half-brother Adonijah threatened to thwart her plans, she moved quickly, using her influence over the ageing David to make him proclaim Solomon king at once. Solomon gained the support of leaders of the priesthood and army. When his father died, Solomon ruthlessly eliminated or exiled his opponents, thus becoming the sole heir to the rich and powerful kingdom of Israel and Judah.

Unlike his father, Solomon was no military leader. He was, though, an able administrator and diplomat. With the wealth that flowed into the royal coffers from internal taxation and international trading enterprises, he carried out an extensive nationwide building programme. The Israelites were conscripted periodically to work on this. Solomon is remembered above all for his building of the Temple in Jerusalem, following plans which had already been prepared by David. Work began in his fourth year as king and was completed in his eleventh. 1 Kings 6–7 describes the splendid appearance of the Temple.

Solomon ruled over a powerful state and he built in a style befitting a true oriental monarch. A treaty was concluded with Hiram of Tyre who 'provided Solomon with all the cedar wood and juniper he wanted' (1 Kings 5:24) in return for wheat and oil. Stone was quarried near Jerusalem. The Temple was built on a high rocky ridge. It stood in the middle of a courtyard and was oriented east to west, with the entrance facing the rising sun. While the outside was probably quite plain, the inside walls were covered with cedar wood and 'carved figures of winged creatures, palm trees and rosettes' (1 Kings 6:29).

Outside the Temple were various burnished bronze cult objects including the altar of sacrifices and the bronze 'sea', a huge basin supported by 12 statues of oxen where the priests purified themselves. There were also ten bronze basins on ornamented wheeled pedestals which were used for washing the offerings. In front of the Temple porch were two free-standing bronze pillars crowned with capitals.

Adjacent to the Temple were Solomon's palace buildings. In a great hall called the 'House of the Forest of Lebanon', 45 cedar columns supported the roof. The cedar-panelled throne room was approached through a colonnaded portico. There, Solomon conducted state affairs, seated on his throne. The throne 'had six steps with a golden footrest . . . and two lions standing beside the arms and twelve lions stood on either side of the six steps. Nothing like it had ever been made in any other kingdom' (2 Chronicles 9:18–19).

Barely a trace of Solomon's Jerusalem has survived. Even the precise location of the Temple and palace complex is uncertain. Many of the details in the Biblical account are unclear, but valuable parallels are found in a range of archaeological evidence. The Temple ground plan is similar to that of many earlier Canaanite temples, while the inspiration for many of the furnishings and cult objects clearly came from Phoenicia.

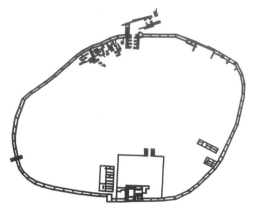

At Megiddo, which guarded the main east–west road across Israel, Solomon built impressive fortifications, a magnificent gateway and several administrative buildings. A ceremonial palace in Syrian style, of fine ashlar masonry, adjoined the city wall on the northeast side.

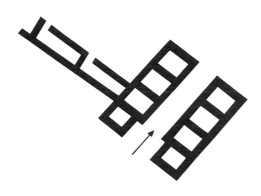

Hazor was Solomon's most important northern stronghold. The defensive wall and gate which he built, shown in the ground plan, *left*, are similar to those at Megiddo. The western part of the mound, which contained monumental buildings, was perhaps a separate royal quarter.

The Temple was built of rectangular stone blocks, **1**, beautifully hewn by skilled masons. All the work was done at the quarry site: 'No sound of hammer or pick or any iron tool was to be heard in the Temple while it was being built' (1 Kings 6:7). The walls may have had a brick superstructure, held together by a wooden framework.

The annex, **2**, erected against all but the entrance wall of the Temple, cannot be reconstructed accurately. It had 3 low storeys, each slightly broader than the one below. It was probably used as a place to store offerings.

The two bronze pillars, **3**, before the Temple were cast by a smith named Hiram, of mixed Phoenician and Israelite descent. The pillars were named 'Jachin' and 'Boaz', the significance of which is still a riddle. Terracotta model shrines from Cyprus and Palestine show similar columns.

Phoenician carved ivory: lioness attacking a Nubian

The Phoenicians: traders and craftsmen

The city states of Phoenicia, the most important of which were Tyre, Sidon, Arvad and Byblos, flourished on trade and commerce. With the advantage of natural harbours, the Phoenicians became seafarers and established colonies and trading posts throughout the Mediterranean. They were masters of shipbuilding, making war galleys, cargo ships and fishing boats. Their coastal plain was narrow but fertile and behind rose the mountains of the Lebanon, where the cedars, coveted throughout the Near East, grew.

As middlemen, the Phoenicians transported raw materials and manufactured goods from other lands. They were also highly skilled craftsmen, working as metalsmiths, weavers, carpenters, ivory carvers and stonemasons. The purple dyes, including the 'Tyrian purple' that coloured the fine textiles, were renowned. The dye came mainly from a mollusc called the murex and to this day mounds of broken shells bear witness to the once thriving industry. Phoenician art shows considerable Egyptian influence, a result of the strong links between the two countries.

Solomon's Temple and palace were largely built by Phoenician craftsmen. The Temple was of typical Canaanite plan. Phoenician and Canaanite religious practices were similar and the Biblical account suggests a close relationship between Solomon's Temple and Phoenician shrines. The Temple's interior decoration has parallels with the Phoenician carved ivories discovered in Assyrian palaces.

Floral motifs recall the 'gourds and rosettes' of the Temple carvings and the winged sphinxes approximate to the 'winged creatures' which guarded the ark of the covenant. Most of the ivory plaques were inlays for wooden furniture – as on Solomon's 'ivory' throne. They were often plated with gold like the example, *above*, which shows a lioness attacking a Nubian. There was also much Phoenician metalwork in gold, silver and bronze among the temple furnishings and cult objects.

Temple practices and rituals

When his Temple had been built, Solomon inaugurated it with sacrifice and prayer. These remained the forms of worship until the Temple was burnt by the Babylonians in 587 BC. Prayer and sacrifice were restored in a second Temple, completed in 516 BC, but destroyed by the Romans in AD 70. Jews still pray thrice daily for the restoration of the Temple and its ritual.

Sacrifice happened every morning and evening when a lamb was wholly burnt on behalf of all Israel, and the 'soothing odour' ascended heavenwards. Sacrifice was once called God's food (Numbers 28:2); it could be motivated by gratitude, as when an individual fulfilled a vow made in distress. In particular, the Israelites believed that all belonged to God, and that a man should return (whether by sacrificing or giving to the priests) the first of all produce – corn, fruit, the fleece of sheep, first-born animals – in order to enjoy the rest. Again, sacrifice served as a 'memorial', reminding God of the sacrificer's needs.

Some sacrifices, called 'peace-offerings', were partly burnt on the altar and partly eaten by the worshipper, apparently to effect communion with God. Yet another purpose of sacrifice was to expiate sin, against God or man. Wrongs against men were an affront to the all-seeing God, who would not accept a sin-offering from one who had not made restitution. A national expiation took place every autumn, on the Day of Atonement: Israel's sins were transferred to a goat, which was then banished (hence the term 'scapegoat') into the wilderness.

Sacrifices might be accompanied, on the three pilgrimage festivals (Deuteronomy 16), by joyous processions and all-night singing (Isaiah 30:29), or, in times of danger, by fasting and solemn assembly (Jeremiah 36:9). The Psalms illustrate the prayers uttered in the Temple and its courts, by commoner, king or all Israel together, in distress and in thanksgiving. Meanwhile the priests presented weekly 12 loaves of bread on the golden table, offered incense twice daily at the golden altar, and kept the golden candelabrum perpetually lit.

Reconstructing the Temple practices, and indeed religious history, is problematic because the dates of the relevant passages are not certain and later generations may project their own practices back to their predecessors. For example, in 837 BC, the seven-year-old prince Joash, surrounded by the royal bodyguard, was marched into the Temple and proclaimed king in place of the tyrannical Athaliah (2 Kings 11). Later, however, laymen were banned from the Temple and restricted to its courts; and so Chronicles, compiled in the fourth century BC, turns the soldiers into Levites (2 Chronicles 23). The great Temple choirs of 1 Chronicles 23 are similarly suspect.

Many scholars prefer to reconstruct the ritual of the first Temple from the Psalms; for example, passages where God speaks in the first person (e.g. 50:7) suggest the presence of Temple prophets, who spoke in God's name. The prophets did not, in fact, reject the Temple ritual, but only condemned insincere or paganised worship (Isaiah 1:11–14).

The dominant view in the Bible is that the Temple became Israel's sole legitimate sanctuary. Some passages, however, imply many more sanctuaries. For example, Elijah repaired and sacrificed upon the Lord's altar on Mount Carmel. Altars at Bethel and Dan became the principal shrines of the northern kingdom after Solomon's death. At Arad, in the Negeb, an altar of earth and rough stones has been found.

The high priest's garments comprised breast-piece, ephod (an apron secured at the shoulders), mantle, chequered tunic, turban with sash and linen trousers. The ephod and breast-piece were made of fine linen and gold, blue, purple and scarlet yarn, all woven together.

The breast-piece was inlaid with 12 gems, but their identity is uncertain. The New English Bible has them as, left to right: sardin, chrysolyte, green felspar, purple garnet, lapis lazuli, jade, turquoise, agate, jasper, topaz, cornelian and green jasper. Each stone was engraved with the name of the ancestor of one of the 12 tribes.

The altar for burnt offerings, **1**, had to be in the open and stood east of the Temple doors. The priest reached it via steps, according to Ezekiel 43:17, despite an earlier prohibition in Exodus 20:26. Southeast of the Temple stood the bronze 'Sea', **2**, where the priests washed and which perhaps represented the primordial waters (Genesis 1:2). There were also five wheeled trolleys with basins, **3**, either side of the Temple for washing sacrificial animals.

Any reconstruction of Solomon's Temple itself must be tentative because the descriptions in 1 Kings 6–7 and 2 Chronicles 3–4 contain many obscure technical terms and omit some crucial details, such as the thickness of the walls and the construction of the roof.

Only unblemished male animals – bulls, rams, goats – could be sacrificed on behalf of all Israel as burnt offerings, on the bronze altar outside the eastern entrance of the Temple. In this stylised stone relief from Sainte Chapelle, Paris, a lamb is being held before the flames of the altar by the priest. The artist was in error, since the lamb ought not to be offered whole but should first have been cut into pieces (Leviticus 1:12).

The priest slaughtered the animal – with a sharp knife to the throat – at the north side of the altar, sprinkled its blood – believed to contain the animal's life force – (Leviticus 17:11) against the altar, flayed the carcass and cut it in pieces, which were set on the altar and wholly burnt. Wine and fine flour mingled with oil, accompanied this sacrifice.

If an individual brought a burnt offering, he first laid a hand on the animal's head. Individuals were permitted to substitute a turtle-dove or pigeon: the priest slit its throat with a finger-nail, discarded its stomach (in case it had eaten the food of others), pressed the wings flat on the altar without breaking them off, and burnt it completely.

Certainly the doors were of olivewood and the walls inlaid with gold, and both were decorated with figures of cherubim (winged griffins), palm-trees and open flowers.

There were five candelabra, 4, on both the northern and southern sides. In the middle stood the golden altar of incense, **5**, with firepans and other accessories, and the golden table, **6**, on which 12 new loaves (the 'shewbread') were laid out for a week every sabbath.

At the back of the Temple, steps led to the Holy of Holies, a cube-shaped area with sides of 20 cubits (30ft/9m). This was entered only once a year – by the high priest on the Day of Atonement in autumn. Here stood the ark of the covenant, **7**, containing the stone tablets on which the Ten Commandments were written, flanked by two cherubim, **8**.

Music and musical instruments

Music, and particularly song, played an important part in both the religious and secular life of the Israelites. Although, in the Bible, music appears to be a predominantly sacred art, incidentally there is evidence of music-making as part of daily secular life.

There are references to vintage songs, to music performed at feasts and processions. There were songs of farewell, as when Laban complained to Jacob: 'Why did you flee . . . without letting me know, so that I could send you on your way rejoicing, with songs and the music of tambourines and harps?' (Genesis 31:27). David soothed Saul's spirits with the sweet sound of his harp and his lament over Saul and Jonathan, 'Does the splendour of Israel lie dead on your heights? How did the heroes fall' (2 Samuel 1:19), was a song that used to accompany archery exercises.

As elsewhere in the Near East, lyric poetry, in all its forms, was popular with the Jews. Their psalms, which represent the greater part of Israel's religious poetry, contain a high degree of poetic language and imagery. The term 'psalm' comes from the Greek word for the stringed instrument ('psalterion') that accompanied those songs or hymns which in Hebrew are called *tehillim* (whose root meaning is 'to praise', or 'exult'). In fact, not all the psalms are songs of praise. There are also psalms of suffering, or laments, and of thanksgiving, while others are particularly connected with the king.

In the historical books of the Bible, there are examples of religious songs linked to specific events, such as the victory song of Deborah (Judges 5) and the song of Moses (Exodus 15). It is impossible to establish when each psalm, or group of psalms, was composed or who created them. It would seem that the various collections had been gathered together by the end of the fourth century, and although some date from after the Jews' exile in Babylon, it is now thought that the period of the kings saw the composition of most psalms.

Tradition has it that David composed the psalms. Some superscriptions relate 73 of the psalms to him. It is not clear, however, whether these superscriptions go further than to establish an unspecified relationship between the persons they name and the psalms. However, David's musical abilities are referred to elsewhere, and so perhaps just as Moses was connected with the law and Solomon with wisdom, similarly, musical tradition was associated with David's name.

The account of David's organisation of the Levitical singers and instrumentalists in 1 Chronicles 15:16–24 gives the greatest existing detail of the musical arrangements in the Temple. Three of the singers were to play the cymbals, eight Levites played the lyre and six the harp, while seven priests blew trumpets. The same chapter tells how the ark was brought to Jerusalem: 'Thus, with war cries and the sounding of the horn, the trumpets and the cymbals, and the music of the lyres and harps, all Israel transported the ark of the covenant of Yahweh' (15:28).

The identity of some of the Israelites' instruments is still uncertain but, in general, there were three types: strings, wind and percussion. The lyre and the harp were the oldest, and the *halil*, probably a double oboe, was also important, as were the tambourines and cymbals. It is hard to know what the sounds of so long ago were actually like, but through the psalms and the liturgical music of church and synagogue, it may be possible to catch a very faint echo of the music of Biblical times.

shofar, **1**: Neo-Hittite musician based on a relief from Carchemish *c*.1000 BC.

toph, **2**: Assyrian musician based on a wall relief from Nineveh, *c*.640 BC.

Dancing is not described in detail in the Bible but in the ancient Near East it often accompanied music in religious ceremonies and secular celebrations. In their performances, Egyptian dancers worshipped Hathor, goddess of love, music and dancing.

Dances could be acrobatic, formal or erotic. Professional dancers and musicians were often slaves or from the lower classes. They had a choice of costume: sometimes they wore veiled garments, sometimes loincloths, as in this tomb painting of the 18th Dynasty (1550–1307 BC).

These musicians are based on wall reliefs and paintings from the ancient Near East.

The *shofar*, or ram's horn, was used on religious occasions and to call the people to war. 'With war cries and the sounding of the horn . . . Israel transported the ark' (1 Chronicles 15:28). It is still used in synagogues today.

The *toph*, sometimes called a timbrel or tambourine, was beaten with the hand. 'Strike up the music, beat the tambourine' (Psalm 81:2).

Selselim, cymbals of brass, seem to have been used in religious ceremonies. 'Praise him with the clamour

The Song of Songs

This Egyptian wall painting from the tomb of Mereruka' Saqqara, during the reign of Teti (*c*.2300 BC), shows Mereruka seated on a bed, with his wife. She is playing the harp to him.

There are close parallels between the Song of Songs in the Bible and the love songs of ancient Egypt. By tradition associated with Solomon, the Song of Songs has been interpreted as an allegory of the love of God for his bride Israel, and by Christians as the love between Christ and his bride, the Church. In fact, the Song is a collection of erotic lyrics of great beauty. Although it contains themes from a much earlier period, it dates from after the exile in Babylon. The Song was probably originally sung at wedding feasts; certainly in the first centuries BC and AD, verses of it were sung by Jewish wedding guests.

The resemblance between the Song and the Egyptian love songs stems from a similarity in themes and imagery. As in the Egyptian songs, the Song expresses love in pastoral imagery: 'My love is a cluster of henna flowers among the vines of En-Gedi' (1:14); an Egyptian love song has: 'I belong to you like this plot of ground I planted with flowers and sweet smelling herbs'. In both the Egyptian songs and the Song of Songs, the lovers call each other brother and sister, and there are references in both to the sweet speech of the beloved and to the luxuries of the time.

selselim, **3**: Assyrian musician based on a wall relief from Nineveh, *c*.640 BC.

kinnor, **4**: Semitic nomad musician based on an Egyptian tomb painting, *c*.1900 BC.

nebel, **5**: Elamite musician based on an Assyrian relief, *c*.640 BC.

mena'anea, **6**: Egyptian musician based on a drawing on papyrus, *c*.1300 BC.

of cymbals, praise him with triumphant cymbals' (Psalm 150:5)

The *kinnor*, rendered as harp in most versions of the Bible, is actually a lyre. 'Jubal was the ancestor of all

who played the harp . . .' (Genesis 4:21).

The *nebel*, or harp, sometimes rendered as the 'psaltery', could be either vertical or horizontal. The *nebel 'asor* was a ten-stringed instrument.

'It is good to give thanks to Yahweh . . . on the lyre, the ten-stringed lyre, to the murmur of the harp' (Psalm 92:1–3).

The *mena'anea* or the sistrum was a kind of rattle, possibly like the

Egyptian instrument associated with Hathor, goddess of love, music and dancing. It was used to generate noise at joyous and mournful occasions. 'David and the house of Israel danced before

Yahweh . . . singing to the accompaniment of harps, lyres, tambourines, sistrums . . .' (2 Samuel 6:5).

Solomon and the queen of Sheba

King Solomon has been called, with some justice, 'the enthroned merchant', a tag which both describes and explains the origin of his fabled wealth. He was, of course, also known for his wisdom and it was both of these attributes that attracted the ruler of a distant Arabian land to visit Israel: 'The queen of Sheba heard of Solomon's fame and came to test him with difficult questions. She arrived in Jerusalem with a very large retinue, with camels laden with spices and an immense quantity of gold and precious stones' (1 Kings 10:1–2).

The Old Testament highlights the relationship between the queen of Sheba and Solomon in terms of their commercial and intellectual partnership. The two monarchs exchanged lavish presents. The queen of Sheba gave him 120 talents of gold 'and great quantities of spices and precious stones'. In return, Solomon gave her the benefit of his famous learning and also 'presented the queen of Sheba with everything that she expressed a wish for, besides what he gave her in exchange for what she had brought the king' (2 Chronicles 9:12).

The romantic implications of Solomon and Sheba's meeting have been endlessly elaborated by later writers from the Jewish, Muslim and Christian faiths. It is supposed in some extra-Biblical legends that the queen returned home to her country pregnant with Solomon's child. The fate of the child has been debated from the Middle Ages to the present day.

On the one hand the Christians of Abyssinia claim that the queen of Sheba's domain was their own country. Meroë, the capital of ancient Ethiopia, was once called 'Saba'. According to Ethiopian legend their first emperor was Menelik, the son of Solomon and Sheba. The claim of the last Ethiopian emperor, Haile Selassie, to such titles as 'descendant of David' and 'Lion of Judah' was based on this tradition, that Selassie was the direct lineal descendant of Solomon.

The Arabian claim, however, as pursued in the Koran, has much better historical grounding. The Arabian kingdom of Sheba, with its wealth of gold, jewels and spices traded by camel caravans, is well known from other Biblical passages. It occupied roughly the position of the modern state of Yemen. Present archaeological evidence of settled states in southern Arabia only extends as far back as the eighth century BC, but there is no good reason to doubt that an Arabian kingdom of Sheba existed earlier. The Assyrian kings of the late eighth century took tribute of gold, precious stones and 'all kinds of spices' from Samsi, queen of the Arabs, corroborating two aspects of the Biblical story – the characteristic luxury products of Arabia and the custom, quite rare in the Near East, of having female monarchs.

Solomon's friendship was obviously worth courting. His wealth was founded, ultimately, on the relatively secure empire which his father King David bequeathed him. Beyond that, Solomon's own skill in diplomacy proved immensely successful. He cultivated the friendship of Hiram, king of the leading Phoenician city of Tyre, and they carried out joint commercial expeditions. An alliance with Egypt was insured by marrying one of Pharaoh's daughters.

What exactly transpired between Solomon and Sheba will never be known. It might have been a 'marriage alliance' that never involved a formal marriage. But whatever the arrangement, it helped Solomon's economic policies and fitted well his own very personal style of kingship and diplomacy.

The Judgement of Solomon
This thirteenth-century miniature from a Hebrew Bible and Prayer Book shows Solomon giving his most celebrated judgement. When two women disputed the parentage of a child, he threatened to cut it in two and give one half to each. One of the women implored him not to – and was thus identified as the true mother. Solomon's great wisdom was thought to be a gift from Yahweh. As well as judicial skills, he was noted for his literary achievements (3,000 proverbs and 1,005 songs) and his knowledge of natural history: 'He could discourse on plants from the cedar in Lebanon to the hyssop . . . on the wall . . . on animals and birds and reptiles and fish' (1 Kings 5:13).

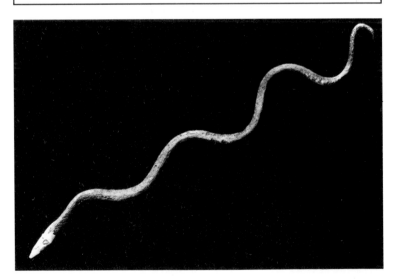

This tiny copper serpent with gilded head was found at Timna in the Negeb, the reputed site of some of King Solomon's mines. Timna is a rich source of copper and mining certainly took place there during Biblical times. But the link with Solomon has always been controversial.

The first excavators of Timna were sure that the mine had been used during the 10th century BC; later work, however, uncovered Egyptian remains, redating the site to the 13th–12th centuries, thereby ruling out the Solomonic link. Yet a recent study, supported by radiocarbon dating,

shows that some of the pottery from the site may date to the 10th century. Indeed, it would seem extremely uncharacteristic if Solomon, who built a port at Ezion-Geber only a few miles to the south, failed to exploit the valuable Timna mines.

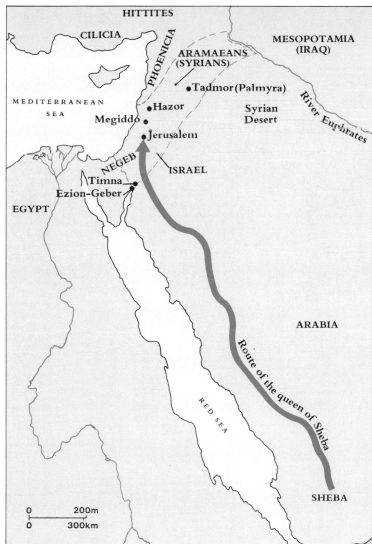

Solomon's empire (broken line) and the route taken by the queen of Sheba's camel caravan is shown on this map, *left*. The Bible describes in detail the network of trading partners developed by Solomon. Spices, gold and precious stones were imported from Arabia. From Ophir, a distant land reached by Solomon and his partner, Hiram, king of the seafaring Phoenicians, came gold, precious stones and rare woods.

Ophir's location, though possibly in India or Arabia, is unknown, as is that of Tarshish, the object of another of Hiram and Solomon's joint ventures, but some scholars think it was in Spain. Every three years, ships returned from Tarshish laden with 'gold and silver, ivory, apes and baboons' (2 Chronicles 9:21). Chariots were imported from Egypt and horses from Cilicia.

How did Solomon afford all these luxuries? The rich copper deposits of the Negeb could have provided one means of exchange. Israel had other mineral deposits as well as agricultural produce – notably grain, wine and oil – and the tribute, including large amounts of copper, from the rich Syrian cities taken by David.

Solomon also exploited the strategic position of his kingdom between Africa and Asia. 1 Kings 10:28–9 shows that Israel profited by being situated between the Hittites and Aramaeans in the north and Egypt in the south. Solomon also developed Tadmor, deep in the Syrian desert, as a staging post for his trade with Iraq.

The queen of Sheba's visit to Solomon is depicted on these medieval Ethiopian panels, which follow the tradition that she came from Ethiopia. According to legend, she travelled part of the way to Jerusalem by ship down the Nile, as indicated by three of the panels, which show messengers and then the queen herself passing the pyramids. After the queen has landed (third row, right of centre), she pitches camp. Then she travels to Jerusalem, where she feasts with Solomon (lowest row, left). Further panels depict their romance. The queen is then shown going home – bearing, according to Ethiopian tradition, Solomon's child.

The destruction of Solomon's empire

Long before Solomon's death, storm-clouds were gathering which, when they broke, would completely disintegrate his empire. With it disappeared the united monarchy of Israel; in its place arose two kingdoms, Israel in the north and Judah in the south, a split ultimately leading to the decline of both kingdoms and their enslavement by foreign powers. While it paints a picture of Solomon's reign as an era of 'peace on all fronts' (1 Kings 4:25), the Bible also gives hints of less healthy developments and of an empire weakening under the attack of jealous rivals raised up by Yahweh to punish Solomon for honouring foreign gods.

To the south of the Dead Sea, Edom rebelled under Hadad, who had taken refuge in Egypt during David's bloody conquest of his country. Hadad returned on the news of David's death and restored a measure of autonomy to the Edomites.

In the north, Damascus was liberated by a military adventurer named Rezon who founded an Aramaean dynasty which was to put constant pressure on Israel's northern border. The loss of Damascus must have prompted Solomon to fortify Tadmor in the Syrian desert as an alternative staging-post for the lucrative trade route to Mesopotamia.

With security weakened by the loss of these strategic areas, other disruptive forces were at work in the heart of Solomon's kingdom. His system of administrative districts, set up to organise taxation and labour, conspicuously omitted Judah, his own tribe. It seems the huge burden of Solomonic luxury was borne largely by the northern tribes of Israel. The favouritism shown to Judah bred resentment and seriously threatened the uneasy union of tribes brought about by Saul and David. Resentment at David's southern origin had already led to a revolt during his reign.

Solomon's policies eventually led to the rebellion of one of his northern governors, Jeroboam. A young nobleman, Jeroboam had been appointed over Ephraim and Manasseh to collect revenue for repairs to Jerusalem's walls. After a bid to wrest control of the northern tribes from Solomon, Jeroboam fled to Egypt. He waited there until Solomon's death and the accession of his son Rehoboam. Ascending Solomon's throne in Jerusalem, Rehoboam then went north to greet the assembly of northern tribes at the traditional meeting place at Shechem.

Jeroboam had now returned from Egypt and joined the assembly in addressing the new king: 'Your father laid a cruel yoke on us; if you will lighten your father's cruel slavery, that heavy yoke which he imposed on us, we are willing to serve you.' Encouraged by hot-headed advisors Rehoboam made a notoriously tactless response: 'My father made your yoke heavy, I shall make it heavier still! My father controlled you with the whip, but I shall apply a spiked lash!' (1 Kings 12:1–14).

The Israelites stoned to death the governor appointed for them by Rehoboam, who fled to Jerusalem. Jeroboam fortified Shechem and assumed the kingship of all the northern tribes ('Israel'), while Rehoboam remained king of Judah. A few years later he was further humiliated by the invasion of Jeroboam's patron, Pharaoh Shishak of Egypt.

Seizing Rehoboam's fortified cities, Shishak threatened Jerusalem itself and had to be bought off with the treasures of Solomon's temple and palace. Meanwhile, Jeroboam set up golden calves at Bethel and Dan as rivals to the temple cult of Jerusalem, completing the political schism with a religious one.

When Egypt invaded Judah

The Biblical Shishak, who invaded Judah shortly after the division of Solomon's empire, is usually thought to have been the Egyptian king, Shoshenq I, founder of the 22nd Dynasty. His reliefs at Karnak (opposite page) describe a victory over the 'Asiatics' of Palestine and include a detailed list of the towns he claimed to have seized. From these a possible itinerary of his campaign can be reconstructed, the plan above following the work of the British Egyptologist Kenneth Kitchen. It seems unlikely, however, that Shoshenq actually conquered all these towns; many may have submitted or sent tribute.

Behind many of the troubles of Solomon's reign can be detected the hand of the Egyptian pharaoh. Solomon formed a marriage alliance with Egypt and as a dowry for the hand of pharaoh's daughter he was given the old Canaanite city of Gezer. Yet the alliance barely masked the fact that Egypt was fostering rivals to the house of David. Hadad, who led the rebellion of the southern vassal state of Edom, had been educated at the Egyptian court and was married to an Egyptian princess. Likewise, Jeroboam, Solomon's most serious rival, was made welcome in Egypt by Pharaoh Shishak.

There can be no doubt that Egypt was jealous of the rapid expansion of an independent Israel under Saul and David. Despite the marriage union, Egypt had no compunction in harbouring Solomon's enemies, and then, when its client Jeroboam had successfully led the northern tribes in rebellion and divided the kingdom, Shishak took the opportunity to invade the weakened southern kingdom of Judah. Rehoboam, Solomon's successor, seems to have considered Egypt, even more than Israel, as his main enemy, judging by the placement of his fortified cities on the southern and western borders of Judah.

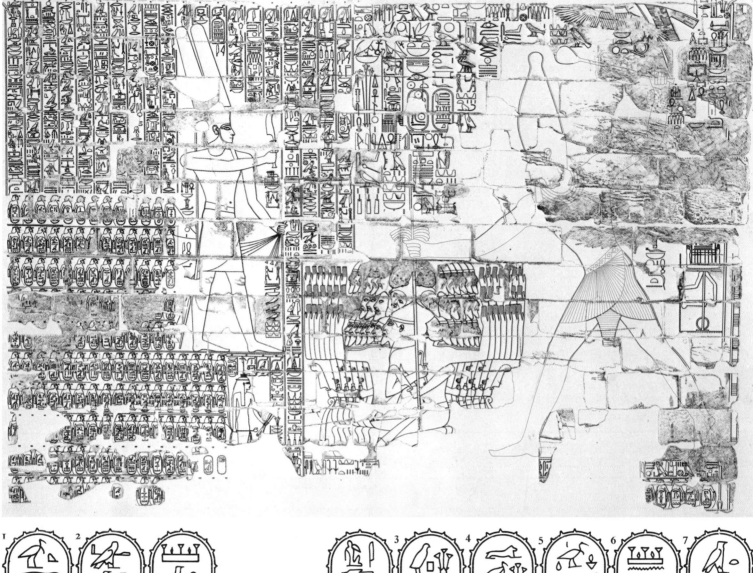

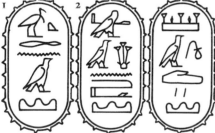

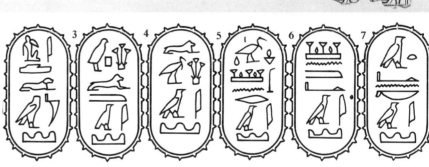

This relief of Pharaoh Shoshenq I at Karnak in Egypt shows him about to club a group of foreigners in the presence of Egypt's chief god, Amun. The figure of the pharaoh, tinted blue, has been superimposed as the original is now largely missing. Behind Amun are rows of oval cartouches with castellated edges, each topped with a bound prisoner. These represent the towns which the pharaoh claimed to have conquered during his campaign in Palestine.

The tinted row of cartouches naming captured towns, shown enlarged beneath the relief, includes, from left to right, Gibeon **1**; Mahanaim, **2** (Israel's capital on the east side of the Jordan); three unknown towns (one damaged not reproduced), then Hapharaim, **3**; next Rehob, **4**, Beth-Shean, **5**, Shunem, **6**, and Taanach, **7**, all towns in the Jezreel Valley and important centres on the Via Maris trade route through central Palestine.

Although Shoshenq I is usually thought to be the Biblical Shishak who attacked the southern kingdom of Judah, few Judaean towns are listed. Most of the places mentioned were within the northern kingdom of Israel, while Jerusalem, target of Shishak's campaign according to the Bible, is missing. Although the inscription is heavily damaged, it is certain that Jerusalem was not included because the list is arranged into geographical sequences which allow no space for the name Jerusalem.

Elijah destroys the prophets of Baal

Elijah is justly revered as one of the greatest of the Old Testament prophets. In the Bible, the legendary stories of Elijah (1 Kings 17–22) are set in the early ninth century during the period of the Omrid dynasty of Israel, some 50 years after the latter had separated from Judah. It was Omri himself who moved the capital of Israel to Samaria, probably prompted by the desire to be somewhere more neutral and free of old tribal associations.

Ahab, Omri's son and successor, married Jezebel from Tyre in Phoenicia and so brought increased wealth to the capital and the kingdom. But, according to the Bible, the marriage also brought into Israel the cult of the Phoenician god Baal and it was for this, and Jezebel's slaying of the prophets, that Yahweh punished the kingdom with a severe drought.

After three years of this drought, with the famine 'particularly severe in Samaria', Yahweh told Elijah to go to Ahab 'and I will send rain on the country'. Elijah went and accused Ahab of ruining Israel by deserting Yahweh. He also proposed a contest between himself and 'the four hundred prophets of Baal who eat at Jezebel's table' (1 Kings 18:19).

The contest was held on Mount Carmel, in the presence of the assembled Israelites, to see whether Yahweh or Baal was the stronger god: which god, when called upon, would bring down fire to the pyres of wood and offerings of dismembered bulls set up by, first, the prophets of Baal and then Elijah.

The prophets danced, mutilated themselves and besought Baal to hear them but to no avail. Elijah mocked their efforts. He then set up his own altar and pyre of wood, and, to emphasise the point, poured water over the pyre so that it flowed even in the trench dug around the altar. Elijah called upon Yahweh whose 'fire fell and consumed the burnt offering and the wood and licked up the water in the trench' (18:38). At Elijah's command, the people seized the prophets and Elijah slaughtered them.

The story cycles of Elijah and his successor Elisha and the Omrid kings well illustrate the clash between king and prophet which recurs throughout the Old Testament. Both Elijah and Elisha, in the early Israelite prophetic tradition, were messengers of God, performing miracles and transmitting their art to the next generation. Thus, after a chariot of fire had borne Elijah up to heaven in a whirlwind, it was Elisha who picked up Elijah's cloak and in whom 'the spirit of Elijah has come to rest . . .'.

The Bible narrative views the Omrids negatively, but their fame was such that even after the dynasty died out, Israel was known to the Assyrians as the 'country of Omri'. Also, the Omrid rule did create a period of relative peace and prosperity in the northern kingdom. For the previous 50 years, after separating from Judah, Israel had been weakened by wars with her neighbours. And her internal stability was threatened by succession problems, in part stemming from the belief of the northern prophets that kingship was conditional on obedience to God's law: if not, disaster would beset the king and his dynasty.

It is against this background that Elijah waged his war against the cult of Phoenician Baal. Although the expansion of Baal into Israel is attributed to Jezebel, there were many Canaanites in Israel who were familiar with Baal worship. However it does seem there was considerable tension between devoted followers of Yahweh, championed by Elijah, and the Israelite court with its pragmatic policy of religious tolerance.

The woman at the window

A popular subject of the Phoenician ivory carvers who embellished the furniture of the palace at Samaria was the 'woman at the window'. Although the piece, *above*, comes from Nimrud, others like it have been found at Samaria. It is thought that this figure, with painted eyes and the frontlets of a whore, represents the goddess as sacred prostitute.

Ahab's marriage to Jezebel increased Israel's cultural links with the Phoenician cities, as evidence from excavations shows. From the palace at the site of Ramat Rahel, there are remains of a window balustrade identical with that portrayed on the ivory. And it was probably from such a Phoenician-style window that Jezebel looked down on and taunted the usurper Jehu after he had just killed her son, King Jehoram. In painting her eyes and adorning her hair, Jezebel was probably preparing to face death with dignity, rather than attempting to ensnare Jehu with her charms.

Jehu ordered Jezebel to be thrown from the window 'and her blood spattered the walls and horses; and Jehu rode over her' (2 Kings 9:33). Later, when they came to bury the body, 'they found nothing but her skull, feet and hands'. The dogs had eaten her, thus fulfilling Elijah's prophecy: 'The dogs will eat Jezebel in the field of Jezreel' (1 Kings 21:24).

Jehu had disposed of Jezebel's son Jehoram in the field of Naboth of Jezreel. For, many years earlier, Jezebel had arranged the death of Naboth so that Ahab could take possession of his vineyard. The king had wanted the land as it adjoined the palace at Jezreel, but Naboth had refused to sell his patrimony. On a fictitious charge, Naboth was stoned to death and his vineyard taken. Elijah had cursed Ahab and his house, but on the king's repentance disaster was transferred to his sons, with whose deaths the dynasty ended.

'Lying on ivory beds and sprawling on their divans' (AMOS 6:4).

This ivory bed-head or chair back, *left*, from the Assyrian city of Nimrud well illustrates the cause of the prophet Amos's railing against Samarian indulgence. Ivory was taken by the Assyrians as booty from the captured cities of the west. Many Phoenician and Syrian ivories have been found in Assyria.

As Israel became increasingly exposed to Phoenician culture, a cosmopolitan court society emerged at Samaria, where Ahab built an 'Ivory House' (1 Kings 22:39). Excavations at Samaria have revealed some 500 fragments of ivory, many carved in the Phoenician style.

A 3rd-century AD wall painting, *above*, from Dura-Europus on the River Euphrates depicts Elijah, to the right of the altar, with staff in hand, at the moment when flames miraculously engulf both altar and bull. At the left, youths bring canisters of water, while below them Israelites cower in awe at the might of their god Yahweh.

The fall of Israel

The fall of Samaria, the capital of the northern kingdom of Israel, was regarded by the prophets as divine retribution for Israel's violation of the covenant with Yahweh. According to the victorious Assyrian king Sargon II, the end of Samaria meant the deportation of 27,290 of its inhabitants. As the Bible puts it: 'At length Yahweh thrust Israel away from him . . . he deported the Israelites from their own country to Assyria, where they have been ever since' (2 Kings 17:23).

It was back in the ninth century that the rising power of Assyria, a land far to the east of Israel, began to affect the nation states of Syro-Palestine. When Shalmaneser III continued the Assyrian expansion west, the local rulers managed to forget their differences and united against this common foe.

In 853 BC, a coalition of 12 kings, including Ahab of Israel (see p.96), met the Assyrian army in battle at Qarqar on the River Orontes. Although the Assryians claimed that the coalition was routed, the victory was not decisive: the advance was checked. Later, however, Jehu of Israel, who usurped power in 842, decided to submit to Assyria.

The main aim of Assyrian military campaigns until the mid eighth century was the acquisition of plunder and tribute. But with the accession of Tiglath-Pileser III (745–727), also known as 'Pul' in the Bible, a systematic policy of territorial expansion began. Vassals who rebelled were mercilessly crushed and deprived of their lands.

After the conquest and annexation of the central Syrian state of Hamath in 738, many neighbouring rulers panicked and offered submission to the Assyrian king, including Menahem of Israel who 'gave Pul 1000 talents of silver in return for his support in strengthening his hold on the royal power' (2 Kings 15:19).

However, Pekah, Menahem's successor, foolishly decided to adopt an openly antagonistic policy towards Assyria. Allied with Damascus, he tried to force Judah to join the resistance. But Ahaz of Judah, ignoring the warnings of the prophet Isaiah, appealed to Tiglath-Pileser for help, offering him bribes from the Temple and the palace treasury.

The Assyrian response was swift and devastating. Damascus was conquered in 732 and its territory made into an Assyrian province. Israel lost Galilee and Gilead and was reduced to a small area around Samaria, its capital. Soon afterwards, Pekah was murdered and Hoshea ascended the Israelite throne as a faithful vassal of Assyria.

But when Shalmaneser V became king of Assyria in 727, Hoshea chanced rebellion, opening negotiations with the pharaoh of Egypt. His action was a grave mistake. Help from Egypt was not forthcoming and the Assyrians moved quickly to suppress the revolt. Hoshea himself was captured and then imprisoned.

The besieged city of Samaria held out for two years after the fall of the rest of the kingdom but finally surrendered in 722. Shalmaneser V died a few months later and the Assyrian army departed.

This breathing space gave the western provinces, including newly-conquered Samaria, their chance to rebel. It was not until 720 that Sargon II, usurper of the Assyrian throne, was able to deal with the western resistance and decisively defeat the allies. Samaria was reconquered and made the capital of a new Assyrian province, Samerina.

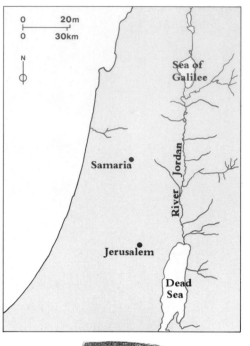

Samaria was founded by Omri (878–871), the father of Ahab, as the new capital of Israel. Strategically sited on a hitherto uninhabited hill, the city was heavily fortified, with massive defensive walls.

The 'Black Obelisk' (c.825 BC) from Nimrud, unearthed in 1846 and standing 6½ft/2m high, commemorates Shalmaneser III's conquests and depicts the tribute received from vassal kings. The inscription above the second panel, **1**, reads, 'The tribute of Jehu, son of Omri'.

Gold and silver objects are listed among the tribute. The Israelite king was included ironically by the Assyrians in the 'House of Omri', although he was in fact a usurper.

Jehu himself is shown, **2**, humbly prostrated before Shalmaneser. This is the only extant representation of a king of Israel. He wears western Semitic dress, a turban and long over-garment.

A relief from Tiglath-Pileser's palace at his capital, Nimrud, depicts the capture of the city of Ashteroth-Karnaim in Gilead, annexed together with Galilee in 733–732 BC. Situated on a mound, the city, with a citadel at one end, is surrounded by a double defensive wall.

In the relief, Assyrian officers drive out sheep as booty and also prisoners of war depicted in western Semitic dress,

carrying bundles.

A regular instrument of later Assyrian policy was to punish rebellious vassal states by deporting large sectors of the population. Sometimes only the ruling classes were deported, but often tens of thousands were removed. It has been estimated that four-and-a-half million people were deported in a period of 300 years. Many deportees were brought to Assyria, where they

were employed on royal building projects.

Craftsmen and artisans were especially valuable. The reliefs of Sargon show deported prisoners of war – among them possibly the Israelites of Samaria – labouring on the construction of the king's grandiose new palace at Khorsabad. Sennacherib said he used Syrian deportees, probably Phoenicians, to build a fleet of ships in Nineveh.

Soldiers were conscripted into the Assyrian army, while other deportees were settled in towns throughout the empire, often in sensitive border areas. Peoples settled in Samaria after the conquest included Babylonians, Syrians and Arabians. Deportation reduced the possibility of national uprisings, increased the labour force and resulted in the blending of cultural and ethnic

groups.

The central panel of the relief has a passage from Tiglath-Pileser's annals, describing campaigns to the north of Assyria. The lower panel shows the king in his chariot, accompanied by his charioteer and a third man holding the royal sunshade.

99

Sennacherib besieges Lachish

In the fourteenth year of King Hezekiah,' some 20 years after Israel had fallen to Assyria, 'Sennacherib king of Assyria advanced on all the fortified towns of Judah and captured them' (2 Kings 18:13). For the death of Sargon and the accession of Sennacherib in 705 BC had prompted rebellions throughout the Assyrian empire.

In the west, Luli, king of Tyre and Sidon, the strongest ruler in Phoenicia, revolted and Hezekiah, king of Judah, led the conspiracy in Palestine. He was joined in his cause by the Philistine cities of Ashkelon and Ekron. There was hope of Egyptian help and the Chaldaean Merodach-baladan also sent messengers to Jerusalem.

Hezekiah prepared well for the inevitable Assyrian attack. He fortified numerous Judaean cities, strengthened the walls of Jerusalem and dug a tunnel from a local spring to the pool of Siloam inside the city walls to ensure a water supply in time of siege. He reorganised the army and 'made quantities of missiles and shields' (2 Chronicles 32:5).

The Assyrian onslaught came in 701 BC. Despite some discrepancies between the Biblical and Assyrian accounts, the general picture is clear. After marching down through Phoenicia and replacing Luli with a pro-Assyrian ruler, Sennacherib went south and conquered several cities belonging to Ashkelon. He then says he defeated the forces of Ekron and Egypt at Elteqeh.

Sennacherib now turned his attention to the destruction of Judah. The climax of the campaign was the conquest of the great fortress of Lachish. Although not described in Sennacherib's annals and only alluded to in the Bible, the siege is immortalised in magnificent wall reliefs from Sennacherib's palace at Nineveh and Assyrian arrowheads and slingstones have been found at Lachish.

The reliefs tell the story in detail: units of the Assyrian army are lined up before the city, which is surrounded by olive trees and vineyards. Battering rams lead the main assault, climbing the mound under cover of a rain of arrows. Defeated inhabitants are shown leaving the city and passing some captured soldiers who have been stripped naked and impaled on stakes. Some distance away, the enthroned Sennacherib surveys the proceedings in front of his tent. His chariot and the royal guard stand by and behind him is the fortified camp.

Some prisoners, probably Hezekiah's men, are beheaded or flayed alive. Others, in bullock carts or on foot, are probably being deported to Assyria. Another Assyrian relief possibly shows men of Lachish employed in the building of Sennacherib's palace at Nineveh. And similar figures appear as members of the royal guard.

Hezekiah sent emissaries and tribute to Sennacherib and 'from Lachish the king of Assyria sent the cupbearer-in-chief to Hezekiah in Jerusalem' (2 Kings 18:17). Hezekiah, however, did not surrender and eventually, for unclear reasons, the besieging force withdrew.

According to the Bible, Sennacherib's army was decimated by a miracle before the gates of Jerusalem: 'The angel of Yahweh went out and struck down 185,000 men in the Assyrian camp. In the early morning, there they lay, so many corpses' (2 Kings 19:35–6). Thus Jerusalem was saved, but Judah was devastated. Hezekiah continued to rule a much reduced land but had to bear the burden of Assyrian domination.

Lachish was surrounded by a massive defensive wall, **1**, with bastions. An outer wall, **8**, protected the lower slopes of the mound. A city's main gate was the focal point for assault. To make this difficult, the approach to the gate was set obliquely to the gate, **2**, in the outer wall.

Archers, **6**, were the main arm of the Assyrian infantry. During siege operations, soldiers covered the archers with huge shields, angled at the top, **4**. Behind the archers, Assyrian slingmen, **5**, fired up the slopes.

Spearmen, 7, were important shock troops in assaults on fortified cities. They wore a helmet and a short tunic and carried a spear in one hand and a small, round shield in the other.

Battering-rams, 3, led the attack on Lachish. Their long, sturdy ramming rods mercilessly hammered at the city's defences until the walls were breached. They had four wheels and light, wooden bodies protected with leather. One of the crew inside the ram ladled out water onto the body to prevent its catching fire.

From the top of the city walls the Lachishites rained down stones, firebrands and even chariot wheels upon the Assyrians. They also threw torches onto the inflammable battering-rams.

At the top of the walls and towers, the defenders of Lachish constructed wooden frames, to which they attached their shields, **9**. Behind this protective screen, the archers could stand upright and shoot a volley of arrows down on the attackers; other soldiers threw down heavy stones.

The grandeur of Assyria

From their homeland in northern Mesopotamia, the Assyrian kings presided over their empire and enjoyed the fruits of their imperial conquests. The great warrior-king Assurnasirpal (883–859 BC) moved his capital from Assur farther north to Calah (modern Nimrud).

There, he built a magnificent palace on the acropolis mound. He celebrated its completion by a huge banquet lasting ten days, during which 14,000 sheep and 10,000 skins of wine were consumed. Among the 69,574 guests were envoys from the states of north Syria and Phoenicia.

Assurnasirpal's successors all lived at Calah until Sargon II (721–705) built a new capital, which he called 'Fort Sargon', at modern Khorsabad. Work gangs from the provinces and prisoners of war from various campaigns, with some of the Israelites deported from Samaria probably among them, did most of the building.

In 707 BC, ten years after the first foundations were laid, Sargon took up residence in his new palace. Only two years later, however, he was killed in battle and his son, Sennacherib, moved yet again, to the ancient site of Nineveh, decried in the Bible as 'the harlot, the graceful beauty . . . who enslaved nations by her harlotries and tribes by her spell' (Nahum 3:4). Nineveh remained the capital until the fall of the empire.

Each Assyrian capital had a citadel where the royal palaces, temples and a few wealthy private houses were located. The booty from military campaigns and tribute from vassal rulers which flowed into the royal coffers were used to adorn temples and palaces. The wealth of Nineveh was famed from afar: 'there is no end to the treasure, a mass of everything you could desire!' (Nahum 2:10).

Court life in the late Assyrian empire was cosmopolitan. Musicians and singers from throughout the empire provided entertainment, the daughters and palace women of foreign kings, among them Hezekiah of Judah, were brought to Nineveh and foreign artisans embellished the royal residences.

The king was surrounded by officials and advisors, including diviners who read and interpreted the omens. The Assyrian kings consulted the omens before taking decisions on all important affairs of state and, on military campaigns, an omen priest usually accompanied the army.

The army was mustered and the military equipment stored in a complex of buildings known as the 'Review Palace' sited on a second mound some distance from the main citadel. The Assyrian troops, efficient and well equipped, were the terror of the ancient Near East: 'Their arrows are sharpened, their bows all strung, their horses' hoofs you would think were flint and the wheels, a whirlwind!' (Isaiah 5:28).

Conscription of soldiers for the standing army was the responsibility of the provincial governors who had to supply the campaigning army en route and provide fodder for the horses assigned to them by the central government. Other duties included levying of men for the upkeep of roads, canals and other building works and the collection of taxes.

Through its well-developed provincial system, the Assyrian empire became the first state in the ancient world to impose an effective central administration on its vast conquered territories. It reached its zenith under the kings Esarhaddon and Assurbanipal, justly famous as Assyria's scholar king, who prided himself on his literacy and created a great library at Nineveh.

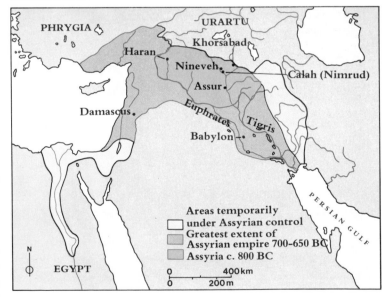

The growth of the Assyrian empire, above, spanned a period of some 250 years. Urartu vigorously opposed Assyrian expansion and Assyria also came into conflict with Phrygia. At its maximum extent the empire stretched from Egypt to the Persian gulf. Egypt was controlled only for a brief period, and Judah and Media retained vassal status. Elam was conquered but not made an Assyrian province.

In superbly carved reliefs from his palace at Nimrud, Assurnasirpal II is shown in combat with majestic lions, *above*. The lions from this relief and the one from Nineveh, *left*, have been carved with great skill.

The royal lion hunt symbolised both the personal valour of the monarch and his power over the forces of nature.

The Assyrian king was portrayed as invincible but not divine. He was the high priest of the god Assur, whose glory he proclaimed throughout the world on his annual campaigns. The coronation ritual took place in the Assur temple.

The king's legitimacy was believed to rest on divine choice, which was confirmed by oracular consultation.

As their servant, the king made rich gifts to the gods and restored and adorned their temples. A prosperous land signified divine approval. The king also undertook civic building works, such as canal construction.

Magnificent human-headed, winged bulls guarded the entrance to the throne room at Khorsabad, Sargon's new capital. They were supposed to impart supernatural protection to the palace and its occupants. The inhabitants of Khorsabad comprised people from many different countries, who were taught Assyrian ways by special officials.

Foreign gods in Judah and Israel

'He built altars to the whole array of heaven in the two courts of the Temple of Yahweh. . . . He had an image of Asherah carved and placed it inside the Temple' (2 Kings 21:5,7). Under Manasseh, son of Hezekiah and vassal of Assyria, Judah relapsed into paganism. Canaanite cults reappeared throughout the land, together with others of Aramaean or Assyrian origin, such as the dedication of horses to the sun.

Although Assyria did not interfere with the local cults of subject states, the mass movements of peoples throughout the empire encouraged a 'syncretism' or amalgamation of different beliefs. Deportees, settled in Samaria after the conquest, brought with them their own gods, including Nergal, the Mesopotamian god of the underworld, associated with the planet Mars.

Nineveh falls to Babylon

Alas, your shepherds are asleep, king of Assyria, your bravest men slumber. . . . All who hear the news of you clap their hands at your downfall. For who has not felt your unrelenting cruelty?' (Nahum 3:18–19). The destruction of the Assyrian capital, Nineveh, in 612 BC, less than 20 years after the death of its last great king, Assurbanipal, shook the ancient world.

For over a century, the Assyrians had expended manpower and resources in attempts to control the tribesmen of southern Babylonia, but no system of government was ever found which was acceptable to all parties. On Assurbanipal's death, fighting broke out between rival factions in Assyria and Babylonia, and for a year Babylon was kingless.

But in late 626 BC, Nabopolassar, a Chaldaean sheikh, seized the Babylonian throne and the next decade saw continual struggles on Babylonian soil. Control of important cities oscillated between different parties. There were several long sieges. During a siege of the garrison city of Nippur, which remained staunchly loyal to the Assyrian king Sin-shar-ishkun, conditions become so desperate that some parents were forced to sell their children to buy food.

By 616, the threat of rising Babylonian power must have become apparent throughout the Near East. For Egypt, which had thrown off the yoke of Assyrian domination some 40 years previously, now joined with her former overlord to fight against Nabopolassar. In 615, the theatre of war shifted from strife-torn Babylonia to the Assyrian homeland. Nabopolassar attacked the ancient city of Assur, but was unsuccessful and forced to withdraw. A new power now appeared on the scene – the Medes, a group of Indo-European tribes on the Iranian plateau, who were a formidable fighting force under Cyaxares.

Cyaxares marched on Assyria in 614. Calah (modern Nimrud) was attacked and Assur captured and plundered. Nabopolassar took advantage of the situation and marched north. He met the Median king near the ruined city of Assur and they concluded a formal alliance. Despite the devastation wrought on their land, the Assyrians confidently dismantled the damaged defences of Calah for repair and in 613 marched south against the Babylonians. Their confidence was ill-founded. In 612, the Median-Babylonian coalition laid siege to Nineveh.

After three months, the great city fell in a terrible onslaught: 'Disaster to the city of blood . . . The crack of the whip! The rumble of wheels! Galloping horses, jolting chariot, charging cavalry, flashing swords, gleaming spears, a mass of wounded, hosts of dead, countless corpses' (Nahum 3:1–3). Sin-shar-ishkun is said to have died in the flames of his palace. The loss of Nineveh was the death blow to the great empire.

The remnants of the Assyrians regrouped at Haran, far to the west, where the last Assyrian king Assuruballit claimed sovereignty over Assyria. There they waited for more help from Egypt. A large Egyptian army under Pharaoh Necho marched through Palestine, but was held up at Megiddo by Josiah, king of Judah. Josiah was killed in the battle but his suicidal attempt to stop the Egyptians meant that Necho arrived in Syria too late to prevent Nabopolassar from taking Haran.

In 609, Assuruballit and the Egyptians made an unsuccessful attempt to recapture the city. The fate of Assuruballit remains a mystery. He is never mentioned again and with his disappearance Assyria, too, disappeared forever.

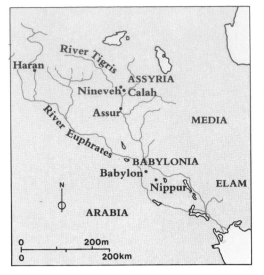

Nineveh was chosen by King Sennacherib as the capital of the Assyrian empire.

He surrounded a vast area north and south of the old city mound with a massive mudbrick wall, faced with ashlar masonry. Access to the city was through huge towered gateways, **3**.

A Babylonian cuneiform tablet, *left*, known as the 'Fall of Nineveh Chronicle', is the main source of evidence for the events leading to Assyria's downfall. The chronicler describes the terrible sack of Nineveh: 'They carried off the vast booty of the city and the temple and turned the city into a ruin heap.'

Precise details of the siege of Nineveh are unknown, but this reconstruction, based on knowledge of the site of the city and contemporary warfare, may give some idea of how the city was 'turned into a ruin heap'.

The Babylonians would have had to negotiate the River Tigris, **1**, which protected the city to the west, and a diverted watercourse, **2**, which protected the north wall.

On the east side there was a second line of fortifications beyond an old wadi bed. On the central mound, an artificial terrace was constructed, where Sennacherib built his magnificent palace, **4**, which he named 'The Palace without a Rival'.

Jonah and the great fish

The story of Jonah, who is shown, *above*, in an illumination from the Kennicott Bible, was probably written after the Exile. It is set in a time before the fall of Nineveh, when the city was a symbol of iniquity. The author chose the prophet Jonah, mentioned in 2 Kings 14:25, as the protagonist for his narrative.

Jonah lived in the eighth century BC, when feeling in Israel ran high against Assyria. When Yahweh told Jonah to go to Nineveh and proclaim its imminent destruction, he rebelled and fled by ship in the opposite direction. During his journey a great storm arose and he was thrown overboard by the sailors to appease the wrath of Yahweh. But he was swallowed by a 'great fish' (popularly identified as a whale), which eventually vomited him onto dry land. Jonah, now obedient to Yahweh, then journeyed to Nineveh. He delivered Yahweh's message to the inhabitants, who repented, and the city was saved. The moral of the story is Yahweh's mercy for all, even the hated Assyrians.

The reforms of Josiah

King Josiah of Judah is remembered for his radical programme of religious reform. He purged the land of the pagan cults allowed by his predecessors and centralised worship at Jerusalem. This reform is associated with the discovery of the 'book of the Law' in the Temple, the precise nature of which is unclear.

The Solomonic sanctuary at Arad in the Negeb desert was seemingly built over at this time, perhaps reflecting Josiah's policy of closing local shrines. One of the aims of centralisation was certainly to improve the collection of revenue.

Josiah extended his reform to the north, taking advantage of the decline of Assyrian power. He 'destroyed all the shrines on the high places which were in the towns of Samaria' (2 Kings 23:19), and expanded Judah's territories. Josiah's death at Megiddo, however, placed Judah at the mercy of the Egyptians.

The siege of Jerusalem 587 BC

In the ninth year of King Zedekiah of Judah's reign, 'Nebuchadnezzar king of Babylon advanced on Jerusalem with his entire army; he pitched camp in front of the city and threw up earthworks round it' (2 Kings 25:1). For 18 months, until the summer of 587 BC, the city lay under siege. So bad were conditions that famine reduced some of the inhabitants to cannibalism.

As the Babylonians advanced into the city, Zedekiah attempted to escape to Transjordan but was captured near Jericho. For breaching his treaty with Babylon, he was taken before Nebuchadnezzer at Riblah where he was made to witness the execution of his sons. He himself was then blinded and led chained into captivity in Babylon where he died.

In the month that followed, the Babylonians burned Jerusalem and its Temple to the ground. The city walls were razed and the population deported, leaving only 'some of the poor country people behind as vineyard workers and ploughmen' (2 Kings 25:12). With this deportation and reduction of the land to 'ruin and desolation' (Jeremiah 25:11) – borne out by archaeological evidence – the kingdom of Judah ceased to exist.

But for many Jews, the Exile had begun a decade earlier when, following Nebuchadnezzar's first attack on Jerusalem, Jehoiachin, the new king, had surrendered. On this occasion, the young ruler's submission had spared Judah from total destruction. However, as both Biblical and Babylonian accounts relate, a considerable quantity of tribute was taken.

Jehoiachin, his mother and most of the upper classes and skilled artisans were exiled to Babylon. Although there are discrepancies in the Bible as to the numbers deported, almost certainly a greater part of the ruling class was taken to Babylon at the time of the first deportation, among them the prophet Ezekiel. Jehoiachin's uncle, Zedekiah, was the new ruler appointed by Nebuchadnezzar.

To understand the reasons for the Babylonian destruction of Judah, it is necessary to trace the events in the years following the demise of Assyria. The collapse of the Assyrian empire created a political vacuum in the Syro-Palestinian area which both Egypt and Babylon sought to fill. As Assyria weakened, so Egypt, her traditional enemy, came to her support to prevent Babylon emerging as the dominant power.

At the same time, Egypt brought some former Assyrian provinces of the Levant under her control. Josiah's clash with the advancing Egyptians and his death at Megiddo in 609 meant Judah was now effectively under Egyptian control.

Egypt was now master of the region west of the Euphrates. But at Carchemish in 605, when the Babylonians defeated the last remnant of the Assyrian army supported by Egypt, the balance of power shifted fundamentally. By 603, Judah was under Babylonian control. Within Judah there were both pro-Egyptian and pro-Babylonian factions, but for two years she remained a faithful vassal of Babylon.

In 601, Necho of Egypt invaded Judah and Jehoiakim, the father of Jehoiachin, seems to have immediately sided with Egypt – despite the prophet Jeremiah's warnings against the alliance. This then led to Nebuchadnezzar's attack on Jerusalem in 597 when Jehoiachin submitted. Incredibly, spurred on by Egypt, Zedekiah pursued an anti-Babylonian policy which was to bring down the wrath of Nebuchadnezzar: the destruction of Jerusalem meant that Judah would now be a people in exile.

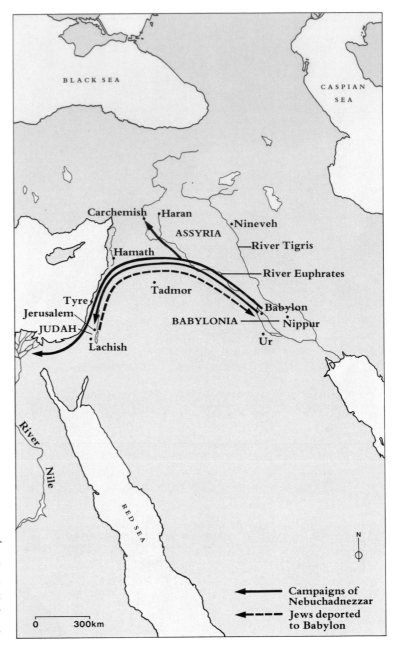

In a series of campaigns which, for Judah, culminated in the exile of 587 BC, the Babylonian king Nebuchadnezzar established the frontier of his empire on the borders of Egypt. In 605 BC, he fought a battle at the city of Carchemish against a combined force of Assyrians and Egyptians sent by Pharaoh Necho. The Babylonians were victorious.

Archaeologists have actually found in excavations at Carchemish arrowheads and a clay seal impression with the cartouche of Necho which testify to the battle fought there. In 604 BC, Nebuchadnezzar marched to Hamath; this cleared the way to southern Syria and Palestine, and in 601 he fought the Egyptians, probably near their border.

In 597, after the Babylonians had attacked Jerusalem, Jehoiachin and the Judaean nobility were exiled to Babylon. In 587, following the Babylonians' 18-month siege of Jerusalem, a second group of Judaeans was exiled. Some were settled in southern Babylonia in the area of Nippur.

Jeremiah was born into a family of priests. As an educated man he was aware of the political upheavals in which Judah was no more than a minor irritant to the great powers, who in turn imposed their will on the region. His prophecies of doom were based on a sound perception of the political forces at work, although they are explained largely in terms of divine retribution for the failure of Judah's people to respect their covenant with Yahweh.

The decline of Assyria provided Judah with an opportunity for reasserting its identity. Josiah's attempts to return to the precepts of the age of Moses were in line with Jeremiah's attacks on pagan rituals and the moral decline in the Temple. But these reforms proved too superficial for Jeremiah – and they were probably irrelevant in the political turmoil that eventually drew Judah back into the Egyptian sphere of influence.

Jeremiah counselled against involvement in the struggle between the great powers – an unpopular view at the time. His contemporaries believed that Judah was inviolate because of divine protection afforded by the presence of the Temple in Jerusalem. Jeremiah was more realistic: he prophesied the catastrophe which eventually overcame Jerusalem – although he attributed it to Yahweh's withdrawing his protection from an undeserving people.

A prophet of doom

Jeremiah's career as a prophet spanned 40 of the most tragic and eventful years in the history of Judah, from 627 BC to the destruction of the Temple in 587 BC. His name is synonymous with unrelieved gloom, but far from being merely a sorrowing and passive witness of the disintegration of Zion, Jeremiah also did all in his power to influence the course of events. Although he failed to prevent Jerusalem's fall, his exhortations, and hope in the future, proved crucial in ensuring the survival of Judaism during the exile in Babylon.

Jeremiah's influence, however, is not due to the fact that he was proved right; it stems from his belief that a better future would be brought about by a genuine commitment to the faith and its underlying values – the renewal of the covenant between the individual and God. His teachings contributed in large measure to the survival of the faith throughout the Exile and to the Jews' steadfast belief in their ultimate return to Zion.

Two of the letters received by Ya'osh, military governor of Lachish during the final Babylonian invasion, are reproduced *above*. These are written in ancient Hebrew script on potsherds, most of which are poorly preserved.

It would seem that the eight that are legible were sent to Hosha'yahu, commander of a garrison at a place somewhere between Lachish and Azekah. Jeremiah (34:7) mentions these places as being the only 'fortified towns of Judah remaining'.

One letter ends: '. . . we are watching for the signals of Lachish, according to all the indications which my lord hath given, for we cannot see Azekah.' This probably refers to a system of smoke signals used for sending messages between cities and military camps.

This clay tablet records the siege of Jerusalem: 'In the seventh year of the month Kislev the king of Akkad mustered his army and marched to Hattu. He encamped against the city of Judah and on the second day of the month Adar he captured the city [and] seized [its] king. A king of his own choice he appointed in the city [and] taking the vast tribute he brought it into Babylon.'

Jerusalem's capture recorded

The Babylonian Chronicle, *above*, first translated in 1956, records Nebuchadnezzar's capture of Jerusalem (2 Kings 24:10–17) on the 2nd Adar of the seventh year of his reign – that is, 15/16 March 597 BC. These chronicles were probably compiled from the astronomical diaries kept by the scribes to record important local events year by year in each king's reign, as well as major events elsewhere which affected Babylonia. The account of the capture of Jerusalem provides invaluable and objective information of the story recounted in the Bible.

Life in Babylon

By the rivers of Babylon we sat and wept at the memory of Zion' (Psalm 137:1). These poignant words express the sadness of the Judaean people exiled far from their homeland. The Jews living in Babylonia represented the political and intellectual elite of Judah. Exactly how many were involved in the three Babylonian deportations of 597, 587 (see pp. 106–7) and 582 BC is uncertain because the Biblical sources are contradictory. Jeremiah 52:30 gives a total of 4,600, but as that probably counts only adult males the exiles perhaps numbered 15,000 to 20,000.

Some of the Jewish deportees, including King Jehoiachin and his family, were settled in Babylon itself. King Nebuchadnezzar had made Babylon the most magnificent city in the ancient world; but for the Jewish writers, it became a symbol of decadence and vice. The River Euphrates flowed through the inner city, dividing it into two sectors.

Nebuchadnezzar had three palaces. The summer palace lay some distance north of the inner city, by the banks of the Euphrates. One of Nebuchadnezzar's interests was antiquarianism and in his northern palace a museum housed his collection of antiquities and the royal library. The main royal residence, the southern palace, was a splendid building with five courtyards surrounded by many suites of rooms. The king received visitors and ministers in his great throne room which had a beautiful facade decorated with a multi-coloured glazed brick frieze of lions, columns and floral motifs.

Jehoiachin was probably held captive in the southern palace. Clay tablets discovered there list rations for people of various nationalities, among them Jehoiachin, his sons and other Judaeans. The Judaean king retained his royal status and was still considered the leader of the Jewish community. He was pardoned by Nebuchadnezzar's successor Evil-Merodach and offered the hospitality of the court.

While Jehoiachin enjoyed the opulence of Babylonian court life, other Jews were settled in southern Babylonia. There was a large Jewish centre at Tell-abib on the River Chebar, a canal which ran from the Euphrates and passed through the large commercial city of Nippur. There they followed the advice of the prophet Jeremiah to 'build houses, settle down; plant gardens . . . marry and have sons and daughters' (Jeremiah 29:5–6).

The Babylonians treated the exiles well. They could meet freely, buy property and practise their own customs and religion. The later archives of a commercial bank at Nippur show that within little more than a century some of the deportees had become quite prosperous. Most of the Nippur Jews were farmers, shepherds and fishermen, but there were also a few who worked as minor city officials.

The exiles, naturally enough, were influenced by Babylonian culture. They adopted the Aramaic language and alphabet and the Mesopotamian calendar, and many people took Babylonian names. At the same time they tried to retain their national identity by attaching special importance to practices such as circumcision, dietary laws and Sabbath observance.

Although life for the Jews in Babylonia was certainly not unpleasant, the period was regarded as one of the fundamental breaks in Israel's history. Prophets such as Ezekiel, who was probably deported at the same time as Jehoiachin, tried to preserve among the people the hope that one day they would return to their beloved homeland.

Babylon was surrounded by a deep moat and a double defensive wall, wide enough – according to the Greek writer Herodotus, who almost certainly visited the city – for a

Map labels: Northern palace, Temple of Ishtar, Southern palace, Esagila, The Processional Way, Double defensive wall, River Euphrates

four-horsed chariot to pass.

The Processional Way went by the northern palace, and proceeded through the Ishtar gate, past the southern palace, and the temple of Ishtar, to the great temple complex of Esagila.

The city was well planned. The main streets, most of them named after different gods, ran either parallel with or at right angles to the river. In addition to the Ishtar gate, there were eight bronze gates in the city walls.

The small temple, **1**, dedicated to the mother goddess Ninmah, was of typical Babylonian plan, with a central court and broad inner cultroom. The towered entrance and recessed walls made optimal use of the contrast of light and shade.

An odd series of vaulted rooms in the Southern palace, **2**, has been interpreted as the remains of the famous Hanging Gardens of Babylon, built for a homesick Median princess. However, as the ration lists

mentioning Jehoiachin were found there, the building may have been some kind of administrative unit.

A broad, paved road known as the Processional Way, **3**, approached the city from the north. It passed between high walls, ornamented with lions, symbols of the goddess Ishtar, in multi-coloured glazed brick relief.

The main entrance to Babylon was through the impressive Ishtar gate, **4**, a double gateway connecting both fortification walls of the city. It was magnificently decorated with bulls and dragons. On festive occasions, great processions of people, bearing the images of the gods, passed through the brilliantly-coloured gateway.

The Persians capture Babylon

When Cyrus of Persia, conqueror of the Medes, took Babylon in 539 BC, the Jews' long exile came to an end. Now they were free to return to Jerusalem, although few, it seems, did so immediately. The Fall of Babylon marks a major turning point in the development of Judaism. For, with the re-establishment of Yahweh's covenant with Israel, his people were redeemed. The exiles who returned from Babylon started the reconstruction of the Temple and established what would become the Judaism of the restoration, with its special emphasis on purity and the Mosaic Law.

Echoes of the events leading to Babylon's eclipse are heard centuries later in the Book of Daniel, where the successive empires of the Babylonians, the Medes and the Persians are likened to visionary beasts. Babylon is depicted as a lion with eagle's wings: 'and as I looked its wings were torn off...' (Daniel 7:4). Evidence for her last years and defeat by Persia comes from Babylonian sources, some of which were composed after Cyrus's victory and are biased towards him.

But the decline of Babylon had begun some 20 years earlier when King Nebuchadnezzar died in 562. The latter seems to have maintained friendly relations with the Medes who, following the fall of Assyria, had taken their boundary west to the River Halys in Asia Minor. However, the construction of a defensive wall north of Babylon shows that towards the end of his reign, Nebuchadnezzar had some anxieties about the Medes' intentions. Little is known of the last years of Nebuchadnezzar, but in the seven following his death, three kings ruled before Nabonidus took the throne in 555.

It is generally claimed that there was considerable opposition to Nabonidus's reign and that Babylon fell without a struggle because Cyrus was welcomed by all. In fact, there is little evidence for this view. Certainly, when the Persians attacked the Babylonians at Opis in October 539, there does seem to have been a fierce struggle.

The Persians then took Sippar and two days later entered Babylon – 'without a battle', according to the Babylonian Chronicle. But it seems there was a two-week delay before Cyrus himself entered the city. During this time there was a strong military presence – 'shield-bearing troops... surrounded the gates of Esagil' – perhaps suggesting that there was resistance to be dealt with before Babylon was deemed safe for Cyrus's arrival.

There is also evidence of some dissatisfaction among the Babylonians. This may have been due to the fact that, early on in his reign, Nabonidus introduced a number of administrative reforms. These included the placing of royal administrators in the temple hierarchy which meant that temple finances were now effectively controlled by the Crown. Those people whose incomes had been reduced by this move, i.e. the temple scribes, may have become disaffected with the king and supported Cyrus. Certainly, the pro-Persian propaganda on the fall of Babylon emanated from the temple scribes who compiled the literature.

For reasons as yet not understood, Nabonidus spent the last ten years of his reign at the oasis of Tema in Arabia. Shortly before his inexplicable departure, Cyrus had attacked the Medes and embarked on extending his rule over much of the Near East. With the fall of Babylon, Cyrus was now ruler of all her domains, including the province of Judah.

Nabonidus, the enigmatic last Babylonian king, is shown on this stele, before the symbols of the moon-god Sin, the sun-god Shamash, and Ishtar, the goddess of love and war.

Haran, where this stele was found, was a major centre of the moon-god cult and Nabonidus carefully restored Sin's temple.

Inexplicably, Nabonidus spent the last ten years of his reign in Arabia. Nebuchadnezzar's madness (Daniel 4:28–31) is probably a telescoping of stories about Nabonidus.

These Persian archers, based on a glazed-brick frieze, made at Susa in the fifth century BC, were part of 'The Ten Thousand Immortals', the king's bodyguard and the élite corps of the Persian army. New recruits instantly replaced fallen members, thus keeping their numbers constant. Here they wear ceremonial attire of spangled robes and the twisted Susian headbands. The bracelets were a mark of distinction. Their cornel-wood spears were tipped with silver blades.

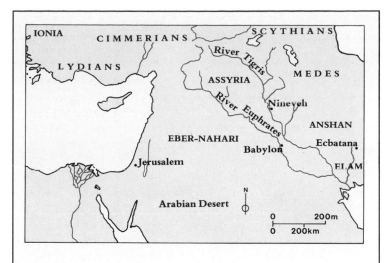

Belshazzar's feast

In Daniel 5 there is an account of Belshazzar feasting with his courtiers using the gold and silver vessels taken from the Temple of Jerusalem. Suddenly a hand appeared and wrote on the wall opposite him the words *mene, mene, teqel* and *parsin*. Since no one could understand their meaning, Daniel, a Judaean exile and a skilled interpreter, was summoned.

Playing on the meaning of words – a traditional Babylonian technique of forecasting – he interpreted them as signifying the end of Babylon as follows: *Mene* ('measure'), the days are numbered; *teqel* ('weight'), the king has been weighed in the scales and found wanting; *parsin*, ('divide'), his dominions will be divided and given to the Medes and the Persians.

Taken literally, these words could also be various weights used for exchange, the mina, shekel and *pêrês* or half-mina, a mina weighing 60 shekels.

Belshazzar was neither king nor the son of Nebuchadnezzar, as described in Daniel. Evidence from cuneiform inscriptions shows him to have been the crown prince, son of Nabonidus. He was in Babylon during his father's long absence at Tema, and it is possible that he lost his life fighting the invading Persians. Such confusions result from the long time span dividing these events from the composition of the Book of Daniel in the second century BC.

The First Cataract of the Nile was traditionally the southern frontier of ancient Egypt. During the fifth century BC, it was guarded by an Aramaean garrison at Syene (Aswan) and a Jewish garrison on the adjacent island of Elephantine. This Jewish settlement, contemporary with Ezra and Nehemiah, is the earliest diaspora Jewish community for which there is extensive documentation.

Legal, epistolary and communal archives, written in Aramaic on papyrus and potsherds, have survived. It is thought that the colony was established by the last native rulers of Egypt around 650 BC. The most interesting insight is that into the religion of the Jewish colonists, since they seemed to have divided their loyalties among a number of deities, and offerings to Aramaean gods are often documented.

Cyrus the Great and the rise of Persia

The Persians were an Indo-European tribe whose name derives from Parsua, one of their earlier areas of settlement. As with the Medes, they are attested in the Assyrian annals. Following the Assyrian Assurbanipal's defeat of Elam in the 640s, Persian tribes moved into the hill country of this ancient kingdom, though it does not seem that they were in control of Susa prior to the fall of Babylon.

For some 200 years, however, before the rise of Cyrus II ('the Great'), the Medes were the dominant power in Persia and the Persians were subject to them. Under their king Cyaxares, the Medes, in alliance with the Babylonians, defeated the Assyrians. Thereafter, they extended their power westwards to the River Halys. Cyaxares's son, Astyages, gave his daughter in marriage to the Persian king of Anshan, Cambyses I. Cyrus was born of this marriage. Greek authors relate various accounts of his birth and emergence as a prince, but these, reflecting traditional royal birth legends of the Near East, lack historical value.

Disregarding legend, it would seem that, on becoming king of Anshan, Cyrus united all the Persian tribes under his rule. According to the Babylonian Chronicle, the Medes rebelled against Astyages and handed him over to Cyrus. Ecbatana, the Median capital, was taken and looted in either 550 or 553 BC. Media became the first province or satrapy of the future empire and Medes were used together with Persians in the army and administration. Cyrus in fact took over much of the apparatus of the Median state.

In 547, Cyrus marched against the Lydian king Croesus, of legendary wealth, and defeated him at Sardis, his capital. With the creation of this satrapy, Cyrus turned his attention to the Greeks of Asia Minor and the Lycians and brought them both under his control. In the east he secured the entire Persian plateau and Gandhara. With the resources of all these lands at his command, he was ready to turn against Babylon.

In Babylon, as elsewhere, there had been a skilled propaganda campaign which extolled Cyrus's clemency and religious tolerance. According to the anonymous prophet who is known as 'Deutero-Isaiah', preaching in Babylon during this period, Cyrus was to be the liberator of the Jews in Babylon: the time of restoration was at hand: 'Thus says Yahweh to his anointed one, to Cyrus whom, he says, I have grasped by his right hand, to make the nations bow before him and to disarm kings . . .' (Isaiah 45:1).

Esther saves her people

The Book of Esther is set in the fifth century BC, 'in the days of Ahasuerus... whose empire stretched from India to Ethiopia' (Esther 1:1). The Persian king Ahasuerus is the well known Xerxes I of the Greek writers. The Biblical account, which reflects Jewish life in Persia, takes place at Xerxes' capital of Susa.

The story begins with the refusal of Ahasuerus's queen Vashti to parade her beauty before the drunken male revellers at a royal party and her subsequent banishment. Some time later, there was a beauty contest for a new queen and Ahasuerus chose the Jewess Esther, cousin and ward of Mordecai, a Jewish exile and royal official. Esther became queen but concealed her Jewish origin. Soon afterwards Mordecai foiled an assassination plot against the king.

Ahasuerus's right-hand man was a noble named Haman. When Mordecai refused to pay him the customary obeisance, Haman was furious and, in revenge, persuaded the king to authorise the extermination of the Jews. This was planned for the 13th of the month called Adar, a date determined by casting the *pur* or 'lot'. Mordecai asked Esther to intercede with the king on behalf of her people. Esther was reluctant to do so, because to approach the king unsummoned incurred the death penalty unless he raised his sceptre to grant immunity. Finally, however, she took the risk.

Esther's gamble was successful, and Ahasuerus accepted her invitation to dine at a banquet together with Haman. Haman, meanwhile, built an enormous gallows and planned to get royal authorisation to hang Mordecai. That night the king could not sleep, so the royal chronicles were read to him and he was reminded how Mordecai had saved his life. Haman arrived the next morning and was immediately commanded to dress Mordecai in royal robes and lead him in honour on horseback through the city square.

Later that day, when the king and Haman were dining with Esther, the queen revealed Haman's plot against the Jews. Ahasuerus stormed off in anger, while the terrified Haman begged Esther for help. When the king returned 'he found Haman sprawled across the couch where Esther was reclining' (7:8). For such a flagrant breach of conduct, Haman was taken away and later hanged on his own gallows.

At Esther's request, the king authorised Mordecai to issue a new edict permitting the Jews to defend themselves against their attackers. So, on the appointed day of 13th Adar and in Susa also on the 14th, the Jews throughout the empire destroyed their enemies. Their celebration after the massacre became a regular festival called the feast of Purim, or 'lots'.

The book of Esther thus explains the Jewish feast of Purim, which was perhaps originally a Persian festival taken over by the Jewish exiles. While the story is full of authentic memories of the Persian period, it is a historical romance and not the record of actual events. There is no evidence outside the Biblical record of the existence of the characters Vashti or Esther, and although an official called Marduka (Mordecai) occurs on tablets from Susa, he probably did not serve during Xerxes' reign.

Ancient historians regard the story of Esther as one of the many tales set in Persia which circulated around the Near East during this period. It belongs in the same category as other stories of women of the Persian court, preserved mainly in the works of classical authors.

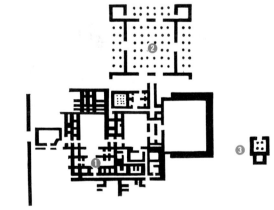

The palace remains show a complex of courts, corridors and rooms. Esther was first brought before Xerxes in the royal apartments, **1**. The great columned audience hall (Apadana), **2**, was doubtless the setting for royal parties and banquets. The palace gate, **3**, suggests the gate where Mordecai regularly sat, as was customary for Persian officials.

Colourful friezes of winged bulls and lion griffins in glazed brick ornamented the palace walls at Susa. According to Darius, the bricks for the palace were made by the Babylonians. This type of decoration was typically Babylonian in style and recalls the buildings of Nebuchadnezzar at Babylon. The bricks were not modelled directly but pressed into a mould. The main colours were blue, white, yellow, green and black. The plan of the palace was also clearly influenced by Babylonian architecture.

Xerxes, king of Persia

When Xerxes, who is known as Ahasuerus in the Book of Esther, succeeded his father Darius in 486 BC, he inherited a vast and well organised empire. He had been designated Crown Prince some years earlier. At the beginning of his reign, Xerxes suppressed revolts in Egypt and Babylonia, but he is remembered above all for his ill-fated invasion of Greece, which began in the spring of 481 BC. The heroic Spartan stand at Thermopylae and the Greek victories at Salamis, Plataea and Mycale are famous.

The Book of Esther and some Greek sources give an unflattering portrayal of Xerxes, who is said to have retired to his harem after the Persian defeat by the Greeks and to have been corrupted by luxury, wealth and court intrigue. There, is however, no evidence of Persian decline during Xerxes' reign. The downfall of the empire took place some 150 years after Salamis and meanwhile Persian gold, in the form of carefully distributed bribes, brought Greece virtually under complete Persian control. Xerxes died in August 465 BC – said to have been murdered in his bedchamber.

The Persian kings built on a lavish scale. Darius the Great chose Susa as his main capital and constructed there a splendid palace complex, which was completed by his son and successor Xerxes. The map, *above*, shows the palace gate, 1, the Apadana, 2, and the River Shaur, 3, behind.

Artisans and materials came from throughout the empire. The Book of Esther reflects the palace's grandeur: 'There were white and violet hangings fastened . . . to silver rings on marble columns, couches of gold and silver on a pavement of porphyry, marble, mother-of-pearl and precious stones' (Esther 1:5–6).

The Persian empire

Peace was maintained throughout much of western Asia for some 200 years by the Persian empire. For knowledge of its history, the Greek writers and historians remain among the most important sources. The empire was largely the creation of its founder, Cyrus, but was extended and reorganised by his successors, particularly Darius I (522–486 BC), who was arguably its greatest monarch. Everything centred around the king, to whom in theory all the imperial lands belonged.

Although not considered to be divine, the king was the elect of the supreme Persian god Ahura-mazda and the fountainhead of justice; in Persian eyes, 'he could do no wrong'. According to the Greek historian Herodotus, when King Cambyses wanted to marry his own sister, the royal judges said that 'though they could discover no law which allowed brother to marry sister, there was undoubtedly a law which permitted the king of Persia to do what he pleased'.

The Persian king is shown as larger than life on many carved reliefs. He supposedly lived largely in seclusion in his palace where he walked on purple carpets forbidden to lesser mortals. Outside the palace his feet were supposed never to touch the ground. At court were the royal family and their households, the king's harem and its staff, the royal bodyguard and a hierarchy of officials.

The court reflected the cosmopolitan character of the empire. There were Greek and Egyptian doctors, Babylonian astronomers and Phoenician explorers. According to the Greek writers, the court moved seasonally from one palace to another, although from Darius onwards, Susa was the main capital.

The empire was divided into provinces or 'satrapies', governed by Persian nobles or princes of the royal house, who were also great landowners. They were responsible for security and tribute collection. Judah was part of the satrapy of Abarnahara. Land was allocated to many different people who had to provide military service or sometimes money payments.

'Darius', to quote Herodotus' report of a Persian saying, 'was a tradesman . . . being out for profit wherever he could get it.' He was almost certainly the first Persian king to issue his own coins, including the famous gold 'darics'. Coins were generally only minted for immediate necessities such as military operations or bribes, otherwise payment was usually in kind.

The kings tended to hoard precious metals that arrived in their treasuries as tribute. Herodotus derides Darius's avarice, saying that on opening Queen Nitokris's tomb at Babylon, instead of the treasure he expected, he found an inscription which read: 'If you had not been so insatiably greedy and eager to get money by the most despicable means, you would never have opened the tomb of the dead.'

Persian authority ultimately rested on the army. Imperial garrisons were stationed in the royal capitals and important satrapal centres. In times of war, the army became a mosaic of different nationalities. Herodotus lists at least 45 different peoples from whom contingents were levied for Xerxes' Greek expedition. They were divided into spearmen, archers and cavalry. The Persian army were not outclassed in the use of the latter until the time of Alexander the Great.

The Persian empire was held together by good organisation and firm discipline. Stability only broke down during the last decades of the empire and Persian authority was finally shattered by Alexander the Great (see pp. 118–19).

The Persian empire, reorganised by Darius the Great into 20 satrapies, embraced a great variety of peoples.

The Royal Road leading from Sardis to Susa, some 1,600mls/ 2,575km long, had 111 staging posts. An extension led to Persepolis. The road was well guarded and travellers were normally escorted.

Another important route ran from Babylon to Ecbatana, the old Median capital and site of a royal palace, and thence to eastern Iran. Bridges were maintained on the main highways.

The eastern staircase of the Apadana at Persepolis depicts tribute delegations from 23 lands, all wearing their native costumes. The leader of each group is escorted by a Persian or a Mede. In the detail, *below*, the Chorasmanians (*top panel, left*) bring a short sword, bracelets, axes and a horse. The Gandarians (*top panel, right*) offer lances and a humped bull. The Indians (*lower panel, left*) carry baskets of vases and lead a donkey, while the Bactrians (*lower panel, right*) bring vessels and a Bactrian camel.

How the cuneiform script was deciphered

Darius I, arguably Persia's greatest king, had inscribed on a remote rock at Behistun in the Zagros mountains an account of his struggles to secure the throne. The king is shown in carved relief with his foot on the body of his predecessor, the usurper Gautama. The accompanying inscription is in Old Persian, Elamite and Babylonian, all in the cuneiform script.

Scholars became fascinated by cuneiform from the late eighteenth century onwards. By 1802, a German scholar named Grotefend had made some progress with Old Persian inscriptions from Persepolis, but the biggest step forward was taken when H.C. Rawlinson, an officer in the British Army, stationed in Kermanshah, visited nearby Behistun.

At great personal danger, Rawlinson scaled the sheer rock face and, between 1835 and 1837, made copies of the Persian and Elamite texts. He first tackled the Persian version, which had fewer signs because it was written in alphabetic cuneiform. He began by isolating the royal names and comparing them with those known in Hebrew and Greek texts, and eventually succeeded in producing a reasonable translation.

The Babylonian inscription was still inaccessible. Rawlinson returned to Behistun in 1847. This time a Kurdish boy offered to help and with great agility crossed the smooth, perpendicular rock. Then, as Rawlinson recounted, 'with a short ladder he formed a swinging seat . . . and . . . took under my direction the paper cast of the Babylonian translation of the records of Darius.' Within a decade, helped by the Old Persian text, Rawlinson and other scholars had deciphered Babylonian cuneiform, thereby providing the key to the understanding of the written records of the Mesopotamian civilisations.

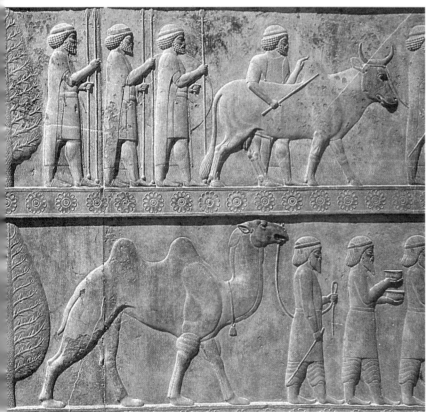

Gods of Persia

The Persians worshipped a triad of deities – Ahura-mazda, seen *above* in a door relief at Persepolis, Mithra and the goddess Anahita. These three are the main deities of the Avesta, the Persian religious texts still preserved by the Parsees of India.

The hymns of the prophet Zoroaster, for whom Ahura-mazda was the one omnipotent god, form the basis of the Avesta tradition. Priests, called the Magi, officiated at Zoroastrian religious ceremonies. Fire was sacred and was tended on special fire altars. The Magi did not cremate their dead, however, but exposed them to be devoured by birds and dogs. According to Herodotus, sacrifices were made without fire.

At the festival of Mithra, an intoxicating drink (*haoma*) was prepared. During the ceremony the king was required to become drunk, and dance in a state of intoxication.

The Persians were, in general, tolerant of other religions and saw reflections of their own deities in foreign gods. For example, the Greek god Zeus, the Babylonian Marduk and perhaps even the Jewish Yahweh, might be likened to Ahura-mazda.

The palace complex built at Persepolis, *left*, by Darius and his successors reflects the wealth and majesty of Persia. On the west of the terrace is Darius's reception hall (Apadana), **1**, with adjoining palaces. The entrance gateway, **2**, was guarded by carved winged bulls. To the east is Xerxes' throne hall, **3**, and the treasury, **4**, where administrative documents have been found.

The return to Jerusalem

Following his victory over Babylon in 539 BC, Cyrus, the Persian king, authorised the return of the Jewish exiles to Judah and the rebuilding of the Temple in Jerusalem. In fact, Cyrus was acting in accord with a general policy of religious toleration followed by the Persians for political expedience. Evidence of this comes from the 'Cyrus Cylinder', an inscription from Babylon, which, although not relating specifically to Judah, records the return of various foreign deities to their native sanctuaries.

Sheshbazzar, 'the prince of Judah', possibly a son of King Jehoiachin, led the first group of Jews back. Into his care was given the Temple treasure taken by Nebuchadnezzar. But the land to which the Jews returned was devastated and impoverished. Edomites (see p.27) were settled in the southern hill country and much of the northern region was now attached to the province of Samaria. The Samaritans were a mixture of those Jews not deported by the Assyrian king Sargon II in 721 (see pp.98–9) and various peoples the latter had introduced into the region. They were religious conservatives and hostility with the returning exiles continued to New Testament times.

Work soon began on the Temple but 18 years later it had not progressed beyond the foundations. Community morale was low as the prophetic books Haggai, Zechariah and Isaiah (ch.56–66) reveal. There were economic tensions, perhaps related to land ownership and a succession of bad harvests.

The community was divided: on the one hand, there were those who had remained and had absorbed much from the pagan world around them; on the other, there were the dedicated followers of Yahweh. In general, the latter were returned exiles, with their devotion to the one God and their concern with 'purity', circumcision and observance of the Sabbath.

The need for the Temple as a focal point for the community became urgent. Spurred on by the prophets, the people resumed construction and the Temple was completed in 515 BC.

Little is known about the community in the 20 years that followed. Groups of exiles continued to return from Babylon and the population increased. The political situation is unclear, but recent archaeological discoveries make it possible to reconstruct the genealogies of governors of Judah and Samaria to the end of the fifth century. It now seems that Judah was a Persian province with its own governor.

The Temple provided the Jews with a defined central place of worship. Nevertheless, the community's morale was still at a low ebb. The prophet Malachi relates that priests offered polluted animals and tithes were not paid. Also, there were many mixed marriages with non-Jews, which, if left unchecked, would have meant, in time, the community losing its identity.

While conditions were in decline in Judah, the Babylonian Jews, lacking, as they did, the Temple, continued to turn increasingly to the Torah (i.e. the Law) and other sacred writings. Through studying their literature, through prayer, readings and expositions, synagogue worship emerged as the centre of their communal life. Also, the existing sacred books were expanded with psalms, prayers and wisdom texts.

It was the Jews in Babylon who gradually established that the continuance of their faith depended on obedience to Yahweh and submission to his laws. The emergence of the *soferim*, the scribes who copied out the sacred scriptures, was fundamental to the transmission of the religion.

From these Babylonian Jews, Ezra 'the scribe' came to Jerusalem with powers to carry out religious reforms within the community. The date of Ezra's mission is uncertain but, according to Biblical chronology, he arrived with more exiles, priests and Levites in 458 BC. He fought against all the religious abuses and disseminated the tenets of the Law.

Ezra was joined 12 years later by Nehemiah, a Jew who was cup-bearer to the Persian king Artaxerxes, and who had been appointed governor of Judah. Although Nehemiah's responsibilities lay in the civic and economic spheres, he shared Ezra's religious aims. In 444, on the Day of Atonement, in the presence of Nehemiah, Ezra read from the Book of the Law of Moses before a large gathering in the Temple court. While he read, professional expounders explained the text. Nehemiah and the people then pledged themselves to obey the Law.

To give the community physical security, it was important to restore the city walls. Nehemiah, therefore, in 445 BC, summoned the leaders of the people to help and the work was completed in 52 days (see opposite page).

Nehemiah was also instrumental in ordering a remission of debts and the elimination of various abuses, such as priestly neglect of duties. Intermarriage, which had taken place even in the family of the high priest, was also combatted.

Ezra and Nehemiah's work laid the basis for the Judaean theocracy – a state ruled by religion based on the Torah. It was the development of this enclosed, exclusive and orthodox community that permitted Judaism to retain its values and survive: religious identity had transcended nationhood.

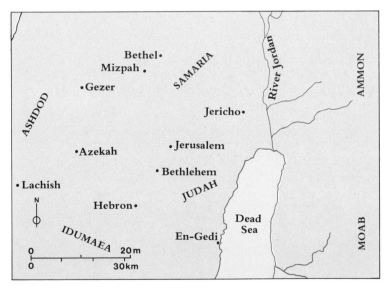

Compared with its former extent, Judah by the time of the return from Exile was greatly diminished. The main settlements and names of district governors are known from Ezra (2:1–35) and Nehemiah (7:6–38). The distribution of sealing impressions with the name 'Yehud' gives some idea of Judah's size: roughly from Mizpah in the north to En-Gedi and from Gezer east to Jericho.

The Babylonians had razed most fortified cities, as excavations at Lachish, Debir and elsewhere have shown. Former Northern Kingdom (Israel) towns, such as Bethel, had remained under Babylonian control and were not destroyed. Edomites were now settled in the southern hill region, hence the later Greek name – Idumaea.

The Cyrus Cylinder, found in Babylon in 1879, is a clay barrel-shaped document inscribed in cuneiform. It was written to commemorate Cyrus's restoration works after his capture of Babylon.

It describes how Marduk, the God of Babylon, turned away from Nabonidus because of his impiety and appointed Cyrus in his place. It contains an account of the return by Cyrus of the various city gods to their original sanctuaries. In a general way this section of the text recalls the decree of Cyrus concerning the rebuilding of the Temple at Jerusalem (Ezra 1:1–3). The cylinder, however, relates only to Mesopotamian sanctuaries.

Silver and gold coins made their first appearance in Judah during the Persian period, when Darius I copied the example of Lydia, which had introduced coinage in the 7th century BC. The Attic drachma was common coinage

in the eastern Mediterranean in the 5th and 4th centuries; the example, *above*, follows that model and bears the owl of the Greek goddess Athene. There have also been discovered coins with the letters YHD, which is the Aramaic form of the name Judah. The Book of Nehemiah suggests that administrative expenses were paid for by levies, in cash or in kind.

Nehemiah, a Jewish cup-bearer and official at the court of Artaxerxes I, was made governor of Judaea in about 445 BC and immediately set about rebuilding the ruined walls of Jerusalem. He made his first tour of inspection secretly at night, then organised workers, both from the city and nearby settlements, into groups; each group was given a section of the wall to rebuild.

Many leaders of neighbouring territories who were hostile to the return of the Jews – notably Sanballat, provincial governor of Samaria – tried to stop their work, alternately by persuasion and force. The Jews duly armed themselves, every worker having a sword by his side. Despite all obstacles, the wall was completed and then dedicated in a solemn service in the Temple.

This reconstruction of Jerusalem's walls, as rebuilt by Nehemiah, shows the course that the walls probably took. Many archaeologists, however, have advanced arguments in support of different patterns. The area has been so often and so heavily built over that the exact course of the wall will probably never be known.

The conquests of Alexander the Great

In 332 BC, a little over a century after Nehemiah (see pp. 116–7), Persian rule came to an end in Judah when Alexander of Macedon took possession of Palestine. On the assassination of his father Philip in 336, Alexander, then only 20 years old, inherited a war with Persia, declared the preceding year by the Greek Confederacy under Philip whose intention had been to conquer Asia Minor; but Alexander's aim became no less than the total destruction of the Persian empire.

Having consolidated his position in Macedonia and Greece, Alexander crossed the Hellespont in 334. Victory over the Persians at Granicus allowed him to take control of Asia Minor. The following year, Alexander faced a huge Persian army led by Darius III Codomanus at Issus. Here, too, the Persians were defeated and Darius fled, abandoning his army and even his mother, wife and daughters to Alexander.

Following the victory at Issus, the east Mediterranean coast came rapidly under Alexander's control. One by one, with the exception of Tyre, the Phoenician cities submitted. Tyre, relying on its island strength, withstood him for seven months. Some scholars see an allusion to Alexander's progress through this region in Zecharaiah 9:1–8: 'Tyre has built herself a fortress. . . . And now the Lord is going to dispossess her; at sea he will break her power, and she herself will go up in flames.'

Once Tyre had fallen, Alexander passed through Palestine. According to the Jewish historian Josephus, the people of Samaria welcomed him but Jerusalem resisted, remaining faithful to the Persians. Josephus relates that Jerusalem eventually submitted to Alexander, but there is no evidence that he did, in fact, visit the city. Alexander tried, as he had done with the conquered regions of Asia Minor, to keep the existing arrangements of government for the cities of Syria and Palestine.

Alexander then advanced to Egypt where the Persian satrap of Memphis surrendered. Hailed by the Egyptians as a liberator, he was proclaimed the 'Son of Ammon' by the priests at the oasis of Siwa. Alexandria, which was to be the largest commercial and cultural centre of the area, was founded in the western delta.

He passed back through Palestine on his way north, and may have put down a revolt in Samaria. Marching to Mesopotamia, he inflicted the final and decisive defeat of Darius at Gaugamela near the River Tigris. Once more Darius fled, only later to be murdered by his own men. With the submission of Babylon, Susa and Persepolis, Alexander was master of the western Persian empire, with great wealth at his disposal.

But even after the defeat of the Persians, Alexander still continued campaigning; first in the northern Persian satrapies as far as the River Jaxartes, then east to the River Indus on the borders of India. These had been the furthest boundaries of the Persian empire at its greatest extent. Indeed, as archaeology has shown, Greek foundations were often on the sites of Persian settlements dating back to Cyrus (d.529). However, when his troops began to mutiny in India, Alexander returned to Babylon. It was there, in 323, that he became ill and died.

Alexander's empire, which was in fact a combination of the old Persian empire and Macedonia, had not been consolidated and was to fall apart after his death. Nevertheless, the effect of his achievement was to spread Hellenistic civilisation and culture into the oriental world of the Near East. For the Jews of Palestine, now brought into the Greek-speaking world, it marked a major turning point.

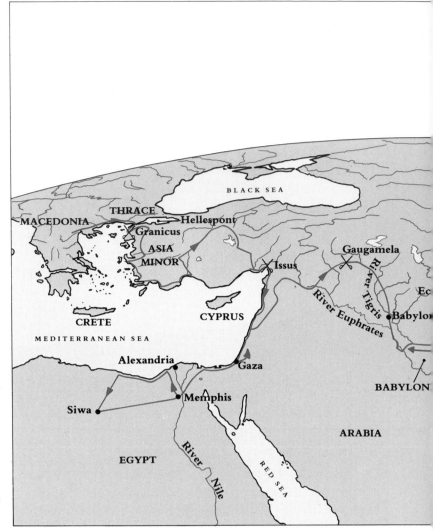

In 334 BC Alexander the Great and his army, accompanied by historians, scientists and engineers, crossed the Hellespont into Asia Minor: his object was the destruction of the Persian empire.

At first, the Persians remained inactive. Within a year, however, Alexander had inflicted heavy losses on them at the battle of Granicus and had liberated the Greek cities along the coast.

The Persian and Greek armies met at Issus in October 333. Darius relied on massive numerical superiority, Alexander on his disciplined phalanxes and the high morale of his troops. In the ensuing battle the Persians were annihilated, losing in the region of 110,000 men. In this one engagement Alexander had, in effect, captured the Persian empire west of the River Euphrates.

Nevertheless, Alexander needed to secure his southern flank and he therefore marched down the Mediterranean coast towards Egypt. There were two obstacles in his path: the fortress cities of Tyre and Gaza. Tyre was in two parts: a mainland town and a citadel 2,500ft/762m offshore. Here Alexander revealed his genius as a military engineer: he captured mainland Tyre, destroyed it and used the rubble to build a causeway to the sea-bound fortress. It took him seven months to subdue Tyre, only one to take Gaza. All Palestine was now effectively under his control.

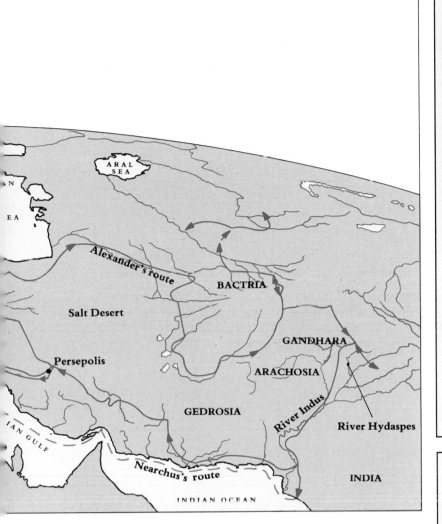

Darius in defeat

This detail from 'Alexander and Darius at the battle of Issus', a late second-century BC mosaic from Pompeii, shows the Persian king faced with a charge by Alexander and his cavalry.

The Macedonian and Persian kings first encountered each other at Issus in October 333. The Persians had advanced slowly to the sea. They first came across the Macedonian sick and Darius ordered that their hands be cut off. Hearing this, Alexander made a forced march and in the morning took the Persians by surprise on their side of the narrow coastal plain. As many as 110,000 Persians were reputedly slain. Darius fled, leaving the royal tent, his treasures and his harem.

In Egypt, in 332, the Persian satrap at Memphis surrendered to him. In 331, he founded the city of Alexandria.

Alexander was now free to resume his march of conquest eastwards. He and his army retraced their steps along the eastern Mediterranean coastline, then turned northeastwards through Syria.

Alexander's army again met the Persians at Gaugamela in 331. The result was the same as at Issus: Darius was defeated, his army destroyed and Persian power was shattered. Darius himself was subsequently murdered.

Alexander then took Darius's great cities of Babylon and Susa, razed Persepolis and in 330 took Ecbatana, the old Median capital. He then resumed his eastward march. He defeated the Indian king Porus on the banks of the Hydaspes, but his army was becoming weary of war and rebelled.

Alexander turned back westwards across the Gedrosian desert, while his admiral Nearchus sailed back along the coast. He died at Babylon, probably of a fever. He was 33 years old and his empire did not for long survive him, but the effects of his career were epoch-making, notably in the bringing of Greek civilisation to Asia Minor and far to the east.

Image of the god king

Alexander did not use his own portrait on the coins that he issued, which had representations of the deities Athena and Herakles. His portrait first appears on the coins of Ptolemy of Egypt and of Lysimachus of Thrace, *above*, where he is represented as Zeus Ammon, wearing the ram's horns of the god Ammon and the royal diadem. As the symbols of the god indicate, this idealised likeness is more than just a portrait; it is an image of the god.

The spread of Hellenism

Greek culture – Hellenism – spread to the already culturally mixed world of the Near East as a result of Alexander the Great's conquests (see pp.118–9). Following Alexander's death in 323 BC, there was a period of long and bloody warfare as his generals struggled for mastery of the conquered territories, with Ptolemy and Seleucus eventually gaining control. From these political confusions there emerged the Hellenistic states which were to retain control until Rome rose to power in the eastern Mediterranean.

The extent to which Hellenistic culture was either embraced or resisted by the peoples of the conquered territories varied from place to place and even within those places, as evidence from Egypt and Judah shows. In general, Hellenism made its greatest impact in the cities and among the conquered aristocracies who, by assimilating Hellenistic culture, were able to gain access to the closed circle of the Graeco-Macedonian ruling class.

Greeks and other peoples of the Near East had long been in touch with each other, particularly in those regions bordering the Mediterranean. Greek craftsmen had carved the tombs of Carian nobles and Phoenician satraps; Greek pottery found in the Levant bears witness to long-standing trading contacts, and Greek mercenaries served in the armies of Egypt and Persia.

With the establishment of the Greeks as rulers, Hellenism became widespread, as Greek officials, merchants and soldiers travelled far and wide. In the Seleucid and Ptolemaic kingdoms, Greeks, though now in a minority, formed the governing class. Soldiers settled on land given to them by the king in return for their military service. This privilege was then passed on to the soldiers' descendants, with the result that a Greek hereditary military class, owing allegiance to the ruler, grew up.

Cities such as Alexandria, Antioch and Seleucia-on-the-Tigris were founded on Greek models. But the personal and absolutist nature of Hellenistic monarchy, an institution rooted in Near Eastern concepts of kingship, by its nature denied to the citizens their traditional freedoms.

An outstanding example of these new Hellenistic cities was Pergamon. Its library was second only to that of Alexandria and it was here that a school of Greek sculpture was developed. There were also many smaller foundations, such as the recently excavated site of Ai Khanum on the River Oxus where, in the mid third century BC, maxims from Delphi were inscribed in Greek on the city's gymnasium.

Greek language crossed frontiers and bound together people from Egypt to Bactria. In his *Moralia*, Plutarch, the Greek writer of the first century AD, says that because of Alexander, 'Homer became widely read [in Asia] . . . the Gedrosians sang the tragedies of Euripides . . .' Greek inscriptions from Kandahar, and recent finds from Tadjikstan in central Asia, point to the wide diffusion of Greek culture in these distant regions.

Nearer to the Mediterranean, with a great increase in Greek penetration of the area, the Jews – among others – migrated and travelled, often adopting the Greek language. In Alexandria the Greek-speaking Jewish population was so large that a translation of the Scriptures into Greek, 'the Septuagint', was made for them. The trade routes, which now radiated to the furthest corners of the known world, bringing silk from China, spices from the east and incense from Arabia, also served as avenues for the diffusion of Hellenism.

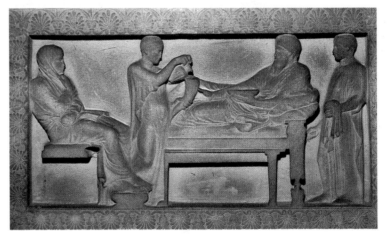

A satrap, from a Sidon sarcophagus, is depicted reclining in the Greek manner and holding a Persian drinking cup. The poses and clothes of the figures reveal the strong influence of the Greek style on western Persia. Satraps were provincial governors under the ancient Persian empire. They had despotic powers but were always subject to the imperial will.

This detail from the Alexander Sarcophagus is generally thought to depict the warrior king, mounted on his horse Bucephalus, attacking and slaying Persian troops. Some scholars, however, deny that this Hellenistic statue has any links with Alexander. Alexander had been nominated by the Greek states to conduct the war against Persia; his success was overwhelming and allowed him to extend his conquests to Egypt (where he founded Alexandria) and India. At his death, his empire degenerated into warring factions.

Ptolemy I (323–283 BC)

Demetrius Poliorcetes (306–283 BC)

Seleucus I (321–280 BC)

Eumenes II (197–160 BC)

Euthydemus I (c.235–200 BC)

The break-up of Alexander's empire
When Alexander died in 323 BC, his empire stretched from Macedonia to the Indus and embraced most of the Near East. He left no heir, and for some 20 years his generals, battling for supremacy, carved up the empire. By 320, following a meeting of the combatants at Triparadeisus in northern Syria, the pattern of the Hellenistic world had begun to emerge, with Macedonia, Egypt and Asia each under separate control. The silver tetradrachm coins, *left*, show Hellenistic rulers after the time of Alexander.

The complex events of the years from 320 to 301 were dominated by Antigonus, who took the title of king in 306 and bestowed the diadem on his son Demetrius. In the following year, Ptolemy followed suit in Egypt, as did Seleucus in Babylonia. The decisive defeat and death of Antigonus at the the Battle of Ipsus in 301, clearly mark the end of the empire.

By the end of the 280s, with Seleucus master of Asia, only the fate of Macedonia remained undecided. There, in 276, Antigonus Gonatas, the son of Demetrius, took the crown and thereby completed the Hellenistic world of territorial states. The subsequent emergence of the Attalids at Pergamon limited Seleucid control in Asia Minor to Cilicia only. In 239, Diodotus established an independent kingdom in Bactria, further reducing Seleucid domains.

One of the main themes in the third century BC is the rivalry between the Ptolemies and Seleucids. Five Syrian wars were fought, although not all in Syria. Egypt retained her control over Coele-Syria until 198, when Antiochus III seized control. Thereafter, Palestine was under the rule of the Seleucids until the rise of the Hasmonaean dynasty.

Antiochus IV persecutes the Jews

After a century of dispute for control of southern Syria, the region passed from Ptolemaic to Seleucid control (see pp.120–1) in around 200 BC, when Antiochus III ('the Great') won the fifth Syrian war. For the Jews of Palestine, the conquest initially brought little change. There is evidence of the spread of Hellenism during these years, but clearly some of the Jewish population resisted it, as is shown by the emergence of a new movement in Judaism.

The *Hasidim* ('the Pious') were a group militantly devoted to keeping the Torah as Israel's law and opposing Greeks and Hellenised Jews as enemies of Israel and its religion. Many scholars, including the *soferim*, belonged to this group, whose viewpoint is reflected in the apocalyptic book of Daniel.

For some years there had been strife between the Jewish aristocratic factions of Jerusalem, who generally favoured Hellenism. The principal protagonists were the Tobiads and Oniads. In 175 BC, Antiochus IV acceded to the Seleucid throne. 'It was then that there emerged from Israel a set of renegades who led many people astray. "Come," they said, "let us ally ourselves with the gentiles surrounding us"' (1 Maccabees 1:11–12). Jason, an ally of the Tobiads, usurped the high priesthood from Onias, hereditary high-priest, on promise of increased revenue for the new ruler.

In return for a further payment, he was granted permission to establish a gymnasium and an 'ephebion' (academy for young men), and 'to register the Antiochists of Jerusalem' (2 Maccabees 4:9–11). The exact meaning of this phrase has been much debated: some scholars interpret it as meaning that Jerusalem became a Greek city with the name of Antioch, while others think a second and parallel government alongside the temple state was created. Either way, Greek institutions had now been introduced into Jerusalem and the Seleucid ruler had chosen the high priest in pursuance of his own financial and political objectives. From now on, the conflict would be more acute.

Three years later, Menelaus, another Tobiad, gained the king's favour and was appointed high priest in place of Jason. His plundering of the Temple on the king's behalf, the murder of Onias, and growing class conflicts between the wealthy Hellenisers and the masses, resulted in riots.

In 169, after Antiochus's campaign in Egypt, Jason returned and killed some of Menelaus's followers. The king then marched to Jerusalem to suppress the disturbances and massacred 80,000 people. Reinstating Menelaus, the king then pillaged the Temple, seizing the sacred vessels, and took 1,800 talents. Shortly afterwards, he instructed his officials 'to force the Jews to violate their ancestral customs and live no longer by the laws of God' (2 Maccabees 6:1).

All religious precepts, particularly the keeping of festivals, observance of the Sabbath and circumcision, were prohibited on pain of death. Possession of the 'Book of the Law of Moses' was made a capital offence and copies were destroyed. The Jewish sacrificial cult was proscribed and pigs' flesh was offered on the Temple altars. The Temple itself was converted to the worship of Zeus and 'was filled with revelling and debauchery by the gentiles, who . . . had intercourse with women in the sacred precincts' (2 Maccabees 6:4).

Many refused to yield and perished as martyrs, while others fled the city. Resistance soon flared into open rebellion, led by Mattathias, a priest of the Hasmonaean family.

Antiochus IV: eccentric but gifted ruler
On his accession to the Seleucid throne, Antiochus took the title 'Epiphanes' – 'God revealed'. A younger son of Antiochus the Great, who had been defeated by the Romans at Magnesia in Lydia, he spent several years in Rome as a hostage and he was greatly impressed by Roman customs and institutions. Always a controversial figure, he seems, like his father, to have been a gifted man, though capricious and given to extravagance. His lavish gifts to the Greek cities were renowned. Ancient accounts portray him as an eccentric personality.

Antiochus was reputedly given to sudden excesses of affection and outbursts of anger. He liked to move among the common people in the city and enjoyed acting and dancing on the stage – unusual activities for a ruler of that period. Polybius has a story of his visiting the public baths, pouring myrrh on the floor and then enjoying the spectacle of people slipping over.

With eccentricity, however, went ambition, manifested in his resolve to restore the Seleucid domains. The emergence of Rome as the greatest power in the eastern Mediterranean was a major factor at this time and, after his humiliating treatment in Egypt, when the Roman legate displayed Rome's great power, Antiochus was relegated to the state of client king.

Nevertheless, his campaigns in Egypt and to the east show that he was an able strategist. Like his brother and father before him, however, he was hampered financially by the terms of the peace treaty of Apamea. The Seleucid war debt to Rome was immense and this could have been a contributory factor in his behaviour towards the Jews, because the Temple was also a financial institution. But his persecution of the Jews has puzzled scholars. For, as a Hellenist, he would have been tolerant in religious matters and nowhere else did he behave in such a way.

Sport was extremely important to the Greeks. They regarded it as training, particularly for warfare. It developed character, and success in the games was seen as a mark of breeding which added lustre to a family name. Running, discus- and javelin-throwing,

jumping, wrestling, shown on the 6th-century BC amphora *above*, and boxing were popular, as were horse and chariot racing.

Athletic contests came to have a religious character and were held at fixed times and at particular sanctuaries. Pictorial representations of

naked athletes were probably an artistic convention, though men seem to have stripped for wrestling and boxing. The gymnasium, a public institution, was open to all citizens and was especially attended by ephebes, youths from 15 to 20 years.

The practice of circumcision

Circumcision is a widespread practice in the Near East and Africa. Its origin is uncertain, but is perhaps connected with the idea of a sacrifice to a tribal god. In some cultures it marks the initiation into manhood and to membership of the tribe. Under the persecution of Antiochus, the Jews were put to death for having their sons circumcised.

In the Bible, the rite was commanded by God as a sign of the covenant made with Abraham. 'This is my covenant which you must keep between myself and you, and your descendants after you: every one of your males must be circumcised' (Genesis 17:11). It was thus a national mark of consecration to the service of God, and individually it represents the offering to him of the human life.

Circumcision of men and boys was practised by the Jews during the captivity in Egypt, as indeed it was amongst the Egyptians. It was discontinued, however, during the sojourn in the wilderness, when even Moses left his son uncircumcised.

Abraham was 99 when he was circumcised and Ishmael was 13. In accordance with the covenantal instructions, Jewish boys are circumcised on the eighth day after birth, as was Isaac. At the ceremony, the child is named.

Circumcision was, like the dietary laws, an important distinctive feature of Jewish religious and national life. It contributed greatly to a specific Jewish consciousness and identity, separating the Jews from the 'uncircumcised gentiles'. Hellenised Jews often tried physically to disguise the marks of their own circumcision. Therefore, the Seleucid attack on this ritual was carefully calculated to antagonise those Jews who wished to remain faithful to their religious traditions.

Zeus: supreme god of the pantheon

Apollo: the god of music, archery and prophecy

Athene: the goddess of war, of arts and crafts

The gods of Greece

The spread of Hellenism also meant the spread of the Greek pantheon. There were many other gods besides those supposed to dwell on Mount Olympus. Cities had their own patron deities (such as the war-goddess Athene at Athens), variously portraying them on coins. Many gods had their sacred shrines, such as that of Apollo at Delphi and Zeus at Olympia. From the fifth century onwards, Olympian religion was under attack, as various philosophies and foreign cults gained adherents.

In the Hellenistic period, Tyche (Fortune) was widely worshipped. As the Hellenistic kings sought religious support to reinforce the claims of their dynasties, the royal houses adopted protector gods. Herakles was the deity of the Antigonids of Macedon; the Ptolemies were devoted to the cult of Dionysus, and Apollo was the protector of the Seleucids – indeed, Seleucus was reputedly the son of Apollo. The gods or their emblems appeared on coinage: Antiochus IV, for example, showed Zeus on his coins.

The Maccabaean rebellion: the Biblical sources

Although sources for the Maccabaean rebellion are relatively abundant, much is still open to conjecture. Historians largely depend on the Jewish tradition in 1 and 2 Maccabees and the Book of Daniel. The latter, though not an historical work, is the only contemporary source. The book is not merely incidental to, but stems from, the rebellion, for it seems to have been a response at the time to Antiochus's persecutions. The language is enigmatic, and it is only with knowledge of the events from elsewhere that Daniel can be used as an historical source.

Daniel is a prime example of apocalyptic literature, in which secret information is revealed about God's plans for the world, and for Israel in particular. Visions, bizarre imagery and symbolic language portray both history and the events of the time. The Day of Judgement would resolve all things, with the redemption of the good and the damnation of the wicked. Daniel's principal importance as a source for this period is that it reflects the Jewish nationalist–religious reaction to Hellenisation.

The stance of 1 Maccabees, composed in about 100 BC, is that of a confident, free nation. Possibly the work of an official historian of the Hasmonaean court, the author's sympathies lie with the dynasty, and his work is imbued with a religious and nationalistic spirit. 2 Maccabees, as the author himself relates (2 Maccabees 2:19), is a condensation of a longer history of the revolt by one Jason of Cyrene, of whom nothing is known.

Whereas 1 Maccabees covers a period of some 40 years (c.175–135 BC), 2 Maccabees deals with events leading up to the revolt and ends with the victory of Maccabeus over Nicanor, in all, a period of not much more than 15 years.

Judas Maccabaeus: the battle of Beth-Horon

Attempts by the Seleucid king Antiochus IV to enforce Hellenism (see pp.122–3) upon Judaea were strongly resisted by many Jews. Among those who escaped persecution by fleeing from Jerusalem into the countryside were Mattathias, a priest of the Hasmonaean family, and his five sons, John, Simon, Judas (nicknamed Maccabaeus, probably meaning 'the Hammer'), Eleazar and Jonathan. They went to their native town of Modein on the edge of the Shephelah.

One day in 167/6 BC, the royal officials responsible for implementing the policy of Hellenisation arrived in Modein to enforce the compulsory sacrifice to the new gods. 'Many Israelites gathered round them, but Mattathias and his sons drew apart' (1 Maccabees 2:16). One of the officials called on Mattathias to 'be the first to come forward and conform to the king's decree' (2:18), but he steadfastly refused. The sight of a Jew about to offer sacrifice aroused Mattathias' anger and he 'threw himself on the man and slaughtered him on the altar' (2:24). Then he also killed the official and destroyed the altar.

This was an open act of rebellion against royal authority. Immediately afterwards, Mattathias and his sons retreated to the hills, where they became a focal point for organised resistance. Among those who joined them were a group known as the 'pious' (Hebrew *Hasidim*). The rebel forces began to consolidate their position by moving around the country and seizing control of the Judaean villages.

When Mattathias died in 166/5, his son Simon assumed an advisory position and Judas Maccabaeus, 'strong and brave from his youth' became the commander of the army. He succeeded in recruiting about 6,000 men. By avoiding open battles and using surprise tactics, Judas gained a series of victories. Although the Seleucid troops were better armed and trained and superior in number, the rebels had greater mobility and good knowledge and control of the area.

The first encounter between the two armies took place at an unspecified location, probably somewhere in the hill country just north of Judaea. The enemy forces were led by Apollonius who 'mustered the gentiles and a large force from Samaria to make war on Israel' (1 Maccabees 3:10). Judas marched out to meet him as he made his way southwards and scored a great victory, in which Apollonius was killed.

The Seleucids now took further action against the rebels, entrusting Seron, commander of the Seleucid forces in Coele-Syria, with the task of restoring control. In late 166 or early 165, he left his northern headquarters at the head of 'a strong army of unbelievers'. He made for Jerusalem, where a Seleucid garrison was stationed, via the coastal route which, if less direct, was safer than the mountain roads. Near modern Lod, he turned east towards the Judaean mountains, passed close to Modein and then began the ascent to the pass of Beth-Horon, one of the main approach routes to Jerusalem from the coastal plain.

Judas was encamped at Upper Beth-Horon, with a force of only 'a handful of men'. When they saw Seron's great army leave Lower Beth-Horon they lost heart. Judas, however, revived their spirits with words of encouragement and 'when he had finished speaking he made a sudden sally against Seron and his force and overwhelmed them'. The attack took Seron and his men by surprise. Judas pursued them down through the mountains and about 800 men were killed. The survivors fled to the Seleucid-controlled Philistine coastal plain.

Seron's army advanced from the coastal plain through the Judaean hills. The small Jewish force waited near the top of the Beth-Horon pass. As the Seleucid troops were nearing the summit, Judas launched a surprise attack. The enemy was routed and fled down the hill.

As the Seleucid army began its march through the Beth-Horon pass, **1**, Judas's men watched from their concealed positions near the top, waiting for an opportune moment to attack. From Lower Beth-Horon, the enemy columns began the long, winding ascent to the upper village, weighed down with their weapons and equipment.

When the first files, **2**, reached Upper Beth-Horon, and began to move along the progressively narrower road to the hill above the village, Judas gave the signal to attack, **3**. The rebels fell on the leading units killing or wounding many.

As the enemy fell back, those behind were pushed down the slopes, Seron himself may have been among the first casualties.

The death of their commander would doubtless have demoralised his soldiers who, in disarray, found themselves at the mercy of Judas's men. Those in the rear turned and fled down the hill, encountering other units, who promptly did likewise. The Jewish forces pursued them down to the plain killing more than 800 men.

After this great victory, the name of Judas 'even reached the king's ears, and among the nations there was talk of Judas and his battles' (1 Maccabees 3:26).

Judas Maccabaeus: after Beth-Horon

The defeat at Beth-Horon further undermined the Seleucid position in Jerusalem and forced the authorities to ask Ptolemy, governor of Coele-Syria, for help. At that time, Antiochus IV was preparing for a campaign against the Parthians in the east. He set out in 165 BC, leaving behind Lysias, one of his relatives, as viceroy. Lysias was given half of the Seleucid army and ordered to suppress the Jews. He left the organisation of the campaign to Ptolemy, who appointed Nicanor as commander of 'an international force of at least twenty thousand men' (2 Maccabees 8:9). Gorgias, an experienced general, was made second-in-command.

The commanders, to avoid their predecessors' mistake of getting trapped in the mountains while on the march, marched to Emmaus, in the Judaean foothills, and set up camp. Judas, meanwhile, mustered all his forces at Mizpah, a few miles from Jerusalem, and waited for the Seleucids to make their next move. Gorgias decided to make a surprise attack on the Jewish forces. He set out under cover of darkness with 5,000 foot soldiers and 1,000 cavalry, while Nicanor remained at Emmaus with the rest of the army.

The Jewish scouts, however, reported Gorgias' movements, and Judas decided to play the Seleucids at their own game. He marched his forces towards Emmaus by a different route. When Gorgias reached Judas' camp at Mizpah, he found it deserted. Wrongly believing that the Jews had fled, he began searching for them in the mountains. Judas' army reached Emmaus at daybreak and soon the enemy troops advanced to join battle. Then 'Judas' men sounded the trumpet and engaged them. The gentiles were defeated and fled towards the plain and all the stragglers fell by the sword' (1 Maccabees 4:13–15).

After pursuing the enemy for some distance, Judas ordered a halt and the Jewish forces returned to Emmaus to deal with Gorgias. However, when Gorgias saw the Seleucid camp in flames and Judas' army drawn up for battle, he wisely avoided an engagement and withdrew to the plain of Philistia.

The reconstruction of subsequent events is problematic because they are described in the two books of Maccabees in different chronological order. Most scholars believe that it was shortly after Judas' victory at Emmaus that Lysias decided to intervene personally in the Jewish conflict. He marched from the south through Idumaea against Judaea and made the border fortress of Beth-Zur his base. Judas assembled his men and, when the two armies met, Lysias suffered an ignominious defeat.

The result of Judas' victorious campaigns seems to have been a revision of Seleucid policies. Lysias negotiated on behalf of the Jews and eventually Antiochus agreed to a compromise. The king's letter to the Jewish people (2 Maccabees 11:27–33) allowed them to 'make use of their own kind of food and their own laws' and granted amnesty to all rebels who returned home within 14 days. Judas then conquered Jerusalem (except for the Acra where the Seleucid forces were garrisoned), purified the Temple and on 14 December 164, reinstated the Temple cult.

Thus Judas achieved the restoration of freedom of worship for the Jews. The struggle, however, was far from over, and he and his successors fought many more battles in the face of changing power politics. It was not until after the death of Antiochus VII, in 129 BC, that Judaea became a more or less independent state and a real Hasmonaean dynasty began under John Hyrcanus, son of Judas' brother Simon.

The value of elephants in war was recognised after Alexander the Great's Indian campaign; thereafter, they played an important part in the wars of his successors.

Elephants could have a devastating effect in battle, particularly against cavalry, since they terrified horses unaccustomed to them. The Seleucids used elephants in one of their later battles against Judas Maccabaeus, which ended in defeat for the Jews.

'These animals were distributed among the phalanxes . . . on each elephant, to protect it, was a stout wooden tower . . . with its three combatants as well as its mahout' (1 Maccabees 6:35, 37).

Judas Maccabaeus' campaigns 166–164 BC

Before the battle of Beth-Horon, Apollonius, commander of the administrative district of Samaria, led the first attack against the Jews in 166 BC. His route probably took him from Samaria to Shechem and then south through the mountains, 1. Judas marched to meet him and battle ensued somewhere north of the Judaean border, 2. Judas scored a great victory in which Apollonius was killed.

The rise and fall of the Hasmonaean dynasty

The history of the Hasmonaean dynasty is known mainly from information in the books of the Jewish historian Josephus and those of the classical writers. John Hyrcanus I (134–104 BC) consolidated and extended Hasmonaean rule. At his death, he left a state comprising Judaea, Samaria, Idumaea, many cities on the coastal plain and parts of Transjordan.

During his reign, John Hyrcanus clashed with the Pharisees, who found his dual role as high priest and secular ruler unacceptable. He therefore joined the Sadducees, the party of the old priestly nobility. His two sons, Aristobulus I (104–103) and Alexander Jannaeus (103–76), succeeded him in turn.

Conflict with the Pharisees degenerated into civil war. When Alexander Jannaeus gained the upper hand, 800 insurgents were crucified. Alexander extended the Hasmonaean state eastwards at the expense of the Nabataeans. His widow and successor, Salome Alexandra (76–67), made peace with the Pharisees and enjoyed a tranquil reign. At her death, civil war broke out between her two sons, and the elder, Hyrcanus, was forced to abdicate in favour of his brother, Aristobulus II (67–63). Hyrcanus, encouraged by Antipater, the rebellious governor of Idumaea, fled to Petra and enlisted the aid of the Nabataeans. Aristobulus became besieged in Jerusalem and both sides appealed to Rome, which had annexed Syria in 64/63.

In the autumn of 63, Pompey moved on Jerusalem and brought it under Roman control. Hyrcanus became high priest – but not king – of a much reduced Jewish state and was made tributary to Rome. Antipater's son, Herod, finally destroyed the dynasty by having Aristobulus's son, Antigonus, beheaded in 37 and by killing most of the surviving Hasmonaeans.

During the Maccabaean period, the Nabataeans, a trading people of Arabian origin, controlled southern Transjordan. They suffered from Hasmonaean expansionist policies and were involved in the struggle for the control of Judaea.

Important caravan routes converged at their capital Petra, in the mountains east of the Wadi Arabah. Petra's most remarkable monuments are the tombs cut out of rock, such as the one *above*, with elaborate façades carved into the beautifully coloured Nubian sandstone.

The greatest achievement of the Nabataeans was their system of water control, a skill vital to survival in their desert homeland.

☐ Seleucids
☐ Maccabaeans

Judas' third encounter with the Seleucids brought him a great victory. Nicanor's troops marched down the coastal plain, then inland to Emmaus, **3**, where they set up camp. While Gorgias tried to make a surprise attack on the Jewish camp at Mizpah, **4**, Judas unexpectedly moved to Emmaus and routed the main army, **5**.

Lysias, whom Antiochus had left in control of Coele-Syria, personally commanded the fourth attempt to crush the rebel forces. He marched down the coastal plain, then round through Idumaea and moved against Judaea from the south, **6**. Judas advanced to attack him and the armies engaged near the border fortress of Beth-Zur, **7**. The Seleucid forces were routed and Lysias withdrew.

The books of Christianity

The New Testament is a volume of early Christian writings that tells the story of the New Covenant between God and the new people of God – the Church. It centres on the life and teaching of Jesus of Nazareth and his sacrificial death. For Christians, Jesus fulfilled the expectation expressed in Jewish scriptures that the 'Messiah' (meaning 'the anointed') would come to deliver the Children of Israel. 'Christ' comes from the Greek word for 'Messiah' and became Jesus' title.

The great events of the New Testament are the crucifixion and resurrection of Jesus: on these the Christian faith was founded. But others were also preserved as equally important such as Jesus' birth, his baptism, episodes of his preaching and teaching, his healing acts, his confrontations with the authorities and his last entry into Jerusalem.

Other great events recorded are the growth of the Church, the day of Pentecost, the conversion of Paul from persecutor to Christian, his long and sometimes dangerous journeys, his arrest and also the extraordinary vision of John that concludes the New Testament. And there are events that form a backdrop to the writings, such as the Great Fire of Rome, the Jewish uprising against Rome and the sack of Jerusalem by the Romans.

The New Testament begins with the 'Gospel' (meaning 'good news') of Jesus' ministry, execution and his rising from the dead. This Gospel has four versions attributed to the evangelists Matthew, Mark, Luke and John. Many think that each Gospel was based on traditions associated with the Churches in one of the great cities, perhaps Matthew with Antioch, Mark with Rome, Luke with Caesarea and John with Ephesus.

The first three ('synoptic') Gospels are closely related to one another. The fourth, John's Gospel, differs from the others, being more spiritual and also more political. A Gospel is not a biography; it is much more like a written sermon or call to faith. The four accounts say little or nothing about the first 30 years of Jesus' life and do not even describe his appearance. Much of their text consists of sayings, or stories of healing, or confrontations, preserved within the Church for different reasons. But each is shaped by one person with interests of his own. All contain a full account of the Passion of Jesus.

After the Gospel accounts stands the Acts of the Apostles, written by the author of the third Gospel, Luke, which tells of the early Church and how it spread beyond the Jews to the gentiles, largely through Paul, a convert.

There then follow 21 letters. Thirteen traditionally bear the name of Paul, seven the names of other Christian leaders, and one is anonymous. It was quite common in the ancient world to attach to a document the name of a well-known figure, and not everyone believes that all these letters were penned or dictated by Paul, Peter or the others. Few, though, would now doubt that a solid block of letters written by Paul himself has survived.

Finally, there is the strange visionary book known as Revelation or Apocalypse, which starts from a sometimes scathing account of several of the Seven Churches of Asia (see p.188), and goes on to a series of visions of conflict and glory.

One scholar has argued that all the New Testament was written by AD 70. Most scholars would place some books between 70 and 100. One or two of the books may have been written in the early second century. There were other Christian writings not in the New Testament. Some are lost; Paul certainly wrote other letters. There were other Gospels but they did not seriously challenge the officially recognised, or canonical, four. By the end of the second century, the main canon was fixed, though not without some disagreement.

Jesus spoke Aramaic, though living in the area known as 'the Galilee', he would have known some Greek. The New Testament was written in Greek; it was translated into Latin in the second century. The documents would have been originally written on papyrus which is thin and fragile. Copies would be made on papyrus, so that they could be circulated more widely.

A few fragments of the New Testament on papyrus survive from the second century, though no very long passage. From the time when Christianity was accepted by Constantine in the fourth century, the best text which could be obtained was written on vellum (a durable sheepskin preparation). The Codex Sinaiticus in the British Library is one of these. From then on, especially in the Middle Ages, literally thousands of manuscripts survive, some exquisitely illustrated, some showing carelessness in copying. The first printed Greek text was published in 1516.

Modern scholars provide us with a text which is as reliable as possible. They have experience in knowing the sorts of mistakes that copyists make, copying by dictation or from capital letters or cursive script. In addition to the early and more reliable manuscripts, scholars use quotations in early Christian writers and some of the early translations into Latin, Syriac or Coptic to try to establish an authentic text, though there are still minor points on which there can be no certainty.

οι ϊουδαιοι ημε ιν ουκ εξεστιν αποκτειναι
ουδενα ϊνα ο λογος του ιησου πληρωθη ον ει
πεν σημαινων ποιω θανατω ημελλεν απο

ЄΡΧЄ
ΤΑΙΟΙϹΚΑΙΛΑΜΒΑ
ΝΕΙΤΟΝΑΡΤΟΝΚΑΙ
ΔΙΔΦϹΙΝΑΥΤΟΙϹ
ΤΟΟΨΑΡΙΟΝΟΜΟΙ
ΦϹ·

An extant portion (highlit) of Greek papyrus, *top*, dating from the first half of the 2nd century AD comprises part of John 18:31 and 32. Papyrus, now almost extinct in Egypt, is a sedge, the stem of which was used to produce a writing material.

Part of John 21:23 from the Codex Sinaiticus, *above*, discovered in 1844 in St Catherine's monastery on Mount Sinai. This 4th-century Biblical manuscript is one of the earliest written in Greek on vellum. The codex, or book, was typical of major Christian documents by the time of Constantine (d.336), replacing the scrolls familiar from Judaism.

**Monogram from
the Book of Kells**,
an illuminated
manuscript of the
Gospels in Latin,
probably written in
the 8th century.

Rome takes over Judaea

In the second century BC, the Maccabees (pp.124–7), in revolt against their Greek rulers and fighting off a threat from Syria, had allied with Rome, at that time an expanding military power. For almost a century they enjoyed virtual independence. But there developed a rift, religious and political, between two powerful factions: the Pharisees and the Sadducees (see pp.156–7). In Jerusalem, Queen Alexandra appointed her elder son Hyrcanus high priest with Pharisee support. The Sadducees backed the younger brother Aristobulus, who, on his mother's death, took over with an army. Hyrcanus won the support of Herod the Great's father, Antipater, who backed him with an army and succeeded in blockading Aristobulus in the Temple.

At Rome, Cn. Pompeius Magnus (106–48 BC), having illegally been consul in 70, was appointed, with popular support and senatorial reluctance, to a series of exceptional military commands. A brilliant operation freed the eastern Mediterranean from piracy. He defeated the dangerous Mithradates, king of Pontus; annexed Syria; established buffer-states, including Armenia; and founded or restored some 40 cities.

The independence of Judaea was doomed – the fraternal quarrel was the pretext for Roman intervention. Both brothers appealed to Pompey who eventually sided with Hyrcanus. Aristobulus's supporters did not give way, and in 63 Pompey stormed the Temple enclosure, although he left the Temple itself unharmed. Pompey left Hyrcanus with the pseudo-independence of a client 'ethnarchy', which, a few years later, was split into five districts. Eventually, out of a period of some chaos, an able usurper named Herod (the 'Great') was established as client-king in 40 BC.

Meantime, Julius Caesar was expanding Roman rule north-westwards. He clashed with Pompey and won, emerging to sole power in 49 BC. His assassination in 44 BC led to further chaos and civil war, until in 31 BC his great-nephew and heir Octavian Caesar, better known by his later title Augustus, was left in control.

Augustus was careful to retain the image of republican government, with the reality of autocratic power. His powers were individually legitimate, but accumulated and permanent. By the end of his long life in AD 14, he had established an

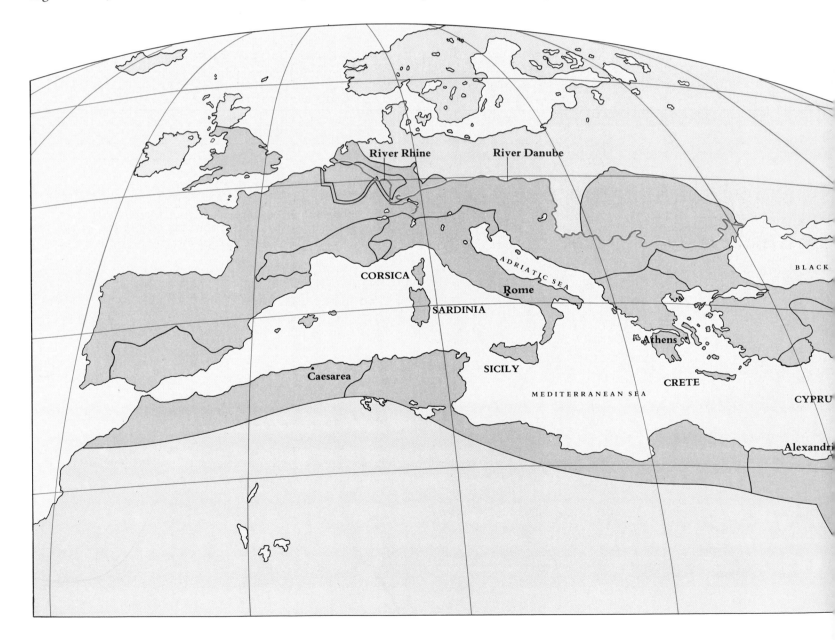

empire. He took personal control of the armies and half the provinces, satisfied the old aristocracy by giving them some control of the other half, and kept the commons quiet by beneficent paternalism.

Rome, a ruthless military conqueror, on the whole governed by consent. By the beginning of the first century AD, the whole of North Africa from Egypt to the Atlantic was policed by one legion (which had a nominal number of 6,000 men). The Romans had an extraordinary facility for assimilating new leaders from North Italy, Spain, Africa, Asia or the Balkans. They kept genuine local loyalties with the promise of Roman citizenship (extended by AD 212 or 214 to virtually all free subjects). Rome, in fact, gave to a larger area of the globe a longer period of untroubled peace than at any time in history, either before or since.

Judaea, however, was Rome's greatest failure. On Herod's death in 4 BC, the client-kingdom was again subdivided. This did not work, and in AD 6 it was brought into direct Roman rule under a special imperial officer called a 'prefect'. In 41 it became again a client-kingdom, but in 44 reverted to direct rule under procurators. Nothing could stave off the disastrous uprising of 66. After the fall of Jerusalem in 70 (see pp. 182–4), the province was governed by legates.

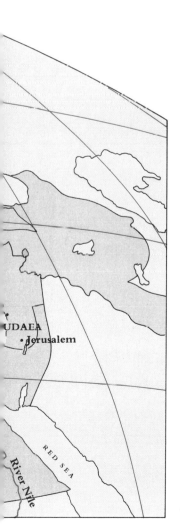

The world into which Jesus was born was dominated by the Roman empire. This map shows the empire at its greatest extent in AD 117. Rome, originally a group of villages, developed into a city in the 6th century BC and slowly gained dominance over the whole of Italy. Rome achieved this with its disciplined army, its diplomatic skill and its generosity in granting citizenship to all those living under its control.

In 264 BC, Rome became involved in the first of the three Punic Wars with Carthage, then the leading power in the western Mediterranean. Despite its terrible defeat at the hands of Hannibal at Cannae in 216 BC, Rome eventually emerged victorious. Carthage was finally destroyed in 146 BC and the western Mediterranean – Sicily, Corsica, Sardinia, Spain and modern Tunisia – fell under Roman control.

The Roman empire, meanwhile, had come into conflict with the Hellenistic kingdoms of the eastern Mediterranean. In the second century BC the Jews under the Maccabees (see pp. 124–7) rose in revolt against their Greek rulers and, fighting off threats from Syria, allied themselves with the expanding Roman empire. For almost a century they enjoyed virtual independence.

Political and religious rifts between the Jewish sects of the Pharisees and the Sadducees led to Roman intervention. Out of the chaos emerged an able usurper, Herod the Great, who was established by the Romans as client-king in 40 BC.

Administrators of the empire

Rome and its empire was administered by officials, and the holders of each rank were charged with specific responsibilities. A *consul*, for example, was one of two magistrates, elected annually, who shared the supreme civil and military power after the kings had been ousted. Under the empire, the office continued although sometimes for part of the year only. The future emperor Vespasian was consul in AD 51, the historian Tacitus in 97. A *proconsul* was an ex-consul holding governorship and command of armies overseas 'in place of the consul'. The emperor always held proconsular power, giving him command of the army.

A *praetor* was a Roman magistrate concerned with administering the law; a *propraetor* was an ex-praetor holding non-military office. Strictly, an *imperator* was the commander of armies, but the term was later applied to the emperor in his capacity as commander-in-chief.

A legionary commander was termed *legatus*. In provinces with only one legion, he was also the provincial governor; in other provinces the legate was subject to the governor. A *praefectus* was one set in charge of various military and civil duties, such as the prefect of the watch and the prefect of the grain supply. The *praefectus urbi* was a senator, responsible for order in the city of Rome; Pontius Pilate was prefect of Judaea.

A *procurator* was a representative or agent. Under the empire, an *eques*, that is a rich non-aristocrat, governed a minor province, such as Judaea. He was a finance officer in a major province and the emperor's representative in a senatorial province.

Herod the Great, servant of Rome

For 40 years, Jewish history was dominated by Herod the Great. He was born in about 73 BC, the son of the Idumaean Antipater, and became a Roman citizen in 47. His father appointed him military governor of Galilee, with the task of clearing the region of terrorists.

In 41, Antony made Herod and his brother tetrarchs, but Herod was not secure and in 40 fled to Rome. There Antony bestowed on him the kingship of Judaea, which he secured with a Roman army in 37. Octavian (the future emperor Augustus) defeated Antony and Cleopatra at the naval battle of Actium in 31, but confirmed Herod in power.

Herod worked assiduously for Rome and retained Augustus's favour. His court was Hellenised and cultured. He founded the Greek cities of Sebaste (Samaria) and Caesarea, with its fine port. He built fortresses and palaces, including Masada, and a magnificent new temple. He also presided at the Olympic Games.

His family life, however, was unhappy. He ruled as an autocrat, supported by police, and, despite his rebuilding of the Temple, to the Jews he remained a detested foreigner. He died in 4 BC at the age of 69.

The first Christmas

The birth of Jesus, the event that ultimately was to change the face of the world through the Christian religion, is shrouded in mystery. Although the traditional events relating to Jesus' birth are well known to Christians, it is not possible to be certain about its exact time or the circumstances surrounding it.

According to Matthew Joseph was going to divorce Mary, to whom he was engaged, because she was pregnant, but was told in a dream that her child had been conceived by the Holy Spirit and should be named Jesus (meaning 'Yahweh saves'). So he took her into his home but abstained from sexual intercourse; later, the child was born.

Next, so Matthew relates, comes the story of the Magi. Jesus was born in Bethlehem in the reign of Herod the Great. The Magi, possibly astrologers from the east, came asking to see the infant king of the Jews, whose star they had seen in the sky. Herod was perturbed, as well he might be: *he* was king of the Jews. His advisers told him that the Messiah, the awaited deliverer of the Jews, would be born in Bethlehem.

The Magi set out for Bethlehem, and saw the star halt over the house where the baby was. They offered gifts of gold, frankincense and myrrh. Joseph was warned in a dream to escape to Egypt. Herod, furious because the Magi did not return to him as he had requested, tried to get rid of a potential rival by killing all the young male children in the vicinity.

Luke starts his narrative, during Herod's reign, from John the Baptist, and tells how the angel Gabriel proclaimed Mary's destiny to her. Mary visited her pregnant cousin Elizabeth and there sang the 'Magnificat', a song about the reversal of human values through the greatness of God (Luke 1:46–55). In due time, Elizabeth gave birth to John the Baptist.

Luke's second chapter deals with the birth of Jesus. The emperor Augustus decreed a census. Quirinius, governor of Syria, had to carry it out. Everyone had to move to his original family home, Joseph going from Nazareth to Bethlehem. Because the inn was crowded, Mary, suddenly in labour, had to lay her new-born infant in a manger. In the fields outside, shepherds had a vision of angels directing them to the birth of the Messiah in Bethlehem and singing in praise of God, and hurried off to find the baby.

On strict historical evidence, it has to be said that there is no certainty as to what actually happened. Some of the problems are as follows. Mark, probably the oldest Gospel, John, probably the latest, and Paul, say nothing at all about Jesus' birth. Matthew sets the events in Herod's reign. Herod died in 4 BC. Luke places them when Quirinius was governor of Syria: he took office in AD 6. Luke also associates them with a census.

There was a famous and unpopular census in AD 6 as part of the Roman takeover of Palestine. There is no record of an earlier census, and a Roman census during Herod's reign in a client-kingdom scarcely would have been possible. Neither is there any historical record of the Romans moving people to their ancestral homes, a fairly chaotic process, for a census.

In Matthew, the child seems to be born in Joseph's home, though the narrative goes on to identify Bethlehem as the birthplace. In Luke, the home is Nazareth, the birthplace Bethlehem. The two offer different family trees, both through Joseph. Matthew emphasises the fulfilment of prophecy. The virgin birth is to fulfil Isaiah 7:14. The birth in Bethlehem is to fulfil Micah 5:1. The flight into Egypt is to fulfil Numbers 23:22 where the original reference is to the Exodus of Israel. The Massacre of the Innocents (Herod's killing the infants) is to fulfil Jeremiah 31:15.

There is no early tradition of the date of Jesus' birth, and no widely celebrated festival documented before the fourth century. Early in the third century, Clement of Alexandria records a tradition that Jesus was born on 20 May.

The first use of 25 December as Christmas Day dates from Rome in the year 336. To the pagan Romans, it was the birthday of the 'Unconquered Sun'. The emperor Constantine's family had worshipped the sun; his vision of the cross came to him from the sun. It was easy to transfer the festival to the Sun of Righteousness. Under St Peter's in Rome, Jesus was pictured driving the chariot of the sun through the sky.

In the East, Christmas was long celebrated on 6 January, and in the Armenian Church still is. More generally this is Epiphany, the appearance of Christ to the Magi – symbolically the gentiles who represent the world outside Judaism.

Matthew tells of a star which guided the Magi. The star of Bethlehem has attracted many theories. Some people have thought that Halley's Comet (visible in 12 BC) may have been the star; the astronomer Johannes Kepler proposed a conjunction of the planets Jupiter and Saturn in 7 BC.

Whatever the exact events, it is certain that Jesus was born of a human mother, Mary. That peasants and intellectuals, Jews and gentiles, may have been the first celebrants of the birth of a different sort of king from Herod and a different sort of authority from Rome, remains significant.

The shepherds of Bethlehem
The fields of Bethlehem look today much as they did when the shepherds saw the Lord's angel. 'In the countryside close by there were shepherds . . . keeping guard over the sheep during the watches of the night. An angel of the Lord stood over them and the glory of the Lord shone around them. They were terrified, but the angel said, "Do not be afraid. Look, I bring you news of great joy, a joy to be shared by the whole people. Today in the town of David a Saviour has been born to you; he is Christ the Lord. And here is a sign for you: you will find a baby wrapped in swaddling clothes and lying in a manger." And all at once with the angel there was a great throng of the hosts of heaven, praising God with the words: "Glory to God in the highest heaven, and on earth peace for those he favours"' (Luke 2:8–14).

+SCS BALTHASSAR +SCS MELCHIOR +SCS GASPAR

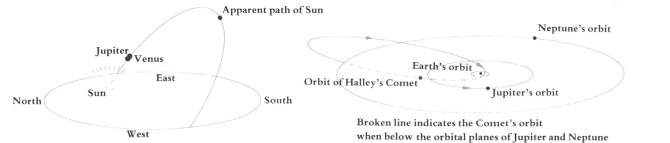

Apparent path of Sun

Jupiter
Venus

East

North

Sun

South

West

Neptune's orbit

Earth's orbit

Orbit of Halley's Comet

Jupiter's orbit

**Broken line indicates the Comet's orbit
when below the orbital planes of Jupiter and Neptune**

An hour and twenty minutes before sunrise on 12 August 3 BC, the planet Jupiter rose in conjunction with Venus, the 'morning star', *above*. This planetary alignment would have created a blazing light in the sky. Jupiter, considered astrologically 'Father of the Gods', when conjoined with Venus could well have been

interpreted as heralding the birth of a king, since Venus is the goddess of fertility.

Also of possible significance to the nativity story is the fact, noted by an American scholar, E.L. Martin, that Jupiter was stationary in the heavens on 25 December 2 BC, having reached its orbital point for retrogression (a

change in its direction of movement). It would also have been in the direction of Bethlehem from Jerusalem. This, he thinks was the date of the Epiphany.

The appearance of Halley's Comet has often been taken as a heavenly portent or omen – for example, it was visible from England in 1066 in the weeks immediately preceding the Battle of Hastings.

Some people have thought that the star seen by the Magi might have been Halley's Comet but astronomers now calculate that it would

have appeared in 12 BC. This date is too early to coincide with the nativity, though there may have been a folk-memory of its appearance in the latter part of Herod's reign, and an assumption that such a spectacular appearance must have heralded Jesus's birth.

An intricate 6th-century mosaic, *top*, of the Magi adorns a wall of the church of Sant' Apollinare Nuovo, Ravenna. In western tradition, there were three Magi. The English historian Bede (d. AD 735) gives their names as Balthassar, Melchior and Gaspar.

Growing up in Nazareth

According to Luke, Jesus' public ministry began when he was about 30 years of age (3:23). But of Jesus' early childhood there is very little in the Gospels except for a fleeting glimpse provided by Luke in the story of the 12-year-old Jesus questioning the doctors of Law in the Temple (2:41–52). Jesus' parents, Mary and Joseph, are presented as faithful Israelites. Thus Jesus was nurtured in simple Jewish piety, first through his home, then through the synagogue, and also by occasional visits to the major festivals in Jerusalem.

Nazareth, where Jesus grew up, was an insignificant agricultural village. However, judging by Jesus' gentle and loving nature, his childhood in Nazareth must have been a happy one. Certainly, it would have provided him with material for the imagery he used in his parables and other teaching, for example, the lilies and the sparrows, the foxes, the lost sheep, the oxen's yoke and the absentee landlord.

The typical dwelling of Jesus' time would have consisted of a small group of rooms around a central courtyard, with the roof sometimes being used as a second storey. The typical family of this period would include the father and the mother, the first-born son and his family along with other, unmarried, children. They would live close to and perhaps share the same courtyard as other married sons and their families. This is indicated in the case of Simon Peter, where his mother-in-law lives in his house, a house in which his own family as well as that of Andrew his brother also live (Mark 1:29, Matthew 8:14, Luke 4:38).

The extended family setting helps to explain some of the debate concerning Jesus' immediate family circle. When Jesus returned as an adult to preach in the synagogue in Nazareth, he was poorly received because he was known to be a carpenter (or possibly the son of a carpenter), the son of Mary and brother of James, Joseph, Judas and Simon. His sisters were also present. It is unclear whether these are full brothers and sisters or whether they are half-brothers and sisters or perhaps only his cousins. Jesus' poor reception was by no means universal. The common people heard him gladly.

Although there is no record of his having any formal rabbinic education such as Paul received under Gamaliel, Jesus' disciples treated him like a rabbi; at times, even the scribes, the official theologians, acknowledged the depth of his understanding of the Law. There is a strong emphasis in the Gospels on Jesus and his disciples teaching the crowds, as well as on Jesus teaching his own disciples.

How a carpenter would obtain this knowledge is difficult to discern. It is known that from about 60 BC, due to the influence of Rabbi Joshua ben Gamala, there had been a concerted effort to educate all Jewish children by appointing teachers for them in every district. These schools were designed to educate Jewish children in their own traditions and thereby minimise foreign influences upon them. The synagogue was certainly a place of reading and induction in the scriptures. Luke says that Jesus went there 'as was his custom' on the Sabbath. It is also known that when Jesus grew up, he became part of the renewal movement led by John and was subsequently baptised by him.

The best clues to the source of Jesus' knowledge are probably those which Luke offers. John, and likewise Jesus, through the piety of humble and faithful believers in Israel as well as through the official channels of teaching and worship, became heirs to a rich heritage of spirituality transmitted down the centuries.

Nazareth, *left*, was, in Jesus' time, a village not far from the Via Maris, a major trade route to Egypt. The village probably had a population of up to 2,000 people. That it was of no great importance is clear from Nathaniel's retort in John's Gospel: 'Can anything good come out of that place?' (1:46).

Jesus was a boy when Judas of Gamala rebelled against Rome and captured Sepphoris, a few miles from Nazareth. The Romans razed the town and crucified the rebels along the road. The boy Jesus must have seen the smoke and the crosses.

As loyal Jews, Jesus' family went each year to the Passover festival in Jerusalem. The 12-year-old Jesus went with them. When they were returning home with a large group of friends, it was presumed that Jesus was part of the company. When he was missed, they had to search for him and after retracing their steps, they eventually found him, among the teachers in the Temple. This 12th-century painting, *left*, from the ceiling of St Martin's church, at Zillis in Switzerland, shows Jesus listening to the teachers and asking them questions. When Jesus was scolded by Mary for the alarm he had caused them, he is reported to have answered: 'Did you not know that I must be in my Father's house?' (Luke 2:49). The significance of this story, as of the rest of the stories of Jesus' birth and childhood in Luke, is that Jesus is here depicted as a pious Israelite in direct continuity with the 'humble pious poor' in Israel, who were waiting for the visitation of God to deliver Israel.

The role of the synagogue

Jewish community synagogues, such as the one, *above*, excavated at Capernaum, are strongly attested in the Gospels. There are frequent references to Jesus preaching and discussing with Jewish leaders and congregations (Matthew 4:23, 9:25; Mark 1:21, 3:1–6; Luke 4:16, 13:10). Some scholars see this emphasis on synagogues as reflecting the post-70 AD situation after the destruction of the Temple by the Romans (see pp.180–3). But synagogues did exist at this time both in Palestine and in the Diaspora. Josephus, the Jewish historian of the late first century, refers to a few synagogues in the north of the Holy Land. Philo, the first-century Egyptian Jewish scholar, attests the presence of numerous synagogues in Alexandria.

At Capernaum, a white limestone building was, as early as 1838, identified as a synagogue. The excavation of 1981 has confirmed that underlying the third-century limestone building are the ruins of a first-century basalt building. This may in fact have been the very synagogue in which Jesus preached.

In Palestine, prior to the destruction of the Temple, the synagogue would have been one of several indigenous organisations in Jewish villages or cities. It may not at first have been specifically built or easily identified as a place of worship. People may have met to read scripture and to pray in the larger houses or even out of doors. Archaeological evidence suggests that, prior to the third century, it was customary to modify existing structures rather than create a new building.

The synagogues were used to teach the young, to house visitors and for communal meals. Philo, Josephus and the New Testament demonstrate that the Bible was interpreted to the people in the synagogues. The Shema and the Amidah or Eighteen Benedictions, important Jewish prayers, were already in use at this period in synagogues.

Baptised in the River Jordan

John the Baptist, described in Mark 1:6 as wearing 'a garment of camel-skin' and as living on 'locusts and wild honey', is said by the Gospels to have baptised Jesus in the River Jordan in Judaea. The Greek text does not indicate the exact manner of baptism, but it is likely that it involved full immersion. Mark's Gospel says that as Jesus '. . . was coming up out of the water, he saw the heavens torn apart and the Spirit, like a dove, descending on him' (1:10).

The great prophets of the Old Testament had visions associated with their call to preach (e.g. Isaiah 6), and, at his baptism, Jesus too was called to fulfil his vocation: 'And a voice came from heaven, "You are my Son, the Beloved; my favour rests on you"' (Mark 1:11). The heavenly voice uses words from Psalm 2 and Isaiah 42; the latter also speaks of God's Spirit coming upon the chosen one.

Jesus' vocation, according to Mark, was to fulfil his destiny as the Messiah, foretold in the prophecies. The coming of the Spirit was a sign of his being anointed king in the royal line of David. But Jesus' submission to John's baptism of repentance raised questions for some early Christians. Luke plays down the event, focusing on the endorsement from heaven.

In Matthew, John hesitates to baptise Jesus, but Jesus suggests that John accept the situation, because 'it is fitting that we should, in this way, do all that uprightness demands'. This may mean that Jesus was identifying himself with the people and their being purified for the 'new world'.

Paul associates baptism with dying and rising with Christ (Romans 6). For Christians, baptism became the rite of initiation in which they put off the old man and put on the new: '. . . for anyone who is in Christ, there is a new creation' (2 Corinthians 5:17). In two of his sayings, Jesus too seems to connect baptism with his death. In Luke, Jesus says: 'There is a baptism I must still receive, and what constraint I am under until it is completed!' (12:50); and in Mark he asks the disciples: 'Can you . . . be baptised with the baptism with which I shall be baptised?' (10:39). Interestingly, Christians later spoke of martyrdom as a 'baptism of blood'.

One interesting question is whether Jesus himself baptised others. In John 3:26, there is a suggestion that Jesus was running a baptism ministry parallel to John's and that some were jealous because he was doing better than John, though this is contradicted by John 4:2. If Jesus' ministry began alongside John's and then took a different direction, it might explain John's changing view of Jesus in the Gospels. Matthew's Gospel (11:3) suggests that John had come to be puzzled by Jesus' identity. But the baptism stories suggest that he recognised immediately who Jesus was.

In John's Gospel, there is no account of the event of Jesus' baptism as such: all that happens is that the Baptist witnesses to Jesus. Also, whereas the other Gospels accept John as being identified with Elijah, the forerunner of the Messiah, in John's Gospel, the Baptist disowns the titles Christ, Elijah and the Prophet (1:21).

John's Gospel, then, emphasises the subordination of the Baptist to Jesus. There is some evidence that there was a rival Baptist movement working alongside the early Church, seeing John the Baptist as the Prophet-Messiah, Elijah. Perhaps John's Gospel is concerned to play down the possibility that Jesus and John led two competing Messianic movements.

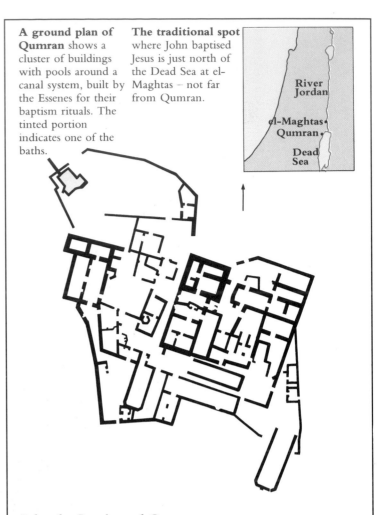

A ground plan of Qumran shows a cluster of buildings with pools around a canal system, built by the Essenes for their baptism rituals. The tinted portion indicates one of the baths.

The traditional spot where John baptised Jesus is just north of the Dead Sea at el-Maghtas – not far from Qumran.

John the Baptist and Qumran

The Gospels suggest that John was an ascetic who came from the Judaean wilderness to preach and to baptise in the River Jordan. It is possible that John was connected with the Qumran monastery (see pp.186–7). Baths for ritual purification have been found there, and the Dead Sea scrolls show that ritual bathing was practised by the Qumran community.

The scrolls reveal a group dedicated to the fulfilment of the prophecies and to belief in the coming of God's kingdom. It was for this that John prepared the people by repentance and baptism. One of the scrolls, the *Community Rule*, concerning entry into the community, refers to a rite in which the flesh is sprinkled with purifying water. Another scroll, the *Manual of Discipline*, talks of the expiation of iniquity 'through practising justice and through the anguish of the refining fire'. All this seems close to what John was proclaiming.

However, a connection with Qumran does not altogether account for John's form of baptism. The monastery's rites of purification, including the initiatory rite, seem to have been repeated every year, whereas John baptised people once only. In that respect, John's baptism resembles the baptism for proselytes (converts to Judaism), who had to submit to a purificatory rite before being circumcised. John, however, baptised those who were already Jews.

John seems to have used baptism as a natural symbol of washing away the old sinful life and to proclaim the need to prepare urgently for the coming of God's judgement and the establishment of his kingdom.

John according to Josephus

In addition to the Gospel stories, Josephus, the Jewish historian, records John the Baptist's activities and his execution by Herod Antipas. Josephus presents John as a philosopher-teacher of the kind who roamed the Graeco-Roman world. The Gospels, however, depict John as heralding the coming of the Messiah, preparing the people for the final judgement. They are likely to be nearer the truth, for Herod would not have been so anxious to get rid of a harmless philosopher as he would someone with a Messianic message who could be a potent political threat.

Josephus himself hints at this when he comments that Herod was afraid that John's influence might provoke a revolt. If the followers of the Baptist did form a rival movement alongside the early Church, it is possible that John himself was a Messianic claimant. Whether or not this is so, he appears to have taken on the role of a prophet and proclaimed the imminence of judgement: 'Even now the axe is being laid to the root of the trees; so that any tree failing to produce good fruit will be cut down and thrown on the fire' (Matthew 3:10).

To escape this fate, the people are urged to repent and be baptised. There is also to be a baptism of the Holy Spirit and fire by the coming Messiah. Luke agrees with Matthew in reporting this judgemental message but adds John's teaching, which seems to assimilate John's message to that of Jesus and is probably, therefore, less reliable than Matthew's.

Mark shows no interest in John's teaching, but he does include a vivid, non-political account of his fate. Herod is depicted as fascinated and awed by John, who was imprisoned at the instigation of his wife, Herodias; John had denounced her marriage to Herod because she had once been the wife of Herod's brother Philip. The Queen engineered John's death by taking advantage of Herod's rash promise to reward her daughter Salome's dancing with anything she requested: Salome's request was John's head on a platter (Mark 6).

Josephus does not mention Salome's dancing and Herod's fatal promise but he does say that John was imprisoned and killed, a victim of Herod's suspicion (*Antiquities* XVIII: 116–19).

A 5th-century mosaic in the Arians' Baptistery, Ravenna, showing the baptism of Jesus by John in the River Jordan. The spirit of God descends on Jesus in the form of a dove, watched by a white-haired old man – the classical personification of the river.

Tempted by Satan

Immediately after Jesus was baptised by John the Baptist and heard the heavenly voice calling to him, the first three Gospels record that he went into the desert, led by the Spirit. He stayed there 40 days, and experienced a period of spiritual testing. Matthew speaks initially of the 'tester' coming to him; Mark names him Satan; Luke calls him 'the devil'. The event is important and of special interest because knowledge of it can have come only from Jesus himself.

Mark does not spell out the tests or temptations. Matthew and Luke speak of three, but place them in a different order. In Matthew's order, the first test was: 'If you are Son of God, tell these stones to turn into loaves' (4:3), and indeed the desert stones would have resembled round loaves of bread.

In the second, Jesus was taken to the parapet of the Temple, to be told: 'If you are Son of God, throw yourself down' (4:6) with a quotation from Psalm 91 apparently guaranteeing his security. In the third, from a very high mountain, he saw all the kingdoms of the world and their splendour, and heard the words: 'I will give you all these if you fall at my feet and do me homage' (Matthew 4:9).

To each of these tests, Jesus answered with a verse from Deuteronomy, each time asserting the total sovereignty of God, at the last dismissing the tempter with the words 'Away with you, Satan!'

It is not necessary to picture a visible 'devil' or miraculous transportation to Jerusalem or to some supra-terrestrial peak to grasp the severity of the tests for Jesus. A voice within and a clear imagination do not make the tests less real. Yet it is curiously hard to pinpoint exactly what Jesus was tempted to do, except that each test meant the use of his powers in ways that were not God's.

The first test is usually thought to be about the selfish use of superhuman powers to satisfy hunger. But Jesus' answer, 'Human beings live not on bread alone but on every word that comes from the mouth of God' (Matthew 4:4), is wider: it links his 40 days with the Israelites' 40 years in the wilderness, and God's gift of manna (Exodus 16; Deuteronomy 8:3). It might even suggest that there are no short cuts. 'By the sweat of your face will you earn your food' is a word of God (Genesis 3:19).

The second test, on the parapet of the Temple, is usually taken to show Jesus being tempted to win the people over by showing superhuman power. Jesus later refused to use miracles to authenticate his identity (Mark 8:11–12).

But Jesus' reply, 'Do not put the Lord your God to the test' (Matthew 4:7), rather asserts that he is to trust in God without testing his power. And if he had used power in that way he would not have been 'one of us' (Hebrews 4:15).

The last test is in some ways the most interesting. The most obvious way to win the kingdoms of the world was by military conquest. The Jews were looking for a military Messiah to overwhelm the Romans. But Jesus came from the desert to teach love of the enemy (Matthew 5:44), and when Peter protested against his saying that the Son of Man was destined to suffer, he called Peter 'Satan' (Mark 8:33) precisely because he was renewing the temptation to achieve worldly power on terms not God's.

So Jesus, having passed through the tests to a clear vision of his calling, went out with a message of repentance, called his first followers, healed the suffering, and taught the way of God.

'Then Jesus was led by the spirit out into the desert to be put to the test by the devil' (MATTHEW 4:1). It was in terrain such as this Palestinian desert, where the stones resemble loaves of bread, that Jesus spent 40 days and nights in fasting and meditation.

'Human beings live not on bread alone . . .' (MATTHEW 4:4). A 12th-century ceiling painting in St Martin's church at Zillis, Switzerland, depicts Jesus' first temptation by the Devil. Jesus, famished after his long fast, rejected Satan's challenge to turn desert stones into loaves of bread (which they greatly resembled) because man lives 'not on bread alone but on every word that comes from the mouth of God'. Medieval art always depicted Satan with a loathsome appearance, his body often composed of parts of malevolent beasts, both real and imaginary.

The Devil: the ultimate opponent

Among the Jews in early times, the power of God was felt to be total. There was no evil power standing against him. The snake in the story of the Fall (Genesis 3:1) is not the Devil; that identification comes only later. Good and evil both came from God. For example, it was God who hardened Pharaoh's heart (Exodus 7:13) and sent an evil spirit on Saul (1 Samuel 19:9). But the prophets declared that God loved righteousness and hated iniquity. How then could he be responsible for evil?

The name Satan originally meant 'adversary' or 'opponent'. In Numbers 22:22, an angel of the Lord is sent to be a 'Satan' to Balaam. The idea of 'the Satan' as a kind of official accuser or tester appears in Zechariah 3:1, and, most familiarly, in Job, where he takes his place among the sons of God (1:6). It has been suggested that this Satan personified, as it were, the self-accusing conscience of Israel. The picture, *above*, is a depiction of Satan from a water-colour by William Blake.

Exiled in Babylon from 597 to 538 BC, the Jews encountered the idea of a cosmic conflict between the Babylonian god Marduk and Tiamat, the dragon of the sea. Then, among the Persians who liberated them from the Babylonians, the Jews found a doctrine of dualism: the Persian religion portrayed life as a battleground between Good Spirit (*Spenta Mainyu*) and Evil Spirit (*Angra Mainyu*) or Ahriman, even between Evil Spirit and the all-good God Ahura Mazda. The influence of this belief on the Jews became strong.

In the period between the Old and New Testaments, there developed the idea of a Satan who is man's opponent. From this emerged the picture of a Satan (or even Satans) who is God's opponent, and who became identified with the snake in Genesis.

In the New Testament, Satan retains the role of tester. But he appears as a mightier power, opposed to God's kingdom, as God's kingdom is opposed to him. The triumphs over the demons of disease are a defeat for Satan (Luke 10:18). The last book of the Bible, Revelation, reflecting the old Persian vision of a cosmic battle, tells of the conflict between God's champion Michael and 'the great dragon, the primeval serpent, known as the devil or Satan, who had led the world astray' (12:9).

The calling of the disciples

The Gospel tradition is quite explicit that one of the most significant events at the commencement of Jesus' ministry is his choosing of 12 disciples, also called apostles, to be with him and to share intimately in his ministry. Apart from Judas, whose surname 'Iscariot' may mean a man from Kerioth in Judaea, all the 12 came from Galilee.

The nucleus of Jesus' disciples was two pairs of brothers, Simon Peter with Andrew his brother and James and John, the sons of Zebedee. These four probably worked together in a small fishing business (Luke 5:10). Thus they were not extremely poor – Mark records that when his sons went off to become disciples, their father was left behind in the ship 'with the hired servants' (Mark 1:20).

The Gospel tradition stresses that it was Jesus who chose his disciples and also that he called them to leave all in order to follow him. Their allegiance was to be to him alone – they were to learn from him and share in his commitment. Though not all disciples achieved it, the ideal was to forsake all. Disciples had to leave their home and work – henceforth they would be dependent on the gifts and hospitality of others. They were at times allowed to carry provisions for only one day and they were to trust in God to give them their 'daily bread'. They could not even carry a staff and basic protection: if attacked they were to 'turn the other cheek'.

But although he called disciples and chose the twelve, Jesus did not found a community with a central organisation or holy place. What 'community' there was consisted in loyal friends like Mary and Martha, residents who would open their homes to these wandering, charismatic prophets. The message they proclaimed was that the kingdom of heaven was at hand. They healed the sick and called them to repent and believe the good news that God had drawn near in these last days to redeem his people Israel. Even though Jerusalem became the acknowledged centre of the Church after the death of Jesus, it is significant that the leading disciples did not live there permanently. In essence the Jesus movement consisted of two groups of people – travelling disciples supported by the hospitality of resident believers in the villages and towns.

Although there are frequent references to Jesus operating in the proximity of the larger cities, his work was essentially rural, moving through the villages and fringes of the larger cities. One reason for this may be that in Palestine the Jews were less attracted into the city precincts of the Graeco-Phoenician cities such as Tyre and Sidon than elsewhere in the Hellenistic world.

Jesus sent his disciples not to the gentiles or the Samaritans but specifically to 'the lost sheep of the house of Israel'. The common (Jewish) people were for the most part untutored in the details of the Law and greatly alienated from the religious leaders in Jerusalem. Some Pharisees were rigid about offences against the Law; in contrast to these, Jesus was described as a 'friend of publicans and sinners'.

The hope that inspired all aspects of Jesus' mission and that of his disciples was 'the restoration of Israel'. The choice of the 12 disciples is thus significant. It indicates the hope of the restoration of the 12 tribes in all Israel. The significance of the twelve is further indicated in 1 Corinthians 15 where Paul states that the risen Jesus appeared to the twelve, and also by the fact that when Judas betrayed his Lord, the disciples soon ensured his replacement by Matthias (Acts 1:15).

'As he was walking by the Lake of Galilee he saw two brothers, Simon, who was called Peter, and his brother Andrew. . . . . And he said to them, "Come after me and I will make you fishers of people"' (MATTHEW 4:18–19). The Sea of Galilee is about 12.5mls/20km long and 8mls/13km at its greatest width. The River Jordan enters it from the north and leaves it from the south. Jesus' Galilean ministry focused on the towns around the Sea of Galilee.

Jesus' disciples

Peter's name always appears first in the list of Jesus' disciples. After the resurrection Acts 2:14 mentions 'Peter standing with the eleven'. Simon (Peter) comes from the Hebrew Symeon. The Greek name Peter means rock or stone.

Andrew, Peter's brother, and Philip are the only disciples with distinctly Greek names. Four of the other disciples' names are Greek in form but of Semitic origin – Bartholomew, Matthew, Thomas and Thaddaeus. There is some uncertainty concerning the last. Instead of Thaddaeus, Luke includes Judas, the son of James (Luke 6:16, Acts 1:13). John refers to a Judas who is 'not Judas Iscariot' (John 14:22).

James and John, the sons of Zebedee, were called 'Boanerges' by Jesus, meaning 'Sons of Thunder'. This may indicate that they were men of thundery temperament. It may also signify that they had strong apocalyptic views, as when they desired to call down fire from heaven on an unfriendly Samaritan village (Luke 9:54). Their prominence is shown by the fact that, with Peter, they were present at the great moments of Jesus' life.

James is to be distinguished from the disciple James the son of Alphaeus, sometimes identified as 'James the younger' (Mark 15:40). Of this disciple little is known. James, the brother of John, suffered a martyr's death at the command of Herod Agrippa but John, according to some traditions, lived to a great age in Ephesus and is credited with the authorship of the Fourth Gospel.

In addition to Simon Peter, another Simon is included in the twelve. Matthew and Mark describe him as 'Simon the Cananaean' but Luke calls him 'Simon the Zealot'. This suggests that the 'Cananaean' is not derived from the geographical term Canaan (or Cana) but from the Hebrew word *kana*, meaning 'man of zeal'. Scholars disagree, however, on whether this should be interpreted as meaning that Simon, the zealous, is a Zealot sympathiser or simply a zealous person. Judas is usually named last in the list of disciples, probably because of his betrayal of Jesus. But he did hold a privileged position as treasurer of the twelve (John 12:5–6; 13:29).

The symbols of the disciples: Key or fish, Peter, **1**; Chalice with snake, John, **2**; Crozier or small cross, Philip, **3**; Saw, Simon, **4**; Transverse cross, Andrew, **5**; Builder's rule or spear, Thomas, **6**; Flaying knife, Bartholomew, **7**; Halberd or lance, Jude, **8**; Pilgrim's hat, James the greater, **9**; Club, James the younger, **10**; Purse, Matthew, **11**; Lance, Matthias, **12**.

Galilee was wide open to foreign influence, especially on its northern borders, an area seldom fully under the control of the Israelites because of its distance from Jerusalem. Religious leaders in Jerusalem and local residents despised the Galileans, considering them yokels, especially when they appeared in Jerusalem for the major festivals. In fact, the Galileans were probably more aware of the political realities of their day than most, because the great trade routes which traversed the region introduced to them many foreigners travelling within the various regions of the Roman empire, itself the ultimate political power of the time.

To the southeast of Galilee, on the other side of the Sea of Galilee, lay the Decapolis, a confederation of 10 cities (shown on the map in capitals) formed after Pompey's campaign (65–62 BC) as a customs union and for protection against the Jews and the Arabian tribes. The cities, which were subject to Roman military service and taxation, were said by Pliny in the first century of the Christian era to be Scythopolis, Dion, Pella, Gadara, Hippos, Gerasa, Philadelphia, Damascus, Raphana and Kanatha. Scythopolis was on the west side of the Jordan, the other cities on the east. The term Decapolis is employed in the Bible to describe the general locality.

Healing the paralytic

According to the Gospels, when, as an adult, Jesus embarked on his ministry, he soon acquired a reputation as a healer. He attracted such crowds that people found it difficult to get near him. To emphasise this point, Mark 2:1–12 relates how, in Capernaum, a paralysed man is let down through the roof of a house where Jesus is preaching, because it is the only way those carrying the man can get him to Jesus.

In response to the faith of these men, Jesus forgives the paralytic his sins, an act which provokes controversy. The religious leaders seize on it as an act of blasphemy, because for them only God can forgive sins. But by healing the man, Jesus proves he has divine authority, since the fact that the man is healed shows that his sins are forgiven.

The connection between sin and physical suffering was often made in Jewish culture at the time. In John 9:2, Jesus' disciples ask him about a blind man: 'Rabbi, who sinned, this man or his parents, that he should have been born blind?' 'Neither he nor his parents sinned,' answers Jesus, flying in the face of accepted belief. But in the story of the paralytic he accepts the link and, by releasing the man from his sin, makes possible the cure.

The story shows that Jesus' power was the power of God. Some scholars believe that it is actually a combination of two stories, the controversy with the religious leaders having been inserted later. In any event, it is designed to link Jesus' power to heal with the power to forgive sins and therefore with divine authority.

There are interesting parallels between this story and the story in John 5 of the paralysed man at the Pool of Bethesda, who cannot benefit from the pool's healing water because he has no one to put him into it. The two stories are set in different places, one in Capernaum, the other in Jerusalem. But both involve a clash with the religious authorities, though the debate in the second story is about Jesus' authority to break the Sabbath.

Both are about a paralysed man, one who has friends to help and one who does not. The command by which Jesus heals both men is identical in the original Greek of the Gospels. There are other stories in the Gospels which have curious links of this kind and there is speculation on how far stories were adapted in different ways before they were collected and written down in their present form in the Gospels.

The need to prove that Jesus' power was God's power arose from the fact that the ability to work miracles was not unique to Jesus. There were many other miracle-workers in the ancient world and the Gospel stories all have a similar pattern or form as other similar stories of Hellenistic origin, though the latter seldom, if ever, involve the need for faith. Hence, Jesus' ability to work miracles could not in itself be regarded as proof of his divine authority. The whole question was by what power he performed the miracles.

One 'message' in the miracle stories in the Gospels emphasises the need for faith. In the early Church, they were probably preserved to encourage trust in the healing power of Jesus. However, in the Gospels, they often seem to point to the need for a deeper awareness of who Jesus is and what his mission is. The other important and recurrent features of the stories are, in Matthew, their emphasis on the compassion of Jesus and, especially in Mark, his reluctance to court popularity. He was not out for gain or celebrity, a charge which was rightly brought against some other miracle-workers.

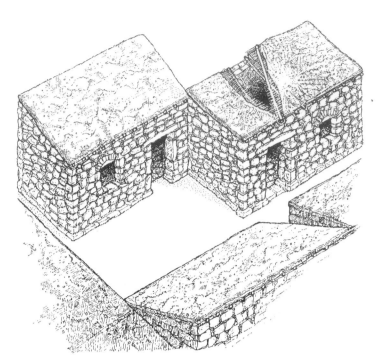

Palestinian houses were built of wood and plaster and had flat roofs. Mark's account of the paralysed man being cured tells of his helpers 'unroofing the roof' and 'digging it out', a fairly quick and easy task. Luke's version, however, is marked by adaptation to conditions in Greece or Italy: the men go up on the roof and let the paralytic in 'through the tiles'. But both Biblical versions dwell on the determination and faith of these helpers. Matthew, whose version is shorter, omits this detail.

'Get up, pick up your stretcher and walk' (MARK 2:9). A 6th-century mosaic shows Jesus, with attendant disciple, miraculously curing the paralytic. Many writers, notably the 2nd-century AD Greek satirist Lucian, ridiculed such 'cures', denouncing the miracle-workers as charlatans.

Carrying the stretcher was often featured in early Christian art, from the catacomb paintings at Rome onwards, because it was felt to provide proof that the cure had been effected and the sin forgiven.

Early and medieval mosaicists depicted Jesus in one of two ways: either as young and beardless or as mature and bearded.

Medicine in the ancient world

Jesus is by no means the only healer known from ancient sources. The idea that the king had the power to heal can be seen from the many cures attributed to the Roman emperor Vespasian. Miracle cures are associated with Apollonius of Tyana, an itinerant philosopher of the first century AD.

Miracles of healing were not confined to the pagan world. The Samaritan Simon Magus (Acts 8:9–25) was alleged to have performed miracle cures in the first century, as also were Jewish 'holy men' such as Rabbi Hanina ben Dosa. All these charismatic healers were accused by the religious authorities of being magicians, as indeed was Jesus (see p.145).

The lot of the poor at that time was appalling. There were no public health institutions, although communities sometimes had a public doctor. Illness could bring ruin, as it did to the woman in Luke's Gospel who spent everything on doctors (some texts of Luke 8:43). Many of the physically and mentally ill were driven from their communities to live as beggars.

Lepers (which in Biblical language means people suffering from any disfiguring skin disease) and demoniacs (those believed to be possessed by demons) were likewise cast out, to fend for themselves as best they might. Lack of hygiene meant that diseases were rife and life-expectancy short. It is thus hardly surprising that a reputed healer, such as Jesus, should be a magnet for great numbers of the sick and disabled.

Medicine was never entirely separated from religion in the ancient world. Among the Jews, religious officials were involved in diagnosis and treatment.

Among the Greeks, 'scientific' medicine was closely linked with ancient religious shrines. The principal Greek god of healing was Asclepius, and the medical school of Hippocrates (from which originated the 'Hippocratic oath') was established on the island of Cos where the god had a shrine. Treatment there was connected with curative springs, but at the Asclepieion in Epidaurus the method used was 'incubation'. Patients slept in the sacred area and claimed to have visions of the god, who produced or prescribed a cure in return for a specified offering.

'Scientific' medicine never succeeded in displacing belief in supernatural causation, although the priests might have had a sound knowledge of specifics, surgery and psychology. Many votive offerings, often clay images of affected parts of the body, have been found in temple areas.

Although Palestine was far removed from Cos and Epidaurus, both geographically and in religious attitudes, similar beliefs are in evidence in the story of the paralytic in John's Gospel: the sick waited around the Pool of Bethesda and the first to enter the (John 5:1 ff).

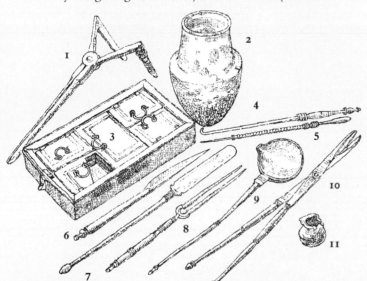

Roman surgical instruments of the first century AD included: rectal speculum, **1**; bleeding cup, **2**; drugs box, **3**; hook, **4**; probe, **5**; scalpel, **6**; spatula, **7**; forked probe **8**; spoon, **9**; forceps, **10**; medicine or ointment jar, **11**. Interestingly, some of these instruments, e.g. the scalpel, forceps and spatula, have not changed significantly down to the present day.

This bronze Roman votive offering, *right*, of the 1st or 2nd century AD would have been dedicated at a shrine of healing, probably on behalf of someone with a diseased or damaged leg.

An Italian wall painting depicts Hippocrates and Galen in conversation although the lives of these great Greek physicians were separated by more than six centuries. Galen (*c.* AD 130–*c.* 199), the most famous doctor of the ancient world, greatly contributed to anatomical research by practising dissection. Doctors of antiquity could perform simple surgical operations, though without anaesthetics. Literature often tells of pain being inflicted in order to heal. Rabbis did not share the same theories about the body and its workings as the Greeks, but there is evidence that similar remedies were known in Palestine.

Jesus the exorcist

Some of the healing miracles in the Gospels are exorcisms. Although, in some respects, Jesus may not have seemed very different from other exorcists and magicians (he sometimes used the same healing substances and commands), for the Gospel writers he was much more: his healing and exorcising are signs of the presence of God's kingdom on earth.

He was challenged, however, by the religious authorities as to by what power he performed these exorcisms. In Mark 3:22 ff., his opponents accuse him of casting out demons by the power of Beelzebul. Jesus' reply seems common sense: since his exorcisms are causing rout among the powers of evil, he implies, they can hardly be the work of the prince of evil: 'How can Satan drive out Satan? If a kingdom is divided against itself, that kingdom cannot last.'

In Matthew 12:28 and Luke 11:20, Jesus goes further: 'If it is through the Spirit (or, in Luke, 'finger') of God that I drive out devils, then be sure that the kingdom of God has caught you unawares.' Jesus further suggests that blasphemy against the Holy Spirit will never be forgiven. What he seems to mean by this is that the kind of spiritual vision which is so distorted that it calls the activity of God the activity of the Evil One is irredeemable.

The accusation made by Jesus' opponents is illuminating because it shows that his exorcisms and healings were not considered an obvious proof of his divine authority in the ancient world. To his contemporaries they could equally be seen in terms of black magic. For magic and astrology played a significant role in the ancient world and exorcism was closely bound up with that world-view.

For Jesus and his followers the exorcisms were signs that the sovereignty of God was invading the territory occupied by the powers of evil. One curious exorcism story which bears this out is the account of the Gerasene man possessed by demons who, according to Mark 5:5, 'would howl and gash himself with stones'.

The name of the demons possessing the man – 'Legion' – is significant, as it stands for the occupying power of Rome. Jesus' exorcism causes the 'unclean spirits' to come out of the man and enter a herd of gentile pigs, 'and the herd charged down the cliff into the lake and was drowned' (Luke 8:33).

Symbolically, the story tells of the fulfilment of the expectations of the people of God that he would come and reestablish his rule in Israel, casting out his enemies. This routing of the powers of evil was not merely magic, but was heralding the beginning of the Messianic age.

And it was not just the demon-possessed whom Jesus liberated: the Gospels also tell how the powers of wind and wave were rebuked as the Christ stilled the storm. In short, the exorcisms are a crucial element in the mission of Jesus, part of his bringing in the kingdom of God.

In fact, all the healing stories are crucial in this last respect. For, the Gospels say, Jesus is not just another 'holy man' or 'magician'. He is *the* one who fulfils the promises of God. This is brought out in the story of John the Baptist who, languishing in jail, questions whether Jesus is the Messiah. Jesus' reply to him sums up his ministry in words which echo the Old Testament prophets and their expectations of the Messianic era: 'the blind see again, the lame walk . . . the dead are raised to life and the good news is proclaimed to the poor' (Matthew 11:4–5).

Miracle-workers: their magic and cures

An important feature of ancient religions was their power, which was often manifested through 'miracles' and magic. In Acts 8, a Samaritan named Simon is said to have practised magic and made claims to be the power which is called 'Great'. He recognised that the 'magic' of the Apostles was more powerful than his own and tried to buy it. This, in fact, seems to be a toned-down account of a certain Simon Magus who, according to early Church fathers claimed to be the Highest Power, higher even than God.

Workers of miracles are quite common in ancient literature. Often religious claims were made by and for them but, as in the case of Jesus, they denied charges of being magicians or sorcerers.

Probably the most famous example is the philosopher Apollonius of Tyana, who was roughly a contemporary of Paul. Philostratus wrote Apollonius's biography in the early third century and made much of his supposed miraculous birth, his teaching, ascetic practices and remarkable cures, which included exorcisms. His end is left mysterious but he is hailed as immortal. He had been brought to trial and, in his defence, rejected charges of wizardry and the allegation that many regarded him as a god.

Some have suggested that Philostratus's book was a counterblast to the Gospels. There are both differences and similarities. If the book is independent of the Gospels, the parallels are the more interesting.

Within the Jewish tradition, the outstanding example is Hanina ben Dosa, a charismatic holy man whom God is said to have addressed as 'Son' and whose prayers were so powerful as to be virtually magical. Through them he could perform cures, though he denied being a prophet.

Exorcism: the casting out of devils

During the past 150 years, the discovery of a large number of papyri in the Near East has widened the understanding of ancient magic. Although the discovered texts are later than the New Testament, it is clear that they are copies of ancient formulae and spells and that there was a developing magical tradition in the ancient world that reached a peak in the fourth century AD.

Magic amulets had long been known and studied, but their significance became clear only with the additional evidence of the papyri. The amulet was supposed to have the effect of a charm bracelet, warding off evil forces and enhancing the wearer's powers. Inscribed on gems, minerals or various metals, their formulae reflect those in the magic papyri.

The object of magic was to manipulate supernatural powers, and a wide range of deities and divine powers figure in both papyri and amulets. Hellenistic magic employed potent names from any religious source. The name of Jesus soon figures, together with corruptions of the secret divine name of the Old Testament God, oriental and Egyptian deities, and the divine beings of Greek mythology and religion; and there is much evidence of magic in the Jewish world of Hellenistic times.

Exorcism is a particularly important element in the widespread culture of magic. Underlying it is belief in invisible powers which can be summoned by secret knowledge of what arouses them, especially knowledge of names. A more powerful supernatural being was invoked to drive out the lesser demon who had taken possession of a sick or mentally ill person.

That Jesus was by no means the only exorcist is substantiated by the saying in Matthew 12:27 and Luke 11:19: 'If it is through Beelzebul that I drive devils out, through whom do your own experts drive them out?'

The illuminated capital letter 'B', *left*, from the 12th century 'Winchester Bible', shows Jesus casting out devils, *top,* and releasing captive souls in hell, *below*, to which he briefly descended after his death.

The ancient Egyptians believed that their fortunes, good or ill, were to some extent influenced by the gods, as well as by the date. Calendars, *below*, were compiled to help people decide when actions should be taken or avoided.

The Sermon on the Mount

Seeing the crowds, he went onto the mountain. And when he was seated his disciples came to him. Then he began to speak. This is is what he taught them: "How blessed are the poor in spirit: the kingdom of Heaven is theirs'" (Matthew 5:1–3). So begins the Sermon on the Mount, which is usually regarded as the kernel of Jesus' teaching.

The Sermon is respected for its moral significance even by non-Christians. It demands exacting moral standards: a lustful look is to commit adultery in the heart, while anger and harsh words are as serious as murder. Hypocrisy is condemned and universal love, even of one's enemies, is enjoined.

Yet it does not provide a comprehensive code for living. Much of it is graphic parables: if someone hits you on the right cheek, offer him the other as well; if someone wishes to go to law to get your tunic, give him your cloak as well.

Many have despaired of ever living up to demands such as these and the Sermon has been called too idealistic for real life. Also, it is permeated by a set of Jewish religious attitudes that cannot be divorced from the ethical teaching.

What the Sermon provides is a picture of life in God's kingdom where earthly values are often turned on their heads. The ultimate demand is to be perfect 'as your heavenly Father is perfect', though the word translated as 'perfect' might also mean 'all-embracing' or 'mature' (i.e. in your love). Jesus proclaims that God's kingdom is imminent and urges his hearers to start living now as already in that kingdom.

A close examination of the text shows that the Sermon is made up of a series of 'sayings' and parables skilfully woven together. Sometimes these are connected by 'catchwords', suggesting that they were placed together for easy memorisation. Sometimes there are sayings which are linked together in Matthew's version of the Sermon but are scattered and separated in the other Gospels, for example, the saying about salt (Matthew 5:13; Mark 9:50; Luke 14:34).

Besides this, there is a 'Great Sermon' in Luke (6:20–49) which overlaps but is not identical with the Sermon on the Mount. Both begin with Beatitudes (declarations of blessedness) and include injunctions against retaliation and on not judging others' behaviour. Both end with the parable of the wise man who built his house on a rock. But Luke says this sermon was delivered on a level piece of ground after Jesus had come *down* from the mountain where he had gone to pray.

Even the material common to both Gospel writers varies: for example, Matthew has eight Beatitudes while Luke has four Beatitudes and four contrasting woes. Much of the teaching in the Sermon on the Mount which the Great Sermon does not contain (e.g. the Lord's Prayer) appears elsewhere in Luke.

Some scholars will accept the Sermon as an authentic record of Jesus' teaching, reflecting that a preacher uses the same material on different occasions in slightly different forms. Others think that the editor of Matthew's Gospel composed the Sermon as it now stands, though some of its sections would naturally translate into Aramaic poetry which, along with similes and stories, appears to have been Jesus' characteristic way of communication in the first three Gospels.

Unlike Mark and Luke, Matthew preferred to collect the brief proverbs and parables, which Jesus used to teach, into blocks, with miracle stories and other material put in between: and the greatest of these collections is the Sermon on the Mount.

The Lord's prayer in Matthew and Luke

'Father, may your name be held holy, your kingdom come; give us each day our daily bread, and forgive us our sins, for we ourselves forgive each one who is in debt to us. And do not put us to the test.' (LUKE 11:2–4).

Our Father in heaven, may your name be held holy, your kingdom come, your will be done, on earth as in heaven. Give us today our daily bread. And forgive us our debts, as we have forgiven those who are in debt to us. And do not put us to the test, but save us from the Evil One. (MATTHEW 6:9–13).

Many phrases of the Lord's prayer have parallels in Jewish religious writing – yet it forms a new and original whole. Luke's version opens simply with 'Father', possibly representing the Aramaic Abba, the intimate address Jesus apparently used and encouraged his disciples to use. Matthew's version, however, is more adapted to Jewish synagogue prayers. Matthew's opening is 'Our Father' – *Abinu*, the usual Jewish address in prayer, together with the typically Jewish description 'the one in the heavens'. Matthew also adds 'Your will be done' which may signify what he, as a Jew, understood the coming of God's kingdom to mean.

Jesus as the new Moses

Early Christian art presented Jesus as a new Moses, an idea first found in Matthew's Gospel. This comes out particularly in the narratives of their births. According to Jewish legend, Pharaoh's astrologers predicted the birth of Moses; Jesus' birth was hailed by the Magi, who were Persian astrologers. As a result, both Pharaoh and Herod the Great instituted the slaughter of Jewish children.

In Exodus 1:22 it says that 'Pharaoh then gave all his people this command: "Throw every new-born boy into the river, but let all the girls live"'. Pharaoh hoped that his infamous order would prevent the Israelites from becoming too strong in numbers and threatening their Egyptian masters. Herod the Great also felt threatened, but, in his case, by the prospect of the birth of 'the king of the Jews'.

Moses and Jesus, in different ways, escaped. Moses was rescued from the river in a papyrus basket, discovered by Pharaoh's daughter, while Jesus was taken to Egypt by Joseph and Mary. Exodus 4:19 says of Moses, 'All those who wanted to kill you are dead'; Matthew 2:19–20 says of Jesus, 'Those who wanted to kill the child are dead'.

These connections and allusions make it likely that Matthew presents Jesus teaching a new Law on 'the Mount' to draw a parallel with Moses receiving the old Law on Mount Sinai. It has also been suggested that Jesus teaching is arranged in five blocks in Matthew's Gospel to suggest a parallel with the five books (known as the Pentateuch) of the Law (Genesis–Deuteronomy).

In this fresco from the museum of S. Marco in Florence, Jesus is depicted preaching the Sermon on the Mount to his disciples. Some think the Sermon was delivered as related, others that it is a compendium of Jesus' teaching. There are a number of traditional sites for its location, one of which is southwest of Capernaum, near the Sea of Galilee.

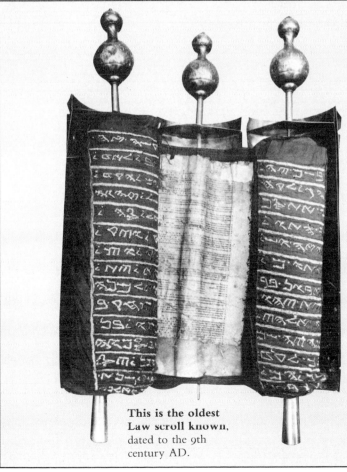

This is the oldest Law scroll known, dated to the 9th century AD.

Jesus and the Jewish Law

In the Sermon on the Mount, Jesus said, 'Do not imagine that I have come to abolish the Law or the Prophets. I have come not to abolish but to complete them. In truth I tell you, till heaven and earth disappear, not one dot, not one little stroke, is to disappear from the Law until its purpose is achieved' (Matthew 5:17,18).

Two facts, however, call into question the idea that Jesus made such a clear statement in favour of the Jewish Law. The first is the presence in the Gospels of many stories about Jesus breaking the Sabbath and coming into conflict with Jewish religious leaders over points of Law-keeping. The second is the fact that the early Church soon came to terms with the admission of gentiles without their requiring the Jewish Law to be kept. This caused debate and controversy in the Church but, if Jesus' mind was unambiguous on the issue, that important debate might not have taken place. Does this strong statement come then from the Jewish Christian faction in the Church? Matthew's is certainly the most Jewish of the four Gospels.

Jesus, of course, was himself a Jew and keeping the Law would have been part of his daily habits and culture. He apparently never attacked the Law as such but engaged in debate about its interpretation. He was also critical of the 'Tradition of the Elders', that is particular applications of the Law deduced from scriptural texts by scribes and Pharisees. Jesus was clearly concerned that outward observance of the Law should not mask inner motivation (see Matthew 5:20ff. and Mark 7:1–23), and that blind devotion to rules should not overshadow God's life-giving intentions (see Matthew 12:1–14). His kingdom is for those whose uprightness exceeds that of the scribes and Pharisees (see Matthew 5:20).

Teaching in parables

J esus' characteristic way of teaching was in parables, two of the best known of which are the Good Samaritan and the Prodigal Son. But interpreting these parables is not as simple as it might seem. They may look like illustrations to a sermon, but that is not what Mark's Gospel suggests.

In fact, for centuries, people assumed that the parables were allegories. So in the parable of the Good Samaritan (Luke 10:29–37), the man who was attacked while going from Jerusalem to Jericho was taken to be humankind. The bandits who assaulted him were the Devil and his angels, who stripped man of his immortality, beat him by persuading him to sin, and left him half-dead. The Good Samaritan who, unlike the priest and the Levite, helped the victim and took him to an inn, was Jesus; the inn was the Church, the inn-keeper the apostle Paul, and so on.

In modern times, scholars have reacted against this sort of interpretation. In the example above, the detailed correspondences seem artificial and can hardly have been the intention of Jesus when he told the story. Although it is now commonly thought that a parable has only one point, this is possibly an over-reaction since allegory was known in the culture to which Jesus belonged.

It is popularly assumed that parables are moral tales showing examples of model behaviour. But because of differences in culture, the original force of the parable is often lost. For example, in the Good Samaritan, the priest and the Levite, by refusing to touch what looked like a corpse, were actually doing the ritually right thing: they were keeping themselves pure so as to perform their religious duties. Even more, it is not usually realised that the Samaritan was the very person a Jew would be most hostile to (see p.116).

With the shock element of the parable diminished, its form and role are obscured. A parable was not really a 'tale', in the modern sense, at all, still less a moral one. The Hebrew word for 'parable', *mashal*, covers all forms of metaphorical sayings, proverbs, similes, allegories and symbols. So nearly all the sayings of Jesus are 'parables', for example the well-known saying: 'It is easier for a camel to pass through the eye of a needle than for someone rich to enter the kingdom of God' (Matthew 19:24). The 'tales' are really extended metaphorical sayings.

The Old Testament suggests that the intention of such parables was often to disturb people out of complacency and force them to wake up. For example, after his appalling behaviour over Bathsheba (see p.85), David is challenged with a parable by the prophet Nathan (2 Samuel 11–12).

Jesus' parables were also challenges that were couched in a kind of riddle form which people either grasped or did not grasp. They often involve a shock to standard assumptions and can arouse moral indignation, e.g. the apparent injustice concerning the payment of the labourers in Matthew 20:1–16.

The basic images of the parables are drawn from the Old Testament. When Jesus speaks of King or Shepherd, he is referring to God. When he speaks of vineyard or flock, he is referring to Israel, the people of God. But the basic message of the parables remains Jesus' message about the kingdom of God, described in graphic images and analogies. Sometimes a series of different short sayings is appended to a parable, doubtless representing various interpretations which had developed before they were written down. Each Gospel has its own way of telling parables, and of interpreting and selecting them.

Two parables of the kingdom

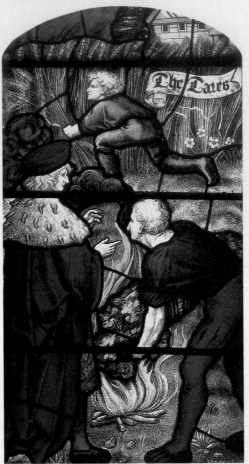

'This is what the kingdom of God is like. A man scatters seed on the land. Night and day . . . the seed is sprouting and growing; how, he does not know. Of its own accord the land produces . . .' (MARK 4:26–8).
In other words, the kingdom comes without human effort. In Matthew's version (13:24–30), however, the point is different: an enemy sows darnel (tares) among the wheat; the man lets the darnel grow with the wheat till harvest when the reapers can separate them, as this 19th-century stained glass shows.
The different versions show how easily the parables got adapted by the early Christians to illustrate different points about the kingdom.

'Again, the kingdom of Heaven is like a dragnet that is cast in the sea and brings in a haul of all kinds of fish' (MATTHEW 13:47).
The parable of the dragnet, which is shown in this 13th-century stained glass from Canterbury cathedral, again underlines Matthew's interest in the judgement that comes before the arrival of the kingdom: other similar parables like the 'pearl of great price' seem to focus more on the idea that nothing is more valuable than the kingdom: you have to be single-minded.

Parables from the four Gospels

'Listen! Imagine a sower going out to sow. Now it happened that, as he sowed, some of the seed fell on the edge of the path, and the birds came and ate it up' (MARK 4:3).

Mark treats the parable of the sower, seen in this 13th-century stained glass from Canterbury cathedral, as an allegory. He suggests that to those who have not been given the 'secret of the kingdom of God', everything comes in parables to prevent them seeing and hearing. In Mark, far from being graphic illustrations, the parables are riddles.

'A man was once on his way down from Jerusalem to Jericho and fell into the hands of bandits' (LUKE 10:30).
Only Luke contains the parable of the Good Samaritan. In this 13th-century stained glass from Chartres cathedral, the bandit is drawing a sword, though there is no mention of one in the text.

Another parable peculiar to Luke is the Prodigal Son (15:11–32). This is typically Lukan, drawing, as it does, a contrast between two characters, the sinner forgiven and the self-righteous put out.

'Ten wedding attendants took their lamps and went to meet the bridegroom' (MATTHEW 25:1).
The parable of the ten attendants, or 'virgins', seen in this 19th-century stained glass, *left*, illustrates the need for Christians to be ready for the coming of Christ ('bridegroom'). Matthew's distinctive parables tend to focus on the Final Coming and the judgement that precedes it.

'I am the good shepherd: the good shepherd lays down his life for his sheep' (JOHN 10:11).
This 6th-century mosaic shows Christ as the good shepherd. John's Gospel does not have parables like those in the other Gospels. But it does have passages which use the same sort of images as the parables, sometimes developing them as allegories which speak of Jesus.

Mary and Martha

According to Luke (10:38–42), in the course of his journey to Jerusalem, Jesus came to a village and was welcomed into the house of Martha and her sister Mary. They were apparently living together, and must have been unmarried or widowed. Mary took what was a highly unconventional step for a woman: she sat at the Lord's feet and listened to him speaking, presumably with the menfolk.

Martha, meanwhile, carried on with her normal domestic role, busying herself about preparations for her guests. It is hardly surprising she felt a little annoyed with Mary, who should have been helping her. In the end, Martha came to Jesus and said: 'Lord, do you not care that my sister is leaving me to do the serving all by myself? Please tell her to help me.' But the Lord answered: 'Martha, Martha, you worry and fret over so many things, and yet few are needed, indeed only one. It is Mary who has chosen the better part, and it is not to be taken from her.'

In the light of what was expected of a woman at that time, Jesus' reaction is startling. A woman was not to concern herself with religious teaching. Her duty was to attend to domestic matters. Here, Jesus is honouring a woman's desire for instruction, recognising her as having the same deeper needs as a man.

The story primarily illustrates a persistent theme in Jesus' teaching, namely that worry and fret over the basics of life can be a distraction from what really matters. Elsewhere, Jesus said: 'Human beings live not on bread alone but on every word that comes from the mouth of the Lord' (Matthew 4:4) and '. . . I am telling you not to worry about your life and what you are to eat . . . Surely life is more than food . . . Look at the birds in the sky. They do not sow or reap . . . yet your heavenly Father feeds them' (Matthew 6:25–6). But the fact that Jesus accords exceptional respect to a woman is still notable.

This accent on respect for women is a particular feature of Luke's Gospel. For example, Luke adds to a summary of Jesus' ministry, typical of all the Gospels, these words: 'With him went the Twelve, as well as certain women . . . Mary surnamed the Magdalene . . . Joanna the wife of Herod's steward . . . Susanna and many others who provided for them out of their own resources' (8:1–3). In Luke, women appear later on, following and mourning on the way to the cross, and some of them are named by Luke as witnesses of the resurrection.

But Luke merely reinforces a noticeable feature of all the Gospels – they all give women surprising prominence. They even present them as the first to discover the empty tomb. This detail probably authenticates the empty tomb story – if it were invented, no one would have given women such a key role.

During his ministry, Jesus cures women, and they feature also in his parables. It was not customary for men and women to converse in the street at that time and place, especially if they were strangers. Yet Jesus talked to women in public, and let them touch him, even when they were 'unclean', like the woman with the haemorrhage. Jesus even let a notorious sinner wash his feet rather than shunning her, and offered her the forgiveness she so badly needed (Luke 7:36–50).

There is another story, found in some manuscripts of John's Gospel, and in others included in Luke, which tells of Jesus not condemning an adulteress. It depicts Jesus as the same kind of figure – one who rises above contemporary social conventions, accepts, respects, cures and forgives women, no matter how serious their pollution, as much as men.

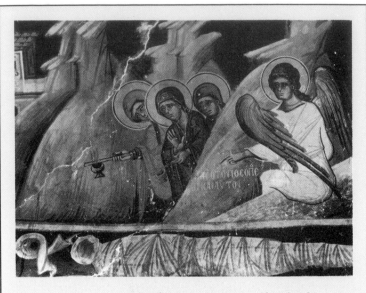

The three women named Mary at the tomb of Jesus: a painting in the Church of St Heracleides in the monastery of St John Lampadistis, Cyprus.

The women named Mary in the New Testament

The name Mary derives from the Greek form of Miriam, a common Hebrew name and familiar as the name of Moses' sister. There are several women named Mary referred to in the Gospels, but the traditions of the early Church often confused them.

The most important is Mary, the mother of Jesus. She figures in the birth stories of Matthew and Luke. In Mark 6:3, Jesus is casually referred to as 'Mary's son' – perhaps a hint that there was something unusual about his birth, since a boy was usually known as the son of his father. Mary is not otherwise mentioned in the first three Gospels, but in John's she is present at the foot of the cross.

Mark and Matthew speak of 'Mary, the mother of James and Joseph (or Joses)', being among the women at the cross. Since James, Joses, Judas and Simon are mentioned as brothers of Jesus in Mark 6:3, perhaps this Mary was Jesus' mother. If she were, however, it seems curious to refer to her as the mother of James and Joseph at the crucifixion. John's Gospel also mentions Mary, the wife of Clopas, the sister of Jesus' mother. It is possible but highly improbable that she was the mother of James and the others; in that case, the 'brothers' of Jesus would in fact be his cousins.

The other important Mary is Mary of Magdala. Luke describes her as one from whom seven demons had gone out, and she is included among those faithful women who followed and supported Jesus during his ministry. She is named as one of the women at the empty tomb in all the Gospels, and in John's version Jesus appears to her first after the resurrection. Christian tradition has identified her with the woman taken in adultery, and the woman who was a sinner and who anointed Jesus. There is nothing in the Gospels to suggest this, except that in John's Gospel the woman who anoints Jesus just before his Passion (a similar but not identical story to the one in Luke 7) is named as Mary. But John is referring to Mary, the sister of Martha, and in Luke's Gospel that Mary is not the same as Mary of Magdala.

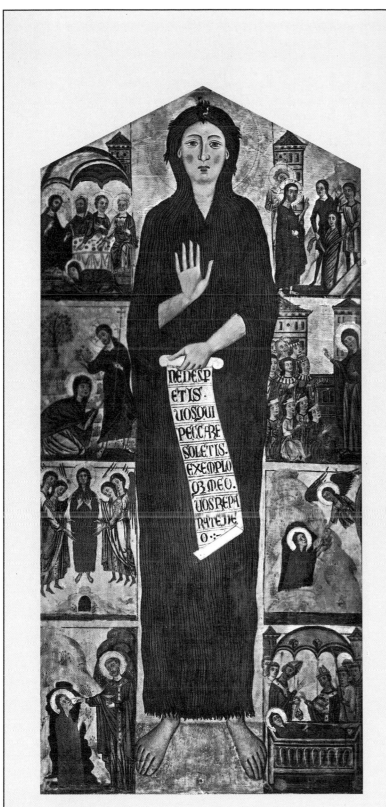

In this 13th-century Italian painting, Mary of Magdala holds a scroll bearing the legend, 'Do not despair, you who have led sinful lives. Follow my example and right yourself with God.' The scenes to either side of Mary show episodes from her life.

The role of women in Biblical times

Apart from their role as ritual mourners at funerals, Jewish women took no part in public life and were largely confined to the domestic scene. A woman was exempt from the commandments requiring attendance at public religious ceremonies, and duties such as studying the Law or *Torah*, making pilgrimage to Jerusalem and reading from the Law in the synagogue. Schools were for boys only, and women probably sat apart from men in the synagogue. Men might not speak to women in the streets.

In the Temple, women had access only to the Courts of the Gentiles and of Women, and during periods of uncleanness (for example, the monthly purification and for 40 days after the birth of a boy and 80 days after the birth of a girl) they were not even allowed there. Yet a woman had her own religious obligations. She was expected to keep *kosher* – indeed, as the one who presided over the kitchen, it would be her particular responsibility to see that the food laws were not infringed. She was to observe the Sabbath, to keep herself ritually clean and to perform significant domestic rituals, for religion affected not only public life but that of the home as well.

Within the household, a woman had much honour and many duties. She was responsible for grinding corn, baking and cooking. She did the washing, the spinning and the weaving, and she cared for the children. She would wait upon her husband and his guests, and was expected to obey him. In rural communities, the women helped in the fields and, among poorer classes, the wife assisted her husband in his trade and often sold his wares.

Respect for father came before respect for mother, but both were required by the commandments. A woman was usually under male protection. Until she married, she was subject to her father; she had no rights of possession and her father acquired the proceeds from anything she produced or found. A father could even cancel her vows and only he could accept or refuse an offer of marriage, which was a contract between male heads of families. If a woman reached maturity without marrying, however, she was free of her father, and even as a minor her consent to a marriage was legally required.

Betrothal signified the legal 'acquisition' of a woman by a man. The marriage contract gave her a certain legal protection from exploitation and it was her property. The marriage-portion had to be given up to her in the event of divorce. In that case, the husband was also required to provide a sum agreed in the contract for her maintenance. A woman could sue for divorce but only the husband could effect it. Marriage usually took place a year after betrothal. By today's standards the age of a girl at marriage was young, often about twelve. Her most important duty was to bear sons for her husband.

In her own domain, a woman's religious and social status was high, but in the eyes of the Law she was inferior, being coupled with minors and slaves in the rabbinical writings of the Mishnah. Her ineligibility to perform in public religious life is reflected in the ancient synagogue prayer: 'Blessed art thou, O Lord God, king of the universe, who hast not made me a woman.'

Feeding the multitude

Jesus' feeding of the multitude in the desert with loaves and fishes is reported in all four Gospels. Two Gospels, Mark and Matthew, repeat the story, though with some differences. Perhaps these stories are variants of one significant event. Alternatively, they may well reflect a memory of Jesus feeding large gatherings more than once.

None of the Gospels puts any stress on how the actual miracle of the feeding was done. Each simply notes the enormous surplus of food gathered up after the fish and bread had been distributed. The feedings are described in terms that anticipate the Mass, Eucharist or Communion Service, when Christians remember Jesus taking bread at the last supper, giving thanks, breaking the bread and then distributing it.

In John, the account of the feeding (6:1–15) is followed by a long discussion about Jesus being 'the bread of life'. Just as God fed the Israelites in the desert with heavenly manna (see pp.38–9), so he provides bread from heaven through Jesus: 'If you do not eat the flesh of the Son of man and drink his blood, you have no life in you' (6:53). So if, as it seems, the last supper is anticipated as Jesus shares the traditional food of the banquet of God's kingdom with his followers in the wilderness, then the memory of more than one feeding may be correct.

But some scholars suggest that behind the Christianised form of the story there are discernible clues which show a turning point in Jesus' career. John's Gospel comments that, after the feeding, the people tried to make him king. It also notes that it was the time of the Passover, which traditionally was the time when the Messiah was expected. At the beginning of Mark's account, people are described as 'coming and going', but for what reason? Was a Jewish nationalist army preparing for an uprising?

There are other clues that might lead to the latter conclusion. Mark's Gospel suggests that John the Baptist had been killed just before the feeding. Could the followers of John have set up a gathering of forces in the desert, and have tried to persuade Jesus to take on the role of Messianic king? After all, John had pointed Jesus out as 'the one to come' – that is, the Messiah.

In a moment of crisis, Jesus may have faced the temptation to take the way of popularity and military success, but then realised that that was not the way he was destined to go. If so, it might explain why he sends off his disciples, dismisses the crowd and goes off up the mountain to pray. It would also indicate that there was in fact only one feeding.

Soon after the feeding, in Mark, comes the discussion between Jesus and the disciples when he asks: 'Who do people say I am?' A variety of suggestions which hint at his being the Messiah are offered. He then challenges the disciples with: 'Who do you say I am?' Peter professes that he is the Messiah. But when Jesus tells them what is in store for him as 'Son of man', namely suffering, rejection and death, Peter rebukes him, presumably feeling that Jesus' Messianic destiny should not conform to such a gloomy prophecy. However, Jesus rejects Peter's remonstration as a Satanic temptation.

Mark then tells the story of how Peter, James and John witness Jesus' 'transfiguration' on a high mountain, when Jesus' clothes became 'brilliantly white' and Elijah and Moses appeared beside him – presumably indicating God's vindication of Jesus' chosen path. He is the fulfilment of God's promises and yet is not the kind of warlike Messiah that some Jews expected.

The feeding: a muster in the desert?

Throughout the years of Jesus' life, Judaea and Galilee were in a state of unrest. Spasmodic uprisings by the Jews against the Romans culminated in the revolt of AD 66 and the destruction of Jerusalem in 70 (see pp. 180–3). A decade or so later than the time of Jesus, a certain Theudas persuaded a great part of the people to abandon their homes and assemble near the River Jordan. He claimed to be a prophet and promised to divide the waters and make a way across. The Jewish historian Josephus describes him as a 'magician'.

In the decade 50–60, guerrilla activity increased and many deceivers and imposters – as Josephus describes them – persuaded the multitude to follow them into the wilderness, claiming that they would manifest wonders and signs. For example, a Jew from Egypt called on the people to assemble on the Mount of Olives and claimed that he would then make the walls of Jerusalem fall down before their eyes. In the event, the Roman garrison killed 4,000 of them and took 2,000 captive.

All these incidents suggest that these nationalist leaders expected God to intervene and support them with miracles like those that are said to have occurred when the Israelites escaped from Egypt, travelled through the wilderness and entered the Promised Land.

The story of the feeding of the multitude has similar characteristics. John's Gospel quite explicitly associates it with the manna, the miraculous heavenly food the Israelites received from God in the wilderness. Mark's Gospel says that Jesus had compassion on the crowds, for they were like sheep without a shepherd. Moses prayed for the people in the wilderness that they might not be sheep without a shepherd: Moses said to Yahweh, 'May it please Yahweh, God of the spirits that give life to all living creatures, to appoint a leader for this community, to be at their head in all their undertakings, a man who will lead them out and bring them in, so that Yahweh's community will not be like sheep without a shepherd' (Numbers 27:16ff).

A Jesus (the Greek form of Joshua) was appointed to lead them. Joshua's task was to lead the people across the River Jordan and to conquer the Promised Land. According to Mark, 5,000 men were assembled in the desert and they sat down in companies, in ranks of 50 and 100 – the units established by Moses according to Deuteronomy 1:15 (cf. Exodus 18:24): Yahweh said: 'I took your tribal leaders, wise, experienced men, and appointed them to lead you, as captains of thousands, hundreds, fifties, tens, and as scribes for your tribes.' Similar provision is made in the Dead Sea scroll concerning 'The War of the Sons of Light'.

In Matthew's account of the feedings, in chapters 14 and 15, there is an addition 'to say nothing of women and children' which may mean 'without women and children'. All this suggests that there may, indeed, have been a muster in the desert and that Jesus reenacted the miraculous feeding of the Exodus. No wonder the people 'tried to make him king' (John 6:15).

This mosaic behind the altar of the Church of the Multiplying of the Loaves and Fishes at el-Tabgha in Israel shows the importance of fish and bread in Christian symbolism. The basket of loaves is full; at the top there are two whole loaves and two halves, each marked with a cross. To either side of the basket there is a fish. In symbolism, though not in practice, fish seem to have replaced the wine of the Eucharist.

All accounts of the miraculous feedings speak of bread and fishes. Tertullian, an early Christian writer, compared the newly-baptised to little fishes, following the great Fish through the waters of baptism. The Gospels themselves speak of the Apostles as being 'fishers' of men and the story of the miraculous catch seems to be symbolic of the success of their missionary work. In John's Gospel, a similar story comes at the end, when the Risen Christ meets the disciples on the shore in the early morning and offers them bread and fish, as they gather round the table of their Risen Lord.

This epitaph, *right*, in the Museo Christiano Vaticano depicts two fish facing each other across an anchor. The Greek inscription reads, 'I-CH-TH-U-S' (Greek for fish), an acrostic for Iesous Christos Theou Uios Soter – Jesus Christ, God's Son, Saviour. The Greek words above the fish read 'Ichthus of the living'.

The triumphal entry into Jerusalem

According to the first three Gospels, as Jesus neared Jerusalem, he sent ahead two disciples to bring back a tethered colt which he had predicted they would find. They brought the colt back and Jesus mounted it. As he moved off, people spread their cloaks on the road and others cut branches to spread in his path. They shouted 'Hosanna! Blessed is he who is coming in the name of the Lord!' Mark adds, 'Blessed is the coming kingdom of David our father!', which may mean that the crowds interpreted Jesus' act as a challenge to the Roman authorities – the words suggesting that the Messiah is coming and that God will ensure his rule on earth.

The suggestion of all three Gospels is that Jesus deliberately set up the entry on a colt. Was Jesus openly proclaiming himself Messiah? He may have been trying to show that he was indeed the Messiah, but that he was coming in peace on a colt, not inciting rebellion on a war-horse, an act which many Jews expected of the Messiah.

John tells the same story, but with a difference. Jesus did not set up the entry himself, but was overtaken by a popular demonstration. All those assembled for the festival in Jerusalem poured out to meet him with palm branches, chanting: 'Blessed is he who is coming in the name of the Lord, the king of Israel.'

In this version, which seems more likely, Jesus responded to a popular attempt to induce him to take on the role of kingly Messiah, by acting in a way that fulfils a prophecy yet which, by riding on a colt, emphasises the non-warlike character of the king. Whatever Jesus intended, the popular response to his entry would have been enough to make the Roman and Jewish authorities nervous.

One interesting question is whether the entry was followed by Jesus' cleansing of the Temple – another provocative and prophetic act. The story of Jesus casting out the traders and money-changers from the Court of the Gentiles follows immediately after the triumphal entry in Matthew and Luke; in Mark it occurs on the following day.

But this chronology of events raises some problems. The reference to palm branches suggests that the triumphal entry happened in autumn at the time of the Feast of Tabernacles, when branches were cut to create 'booths' to live in, commemorating the sojourn of the Jews in the wilderness (see pp. 38–9). The first three Gospels imply, however, that the cleansing of the Temple was what drove the authorities to proceed against Jesus, and that his trial and death happened at Passover, the spring festival. John's Gospel confirms that it was Passover when the cleansing of the Temple happened but places the event at the beginning, not the end, of Jesus' ministry.

It is difficult to be sure of the precise sequence of events, but both incidents appear to be deliberate demonstrations that the Old Testament prophecies are being fulfilled; and both acts would have inevitably incited the crowds gathered in the Holy City for one or the other religious festival. Also, both would have worried the Jewish authorities whose one desire was to find some way of surviving under Roman rule.

Indeed, the discussion among the chief priests and Pharisees reported in John's Gospel rings true to the political situation. 'If we let him go on in this way everybody will believe in him, and the Romans will come and suppress the Holy Place and our nation . . . one man should die for the people, rather than the whole nation perish' (11:48–50).

This inscribed stone fragment from the Temple indicates the point beyond which gentiles were forbidden to pass. It is this barrier through which Paul was thought to have taken Trophimus (Acts 21:28–9). According to Josephus, the complete text originally read: 'No foreigner is to enter within the balustrade and enclosure around the Temple area. Whoever is caught will have himself to blame for his death which will follow.'

Jesus and the money-changers

Jesus went into the Temple, the Gospels relate, and began driving out the traders and upsetting the tables of the money-changers. What were these men of trade doing there?

The Temple was a large, enclosed area with various courts of increasing sanctity, built around a temple-house to which only priests had access. The traders were in the court of the Gentiles, the large outer court open to all but beyond which they were forbidden to go, *above*. The traders were important to Temple worship because they provided the animals necessary for sacrifice, and converted standard currencies into the special coinage required for paying the Temple tax. Their activities were not regarded as causing pollution under the Law.

Why, then, did Jesus 'cleanse' the Temple? The first three Gospels record his quoting Isaiah: 'My house will be called a house of prayer . . . but you have turned it into a bandits' den.' Jesus' act is a fulfilment of prophecy, ending the Temple's desecration. It reinforces his identification with those who looked for God's kingdom to bring an end to the corrupt state of Temple worship.

Mark adds that Jesus would not let anyone carry anything through the Temple – in other words, desecrate it by using it as a short-cut. But Mark's version has a further dimension. He quotes Isaiah's words in full: 'a house of prayer for all peoples'. Jesus is thus making ready the Court of the Gentiles for the time when all nations would flow to the holy city to worship the one true God, a further indication that the act implied expectation of the immediate arrival of God's kingdom. This was certain to be politically provocative.

John's Gospel has different timing, different wording and different prophetic quotations. It links the story with the saying, 'Destroy this Temple and in three days I will raise it up', so implying that Jewish Temple worship has been fulfilled and ended in Jesus.

Entering Jerusalem

The route of Jesus' triumphal entry into Jerusalem is clear. Jesus was travelling from Bethany and came to the Mount of Olives, **1**. From the Mount of Olives there is a striking view across the Kidron valley, **2**, to the hill on which the old city stood and the Temple area, **3**. Luke records that as Jesus neared Jerusalem – presumably when he could see this panorama of the city – he wept and predicted its destruction.

People in the city would have had a clear view of a party coming over the Mount of Olives from Bethany and, as John's account suggests, the crowds of pilgrims gathered for the feast could make their way across the valley to meet Jesus.

The Kidron valley is steep, especially on the city side. Jesus presumably entered by the gate near the pool of Siloam, **4**, and made his way up towards the plaza where pilgrims gathered before entering the Temple gates. As the drawing of a model of the Temple, *below right*, by Dr C. Schick in Jerusalem shows, Jesus would then have entered the Court of the Gentiles, **5**, through the Double ('Huldah') gate, **6**, when he would be on the Temple platform. The mosque known as the Dome of the Rock now stands where the Temple and its courts once stood.

Herod the Great had initiated the rebuilding and refurbishing of the Temple, and the work continued throughout Jesus' life. According to Josephus, Herod removed the old foundations, enlarged the whole Temple area and considerably increased the height of the structures. The Temple gate was adorned with a golden vine and the doors were covered with embroidered veils.

Around the Temple courts there were large cloisters. The 'beautiful gate' referred to in Acts was the Nicanor gate, **7**, which led from the Court of Women, **8**, to the Court of Israel; it was made of Corinthian bronze, which shone like gold and far exceeded the others in value. The remaining gates were gilded. According to Josephus, the whole Temple was gleaming with gold. But the Talmud – the body of Jewish civil and ceremonial law – says that wise men dissuaded Herod from fulfilling his intention to overlay it with gold on the grounds that it was more beautiful as it was.

It is not surprising that people tried to elicit Jesus' admiration of the Temple, as reported in Mark's Gospel: 'As he was leaving the Temple one of his disciples said to him, "Master, look at the size of those stones! Look at the size of those buildings!" And Jesus said to him, "You see these great buildings? Not a single stone will be left on one another; everything will be pulled down"' (Mark 13:1–2).

The Temple was completed in the time of Albinus' governorship (AD 62–64); following the Jewish revolt, it was razed to the ground by the Romans in AD 70.

Paying tribute money to Rome?

In the Gospels, the dominant occasions of conflict for Jesus and his disciples appear to emanate from the Pharisees. In Mark 12, the Pharisees and 'some Herodians' try to catch Jesus out with the question: 'Is it permissible to pay taxes to Caesar or not? So, Jesus asks to see a denarius. 'They handed him one and he said to them, "Whose portrait is this? Whose title?" They said to him "Caesar's." Jesus said to them, "Pay Caesar what belongs to Caesar – and God what belongs to God."

It was not unreasonable to expect of someone professing to teach the way of the Lord that he should know whether payment of tax to Caesar was obligatory or not. The payment of the poll tax imposed on provincials in Judaea, Samaria and Idumaea was deeply resented. It was a perennial reminder of the Roman yoke and had to be paid in currency that bore Caesar's name and image. In AD 6 this poll tax had provoked a revolt by Judas of Galilee which the Jewish historian Josephus connects with the subsequent rise of the Zealot party, a fanatical group dedicated to the forceful removal of Roman rule.

The dilemma with which his opponents faced him appeared to give Jesus the option of either saying that the tax should be paid and thus offending the nationalists, or of affirming that it should not be paid and thus offending the Romans and their sympathisers. The likely outcome of the latter course would be death for treason.

Jesus' response to the catch question is revealing. According to Mark 12:15 he says 'hand me a denarius' and then proceeds to use the coin as part of his reply. The inscription on the coin – Tiberius Caesar, Son of the Divine Augustus, High Priest, indicates both the ultimate owner of the coin and also his right to rule and exact taxes. In pointing to this, Jesus was indicating that everyone who in his daily life used these coins was implicitly recognising the fact that he lived under Tiberius' rule and economy. Further, the scene is the Temple court and no human image should have been found there.

Jesus' pronouncement – 'Pay Caesar what belongs to Caesar – and God what belongs to God', recognises a certain limited sphere of authority for Caesar with its special obligations. But his emphasis falls on paying to God the complete and absolute obedience that he alone can command. It is this challenge that Jesus presented to the political and religious groups of his day – whatever other responsibilities one may be involved in, there is no escaping the radical demand of obedience to the divine will. Jesus' reply shows his refusal of the Zealot way of violence while giving no room for unthinking obedience to Roman rule.

The opposition to Jesus is recorded elsewhere in Mark 12: there are references to the Herodians and Pharisees plotting against Jesus; the Sadducees provocatively question Jesus about the resurrection of the dead (12:18–27). The latter group came mainly from the priestly and aristocratic class and were inclined to cooperate and to compromise with the Romans in order to preserve their privileged position.

The Pharisees believed more in divine providence and faithful observance of the law as the way to deliverance. This was in strong contrast to the Zealots who were seeking to secure the kingdom by force. It is unclear in Mark whether the Herodians are being presented as a nationalist group opposed to the payment of Roman taxes. What is clear is that both they and the Pharisees are seeking to trap Jesus with a burning issue on which they believe he will be unable to avoid taking sides.

Pharisee

Scribe

Religious and political parties

Because of the conflict between Christians and Jews in the early period of the Church, the Pharisees are given a poor image in the Gospels. Matthew is the harshest of all and calls them hypocrites, vipers and blind guides (Matthew 23). Luke is less critical and, in 7:36, Jesus is depicted as eating in the house of Simon, a Pharisee.

Moreover, the Pharisees try to warn Jesus of Herod's plan to kill him (Luke 13:31). The Pharisees were characterised by their emphasis on strict observance of the laws of purity. They cleansed themselves and their utensils meticulously and excluded 'unclean' persons, such as tax collectors, the mentally or physically ill, even the physically handicapped, from eating at the same tables as themselves.

The richest and most powerful people in Jewish society were the Sadducees. They occupied a majority of seats in the Sanhedrin, Israel's highest court, and though they were not all priests, the Temple administration and worship were controlled by them. They interpreted the scriptures literally, regarding the Pentateuch as the supreme authority, and refused to believe in new doctrines, such as the resurrection of the body. 'For the Sadducees say there is neither resurrection, nor angel, nor spirit' (Acts 23:8).

Little is known of the Herodians, except that they were probably supporters of the rule and policies of Herod Antipas. He was a son of Herod the Great and ruled Galilee and Perea from 4 BC to AD 39. He is 'that fox' referred to in Luke 13:31–32 and the Herod most frequently mentioned in the Gospels.

All these religious and political groups, though they comprised the richest and best educated classes, made great use of scribes. These were originally Jewish scholars who knew the art of writing; later the term came to mean an official teacher of Jewish Law based on the Hebrew Bible and on tradition.

The coinage of Israel

The coin referred to by Jesus during his pronouncement on payment of tribute to Caesar was almost certainly a denarius, a small silver coin whose value was equivalent to a labourer's wage for one day's work (Matthew 20:2). Prior to the Jewish–Roman war, the Temple tax was equal to two denarii. Payment of this tax could be made from home during the month preceding Passover, or within the Temple precincts during the 20 days immediately prior to the feast. In New Testament times, there were important mints for Roman imperial coinage at Pergamon, Ephesus, Antioch and Alexandria in the east. Unlike small local coinage, which usually bore neutral images, such as grapes or pomegranates, the Roman coinage had religious symbols.

The small coin mentioned in Mark 12:42, the widow's mite, was a Greek 'lepton', the coin of least value then in circulation. The 30 pieces of silver paid to Judas Iscariot (Matthew 26:15) were probably silver shekels and equivalent to about 120 denarii. This was the amount of compensation or 'blood money' payable for an accidentally slain slave, according to Exodus 21:32.

At the time of the Jewish–Roman war, coins were struck with the inscription 'shekel of Israel', the likeness of three pomegranates and the words 'Jerusalem is holy'. But when the revolt was suppressed, Vespasian and Titus issued coins with the Latin inscription, 'Judaea in captivity'. At the same time, the Temple tax was increased to a half-shekel, that is two denarii, and became payable to Rome. It is impossible to value in modern terms coins in use so long ago, only their worth in relation to each other.

Coin showing a barbarian holding out a child to Augustus

A denarius 'tribute penny': Tiberius AD 14–37

A denarius: Augustus 27 BC–AD 14

Coin of Nero's reign showing Ostia harbour and Neptune

These silver coins and bronze pot, *above*, from the last centuries BC and the 1st century AD were found during an archaeological excavation and are kept in the Israeli Museum, Jerusalem. Coins are especially valuable finds because they can be accurately dated.

Because of the variety of moneys in circulation in Jerusalem, due to its cosmopolitan nature and particularly during the influx of pilgrims at times of major festivals, money-changing as a trade flourished.

The money-changers were seated at the gate of a city or close to important buildings, such as the Temple. In addition to exacting a fee of four to eight percent and thus contravening Jewish laws concerning usury, there were great temptations on money-changers and some of them cheated in the payments for sacrificial animals. Hence Jesus' anger with them in the Gospel story (Matthew 21:12–13; Mark 11:15; Luke 19:45–46).

The last supper

On the night in which he was betrayed by Judas, Jesus ate his last supper with his disciples. The apostle Paul, writing to the Corinthians in about AD 57, gave an account of what happened. Paul needed to put them straight about what it meant to join in the supper of the Lord, which clearly was repeatedly commemorated. Jesus had taken bread, blessed it, broken it and given it to the disciples, saying, 'This is my body, which is for you'. He had then taken a cup of wine, given thanks, and passed it round, saying, 'This cup is the new covenant in my blood'. Paul suggests that every time Christians do this in memory of Jesus, they proclaim his death until his coming again.

Paul's account of the last supper is the earliest written record. The Gospels all contain accounts of it too. In Matthew and Mark, the wording is slightly different, no doubt because different Churches repeated the words in their liturgy in slightly different ways, which then influenced the Gospel accounts.

Luke's account of the supper is rather puzzling: the manuscripts give two different forms of the text, and it looks as though the longer form was produced by scribes who added in bits from Paul and Mark. The shorter form of the text has some odd features, and some scholars think that Luke may have known a different, possibly older, form of the story. In this, the interpretation centred not on the death of Jesus, but on the idea that this celebration anticipated the feast of God's kingdom.

John's Gospel says nothing about the bread and wine, though his account does overlap with the others. Instead of distributing bread and wine, Jesus washes the feet of the disciples. Even so, the author of this Gospel must have known about the giving of bread and wine because in the discourse following his version of the feeding of the multitude (see pp.153–3), Jesus says: 'If you do not eat the flesh of the Son of Man and drink his blood you have no life in you.'

In John, the last supper cannot have been the traditional Jewish Passover meal, which commemorated the escape of the first-born Jewish children from the angel of death in Egypt (see pp.34–5). Jesus was crucified at the sixth hour on the Day of Preparation – the time, in fact, when the Passover lambs were being killed in the Temple for the feast. Also, Paul says in 1 Corinthians 5:7, 'For our Passover has been sacrificed, that is, Christ', which supports John's account.

The other Gospels, however, identify the last supper as the Passover meal, although there is no description of the full meal, no mention of the customary bitter herbs nor the Passover lamb. But then the accounts have been 'streamlined' by their use in the Church, and concentrate solely on what was, and is, significant for Christians. There are some hints that it may have been a Passover meal: even in John there is mention of people 'dipping' in a common dish, which, like the blessing of several cups of wine, is a feature of the meal.

But Luke hints that in that year Jesus did not actually eat the Passover meal, but anticipated it: 'I have ardently longed to eat this Passover with you before I suffer; because, I tell you, I shall not eat it until it is fulfilled in the kingdom of God' (22:15). Whether or not the last supper was the actual Passover meal, the death of Jesus clearly took place at Passover time, and his last supper signified what his death was about. Just as the blood of the Passover lamb had saved the people of God from the angel of death, so the blood of Christ provided the way of salvation.

The death of Judas
According to all four Gospels, Jesus predicted his betrayal during the last supper and the identification of Judas as betrayer is generally associated with Jesus dipping the sop of bread (John 13:26). Possibly Judas had been a Zealot, was attracted by Jesus' promise of God's kingdom and then became disillusioned. Possibly he was impatient and was trying to force Jesus' hand rather than destroy him. That might explain his subsequent suicide by hanging (Matthew 27:5), depicted, *above*, in a twelfth-century bas-relief in the cathedral of Autun, France.

The washing of the feet
John's Gospel alone tells us of Jesus washing his disciples' feet at the last supper, as shown in this twelfth-century painting in St Martin's church at Zillis, Switzerland. Peter protested at the action. A dialogue ensued which perhaps points symbolically to baptism and the cleansing from sin which Jesus brought. The act, however, is also a demonstration of Jesus' reversal of values; for it was the duty of a wife or a slave to wash the master's feet: Jesus proceeds to glory and kingship, not by the way of power, but by the way of the cross.

Luke's Gospel, unlike Mark's and Matthew's, emphasises this reversal of values by placing at the last supper the disciples' dispute about greatness, and Jesus' reply: 'the greatest among you must behave as if he were the youngest . . .' (22:26).

Christian art has usually made the event of the last supper contemporary, since it survives in the repeated commemoration of the Church's Mass or communion service. In his famous Milan mural, Leonardo da Vinci painted the scene on the end wall of a refectory and depicted Jesus and his disciples sitting at the high table. By the 12th century, the apostles were usually depicted seated at a table, as seen in the miniature, *right*, from a Syriac codex. The Gospels, however, show that they reclined to eat. This was common in the ancient world, and in earlier Christian art, like the 6th-century mosaic, *above*, in Sant' Apollinare Nuovo, Ravenna, it was depicted in this way.

It has been suggested that this reclining posture is another hint of the special Passover character of the meal. However, since the Greek word for reclining at table is used quite naturally elsewhere in the Gospels, for example when Jesus eats with tax collectors and sinners at the house of Levi (Mark 2:15), the argument does not seem to be strong.

One argument against Jesus' last supper being a Passover meal is the fact that it was not a family occasion – neither women nor children being present. It seems more like the private fellowship-meal of a close-knit religious group (a Chaburah). Since the discovery of the Dead Sea scrolls, however, the taking of meals as it is described there, with prayers and stipulated food and wine, has been seen as a more striking parallel to the last supper. Members of the Dead Sea sect apparently blessed bread and wine to anticipate the feast of God's kingdom.

Jesus' arrest and trial

The final stages of Jesus' life are well known. Each Gospel tells of his arrest in the Garden of Gethsemane, of a series of trials, and the death sentence passed by Pilate. But the accounts do not precisely correspond (e.g. Jesus' trial before Herod Antipas is found only in Luke), and they raise all kinds of questions about what actually happened. Who was really behind the move to get rid of Jesus? What was the real nature of the charges brought against him?

The first three Gospels suggest that the chief priests and elders of the people were responsible for Jesus' arrest, that he was tried before the Jewish Sanhedrin, and that the Jewish authorities, supported by the crowds, then engineered his condemnation and execution by the Romans. The tendency of all the Gospels is to exonerate the Romans and blame the Jews. But there are hints that this may not be the full picture.

According to John's Gospel, soldiers, presumably Roman, were involved in the arrest; according to Luke, Jesus faced specifically political charges before Pilate; and the one point the Gospels are definite on is that Jesus was put to death by the Romans. Crucifixion was a Roman punishment. The Jewish punishment for blasphemy was stoning to death. So it was not a Jewish court which passed the crucial sentence.

In Mark 14, the report of Jesus' trial by the Sanhedrin is problematic. Evidence suggests that the procedures described were highly irregular – it was probably not a formal trial but a preliminary investigation. Luke has no night trial. The Jews drew up charges against Jesus which would cut some ice with the Roman authorities: 'We found this man inciting our people to revolt, opposing payment of tribute to Caesar, and claiming to be Christ, a King' (23:2). That Pilate was responding to charges of this kind is clear from the *titulus* on the cross: 'This is Jesus, the King of the Jews.' Jesus was condemned as a disturber of the peace, presumably as a 'Zealot' – a Jewish freedom-fighter.

The Gospels present Jesus as innocent of such charges, suggesting that they were trumped up by the Jewish authorities who had religious reasons for getting rid of him. The Jews accuse Jesus of blasphemy for claiming to be the 'Christ the Son of the Blessed', i.e. the Messiah. But claiming to be the Messiah was not technically 'blasphemy', and the idea that Jesus was condemned for making this claim may reflect Christian frustration at continuing failure to convince the Jews of Jesus' Messiahship.

A more plausible case for blasphemy may be found in the charge that Jesus said he would destroy the Temple, presented as a 'false' charge in Mark 14:58, though a similar saying is actually reported on the lips of Jesus in John's Gospel (2:19). Certainly, all the Gospels suggest that Jesus antagonised the various religious authorities over sensitive issues like keeping the Sabbath and strict observance of the Law.

In terms of the historical context, the real reason why Jesus was put to death may well lie in the highly charged atmosphere created by Roman occupation, and the constant need for the Jewish authorities to find a way of living with a hated necessity.

The remark of the high priest Caiaphas to other Jewish leaders, reported by John, is a telling one: 'You do not seem to have grasped the situation at all; you fail to see that it is to your advantage that one man should die for the people, rather than that the whole nation should perish' (11:49–50). In other words, it is better to get rid of anyone who might upset the status quo, rather than risk confrontation with the Romans.

The strange story of Jesus Bar-Abbas
The Gospels tell us that Pontius Pilate tried to save Jesus by exploiting a custom whereby a prisoner was released at the Passover. Instead, the crowd demanded that Barabbas be freed, a man described as a 'bandit' who had instigated rebellion and committed murder. The word translated 'bandit' is the one the Jewish historian Josephus uses for 'Zealot'. So the Gospel story is full of dramatic irony: a presumed freedom-fighter is released and one innocent of such activities is condemned.

This story has so many curious features that it has led to much speculation. One suggestion has been that Jesus and Barabbas were together involved in an attempted coup – while Jesus took over the Temple, Barabbas stormed the citadel. Both were arrested when the attempt failed. Although some nationalists may have hoped that Jesus would lead a fight for freedom, such a reconstruction of events seems implausible.

The main difficulty about the story as it stands is that there is no evidence anywhere else of the custom of releasing a prisoner at feast time. If Barabbas had been condemned to death, only the Roman emperor could have released him, and it is unlikely that anything could have induced a responsible governor to release a notorious nationalist. It is entirely out of character with what is known of Pilate from Josephus.

Even more curious is the man's name. One of the texts seems originally to have read Jesus Bar-Abbas. Presumably the 'Jesus' was removed from the manuscripts of Matthew because it was offensive to attribute such a sacred name to such a man. A further oddity is that Bar-Abbas means 'Son of the Father', precisely what Jesus claims to be in John's Gospel. It remains possible that the whole story developed out of a misunderstanding.

Pontius Pilate: man of caution or tyrant?
Found in the theatre of Caesarea, this stone has the only known inscription of Pilate – '[Pon]tius Pilatus' – seen below 'Tiberieum' (*top*). According to the Jewish historian Josephus, while he was governor of Judaea, Pilate was involved in several confrontations with the Jews. He was a harsh ruler and one determined to maintain law and order in a particularly sensitive Roman province. He knew that Jewish religious sensibilities had political implications and he could not afford to be tolerant.

This is hardly the character indicated in the Gospels. Such a man would scarcely be moved by questions of innocence and truth or give way to the mob. But Pilate was an appointee of Tiberius' minister Sejanus, who was condemned for treason in AD 31. His associates were suspect. If the crucifixion was after that date, the threat 'If you set him free you are no friend of Caesar's (John 19:12) would be a grave one.

After the verdict

'Pilate then gave his verdict: their demand was to be granted. He released the man they asked for, who had been imprisoned because of rioting and murder, and handed Jesus over to them to deal with as they pleased' (Luke 23:24–5).

Jesus, after carrying his cross to the place of execution, was crucified between two 'bandits'. With the possible exception of being burnt alive, crucifixion was the most dreadful of punishments. Many people thought it unfit for free men.

There was only one 'merciful' aspect to this form of execution: the most severe scourging was inflicted prior to crucifixion to weaken the condemned man's resistance and cause him to die sooner. The instrument used was the *flagellum*, a savage type of scourge which might be embellished with flesh-tearing hooks and which, with every lash, encircled the body.

The exact route taken by Jesus from his place of trial and condemnation to Calvary is uncertain because the destruction of Jerusalem in AD 70 and its later rebuilding by the Romans effectively erased the city as it was in Jesus' time. Moreover, it is uncertain whether Jesus was condemned at the Antonia, **1**, close by the Temple, **2**, or whether Pilate was at the time residing at Herod's upper palace, **3**.

Modern scholars tend to accept the latter, in which case Jesus' way to Calvary, **4**, would have followed line **5**, but the earlier supposition has not been disproved and Jesus may therefore have gone along the other route, **6**. The third line, **7**, indicates the possible path taken by Jesus after his arrest in the Garden of Gethsemane, after which he was taken to the house of Caiaphas, situated at either **8** or **9**.

Whichever route Jesus took to Calvary, a number of incidents occurred between his being condemned and his being laid to rest in the Holy Sepulchre, and are revered as the 14 Stations of the Cross. The first is where Jesus was condemned to death, the second where he received his cross and the third where he is thought to have fallen for the first time. The fourth station marks the spot where he met his mother and the fifth where Simon of Cyrene was ordered to carry his cross. At the sixth station a lady of Jerusalem named Veronica wiped his face with a handkerchief, on which his features were said to have become imprinted. At the seventh station, Jesus fell for the second time. At the eighth, he met a group of weeping women and urged them to think not of him but of themselves. Jesus fell again at the ninth station, and the tenth marks the spot where he was stripped of his clothes. The remaining four stations mark his being nailed to the cross, dying on the cross, being taken down from the cross and being laid in the sepulchre respectively.

The Third Station of the Cross, *below*, marks the spot where Jesus fell for the first time under his heavy burden. This incident is not mentioned in the Gospels but belief in it is ancient, and shortly afterwards Jesus needed help to carry the cross. This sculpture is above the entrance to the Polish Chapel in the Via Dolorosa.

Crucified

He was crucified under Pontius Pilate – the words from the traditional Christian creeds – records an event that is one of the cornerstones of the Christian faith. It is also a solidly based historical event. The Roman historian, Tacitus, writing of the Christians, says that 'Christ, the originator of their name, had been condemned to death by Pontius Pilate in the reign of Tiberius' (*Annals* 15.44).

The Gospels record that, after his trial, Jesus was taken outside the city and crucified with two 'bandits' or guerrillas, before the eyes of the women of his circle and jeering bystanders. Then there is said to have been a spreading darkness and, at his death, an earthquake and damage to the Temple curtain.

The Roman punishment of crucifixion was, according to the Roman statesman Cicero, the extreme penalty. It was only rarely applied to Roman citizens and was the typical penalty for slaves; it is sometimes called 'the slaves' sentence'. Jesus, of course, was not crucified for being a slave, but early Christian writers were quick to use the link: they identified Jesus with the image of the Suffering Servant (or Suffering Slave) in Isaiah, and in the hymn which Paul quotes in writing to Philippi, Christians sang how Jesus took the form of a slave and was crucified (Philippians 2:7–8).

More particularly, crucifixion was a penalty for rebellion against Rome. It was also a penalty for banditry: freedom-fighters were nicknamed 'bandits'. The *titulus* or notice affixed to the cross over his head gave the charge (Mark 15:26). The four Gospel writers present it in slightly different forms, but all include 'The King of the Jews'.

Jesus was not executed as a blasphemer (for which the Jewish penalty was stoning - see Leviticus 24:13–16; Acts 7:57), but as a revolutionary, who set up his authority against that of Ceasar. Jesus was seen as a danger to the values of the establishment, whether in Judaea or Rome. But Jesus was an unusual revolutionary who opted for nonviolent, as opposed to violent, action.

In a typical crucifixion, the agony of the condemned man started before he was nailed to the cross. First, he was scourged, which would leave him weak. Then, he was expected to carry the beam of the cross through the streets with the notice of his crime preceding him or hung round his neck. The upright was secured in position at the place of execution. On arrival, the condemned man was stripped and laid flat on his back. The crossbeam was pushed under his neck, and his arms were tied to it. The hands were then nailed in position.

The beam was lifted by ropes and nailed to make a 'T' with the upright, with a small projection for the notice; the weight of the body was taken by a peg. The feet were then nailed to the upright. Victims usually survived till death by exposure or hunger; there is evidence that a lance wound was sometimes given to accelerate death. The body was usually left to decay, but might be released to the victim's friends.

Crucifixion was regarded as shameful, ignominious, in-famous, and the pagans made the most of this in their attacks on the young Church. The Christians could well understand that their proclamation of Christ crucified was 'to the Jews an obstacle they cannot get over, to the gentiles foolishness' (1 Corinthians 1:23). But they could discern God's power and wise purposes through the apparent shame and failure. They saw God reigning from the cross (Christian versions of Psalm 96:10).

Roman crucifixion
The drawing shows a typical Roman crucifixion with the nails going through the man's wrists, the legs bent and the feet affixed to the cross by a nail and piece of wood. The Gospels state that nails pierced Jesus' palms which almost certainly would not have borne his weight, unless his arms had been bound to the crossbeam.

A Roman jibe at Jesus?
One of the earliest known depictions of Jesus' crucifixion is this graffito on the wall of a house on the Palatine Hill in Rome, in which he is satirically depicted with an ass's head. (There was a current slander that the Jews worshipped an ass-headed god.) Nearby a male figure stands with an arm raised in prayer. Below is the legend, 'Alexamenos worships God', suggesting that it was derisively aimed perhaps at a slave who had become a target of his fellows for his belief in Christ.

Jesus on the cross, a painted wooden crucifix in the church of S. Croce, Florence. The figure by his right hand is that of Mary, his mother, and to his left the apostle John.

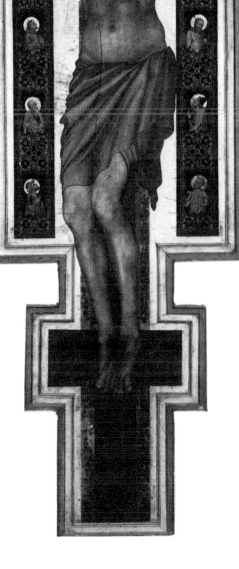

כלן היהודים

REX IVDAEORVM

OBACIΛEYC TωNIOYΔAIωN

According to John (19:19–24), Pontius Pilate wrote out the *titulus*, or notice, for the condemned Jesus. The *titulus* was hung around a criminal's neck on his way to execution and then affixed to the cross above his head. John records that Jesus' *titulus* read: 'Jesus the Nazarene, King of the Jews'. The other Gospel writers give different versions of the *titulus* but all include the words 'King of the Jews', written in Hebrew, *top*, Latin and Greek.

Seven sayings by Jesus on the cross are recorded: three in Luke only, three in John only, and one in Mark and Matthew. The first calls for forgiveness of his crucifiers; the second a promise to one of the bandits crucified with him; the third commends John to Mary and Mary to John. Then follows a cry of despair from Psalm 22 and a statement of his thirst. The last two appear in John and Luke as his final words, both showing that he died in faith.

'Father, forgive them; they do not know what they are doing' (Luke 23:34).
'In truth I tell you, today you will be with me in Paradise' (Luke 23:42).
'Woman, this is your son. . . . This is your mother (John 19:27)
'*Eloi, eloi, lama sabachthani*?' ('My God, my God, why have you forsaken me?') (Mark 15:34; Matthew 27:46).
'I am thirsty' (John 19:28)
'It is fulfilled' (John 19:30).
'Father, into your hands I commend my spirit' (Luke 23:46).

Resurrected from the dead

After Jesus had died on the cross, all four Gospels relate that Joseph, a man from Arimathaea (a place not certainly identified), went to Pilate to ask for Jesus' body. An apocryphal writing describes Joseph as 'a friend of both Pilate and the Lord', which may be right. Pilate granted the request. Joseph took the body away, wrapping it in a linen cloth, helped according to John by Nicodemus, a Sanhedrin member.

With the Sabbath approaching, the work had to be done quickly. The body was placed in an unused rock-cut tomb, perhaps bought by Joseph against his own burial. John says that it was in a garden near the place of crucifixion. The tomb was sealed, as normally, by a heavy wheel-shaped stone. Matthew says that in addition a guard was set.

Exactly what happened next is not known. Matthew alone tells of an earthquake. All the Gospels agree that Mary of Magdala, with or without the other women, came early to the tomb (with spices for the body), and found the tomb open and the body gone. Mark says that they saw a man in a white robe, Luke two men, Matthew an angel, who told them that Jesus was risen, as he had promised. John has the beautiful account of Mary of Magdala wandering disconsolate, and seeing a figure she took to be the gardener. She found it to be Jesus, who would not let her touch him. An interesting aspect of this is that a manual worker might well strip down to his loincloth, probably the sole garment of the crucifixion.

The Gospels give a number of accounts of Jesus appearing to the disciples individually and in groups. One of the most attractive is of two who encountered him as they walked to Emmaus, not recognising him until he sat down to supper with them and in a characteristic gesture broke bread.

But the body with which he appeared was no ordinary body, for though there is the story of 'doubting Thomas' being invited to touch him and another story of his eating with them (both in John), there are also stories of his appearing in a room with locked doors or suddenly disappearing. Paul ranks his vision on the road to Damascus with the other resurrection appearances (1 Corinthians 15:8).

The appearances continued for a period; then Jesus took his disciples to the Mount of Olives, blessed them, was lifted up and vanished from them in a mist. This is called the ascension. They then went back to Jerusalem, and waited for the coming of the Spirit.

Whatever happened, one thing is certain. The disciples who, denying their Master, had run away from those with powers of arrest and execution were found defying them within a few weeks and proclaiming Jesus. They said it was because he had risen from the dead.

If Jesus had not really died but swooned, this would not explain their conviction nor the strange nature of the appearances. If the body was stolen, it would explain the empty tomb, but not their experience of his presence. Were the disciples suffering from mass hallucination? But the appearances, over a number of weeks, were sometimes to individuals. Were they making fraudulent claims? If so, it was the most successful fraud in history! But this does not fit their behaviour.

What is certain is the disciples' conviction that they had experienced the living presence of Jesus after his crucifixion. Those experiences, however explained, not the empty tomb, were the foundation on which the Christian Church was built.

A stylised 6th-century mosaic, *left*, in the church of Sant' Apollinare Nuovo, Ravenna, depicts an angel, with Mary, the mother of James, and Mary of Magdala. They stand in awe before Jesus' tomb, now empty following his resurrection. 'And suddenly there was a violent earthquake, for an angel of the Lord, descending from heaven, came and rolled away the stone and sat on it' (Matthew 28:2).

Wheel-shaped stones, *below left*, were used in Jesus' time to impede grave-robbers, since the custom was to leave precious objects with the deceased. The stone was usually located on a slope, so that a wedge was needed to fasten it open before the grave was entered.

Jesus' ascension into heaven is portrayed on this 16th-century icon on the screen of the church of S. Neophytos, near Paphos, Cyprus. After his resurrection, Jesus appeared several times to his disciples before his ascension into heaven.

The Turin mystery: Jesus' shroud or medieval fake?

The cathedral at Turin has, since 1578, housed a linen cloth, suitable for a shroud, bearing the imprint of a well-proportioned male figure, 5ft 11½in/1.8m tall, of majestic countenance, with Semitic features and bearded. The figure had been scourged – there are lash marks on the back of the image – and crucified, with nails through wrists and feet. The cloth is compatible with weaving at the time of Jesus; pollen grains in it include those of plants characteristic of Jerusalem and Edessa. Might the cloth be the shroud that wrapped Jesus' body?

The cloth came to Italy from France; so much is certain. All else remains speculation. But there is a tradition that after the crucifixion, Thaddaeus, one of the disciples, brought a portrait to Edessa, in south central Turkey, where King Abgar V was converted to faith in Christ. This cloth, called the mandylion or the 'Edessan image', was rediscovered in 525 in a niche above Edessa's west gate and the likeness on it seems to have affected representations of Jesus in art. The mandylion passed to Constantinople, then disappeared during the city's sack by the Crusaders in 1204. Many think it was taken to France and that it is identical with the Turin Shroud, and that the portrait that Thaddaeus took to Edessa was in fact the shroud of Jesus.

Scientists are investigating. Analysis by Walter McCrone, head of the McCrone Research Institute in Chicago, led him in 1986 to suggest that the image was painted on the cloth during the Middle Ages, because there is no blood in the cloth; the red particles adhering to the flax fibres, he argued, were iron oxide, such as is found in red paint. Other specialists, including Ian Wilson, a British expert on the Shroud, claim that the red particles are organic and therefore cannot be iron oxide.

The day of the Pentecost

Originally a festival of harvest, the Jewish feast of Pentecost was also the commemoration of the gift of the Law at Sinai (see p.40). It was a time when Jews from many different places came to Jerusalem to celebrate at the Temple.

That Pentecost morning described in Acts 2, the disciples of Jesus were together in an upper room, when suddenly a powerful gust of wind blew into the house and what seemed to be 'tongues of fire' rested on the head of each. Wind and fire were familiar attributes of God's intervention, as when he gave his Law to Moses on Mount Sinai (Exodus 19:16). But now they signalled the coming of the gift promised by Jesus: the Holy Spirit.

In the past, when God's spirit came upon people, it transformed them, giving them the power to work wonders and making them prophesy with inspired language (Numbers 11:25). So now, when the flames came upon them, the disciples of Jesus were filled or 'baptised' with the Spirit and began to speak in different languages (Acts 2:4).

The 'sound as of a violent wind' was heard not only by the disciples, but also by the crowd that gathered from 'every nation under heaven', an obvious, if discreet, allusion to the story of Babel when Yahweh caused the people of the world to speak different languages (see pp.16–19).

It is uncertain whether the disciples spoke the diverse languages of all these different nationalities or their Galilean dialect. Perhaps they spoke, not in an intelligible language, but in 'ecstatic sounds'. However the disciples did, in fact, speak, the crowd could still understand that, though they appeared drunk, the disciples were praising God and telling of his mighty works (Acts 2:11).

After this, Peter began to preach, explaining, in terms to which Jews could relate, the importance of Jesus as Messiah, and telling of his resurrection. At the end, a great number of people believed and were baptised. It was in this way that the Church began.

For Luke, the author of the Acts of the Apostles, the descent of the Holy Spirit upon Jesus' disciples gathered in Jerusalem, is a decisive turning point. In his Gospel, Luke relates 'what Jesus had done and taught' in person. In Acts, he shows what Jesus continued to do through his witnesses, the disciples. With this new presence of Jesus through the Holy Spirit, the believers became the Church, and were sent to be witnesses of Jesus 'not only in Jerusalem, but throughout Judaea and Samaria, and indeed to earth's remotest end' (Acts 1:8).

The city of Jerusalem, where the Christian Church was born, has a symbolic significance. In the Old Testament, it was foreseen that God would bring the glory of all the nations back to Jerusalem (Isaiah 66), and also that messengers would go out from there to the lands that had not heard of God's name (Isaiah 66:19; 2:3).

Luke's Gospel presents Jesus initially as journeying towards Jerusalem; it closes as he meets the disciples after the resurrection and charges them with preaching the message of salvation and forgiveness of sin. Acts opens with a reminder that this task will start from Jerusalem, but not until the disciples have received the power of the Holy Spirit. In this way, Acts tells of the growth of the Church, always making clear the crucial role of the Spirit in giving power to those who preached the word.

The power of the Spirit

Throughout the Bible there are many different references to the Spirit, the Spirit of God, the Holy Spirit or the Holy Ghost. In the Old Testament, qualities of leadership and strength were given by the Spirit and attributed to the Spirit's power. The insight which gave the prophets the ability to see and understand what was hidden from others was a particular gift of the Spirit.

This gift allowed them to proclaim with absolute assurance that their message was the Word of the Lord. Through the guidance given to the leaders and the inspiration given to the prophets, God called his people to himself and enabled them to follow his bidding. When the people proved disobedient, he nonetheless promised to send his quickening Spirit on them and all humankind (Ezekiel 36:27; 37:1–14; Joel 3:1–2).

Jesus is shown in the Gospels as having received the Spirit at his baptism. He himself quotes Isaiah 61:1–2 early in his ministry: 'The Spirit of the Lord is upon me' (Luke 4:18). Jesus' works, the wisdom of his teaching and the good he did, are attributed to the workings of the Spirit through him. He promised the gift of the Spirit to the disciples (John 14:17, 26) and on almost every page Acts shows the Church inspired and guided by the Spirit. The presence of the Spirit is manifested through the various gifts received by members of the community, all given by the Spirit to be shared among God's people (1 Corinthians 12:1–11). So, from knowing God in the traditions of Israel as creator and Lord of nature and history, in Jesus, and in the presence of the Spirit, Christians came to the belief that God is One, yet also Three, Father, Son and Holy Spirit.

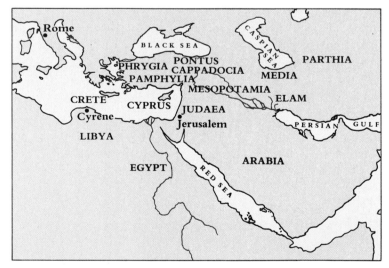

'Men living in Jerusalem from every nation . . . Parthians, Medes and Elamites; people from Mesopotamia, Judaea and Cappadocia, Pontus and Asia, Phrygia and Pamphylia, Egypt and Libya round Cyrene, residents of Rome – Jews and proselytes – Cretans and Arabs' (ACTS 2:9–10). Were these 'men living in Jerusalem' pilgrims or, more probably, residing in the city? The 'assembly' in Jerusalem represented the whole known world. The list of peoples probably reflects ancient astrological documents, in which nations are listed geographically from east to west and from north to south.

Christians celebrate Pentecost to this day in commemoration of the coming of the Spirit.

Simon Peter, *above*, was the accepted leader of the early Church. It was he who came forward to explain the meaning of the events of Pentecost. His name was Simon, his home Bethsaida near Lake Tiberias, his profession that of fisherman. His brother Andrew brought him to Jesus, who nicknamed him Cephas – Peter or 'Rock'.

In character he appears vigorous and impetuous. Jesus saw his failings, and saw the strength and loyalty which would overcome them; when there was a small group close to Jesus, he was always there. At Caesarea Philippi, it was he who called Jesus the Messiah and was commended in the words 'On this rock I will build my community' (Matthew 16:18).

Yet, when Jesus showed that Messiahship meant suffering, Peter protested, and was rebuked. It was he who in Gethsemane tried to protect Jesus by violence; after the arrest he denied his master three times. After the resurrection, he three times asserted his love for Jesus, who told him to feed his sheep.

So Peter went out preaching and healing, facing punishment with courage. He admitted the gentile Cornelius to the Church, though Paul complained that he did not stand by this. At some point he probably went to Rome. When persecution came he tried to escape, but one tradition says a vision of Jesus sent him back, and he was crucified traditionally head-downwards.

This illumination, from a 13th-century psalter, *left*, shows the ascension in the top panel and Pentecost below. Pentecost (the '50th' day after the Passover) is an important Christian and Jewish feast, held in spring at the end of the grain harvest. It was on the first Pentecost after the resurrection of Jesus that the Holy Spirit descended on the disciples. Christians celebrate Pentecost or Whit Sunday as the festival of the coming of the Spirit.

167

Philip converts the Ethiopian eunuch

On the road from Jerusalem to Gaza, according to Acts 8:26–40, Philip, one of the Jerusalem Christians, came across a man in a chariot who was a eunuch and court official of the queen of Ethiopia. Philip noticed that the eunuch was reading Isaiah and asked him whether he understood it. The eunuch invited Philip to guide him on the text and Philip, starting with the Isaiah passage, went on to explain the Good News of Jesus to him.

Soon they came to some water and the eunuch asked Philip to baptise him in it. When Philip had done so, he 'was taken away by the Spirit of the Lord, and the eunuch never saw him again but went on his way rejoicing' (Acts 8:39).

The story of Philip and the Ethiopian eunuch indicates a significant development in the early Church. At first, the group of Jesus' disciples appeared to be an association within Judaism, but soon the radical distinction between the new faith and the traditional Jewish religion became clear. To become a member of the Church it was no more necessary to submit first to the Jewish Law (Acts 15).

Philip was one of the seven disciples elected to ensure a fair distribution of material goods among the Jerusalem Christians, after the Greek-speaking or Hellenist community had complained that their needy members were being overlooked (Acts 6:1–6). The names of the seven sound Greek: probably they were chosen from this group of 'Hellenists', that is, those who had come to Palestine from the different countries of the Jewish dispersion. The Hellenists seem to have formed distinct groups, with separate synagogues according to their countries of origin, and were different from the Hebrew-speaking indigenous Jews, perhaps even in their religious thinking and customs.

It is possible that Christians from this group were more prepared to preach to non-Jews than the strictly Palestinian Christians, and so they led the way in this. Stephen and his fellow deacons certainly did not restrict their activities to social concerns. Stephen was stoned to death for his bold preaching, and the Hellenistic Christians were then forced to leave Jerusalem in the persecution that followed. While some went to Phoenicia, Cyprus and Antioch, Philip's evangelistic initiative was in Samaria.

His meeting with the Ethiopian is inspired by 'the angel of the Lord'. Ethiopia here probably refers to the northern Sudan, where in apostolic times the Kushite kingdom of Meroë in Nubia was still flourishing. He is called a eunuch, which, if taken literally, would have excluded him from participation in Jewish religion (Deuteronomy 23:1). In oriental court language, however, officials were often called eunuchs, even if they were not so physically. Perhaps the designation is deliberately given here to show that Christianity excluded nobody on such human grounds: Philip freely preaches to him the Good News of Jesus so that this pilgrim, who had gone to seek God among the Jews, finds in the new faith what he was seeking.

The punchline in the story seems to lie in the eunuch's question to Philip: 'Is there anything to prevent my being baptised?' The answer is, of course, 'Nothing'. From now on there is to be no distinction between Jews and gentiles, between slaves and freemen, between men and women (Galatians 3:28). The faith could now spread freely to all nations, even through this new convert returning home and bringing the Good News of Jesus to his fellow citizens of Nubia.

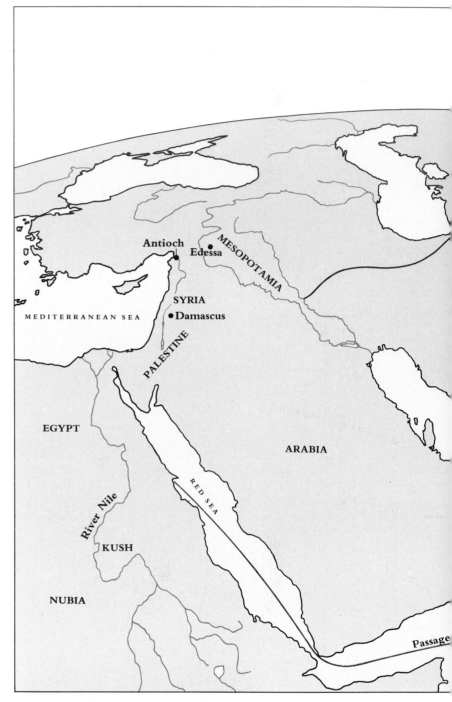

'Like a lamb led to the slaughter house, like a sheep dumb in front of its shearers' (ACTS 8:32) The eunuch was reading this passage of Isaiah (53:7) when he was approached by Philip. Among the manuscripts discovered in caves near the Dead Sea (see pp. 86–7) was the famous Isaiah scroll, part of which is shown *above*.

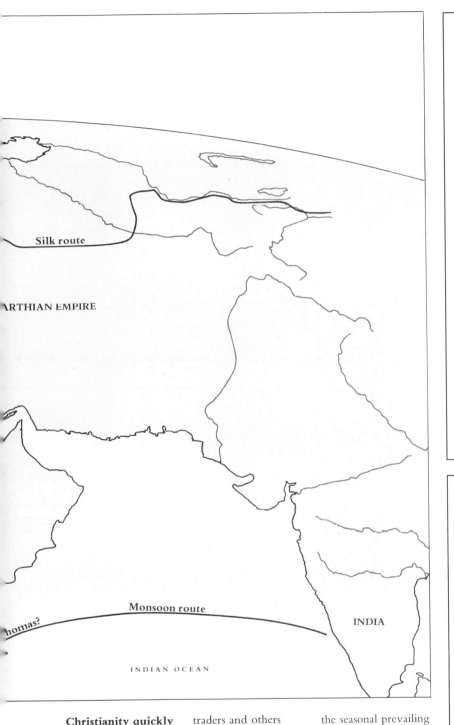

Silk route

ARTHIAN EMPIRE

homas?

Monsoon route

INDIA

INDIAN OCEAN

Antioch: the second city of early Christianity

'Some of them . . . went to Antioch, where they started preaching also to the Greeks, proclaiming the good news of the Lord Jesus to them' (Acts 11:20). Antioch, famous for its 'cave church', *above*, supposedly the first church in Christianity, was where the disciples were first called Christians.

It became the centre for the mission to the gentiles. It was to Antioch that Barnabas came from Jerusalem and Paul from Tarsus to be 'set apart by the Spirit for the special task'. Antioch grew into the most important Christian centre after Jerusalem and it was from there that Paul set out on his three missionary journeys.

Christianity's early expansion

The episode of Philip and the Ethiopian official exemplifies the links that existed for many centuries between Palestine and the lands of present-day Africa. Egypt, land of the pharaohs, is better known in the Bible than the countries farther south, which are mentioned less frequently. Egypt, however, was in contact with the kingdoms which flourished farther up the Nile valley and along the Red Sea in what are today Sudan and Ethiopia.

The kingdom of Kush in Nubia, between Aswan and Khartoum, was even strong enough to wrest power from the pharaohs in the eighth century BC and rule all Egypt for 100 years. The name of Ethiopia in ancient texts referred to this Nubian area, with its capital first at Napata, then at Meroë, rather than to present-day Ethiopia, which is linked with another ancient kingdom, that of Axum, lying farther southeast, near the Red Sea. Christianity became firmly established in Axum, certainly in the time of King Ezana around AD 340.

Christianity may have come even earlier; there is a local legend that the apostle Matthew evangelised Ethiopia. It is doubtful, however, that the Ethiopian official in Acts was Axumite; it is more likely that he came from the Nubian kingdom of Meroë.

Women rulers, most probably queen mothers bearing the title of Candace, are mentioned in ancient literature about the Nubian kingdom and their tombs can still be visited. That a minister of the Meroitic Candaces was on a pilgrimage to Jerusalem and was reading the Jewish scriptures, suggests more than a passing acquaintance between Palestine and Kush (see also Numbers 12:1). It is equally an indication that Christianity could have reached these ancient African kingdoms quite early.

Christianity quickly spread southwards and eastwards, the message being taken by missionaries along ancient routes into Africa and into Syria, Mesopotamia and perhaps as far east as India.

Thriving Christian communities developed early in Egypt, Palestine's neighbour. Using the water route of the Nile, Christian sailors, traders and others could easily reach the kingdoms of ancient Kush, Nubia in modern Sudan, and beyond. Traces of old Christian settlements have been discovered in those areas.

India was evangelised, traditionally, by the apostle Thomas travelling by sea across the Indian Ocean, perhaps via the monsoon route, using the seasonal prevailing winds. Certainly, Syria, with its great cities such as Antioch, Damascus and Edessa, was a centre of Christian expansion. Syrian monks and evangelists are known to have used the caravan routes towards Mesopotamia and onward to the Far East and missionaries were active in pre-Islamic Arabia.

Paul's conversion: the road to Damascus

The conversion of Paul from persecutor of the Church to, arguably, the most important and famous of Christians took place in the mid thirties of the first century – within a few years of Jesus' death. Paul refers to this event in Galatians 1 and 1 Corinthians 15, and Luke reports it three times, in Acts 9, 22 and 26.

Luke's accounts agree in presenting Paul as a former persecutor of Jesus' followers. But some scholars question whether Paul's conversion happened as Luke describes it many years later. Two of the Acts accounts are in speeches which may highlight only certain aspects.

Acts 9 says that Paul (or 'Saul', his Hebrew name: as a Christian he used his Roman name) was going to Damascus to arrest and extradite for trial in Jerusalem radical Christian disciples as part of the persecution authorised by the high priest. As he approached the city, a light from heaven shone all around him. He fell to the ground and heard the words: 'Saul, Saul, why are you persecuting me?' 'Who are you Lord?' he asked. 'I am Jesus whom you are persecuting.' This brief exchange is the common element in the three accounts in Acts.

According to Acts 9, the vision caused Paul to lose his sight and he was led to Damascus by hand. Later, a disciple named Ananias came to Paul, helping to restore Paul's sight, enabling him to understand what had happened and having him baptised into the faith. But it was probably some years before Paul realised the full implications of his vision (Galatians 1:16–18). At the time, Christianity was still a sect of Judaism, so at first it was more a call within that religion than a conversion to an entirely different one.

That Paul himself believed that the risen Christ had appeared to him on the road to Damascus is indicated by what he writes in Galatians 1 – 'God . . . chose to reveal his Son in me.' Likewise, according to 1 Corinthians 15, he includes himself among the witnesses to whom Christ appeared. Like the great prophets of the Old Testament, Paul sees himself as chosen by God for a specific task – to be apostle to the gentiles.

Earlier this century, there was interest in a psychological understanding of Paul's conversion and how prepared Paul was for it. Was it as sudden as Acts suggests? In Romans 7, Paul appears to be describing an inner struggle with the demands of the Law. This has been interpreted as referring to Paul's own struggle and thus his conversion has been understood as the outcome of a long period of dissatisfaction with Judaism.

But the weakness of a merely psychological explanation of Paul's conversion is that it suggests that Christ's revelation was the necessary result of Paul's inner struggle. Also, in Philippians 3, he says that as regards the Law he was blameless. An alleged deficiency in Judaism or any explanation other than the appearance of the risen Christ does not adequately account for Paul's own theology and statements and the changes in his subsequent life.

If anything, it was the faithful witness of disciples like Stephen that may have raised questions in Paul's mind. Paul had watched while Stephen was stoned to death by the Jews for alleged blasphemy. Despite the difference in behaviour before and after his conversion, there is a measure of real continuity in Paul's experience. Before his conversion, Paul was emotionally involved against faith in Christ. Afterwards, he was emotionally involved in promoting the same faith.

The Conversion of Paul

'It happened that while he was travelling to Damascus and approaching the city, suddenly a light from heaven shone all round him' (Acts 9:3). The sequence of events leading to Paul's conversion are shown in this ninth-century manuscript. Paul's family were Pharisees of the tribe of Benjamin. He was named Saul, after King Saul, and was also given a Graeco-Roman name – the Latin *Paulus*. His home was in Tarsus in Cilicia, a free Hellenistic city and centre of Greek culture. By birth he was a Roman citizen but received his education at the renowned Gamaliel's rabbinic academy in Jerusalem. As was customary for Jews, Paul probably learnt a trade – in his case, tentmaking.

Paul first appears in the Bible as a willing witness to the stoning to death of Stephen, who had proclaimed that Jesus was the Messiah. Because of the persecution in Jerusalem, many Christians fled the city. Paul, an extremely ambitious man, went to the high priest and asked for, and was granted, letters of authority to bring Christians from Damascus for trial in Jerusalem.

His precise route is unknown but somewhere along the way Paul reached the turning point in his life. After his conversion, Paul, blinded, was led to Damascus. There, his companions took him to a street called Straight and the house of a man named Judas. Renouncing food and water, Paul passed his time in darkness and constant prayer. On the third day Ananias, a Christian, came to him, as instructed in a vision, laid his hands on him and said, 'Brother Saul, I have been sent by the Lord Jesus, who appeared to you on your way here, so that you may recover your sight and be filled with the Holy Spirit' (Acts 9:17). Then Paul could see again. 'So he got up and was baptised, and after taking some food he regained his strength' (Acts 9:18–19).

Both Acts and Paul himself describe his experience on the road to Damascus in terms typical of the call of a prophet. These are six in number: a meeting with a bright light; a vision of the Lord on a throne; the prophet falls to the ground; the prophet is raised to his feet; and he is given a call to prophecy. Finally, the prophet feels a sense of divine compulsion both during the vision and throughout his life.

Roman citizenship: its rights and obligations

Paul of Tarsus was by birth a Roman citizen (Acts 22:28). Roman citizenship was originally confined to free natives of Rome, but as Roman control extended throughout Italy and far beyond, individuals and communities, not Roman by birth, were admitted to this privileged class. Soldiers recruited in the provinces were usually made citizens. Paul's family was a strict Pharisaic one and hostile to other cultures, so the award of citizenship was probably for services rendered to the state.

A new citizen would take on the first two names, the *praenomen* and the *nomen*, of the official granting his admission, and would retain his own name as the *cognomen* or third name by which he would generally be known. The most likely explanation of Paul's *cognomen* 'Paulus' is that it was chosen because of its similarity to the Hebraic 'Saul'.

New citizens were given a document called a *diploma civitatis Romanae* or *instrumentum*. Merchants and soldiers who had to travel far from home used this as an identity card. A person such as Paul, born a Roman citizen, may have carried a certificate of birth registration for identification purposes.

A Roman citizen of any social class enjoyed strong legal protection. Magistrates were forbidden to scourge a citizen, and he retained a right of appeal from their jurisdiction to that of the emperor (Caesar) in person. Neither might they prevent him going to Rome to lodge an appeal. Hence Paul's protest that at Philippi he, a Roman citizen, was beaten without even a proper trial (Acts 16:37). Poorer citizens, however, might not have been able to find witnesses able to afford the journey to Rome and hence may have seen no advantage in appealing to Caesar. Even

in death, the Roman citizen had to be respected. He was not put to death by crucifixion but only by the sword.

Citizenship involved other rights besides legal protections. The most important were the right to contract legal marriages and the right to enter into legal contracts enforceable under Roman law. A third right, that of voting in the Roman assemblies, had always been excluded from some grants of limited citizenship, and under the empire, with the abolition of the assemblies, became non-existent.

One of the great advantages of having Roman citizenship was the right to marry the woman of one's choice, *left*. The right of *commercium* meant that a tradesman, such as this coppersmith on a stone relief from Pompeii, *above*, if a Roman citizen, had the protection of the Roman courts in validating his contracts.

Roman citizenship also carried responsibilities: a five per cent inheritance tax on large sums bequeathed to other people than close relatives was levied on every Roman citizen; and the extension of the citizenship increased the income considerably. There

were other taxes as well.

In early times, the most important public obligation (*munus*) was military service, but voluntary enlistment did away with this. (The Jews were exempt from military service anyway on religious grounds.) The citizen's main obligation was support for the local community by holding office: this eventually led to a crippling responsibility for the imperial taxes.

But the privileges far outweighed the disadvantages and it is clear that Paul and his contemporaries valued Roman citizenship highly.

Paul's first two journeys

After his conversion, Paul left the Damascus area and spent some time in Arabia, the area east and south of the Dead Sea. This was then not simply a desert area. There were Bedouin nomads with their flocks; caravans of Nabataean traders en route from the Dead Sea to the Mediterranean; great cities such as Petra, the rose-red sandstone capital of Nabataea.

Paul then did mission work in his own home area in Syria and Cilicia. It is probable that even at this period of his work, Paul did not restrict his Gospel message only to Jews, but preached to gentiles as well. How fruitful Paul's work was at this period is not known. The fact, however, that he lacked any connection with the Jerusalem Church and had not yet developed structures of his own to oversee his converts, probably meant that he was not too successful.

The development of Paul's missionary work owed much to Barnabas who had been sent from Jerusalem to work with the Church at Antioch. He realised that Paul had special gifts, and brought him from Tarsus to Antioch, 1, where the two worked together for a time. About AD 47 Barnabas took Paul with him on their first main missionary journey, which began in Cyprus.

From there they proceeded to the cities along the military road in the southern part of Asia Minor, through Pisidia and Lycaonia, passing through Pisidian Antioch, 2, Iconium, 3, Lystra, 4, and Derbe, 5, before retracing their steps to revisit the congregations they had founded. But instead of returning to Cyprus, they sailed from Attalia, 6, back to Antioch, 1.

According to Acts, it was in Antioch that some Greek-speaking Jews from Cyprus and Cyrene had first preached the Gospel to non-Jews. It was fitting, therefore, that Paul and Barnabas should defend this practice before the apostles in Jerusalem, 16, – the Jerusalem Council – held in about AD 49.

The issue was that the Jerusalem apostles should recognise the legitimacy of preaching to gentiles and of the right of the latter, after they had become Christians, to continue to live as gentiles rather than becoming Jews. The outcome was that two parallel missions were recognised – the one led by Peter to the Jews, the other led by Paul to the gentiles.

The gentile mission was thus fully endorsed. The only stipulation was that converts should refrain from certain practices, such as eating meat sacrificed to idols, in order to

This map shows the first and second journeys, red and blue lines respectively, of Paul. During the second, Paul recruited Timothy at Lystra, 4. Timothy's mother was a Jew but his father was a Greek; so Paul had to have Timothy circumcised 'on account of the Jews in the locality where everyone knew his father was Greek' (Acts 16:1–3).

One night at Troas, 7, 'Paul had a vision: a Macedonian appeared and kept urging him in these words, "Come across to Macedonia and help us." Once he had seen this vision we lost no time in arranging a passage to Macedonia, convinced that God had called us to bring them the good news' (Acts 16:9,10).

facilitate good relations with Jews. In addition, it was agreed that gentile Christian congregations should contribute alms for the poor in Jerusalem.

A second missionary journey was envisaged to strengthen the congregations founded on the first journey. But Paul and Barnabas differed over the suitability of the disciple John Mark for the journey, and also possibly because Paul was now adopting a more radical stance concerning the rights of gentile believers. So Barnabas and John Mark sailed to Cyprus. Paul took Silas with him to his home area and from there to Derbe, **5**, Lystra, **4**, and Iconium, **3**.

Having travelled through Phrygia and north Galatia, Paul arrived at Troas, **7**. A vision in the night persuaded him to cross over into Europe. He travelled along the Egnatian Way through Neapolis, **8**, Philippi, **9**, and on to Thessalonica, **10**. After visiting Beroea, **11**, and Athens, **12**, Paul went to Corinth, **13**.

He then returned briefly to Antioch, **1**, by way of Ephesus, **14**, and Caesarea, **15**. A reference to Gallio being the Roman proconsul in Corinth means Paul was there in the year 51–52, so the second missionary journey can be dated to the years 49–52.

Paul: a leader of men

Paul was the leader and coordinator of a team of workers. More than 100 names are associated with him in Acts and in his letters. Twelve of these people appear to have had a lengthy association with him. They acted as his staff, travelling with, or for, him as his full-time assistants.

Paul worked in close cooperation with men such as Barnabas, Apollos and Silvanus (Silas), who had high status in their own right and later worked independently of him. Titus, Paul's companion to the Jerusalem council, may also have later worked on his own in Dalmatia and Crete.

Mark is called Paul's co-worker and, with interruptions, continued to assist him over many years. Tychicus carried Paul's letters and Erastus worked with Timothy in Macedonia. Timothy, a half-Greek, half-Jewish young man and one of Paul's closest assistants, represented him to the gentiles for some 15 years. Others, such as Luke, Priscilla and her husband Aquila, helped Paul both in tent-making and evangelistically in various centres during his mission to Greece.

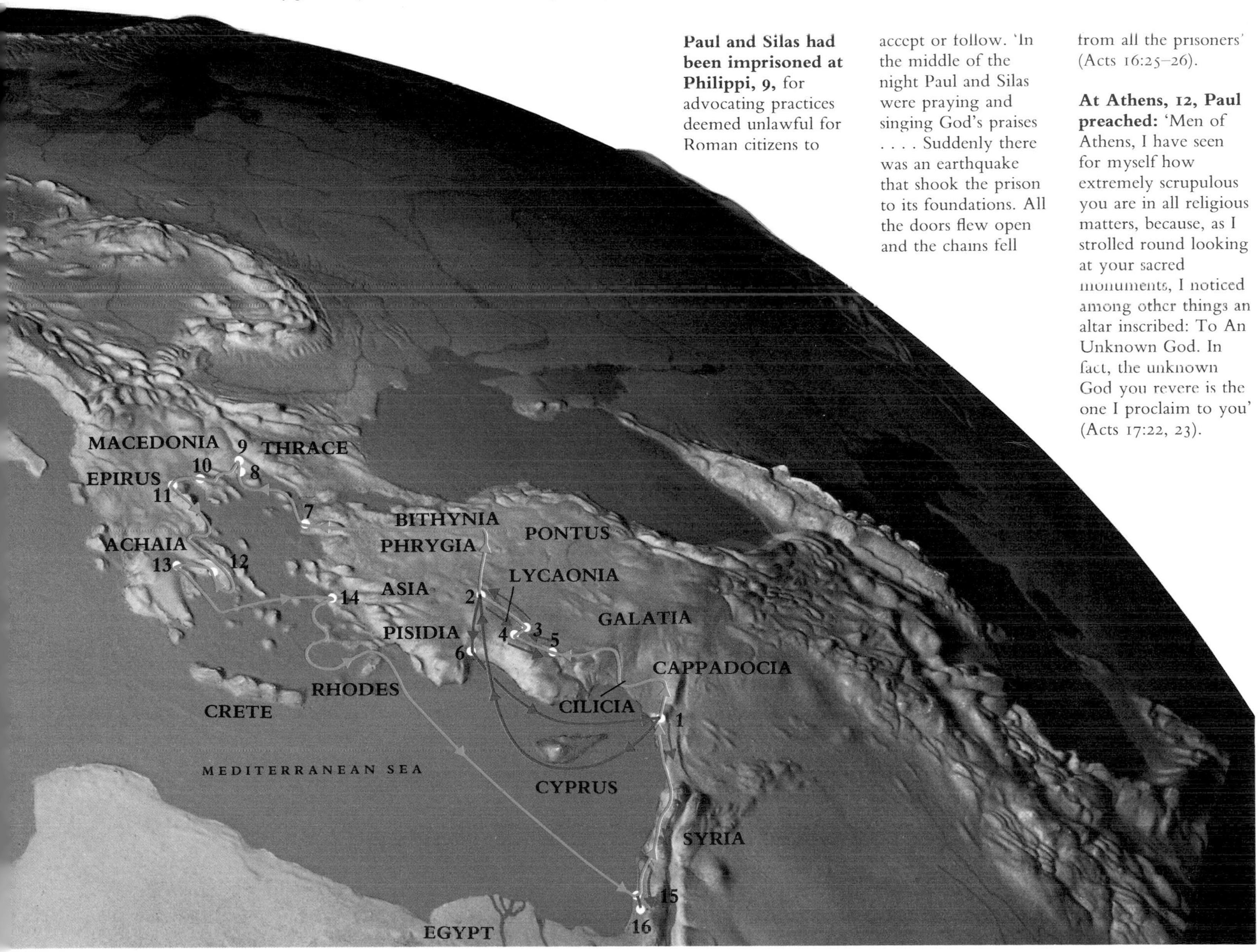

Paul and Silas had been imprisoned at Philippi, 9, for advocating practices deemed unlawful for Roman citizens to accept or follow. 'In the middle of the night Paul and Silas were praying and singing God's praises . . . . Suddenly there was an earthquake that shook the prison to its foundations. All the doors flew open and the chains fell from all the prisoners' (Acts 16:25–26).

At Athens, 12, Paul preached: 'Men of Athens, I have seen for myself how extremely scrupulous you are in all religious matters, because, as I strolled round looking at your sacred monuments, I noticed among other things an altar inscribed: To An Unknown God. In fact, the unknown God you revere is the one I proclaim to you' (Acts 17:22, 23).

MACEDONIA 9 THRACE

EPIRUS 10 8

11

ACHAIA 7

13 12 BITHYNIA PONTUS

PHRYGIA

ASIA LYCAONIA

14 2

PISIDIA 4 3 5 GALATIA

6

CAPPADOCIA

RHODES CILICIA

CRETE 1

MEDITERRANEAN SEA

CYPRUS

SYRIA

EGYPT 15

16

Letters to the Churches

Almost half of the New Testament comprises letters attributed to Paul. They are important because they are the earliest written documents of the Christian faith. Paul's authorship of seven letters, i.e. Romans, 1 and 2 Corinthians, Galatians, 1 Thessalonians, Philippians and Philemon, is universally accepted.

Other letters are perhaps more likely to have been written by his followers; some such as 1 and 2 Timothy and Titus, may have been written only 30 years after Paul's death. But the undisputed letters of Paul were probably written mainly between AD 50–60 and retained by Churches or individuals to whom they had been sent. They were eventually put together into a collection around AD 100, perhaps even by Onesimus, the slave in Philemon, who may be identical with the Onesimus who is known to have been the bishop of Ephesus.

In the first century AD, letter-writing flourished in the Hellenistic world. Paul's virtue was that he popularised this form so that it became the normal vehicle of communication within the Church.

Paul's letters are not just theological essays; they are real letters. Paul considered it proper to relate his deepest theological convictions to contemporary issues in the Churches he founded. Thus he writes to the gentile churches in Galatia to warn them not to submit to circumcision but to stand fast in the freedom of Christ. He writes to the Church at Corinth to oppose divisions among themselves and to answer questions put to him by the Corinthians concerning sexual relations, meat offered to idols, the Lord's Supper and spiritual gifts.

Paul's letters are neither casual nor informal. They are the carefully structured creations of an educated man. His rhetorical skill is most obvious in 2 Corinthians 10–12 where he makes full use of irony in a comparison into which he is forcibly drawn by his opponents. While acknowledging that he is behaving like a madman in boasting at all, he takes up their challenge and boasts of his sufferings for Christ rather than in his own eloquence or wisdom.

Elsewhere, he skilfully writes in the dialogue style of the diatribe (Romans 2), composes a hymn to love (1 Corinthians 13) or uses Christian traditions (Galatians 3:28) or Old Testament citations to substantiate his teaching (Romans 9–11).

Paul's letters are personal communications but they are more than this. Paul, as an apostle, sees himself as commissioned by the risen Jesus to represent his master. And he regarded the letter as mediating his presence and power to the Churches just as much as his being there in person. In fact, in his own time, his letters were acknowledged as being weighty in contrast to his personal presence which some thought was unimpressive (2 Corinthians 10:10).

In one of the latest New Testament letters (2 Peter 3:15–16), we find evidence of Paul's letters coming to be regarded as sacred scripture but also having a reputation for containing some things hard to understand. However, his letter-writing must have proved effective because it became a model for subsequent Christian correspondence.

In the New Testament, Peter is credited with having written two letters; alongside these there are three epistles of John with one from James differing greatly from these others. Even the Revelation to John has the framework of a letter and includes letters to the Seven Churches.

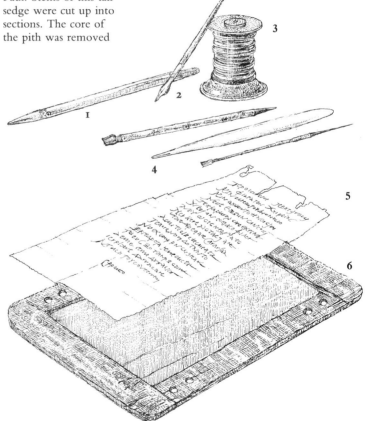

The English word 'paper' derives from the Egyptian papyrus plant (Greek *papyros*), the pith of which was used as writing material at the time of Paul. Stems of this tall sedge were cut up into sections. The core of the pith was removed and sliced into thin, tape-like strips and laid alongside each other. Similar strips of pith were laid across these at right angles, and the whole was then beaten into flat sheets. These could be pasted together to form a roll.

The Greeks used a wooden writing tablet, **6**, the inner panel being coated with wax and the frame pierced with holes to enable it to be joined to other tablets. A stylus, **4**, made of bronze, ivory or wood, was used for incising letters into the wax, while the broad end could be employed for erasing. Alternatively, the Greeks wrote on sheets of papyrus, **5**. Ink pots, **3**, were usually of bronze. Other writing equipment shown here includes a reed pen with a split nib, **2**, and a bronze pen, **1**.

1. The opening address of Paul's letters begins with Paul and his designation – apostle of Jesus Christ etc. Often, as here, Paul includes another person with him in the sending of the letter. This is normally followed by the naming of the addressees. The implication is that what Philemon does in response to this letter will have repercussions for the Church in his house, i.e. this is not simply a private letter. Paul's greeting is more than a wish for good health. It is a Christianised form of the Jewish modification of the secular letter greeting.

2. After the opening greeting, Paul thanks God for some spiritual quality or activity on behalf of his recipients (v.5). This is followed by the expression of a desire for this to increase and to prove more useful, i.e. this indicates indirectly Paul's future expectations of them. Normally, this part of the letter relates back to some aspect of Paul's previous relations with the recipients. Paul's, like any other useful letter, serves the function of updating past shared experiences or events and of outlining future expectations in relation to matters of mutual interest.

3. Paul has sent the runaway slave Onesimus (whose name means 'useful') back to Philemon, who has several options: a) he could accept Onesimus as an escaped slave and demand full legal retribution; b) he

could accept him as a slave but withhold punishment and overlook his debts; c) he could accept him as a slave but turn him over or lend him to

another Christian master, i.e. Paul, to avoid confrontation; d) he could accept him as a brother and pay for his legal manumission.

4. That Paul wants Onesimus to be freed is shown by his words in verse 16. Paul hopes Philemon will accept Onesimus as a Christian brother

and pay to set him free. Only the magnitude of the request can explain Paul's stress on the theme of debt and of brotherhood.

The Letter from Paul to Philemon

Address

From Paul, a prisoner of Christ Jesus and from our brother [1] Timothy; to our dear fellow-worker Philemon, 'our sister [2] Apphia, our fellow soldier Archippus and the church that meets in your house. ·Grace and the peace of God our Father and the [3] Lord Jesus Christ.

Thanksgiving and prayer

I always thank my God, mentioning you in my prayers, ·because [4,5] I hear of the love and the faith which you have for the Lord Jesus and for all God's holy people. ·I pray that your fellowship in faith [6] may come to expression in full knowledge of all the good we can do for Christ. ·I have received much joy and encouragement by [7] your love; you have set the hearts of God's holy people at rest.

The request about Onesimus

Therefore, although in Christ I have no hesitations about telling [8] you what your duty is, I am rather appealing to your love, being [9] what I am, Paul, an old man, and now also a prisoner of Christ Jesus. ·I am appealing to you for a child of mine, whose father I [10] became while wearing these chains: I mean Onesimus. He was [11] of no use to you before, but now he is useful both to you and me. I am sending him back to you – that is to say, sending you my [12] own heart. ·I should have liked to keep him with me; he could [13] have been a substitute for you, to help me while I am in the chains that the gospel has brought me. ·However, I did not want to do [14] anything without your consent; it would have been forcing your act of kindness, which should be spontaneous. ·I suppose you [15] have been deprived of Onesimus for a time, merely so that you could have him back for ever, ·no longer as a slave, but [16] something much better than a slave, a dear brother; especially dear to me, but how much more to you, both on the natural plane and in the Lord. ·So if you grant me any fellowship with [17] yourself, welcome him as you would me; ·if he has wronged you [18] in any way or owes you anything, put it down to my account. ·I [19] am writing this in my own hand: I, Paul, shall pay it back – I make no mention of a further debt, that you owe your very self to me! ·Well then, brother, I am counting on you, in the Lord; set [20] my heart at rest, in Christ. ·I am writing with complete [21] confidence in your compliance, sure that you will do even more than I ask.

A personal request. Good wishes

There is another thing: will you get a place ready for me to stay [22] in? I am hoping through your prayers to be restored to you.

Epaphras, a prisoner with me in Christ Jesus, sends his [23] greetings; ·so do my fellow-workers Mark, Aristarchus, Demas [24] and Luke.

May the grace of our Lord Jesus Christ be with your spirit. [25]

5. Paul may sometimes have had the help of a secretary in the actual writing of his letters. But whenever he wishes to emphasise the seriousness of some item or to indicate his own deep involvement, he states explicitly that he is actually writing that part of the letter in his own hand. In the case of Philemon this personal signature shows that he himself guarantees to meet any debt incurred by Onesimus.

6. Debt is a central theme in Philemon. Possibly Onesimus was in debt to his master both because he had run away and because he may have stolen something when he did. Paul is now in debt to Onesimus because he has been helping Paul in prison. Onesimus is also indebted to Paul because by winning him to faith, Paul has become his father in Christ. Paul also pointedly reminds Philemon that he, being converted by Paul, owes a great debt to Paul.

7. The closing section of Paul's letters normally has three parts: a) the doxology (praising of God); b) greetings and requests for prayers; and c) a benediction. Philemon includes a specific request to prepare a guest room for Paul to stay in as soon as he is freed from prison. Greetings are often included from fellow-workers (no less than five in Philemon; they doubtless supported Paul's appeals in the letter).

Paul's third journey: the riot at Ephesus

Ephesus was the main city of the Roman province of Asia. In New Testament times it was an important port and trading centre. Because of its strategic location and easy access both by sea and road, Paul chose it as a centre from which to keep in touch with congregations he had already founded, and as a base for new operations. As well as the temple of Artemis (Diana), one of the seven wonders of the ancient world, the city had marble-paved streets and enjoyed fine baths and libraries, a market place and a theatre.

According to Acts, Paul enjoyed hospitality with the Jewish community in Ephesus for several months. Eventually he was forced to find other accommodation – in the hall of Tyrannus. One version of Acts 19:9 ('the Western Text') says that Paul had the use of this building from the fifth hour to the tenth, that is, from 11.00 a.m. to 4.00 p.m. – the hottest hours of the day. Paul would probably have spent the earlier part of the day, from dawn or even earlier, as well as the evening, working at his trade of tent-making in order to support himself. He tells the Ephesian elders in Acts 20:34 'these hands of mine earned enough to meet my needs and those of my companions'.

Paul evoked much interest, and some strong opposition, in his evangelism at Ephesus. After a time his influence was significant enough to arouse the enmity of a guild of silversmiths whose income from making statuettes of Diana for her devotees was being threatened by Paul's message of the one true God.

These tradesmen were the sort of people Paul tended to convert to Christianity. The Churches he founded had a few wealthy people, and some poor people and slaves, but many skilled craftsmen. These middle-class groups had few political opportunities. They had formed themselves into 'collegia,' or guilds, which existed basically to provide a social life for their members and which were wary of anything that threatened their economic prospects or interfered with their rights.

Luke, the author of Acts, intends his readers to see the hall of Tyrannus as a meeting-place like one for the 'collegia'. Tyrannus might have given his name to the hall as patron of one of the guilds. Thus Paul appears here as a workman in contact with other craftsmen and in the company of Aquila and Priscilla, his fellow-workers. It was Demetrius, president of the silversmiths' guild and possibly also one of the goddess's vestrymen, who instigated a riot from which Paul escaped only through the intervention of the town clerk and local officials. But although Paul was not captured in this instance, there is good reason to think he did spend some time in prison in Ephesus.

In addition, Paul recounts that Aquila and Priscilla 'risked their necks for him' and describes Andronicus and Junia as 'fellow prisoners' (Romans 16:4–7). He almost despaired of life at one point – perhaps through illness but possibly also through persecution and imprisonment (2 Corinthians 1:9).

However, the Ephesus period was the crown of Paul's ministry. He wrote some of his major letters at this time, perhaps including some of the 'captivity' epistles, such as Philippians. Also, Paul's theological development was at its peak. This is supported by the fact that he now devoted a lot of time to organising a collection to be taken by representatives of his gentile churches for the poor in Jerusalem. He was now confident of his own achievements but longed for full acceptance of this collection as evidence of unity between the Jewish and gentile parts of the Church.

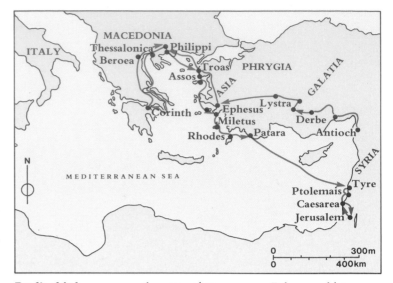

Paul's third missionary journey began with a pastoral tour through Galatia and Phrygia to strengthen the congregations already founded there. He then moved to Ephesus, which he made his regional headquarters for almost three years. From there, he made a brief visit to Corinth. He returned to Ephesus and later travelled to Troas and Macedonia. Paul finally returned to Corinth for a stay of three months early in AD 57. From there he proceeded to Philippi.

This statue of Artemis, an earth-goddess linked with wild nature, was made in the 2nd century AD and was discovered at Ephesus. The protuberances on the statue may represent many breasts, or perhaps the ova of the sacred bee. The temple of Artemis was a vast structure, four times the size of the Parthenon in Athens. It had 127 columns, each 60ft/18m high, adorned by the most gifted sculptors of the day.

The temple housed an unshaped icon of the goddess; this was believed to be of divine creation since it had allegedly fallen from the sky. The cult had a long history at Ephesus, dating back to pre-Ionian worship of the Anatolian mother-goddess. In mainland Greece, Artemis, Mistress of the Animals, appeared as a virgin huntress.

The theatre of Ephesus

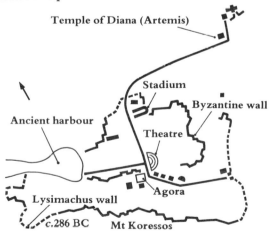

Temple of Diana (Artemis)

Stadium

Byzantine wall

Ancient harbour

Theatre

Agora

Lysimachus wall

c.286 BC   Mt Koressos

In Paul's time, Ephesus, *above,* was one of the finest cities in the Roman empire: it was a religious, political and trading centre and an important seaport. The theatre and the temple of Artemis were among the finest in the Graeco–Roman world.

Paul spoke daily in the synagogue and later held daily discussions with his followers in the lecture room of Tyrannus. According to Acts, so remarkable were his miracles at this time, that handkerchiefs which had touched him were taken to the ill and they were cured.

The city Paul knew was founded by Lysimachus about 290 BC following two earlier cities on different sites. Despite ravaging by the Goths in AD 263, it remained in occupation till AD 1000; but a new and prosperous centre developed nearby around the Church of St John, taken over by the Turks in 1426.

Paul's missionary success in Ephesus began to damage the silversmiths' trade, which largely comprised making votive images for sale to the many pilgrims who came to the temple of Artemis. One of the silversmiths, Demetrius, organised his colleagues in an attempt to convince the citizens that Paul and his associates were not only ruining their trade but threatening the worship of the goddess Artemis.

People quickly gathered and soon formed a rioting mob, making for the theatre, *above,* a giant structure which could take 24,000 people. Two of Paul's companions were seized and forced to go with them. Paul wanted to assist his companions but was restrained from doing so by his friends.

Pandemonium reigned in the theatre for two hours, with the crowd shouting, 'Great is Diana [Artemis] of the Ephesians'. Finally, city officials managed to pacify the crowd by warning them that the Roman garrison would soon come to suppress the disorder. The crowd dispersed and shortly afterwards Paul left the city.

Paul's voyage to Rome

After Paul had returned from his third missionary journey, he went to Jerusalem despite a prophetic warning that he would be arrested should he go there. Nevertheless he went, and his presence caused some of the Jews to riot against him, since they thought, wrongly, that he had broken Jewish law by taking a gentile into the Temple. The riot led to his arrest by the Romans. They were about to flog him when Paul saved himself by revealing his Roman citizenship.

To avert an assassination attempt on Paul by the Jews, the Romans removed him to Caesarea. Here he appeared before successive governors, Antonius Felix and Porcius Festus, the latter being accompanied by Herod Agrippa II and his sister Berenice. To avoid being sent to the Jewish Sanhedrin at Jerusalem for trial and to have the chance to carry on his witness to Rome (Acts 23:11), Paul claimed his right as a Roman citizen to tried at Rome. His request was duly granted.

The voyage to Rome was held up by adverse winds but Paul's ship reached Myra in Lycia where they changed ships for an Alexandrian vessel bound for Italy. Instead of wintering in Crete, they pressed on and were shipwrecked off Malta. Three months later they picked up another ship from Alexandria which took them to Puteoli in the Bay of Naples, where Paul stayed a week with fellow-Christians before travelling overland to Rome. There, he remained for two years in private lodgings under guard, proclaiming the Gospel to visitors (Acts 28:30–1).

At this point, probably in AD 63, the Book of Acts ends. It is not known if the book was written in 63 before Paul's death or if it was written later, and, if so, whether the author intended a third volume, following Luke and Acts.

Nor is it known for certain what happened to Paul. There was a persistent tradition in the second century that he made a missionary journey to Spain. This presupposes either his acquittal or the lapsing of the case against him and his release. If the Pastoral Letters to Timothy and Titus were written by Paul or contain an element authentic to him, they presuppose a further journey in the east, and a final imprisonment in Rome. Some scholars think that they were written by one of Paul's followers and attributed to him.

Whatever view is taken of the Pastoral Letters, some scholars find the tradition that Paul was executed in AD 67 convincing, and this would fit with his release, the journey to Spain he was set on making (Romans 15:23), a natural and understandable return to the east, further visit to Rome, rearrest and execution.

There is also a tradition that Peter was in Rome and was martyred there, though there is no early evidence that he was bishop for 25 years before his death. That he was crucified is suggested by John 21:18; that he was peculiarly, with Paul, associated with the Church in Rome is clear from the early Churchmen Ignatius and Irenaeus, and from the relics under St Peter's Cathedral.

A marvellous apocryphal story tells how he was trying to escape from persecution but met Jesus going in the opposite direction: 'Domine, quo vadis?' he asked – 'Lord, where are you going?' 'To be crucified a second time.' Peter turned round and went to his death, asking to be crucified upside down, since he was not worthy to suffer his Master's precise fate. The deaths of Peter and Paul are universally associated with a persecution of the Christians in the reign of Nero but there is conflicting evidence about the circumstances.

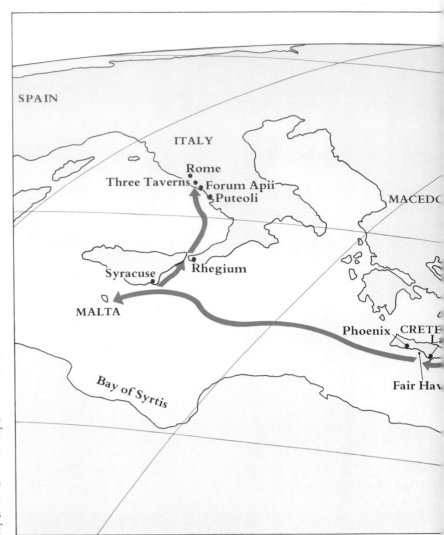

'But it was not long before a hurricane, the "north-easter" as they call it, burst on them from across the island' (ACTS 27:14–15). Throughout the Roman empire, troops and travellers were transported by sea, and there was also extensive trade. The grain of Egypt, which would have been brought in Roman ships such as that pictured, *above*, fed the people of Rome.

Sea travel was not without danger. The Romans had done much to clear the seas of pirates, but ships of the period were vulnerable to winds and turbulent seas. The ships were propelled with the aid of fairly simple sails, oars or both.

One of the first concerns of sailors during a storm, such as that which assailed the ship on which Paul was travelling to Rome, was to hoist on board the ship's lifeboat. This could be a difficult task, but was essential to ensure that it was not carried away by the wind or smashed against the ship. Roman mosaics often depict the lifeboat as attached to the vessel's stern.

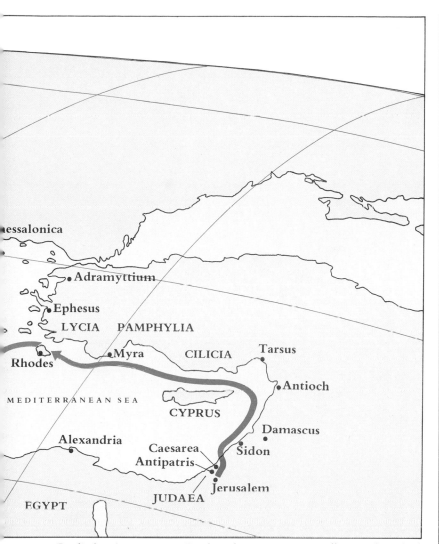

Bust of Nero: Museum of the Terme, Rome

Paul's last journey – to stand trial in Rome – started at the port of Caesarea. The ship put in at Sidon, then sailed on to Myra in Lycia. There, Julius the centurion found an Alexandrian ship bound for Italy and put the prisoners aboard it. Paul's ship made slow headway and it was late in the year when it reached Fair Havens on the island of Crete.

Paul advised delaying in Crete but was overruled and the ship set sail again. A slight breeze soon turned into a raging north-easter that drove them across the opening of the Adriatic and finally grounded the ship on the shores of Malta.

During the storm, Paul admonished the crew: 'Friends, you should have listened to me and not put out from Crete.' But he reassured them that all would survive the tempest because of the promise of an angel of God who had appeared to him (Acts 27:24).

The Maltese made the travellers welcome by lighting a huge fire. Paul was putting sticks on the fire when a viper attached itself to his hand. Bystanders at once took Paul to be a murderer who, though he had escaped the storm, was to be a victim of divine justice. The apostle, however, shook the creature into the fire and, when he did not

swell up or drop dead, was taken for a god.

Paul is credited with a miracle cure on Malta, when he healed the father of the man designated by the Romans to rule the island. When the weather improved in the following spring, prisoners and Paul's friends who had accompanied him throughout the journey, set out for the Italian mainland. They landed at the harbour of Puteoli, near Naples. A delegation of Christians from Rome had travelled along the Appian Way to meet him and escort him to the capital – and ultimately martyrdom.

Nero's persecution of the Christians

Tacitus (c.AD 56–115) wrote one of the first surviving accounts of the early Christians of Rome. Here, he is writing of the Great Fire of AD 64:

'To dispel the rumour [that he had started the Great Fire] Nero put into the dock instead the group whom the man in the street detested for their vices and nicknamed "Christians", finding highly recondite punishments for them. The name originated with one Christus, executed on the authority of the governor Pontius Pilate during Tiberius's reign . . . Their execution was accompanied by mockery. They were sewn up in animal skins to be torn to death by hounds, or set on crosses, or prepared for the brand and burned to give light in the darkness when daylight faded. Nero had opened his private gardens for the spectacle, and offered an exhibition in the circus, mixing with the crowd in a charioteer's uniform or riding in a chariot.

Suetonius (c.AD 69–135) separates his account of the punishment of the Christians, 'a group of people practising an innovatory, degraded and dangerous superstition', from the fire, which he attributes to Nero. Clement of Rome, writing as a Christian at the end of the first century, attributes the deaths of Peter and Paul to jealousy. Dio Cassius, an historian of the early third century, does not mention the Christians at all and blames the fire on Nero's agents.

The historian Eusebius, writing in the early fourth century, reports the persecution but does not associate it with the fire. 'Nero was the first to be proclaimed an opponent of God, appearing for the slaughter of the apostles. History relates that Paul was beheaded, actually in Rome, during his reign; similarly, Peter suffered crucifixion.' Jerome (c.342–420), a scholarly Christian writer, follows Eusebius in placing the fire in 64 and the persecution in 68.

The siege of Jerusalem AD 70

Jerusalem, wrote the Jewish historian Josephus, was twice laid desolate, once by Babylon and once by Rome. The siege of the city and its destruction by the Romans in AD 70 was a decisive calamity for the Jews.

To the Romans the Jews were awkward subjects, nationalistic and religiously exclusive. The census of AD 6 led one Judas to a military uprising; he is said to have founded a new religious sect which continued to create trouble for 60 years. These freedom-fighters were usually called 'bandits'. Barabbas was one. So was the Egyptian mentioned in Acts 21: 37–8. One group were the *sicarii* or dagger-men. Jewish freedom-fighters were first called Zealots in the great uprising of 66.

On the whole the Roman governors of Judaea were second-rate and maladroit. Some were corrupt, and to the nationalists they were symbols of oppression. Pilate was careless of Jewish religion. Porcius Festus (Acts 25:1–9) (60–2) is the only one against whom there is no major criticism. But the Roman historian Tacitus actually says, 'The Jews put up with things until the procuratorship of Gessius Florus', a strong indictment of the whole succession.

Many other factors – social, economic and nationalistic – contributed to the uprising, notably racial tension in Caesarea between Graeco-Syrian citizens and the Jews. The situation was unstable. In 66 Florus demanded 17 talents from the Temple treasury in part payment of tribute already owing. To mock the procurator's poverty, demonstrators held a street collection for him. Florus came to Jerusalem with an army, demanded the arrest of the offenders, and imposed martial law; in the subsequent riots over 3,000 were killed.

Florus had gone too far. He withdrew to avoid further provocations – but too late. There was now open rebellion; sacrifice for the emperor ceased. The Roman garrisons in Jerusalem and Masada were massacred. That of Jerusalem had taken refuge in three fortified towers of Herod's palace, where they were fairly secure but powerless. They were allowed to leave unarmed, but once they were out of the city they were treacherously attacked and killed.

Pogroms and counter-massacres ensued in Caesarea, the Decapolis, Alexandria. Cestius Gallus, the governor of Syria with military responsibility for Judaea, advanced on Jerusalem with the Twelfth Legion and support troops. After an initial success he withdrew, was ambushed, and was fortunate to escape with the loss of nearly 6,000 soldiers together with much equipment.

Now war was inevitable. The Jews were divided into factions. Despite this, they organised themselves into systematic divisions of responsibility. Some of their commanders were young and inexperienced. Josephus, the historian, was only 30 when he was given command in Galilee.

Nero gave the command in the war to T. Flavius Vespasianus, who had fought in Britain and governed Africa. He had three legions, and in all perhaps 60,000 men. He systematically reduced northern Palestine: Josephus surrendered, told Vespasian that he would become emperor, and was spared. The Christians, refusing to fight, left Jerusalem for Pella. Vespasian was in no hurry to assail the capital. In 68–9 he secured the rest of the country except for Masada and two other fortresses.

Meanwhile Nero was overthrown and committed suicide. Civil war at Rome ensued. Galba, Otho, Vitellius succeeded one

Titus first encircled Jerusalem to starve the freedom-fighters into submission. Then he stormed the city, first securing and then destroying the Antonia Tower, **1**.

The besieged were forced back into the Temple, **2**. There they laid a trap for the Romans by seeming to withdraw and firing the western cloister of the Court of the Gentiles, **3**.

Titus, thinking that the Jews themselves had started to burn down the Temple, which the Romans would not have attacked, turned to a final assault.

Battering-rams were brought up against the inner Temple and scaling-ladders were used, but without success.

Titus then gave the order to fire the gates. This destroyed the outer defences and the Romans made their first breakthrough. A counter-attack through the east gate of the inner Temple was repulsed.

According to Josephus, Titus was unwilling to destroy the Temple and gave orders for the fires to be checked. But a soldier snatched up a blazing piece of wood and threw it through a window, where it fell on inflammable material.

Widespread commotion followed on both sides. Roman soldiers rushed in without orders, trampling on one another, succumbing to the fire themselves but also slaughtering the Jews, who were preoccupied with the disaster overwhelming their Temple.

Titus's commands to save the Temple were either inaudible or ignored. Looting was widespread, and one soldier spread the fire in the darkness of the inner sanctuary. The defenders were driven out of the inner court into the outer, then into the lower city and finally to a last stand in the upper city.

Some of the priests actually used the metal spikes, which protected the Temple from birds settling on the holy place, as javelins against the Romans. But by now the Temple could not be saved. The Roman soldiers, totally out of control, burned down the treasury (with all the sacred garments) and one of the outer cloisters, where refugees, including many women and children, were huddled together.

The siege of Jerusalem (continued)

another as emperor. The eastern legions proclaimed Vespasian emperor. Vitellius was murdered and Josephus' prophecy fulfilled. Vespasian left his son Titus in charge of the war. A spectacular victory was now needed for Vespasian's prestige. Jerusalem must be taken. This was a task of great difficulty. The city was almost impregnable on three sides because of the steepness of the valleys beneath its walls, while the northern side was protected by three lines of defences, comprising strong walls and towers.

Titus advanced in the spring of 70, driving the Passover pilgrims before him to increase the mouths to feed. He nearly lost his life while reconnoitring, showing great courage. The Jews, realising that their fate in defeat would be crucifixion or slavery, defeated the Romans by sallying from the gates. The success was temporary. The Roman camps were soon established.

The freedom-fighters were divided into three factions led by John of Gischala, Eleazar and Simon bar Giora. They fought among themselves. Eleazar had the worst of it. John and Simon joined forces and made a daring sally against the Roman siege-towers.

But the towers remained and drove the defenders back from the walls, the battering-rams breached the outer wall, and Titus secured the northeastern quarter. The second wall was breached, but in the narrow streets the Romans were repulsed. Not for long: four days later they re-entered and demolished the wall.

Now Titus invested the city with a wall to prevent escape or the admission of supplies. Famine spread; the bodies of the dead were dropped over the walls into the valleys to avoid plague. There is even a record of cannibalism. Fugitives who fell into Roman hands were crucified in sight of the city, to the number of 500 a day.

At the end of June the direct assault was resumed. The Antonia fortress was captured and razed. In July the daily Temple sacrifice ceased. On 6 August the Temple was stormed, and against Titus's orders destroyed by fire. The revolutionaries made their last stand in the Upper City. This was finally breached, and after five months' siege the city taken and razed to the ground. Prisoners were forced into the arena as gladiators. Seven hundred, including Simon and John, were displayed in triumph at Rome with spoils from the Temple.

So were fulfilled the words of Jesus in Luke: 'When you see Jerusalem surrounded by armies, then you must realise that it will soon be desolate' (21:20); '. . . the time will come when not a single stone will be left on another, everything will be destroyed' (21:6).

There were isolated pockets of resistance left, such as Masada (see pp. 184–5). But the Jewish state had ceased to exist, and with it the Sadducees as well as the nationalists. A pagan shrine was established on the Temple site. The pilgrimages to Jerusalem were at an end. The Temple-tax, paid by Jews of the Dispersion for the upkeep of the Temple, was transferred, at least for a time, to the Temple of Jupiter Capitolinus in Rome. Judaea became an independent province. The economy suffered severely in the war; the best land was confiscated by the Romans.

But the Pharisees, with their genius for practical devotion, remained strong. A new centre for the study of the Law was established at Jabneh. The religious life of Judaism survived the destruction of the Temple.

The Arch of Titus, which stands at one end of the Roman Forum, is decorated with reliefs commemorating Rome's capture of Jerusalem, with Jewish prisoners and Titus triumphant. This section shows the booty from the Temple being carried in procession. Objects include trumpets, the table for the shewbread, and the seven-branched candelabrum, with placards being brought up in the rear.

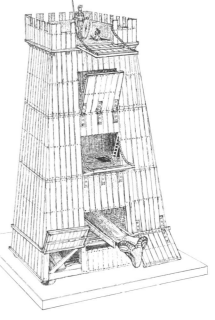

In ancient warfare, the Greeks developed catapults for breeching enemy fortifications, but it was the Romans who invented the most sophisticated weaponry, notably the siege tower. This enabled them to cast a drawbridge across the top of a citadel's walls. At the same time, the tower housed a massive wooden battering-ram, fitted at the striking end with a lump of iron in the shape, according to Josephus, of a ram's head (hence the name). The ram was supported at its middle by ropes, allowing gangs of soldiers to pull it back into the interior of the tower and then thrust it outwards with great force.

'I [Josephus] have been sent by God to you. . . . You, Vespasian, are Caesar and Emperor.' Josephus: *The Jewish War*.

Josephus: patriot or traitor?

Born in AD 37 or 38, Josephus was reluctantly drawn into his people's revolt against Rome in AD 66. After the stronghold of Jotapata fell, he escaped with 40 others. These, realising their position was hopeless, entered into a suicide pact. Josephus and one other, however, surrendered to the Romans and Josephus sought to win Vespasian's favour by predicting that he would one day become emperor. The prediction came true in 69 and Josephus, now in imperial favour, was attached to the Roman army during the siege of Jerusalem. For these acts he was stigmatised as a traitor by his people, but later in Rome he devoted his time to writing their history.

'If then it takes the experience of years to make good government, we have Vespasian; if the vigour of youth, Titus.' Josephus: *The Jewish War*.

Vespasian: architect of Jerusalem's fall

Titus Flavius Vespasianus (AD 9–79) was a Sabine (a people of Central Italy) born to middle-class parents. He made his way in the army by sheer ability and hard work. He served in Germany and later in Britain, where he captured the Isle of Wight. In 51 he was made consul and later served Nero as proconsul in Africa. In 66 he was appointed to command the Roman army in the war against the Jews. While he was in Judaea, Nero died, and after some usurpations, Roman soldiers in Alexandria, Judaea and Syria proclaimed him emperor. He returned to Italy to make good his claim, leaving his son Titus to prosecute the Jewish war. As emperor, Vespasian lived frugally, in contrast to Nero, restored the state's finances and inaugurated a period of prosperity and peace that lasted a century. Vespasian was succeeded by his son Titus and later by Domitian, his other son.

This coin was minted in Rome between AD 69 and 79 to commemorate the capture of Jerusalem. One of a series of coins, in gold, silver and bronze, it depicts the emperor Vespasian on the obverse and, on the reverse, *above*, a symbol of defeated Judaea, a grieving woman under a palm tree. The inscription IVD CAP means 'Judaea in Captivity', and SC 'by decree of the Senate'.

The fall of Masada

After the fall of Jerusalem in AD 70, the scene for the last Jewish resistance took place two years later at Masada. One of the most spectacular fortresses of antiquity, Masada stood on the edge of the desert above a sheer drop of 1,300ft/397m to the Dead Sea. Herod the Great made it a major citadel, with walls and towers, rainwater cisterns, stores, barracks for soldiers, and palaces.

When the Romans took over from Herod's successors, they garrisoned the stronghold. However, the Romans were annihilated by a guerrilla named Menahem and his followers in AD 66. The Zealots then held the fortress, reinforced by a few refugees from the capital. From there they carried out guerrilla raids on the Romans. In 72, the Roman governor Flavius Silva determined to eliminate this final bastion of the Jewish resistance movement. He had at his disposal the Tenth Legion – nominally, 6,000 men, though not always up to strength – supported by auxiliaries and forced labour for transport.

Flavius Silva used traditional Roman siege techniques. A series of camps was established around the foot of the great rock, so that there was total encirclement. At the western side of the fortress, he built a ramp of rocks and beaten earth. On this ramp he established a siege-tower and used this for covering fire to enable a battering-ram to be employed against the wall of the citadel, finally breaching it.

The Jews employed considerable ingenuity in providing an inner line of defence by piling up wood and earth: the effect of the ram was thus to solidify this structure. The Romans succeeded in setting fire to the wall only to find a sudden northerly wind carrying the flames towards their own positions. A change of wind left the wall breached by the fire.

There were 960 men, women and children in the citadel and the defenders of Masada now reviewed their precarious situation. Their whole campaign had been to reject servitude to the Romans. For the men, death freely chosen was preferable to being slaughtered by the Romans, for the women and children it was better than the abuse and slavery they would suffer. The Jews had an old saying: 'We are born that we may die and die that we may live.' So the people took their own lives, first drawing lots to decide who should be the executioners.

The Romans armed themselves for the final assault. There was no resistance – only an awesome silence. Two women and their five children had opted for life rather than death, and lived to tell the story. Josephus says that the Romans, admiring the courage shown by their adversaries, could take no pleasure in their victory. For a period, Flavius Silva left a garrison in the fortress. Then, as the dangers to Roman rule within Palestine receded, the site was abandoned. In the fifth and sixth centuries, some Christian monks occupied the hillfort and built a chapel there.

In the early 1960s, Professor Yigael Yadin, an eminent Israeli archaeologist, mounted an expedition to Masada. His team found the refined architecture and painted walls of Herod's luxurious palace, they found evidence of religion – a synagogue and a ritual bath; they also found scrolls, coins and jars, food, rings, weapons, and fragments of clothing. They found potsherds which may have been the ones used to draw lots as to who should kill the others. Finally, although the Romans had cleared away most of the bodies, they found the skeletons of a man, woman and child. The woman's dark plaited hair had survived, a vivid reminder of the defenders of Masada.

Masada was fortified as a royal citadel, fortress and palace by Herod the Great. On the northern cliff face there was a villa on three terraces, **1**, connected by staircases and containing magnificent frescoes.

The Roman commander, Flavius Silva, **7**, mounted and directing operations, surrounded the foot of the citadel with a wall to prevent escape. He found only one point from which to mount a direct attack – on the west side, where a promontory enabled him to build an earth ramp, **4**, 219yds/200m long and 109yds/100m high. This was made even higher by the addition of stones, reaching almost to the casement wall – a remarkable feat of military engineering for the time.

Roman siege techniques were advanced and efficient. They had powerful catapults, **8**, and these at the siege of Jerusalem lobbed boulders of 55lb/24.5kg a quarter of a mile/0.4km. Smaller catapults, called 'scorpions', **9**, worked like the later crossbow. The catapults shown would not have been used from these positions but would later have been advanced for the attack.

The legionaries, 5, wore leather or metal body armour, bronze helmets with iron skull-plates, and boots. They carried large, curved shields, javelins, swords and daggers.

One hundred and twenty horsemen were attached to each legion to act as dispatch riders and scouts.

The most important siege-engines were the battering-rams (topped with a ram's head of iron), protected by a strong, wheeled shed called a tortoise, mobile towers of wood, **3,** ironclad and with a strong roof, plaited screens of iron or leather, and metal hooks for dislodging masonry.

Supplies and siege equipment were brought forward by two-wheeled carts, **6.**

The ramp, 4, and the tower, 3, enabled the Romans to clear the defenders from the walls and also to cover the use of the rams. The foreground legionaries waited to attack after a breakthrough had been effected. When this came, the Zealots built another wall of earth and wood. The legionaries set this on fire, **2;** a change of wind nearly destroyed the siege-tower but a further change of direction consumed the defenders' last protection.

The Dead Sea scrolls

In the spring of 1947, a Bedouin boy, Muhammed ed Dib, while tending his goats, tossed a stone into a cave on the northwest corner of the Dead Sea. He heard the stone strike something and, on further investigation, found a number of Hebrew scrolls in large clay jars. This was the first of several such momentous finds.

Scholars soon realised that the scrolls were ancient documents hidden away prior to the Roman siege of Jerusalem in the war of AD 66–70 against the Jews. The discovery of the 'Dead Sea scrolls' has proved to be of immense significance for the study of first-century Judaism and of early Christianity. For the scrolls portray the world-view of Jews contemporary with the New Testament era. They contain differing forms of Jewish texts of scripture as Jesus or Paul would have known them. Apart from Esther, at least a portion of every canonical book in the Hebrew Bible was found at Qumran. More valuable still are the numerous commentaries produced on books of scripture.

The monastic-style community of the group which produced the scrolls has been excavated on a plateau overlooking the Dead Sea, near the Wadi Qumran – Qumran giving the sect its name. The site included a central building with common rooms, a 'scriptorium' for copying sacred texts, and next to it a banqueting and assembly hall. Near to the main building, remnants of agricultural buildings – storehouses, mills, stables, and a pottery with a kiln – were found. There were also cemeteries with a total of about 1,100 graves.

The members of the Qumran community understood themselves to be the true people of God, preparing themselves for the imminent end of the world and judgement of God. The community was established in order to make it possible for its members to conduct their lives according to this perspective. Thus elaborate water systems of reservoirs, ritual baths and irrigation channels were created to facilitate both the physical survival and liturgical needs of the group. Enough water was stored to provide for the needs of several hundred people in the dry season.

Preservation of the religious purity of community members was a central concern. The basis for this was their interpretation of the Law – the point at issue which distinguished Qumran members from other Jews.

New members of the community had to pledge obedience to all that had been revealed to the Zadokites, the priests. Initiation was followed by a probationary year, then two years as a novice. On successful completion of these, the member was given the white linen robe and allowed to share in the common meal.

The beliefs of a group that existed side by side with earliest Christianity are of great interest. A basic 'dualism' pervaded their thought, which meant that they believed they were witnesses to a climactic, cosmic struggle between the forces of light and darkness – between good and bad angels as well as humans. They regarded themselves as God's elect. They expected two Messiahs, a priestly Messiah of Aaron and a royal Messiah of David, as well as a third, prophetic figure.

But they did differ from Jesus and his followers. Jesus welcomed women, the handicapped and the diseased; Qumran excluded them. Qumran stressed love of the insider and hatred of the enemy, while Jesus stressed love of all, including enemies. Doubtless study of the scrolls will continue to shed yet more light on Judaism and on Christianity's origins.

Who were the Essenes?

The existence of the Essenes had long been known from first-century writers, such as Philo of Alexandria. He described their life of ascetic withdrawal, communal sharing and self-sufficiency, 'preparing the way of the Lord in the wilderness'. Both Philo and Josephus noted the strict, almost military discipline of the sect, whose members had to adhere rigidly to regulations. The Essenes regarded themselves as soldiers who would fight only in the final battle between themselves, 'the sons of light', and evil men, 'the sons of darkness'. However, they refused all contact with weapons.

It is now reasonably certain that the Jewish sect at Qumran was identical with the Essenes. But not all Essenes lived at Qumran, for one of the scrolls, the *Damascus Document*, seems to have been written for members who lived as ordinary married citizens throughout the country.

The Essenes probably originated as a priestly group within the general opposition to Hellenisation that culminated with the Maccabaean revolt. Qumran was certainly occupied briefly between 160 and 134 BC. The withdrawal to Qumran probably took place when a Jew named Simon became high priest in about 140 BC. It is thought that he was the 'Wicked Priest' who persecuted the founder of the sect, the 'Righteous Teacher'.

A view from a cave at Qumran shows the terrain as inhospitable today as it was in the time of the Essenes.

The Isaiah scroll, *left*, the oldest manuscript of a complete book of the Old Testament, was found in Cave 1 at Qumran. It comprises 17 pieces of leather, sewn together to form a roll more than 24ft/7.3m long. The average length of each column of text is 10in/25cm.

Daily life at Qumran

One of the Qumran scrolls, the *Community Rule*, lists regulations and obligations for full-time members of the sect who lived there. These were all male and celibate. Members rose to pray before dawn, then worked at their crafts and agricultural tasks until the fifth hour (11 am). They then reassembled, bathed and donned sacred white garments for the ritual meal. Daily meals, preceded and followed by prayers, were taken communally. Some scholars see similarities between these meals and the last supper.

Each able-bodied man had to stand watch for a third of all the nights of the year, to read the Book and to study the law as well as to care for the sick and aged of the community. The law was recited and prayers were said by the group on duty during the three watches of the night.

A strict ethical code was prescribed to maintain purity. Rigorous Sabbath observance precluded lighting a fire, preparing food or even defecation on the holy day. The Essene calendar was arranged so that major festivals never fell on a Sabbath. The taking of oaths, spitting or sleeping in the holy assembly, exposing their nakedness, lying about their possessions and even scornful laughter were all expressly forbidden.

The Jewish sect that resided at Qumran was almost certainly the Essenes, though not all of them lived there. This ground plan shows the probable location of: the entrance **1**; a kitchen **2**; a 'scriptorium' for copying texts, **3**; a bath, **4**; storerooms, **5**; cisterns, **6**.

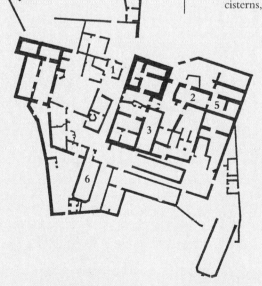

Expulsion from the community for limited periods was used to enforce the rigid communal discipline. This was presided over by a priestly hierarchy. The community was divided into 'camps' of ten persons, each directed by a priest, and a single priest with supreme authority over them all. This strict discipline was regarded as the necessary preparation for God's final visitation.

The Revelation to John

The Revelation to John, the last book of the New Testament, was probably written at about the time of the Roman emperor Domitian (AD 81–96). It is an account of the vision granted by God to John, probably not John the Apostle or John the Evangelist, but a Church Elder from Asia Minor, exiled to 'the island of Patmos'. In the vision, John received a message for the Seven Churches of Asia which, in the first three chapters, he records in the form of letters to them, full of guidance, correction and encouragement.

In chapters 4–21, there is a general message for the whole Church. The Christian readers are called to stand firm in the face of persecution, and to refuse to give divine honour to the Roman emperor. This basic message is repeated with different images. First the Lord Jesus, symbolised by the Lamb, opens 'the seven seals' of world history, revealing disasters that will befall the earth. These include the four horses with their riders, 'given authority over a quarter of the earth, to kill by the sword, by famine, by plague and through wild beasts' (6:8).

Then seven trumpets introduce the Lamb's plagues of judgement and the triumph of the faithful (8–11). Next, there is the struggle between God's representatives, symbolised by the woman and her child, and his opponents – the Dragon and his accomplices – and the destruction of Babylon, symbolising Rome. After this comes the saints' final victory, beginning with the reign of a thousand years, and ending with the final triumph in the new Jerusalem.

The Revelation to John, with its strange visionary symbolism of angels, evil spirits, earthquakes, victory over the powers of darkness, is so esoteric as to have daunted many readers. Perhaps the best way of understanding it is to see it as an example of a type of literature which flourished among the Jews, especially between 170 BC and AD 70 – a period of persecution by various gentile powers.

In former times, guidance during times of crises would have come from the prophets. They spoke in God's name, analysing the situation and summoning the people to obey their God. But during times of persecution, such straightforward language was too incriminatingly dangerous. Instead, guidance and encouragement were given in a new form of writing known as 'the apocalypse' ('revelation' in its Latin form). The message was that the people should remain firm: the present tribulations were only temporary and God would soon destroy their persecutors.

The typical apocalypse expressed current events and personages in strange images, symbolic colours, numbers and creatures, which, to an outsider, would be meaningless, but which initiated readers could interpret. It was often written as though a figure from Jewish history had been given a 'revelation' of things to come, and had been commanded to write it down for a future generation – though actually it was for contemporary readers. The idea was to hide the identity of the real author. Many such apocalypses were written in the years just before and after the time of Jesus, but only two whole books are included in the Bible: Daniel and Revelation.

This explains the presence of the complicated symbols and figures in Revelation. But the book's real message is clear: God and those faithful to him are the final victors in the drama between good and evil. This message was valid for the time of the writer, is relevant today, and gives a religious understanding of the whole of human history.

Patmos is an island in the Aegean Sea. Revelation 1:9 says the author, named John, was punished for preaching about Jesus by banishment here.

In the 2nd century, Irenaeus said that the work was written in Domitian's reign (AD 81–96), though some scholars place it near the end of the reign of Nero (d.AD 68) or Vespasian (AD 69–79). Justin (AD c.100–165) attributes it to the author of the Fourth Gospel; many have rejected this on grounds of style, and because an apostle would hardly be called 'John the Divine'

[= Theologian].

Others think it was the apostle, and that after the emperor's death, he returned to Ephesus, where he died.

The Monastery of St John of Patmos was built in the 11th century to commemorate his exile.

'The number of the Beast . . . is 666'

This riddle from the Revelation has exercised and taxed the human imagination over the centuries. Revelation identifies the Beast quite clearly as a loathsome 'human being'.

In both Greek and Hebrew the letters of the alphabet did double duty as numerals. The number of Jesus is 888 in Greek (I = 10, H = 8, S = 200, O = 70, Y = 400, S = 200). 666 parodies this. Probably the best solution is that it conceals 'Neron Kaisar' (the emperor Nero) transliterated into Hebrew: this does not tell us whether it refers to Nero or to Domitian (who was called 'a bald Nero'). This would fit one of the book's major themes – Rome and its emperors. Babylon symbolises Rome, and the first monster (13:1) has seven heads which symbolise the Roman emperors, though there are difficulties in identifying which.

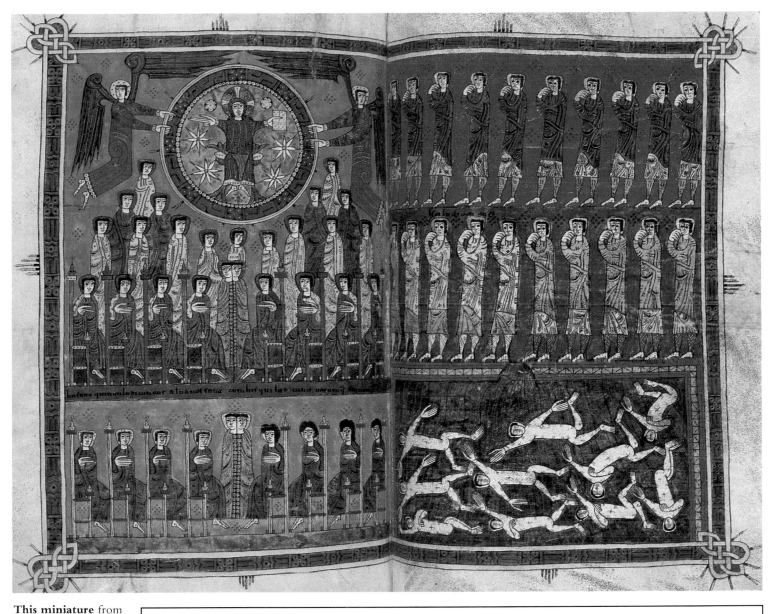

This miniature from the 12th-century Silos Apocalypse manuscript in the British Library shows, *top left*, Christ enthroned in majesty and surrounded by stars in a mandala, flanked by two angels. The figures below him are probably the 24 elders, while those seated in the bottom panel represent the already blessed.

The figures on the right-hand page have come to judgement. Those in the top two panels are in attitudes of adoration; below are the damned, probably in the burning sea of sulphur (Revelation 21:8).

Dreams, visions and symbols

The Book of Revelation takes its readers into a world of visions, dreams and prophecies, where an understanding of hidden realities is communicated from the invisible world to that of the living. This often takes place when the subject is not in the ordinary state of consciousness, that is, in sleep, in torpor or in ecstasy. In most cultures of the past, and in many societies today, it is accepted that there is interaction between the two worlds, and that influences of all kinds can be exerted on the visible world by the higher powers, spirits and divinities of the invisible.

Some readers of St John's Revelation find it obscure today because, unlike the original readers, they do not possess the 'key' needed to interpret the symbols and figures used in apocalyptic literature. Symbols are a language of images and, like the words we use in speech, they are 'conventional' – that is, their meaning depends on a common understanding. Some are shared fairly widely because there is a clear similarity between the symbol and what it brings to mind, such as the lion evoking majesty and strength. But others are in secret language, meaningful only to an initiated circle.

The symbolic language of Revelation comes mostly from the Old Testament and recalls events and figures significant in Jewish history and familiar to Christians. Although modern readers cannot break this code completely, the general meaning can still be recaptured by reference to sayings in the Bible. For example, the Lamb is Jesus and the Bride is the Church; the 'Woman' evokes Eve, the people of Israel and the community of Christian believers, while Babylon signifies Rome, the most hostile of earthly powers. The Dragon or Serpent is Satan, who used the powers of the earth (Beasts) to persecute the faithful. Numbers and colours are also common symbols. For example, 7 means complete, 6 (or $7-1$) signifies incompleteness. The meaning of these symbols is conveyed not as a logical discourse or in a way that makes sense visually, but more like music, which communicates meaning to those who are sensitive to its message.

The early growth of the Church

Jesus left behind him a community of men and women brought up on the Jewish faith, some Jews and some Greeks or other proselytes. The first Jerusalem Christians held their possessions in common, worshipped regularly in the Temple, and met in private houses for prayers and 'the breaking of bread', probably a common meal, incorporating the Eucharist (Acts 2:42–7; 4:32–5). They cared for those in need and, while it is wrong to deny or underestimate the tensions and conflicts between them (Acts 5:1–11; 6:1), there was a remarkable fellowship. These early Christians continued to preach and heal; they record the power of the Holy Spirit upon them.

As the years passed, changes were bound to come. The expectation of the imminent return of Jesus in glory receded, though always remaining a hope. Gentiles were admitted to the Church without having to submit to circumcision or Jewish food laws. Periodically, Jews opposed the new movement, sometimes violently; Nero set a precedent for Roman persecution of Christians. Both were aggravated by Christian pacifism, which was regarded as treacherous to Jewish liberation movements and Roman patriotism alike. The relative informality of a house-church was no longer appropriate to a worldwide movement. There was anxiety about divergence of belief.

Christianity spread rapidly in Syria, Asia Minor and Greece. By the time Paul wrote to Rome, there was a Christian community of some size there, as well as round the Bay of Naples. Paul may himself have taken the Gospel to Spain, his disciple Crescens perhaps to Gaul (2 Timothy 4:10). Certainly, by the second century, there was a healthy community in the Rhône valley. In Britain nothing of early Christianity is known beyond legends and vague statements. There were, however, three British bishops at Arles in 314. By the second century, the Church was strong in North Africa, where the Bible was first translated into Latin, and in Egypt in Alexandria. There is some suggestion of early outreach into Black Africa, Edessa the capital of Osrhoene, and even India (through Thomas).

The original apostles were missionary leaders; alongside them were prophets and others endowed with spiritual gifts, accredited teachers, and administrators. Preaching was done outside the churches, teaching inside. Already in the New Testament there is a distinction between 'bishop' (superintendent) or 'presbyter' (elder) who presided over a local Church or group of Churches, and deacon (administrator). The one office was not a stepping-stone to the other. In the New Testament, women presided over certain local Churches (Colossians 4:15) and held administrative office (Romans 16:1). As the Church spread, the bishop of Rome naturally acquired prestige, but he was not the only 'pope' (from *papa* 'father'), and the exclusive claims of Rome are clear only from the sixth century.

A second-century document, the *Didache* ('teaching'), tells of Church life: baptism, fasts on Wednesdays and Fridays, the Eucharist and appropriate prayers, the Lord's Prayer (three times each day). The Roman Pliny recorded that the Christians met on a set day before daybreak, sang a hymn antiphonally to Christ as God, and took an oath of upright behaviour, dispersing and meeting again in the evening for a common meal.

Two things fostered the growth of Christianity – quality of life and quality of death. The bearing of the martyrs ('witnesses') was such that the early Christian theologian Tertullian (*c*.160–*c*.230) said, 'The blood of Christians is seed'.

The persecution of early Christians in Rome was one factor in their adopting allusive symbols – doves, fish, ships and marine anchors – on their seal-stones and on walls. These peaceful images had meaning for Christians but were not incriminating, even in times of intense persecution.

The mosaic, *top left*, was found under one of the arches of the baptistery of Albenga, Italy. The three concentric circles probably signify the triple immersion in the name of the Father, the Son and the Holy Spirit.

The carving, *below left*, is on a wall of the Basilica of St John at Ephesus, built by the emperor Justinian. This early Christian symbol was based on the ancient forms of cross and circle and is similar in design to that of early rose windows. The sun, symbolised by circle, wheel or swastika, was an object of reverence in antiquity, and the Christians adapted it to the 'sun of righteousness'.

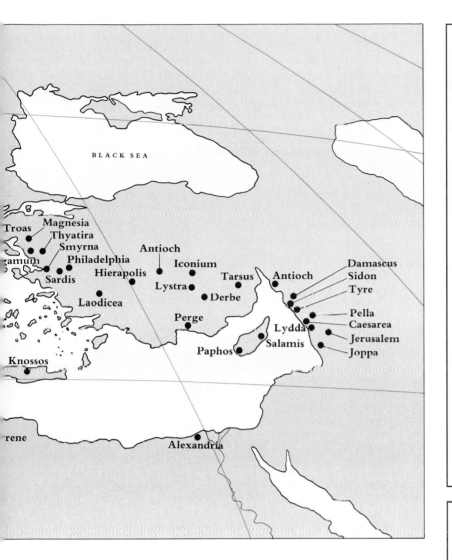

The first monks

Asceticism, including celibacy, is a spiritual discipline in many religions. The Christian Eusebius saw the Essenes (see pp. 186–187) as forerunners of the monks.

Monk (Greek *monos*) means one who lives alone. In about 285, St Anthony of Egypt retired to an ascetic life in the desert. Others followed. A Syrian hermit named Simeon started a movement of 'stylites', each living, solitary and exposed, on top of a pillar.

In general, the Christians, under the influence of Pachomius and Basil in the east, and Martin, John Cassian and, later, Benedict in the west, followed the cenobitic or communal life, disciplined and austere, in work and prayer. Monasteries, such as that at Inishmurray, Eire, *above*, were usually in isolated places.

The Christian heretics

The word 'heresy' means choice. It was used of a school of philosophy and came to be applied to those who set up their own 'choice' or opinion against that of the wider Church. To some extent, orthodox Christian doctrine was reached by rebutting heresies. Many, but not all, the heresies had to do with the nature and person of Jesus Christ. The beliefs of the more important of the heretical groups are as follows:

Apollinarians held that Jesus had a human body and soul but that instead of a human spirit he had the divine Word. *Arians*, named after Arius, a fourth-century Libyan-born theologian, believed that the Son of God was created, not eternal, and that therefore Jesus Christ was not fully divine. *Docetists* held that the Word (John 1:1) only *seemed* to become flesh, and that Jesus only *seemed* to suffer. *Ebionites* were Jewish–Christian ascetics, adhering to the Law of Moses, and holding that Jesus was humanly born, and *Encratites* carried asceticism to extremes.

The *Gnostics* (Greek *gnōsis* means 'knowledge') held that salvation comes through knowledge of God and of the origin and destiny of humankind revealed only to those 'in the know', often with a complex belief-system. *Monarchians* safeguarded the authority and unity of God the Father by subordinating the Son, and *Patripassians* were Monarchians who held that God the Father suffered on the cross. *Montanists* opposed institutionalism and believed in direct possession by the Spirit and ecstatic prophecy, combined with stern moral discipline. *Pelagians* were also stern moralists. They held that individuals were responsible for their own sins and that they must themselves take the initiative in responding to the work of God in Christ.

By the end of the first century, Christianity had begun to spread widely through the Mediterranean basin. The map, *above*, shows the locations of Christian Churches at this time. Paul was the main but not the sole agent. The names of the Churches he founded are known, as are the Seven Churches of the Revelation and a few others from the New Testament – for example, Hierapolis (Colossians 4:13) and Puteoli (Acts 28:13). It is curious that there is no indication of a Church in the great cosmopolitan city of Miletus.

Sometimes there is written evidence of Churches. Ignatius tells of Churches in Magnesia and Tralles; Eusebius in Alexandria and elsewhere. The pagan Pliny records Christians in Bithynia and Pontus, perhaps in Sinope among other places.

Archaeological evidence points to there having been a Church at Pompeii, but at Herculaneum a cross in plaster is more probably a bracket mark.

Later it was normal for Churches to claim apostolic or early foundation. Such claims must generally be discounted. It is not likely that Joseph of Arimathaea went to Glastonbury, in England, but there is a strong tradition that Thomas took the Gospel to India.

Bibliography

This list includes books which the publishers and the authors have consulted in the preparation of *Great Events of Bible Times* and also some suggestions for further reading.

Achtemeier, Paul J. (Ed) *Harper's Bible Dictionary* Harper & Row, New York, 1985

Aharoni, Yohanan *The Land of the Bible, 2nd rev ed* Burns & Oates, London, UK; Westminster Press, Philadelphia, USA, 1979

Albright, William F. *The Archaeology of Palestine* Penguin Books, Harmondsworth, UK, 1949; Fleming H. Revell, New Jersey, USA, 1932

Anderson, Bernard W. *The Living World of the Old Testament, 3rd ed* Longman, London, 1978

Anderson, Hugh *The Gospel of Mark–New Century Bible* Marshall, Morgan & Scott, Basingstoke, UK, 1976

Baines, John and Málek, Jaromír *Atlas of Ancient Egypt* Phaidon, Oxford, UK, 1980

Bainton, Roland H. *The Horizon History of Christianity* American Heritage/Harper & Row, New York, 1964

Bammel, E. and Moule, C.F.D. *Jesus and the Politics of his Day* Cambridge University Press, Cambridge, UK, 1984

Bierbrier, Morris *The Tomb-Builders of the Pharaohs* British Museum, London, 1982

Boardman, John *Greek Art* Thames & Hudson, London, 1964

Bouquet, A.C. *Everyday Life in New Testament Times* Batsford, London, 1953

Brandon, Samuel G.F. *Religion in Ancient History* Allen & Unwin, London, UK, 1973; Charles Scribner, New York, USA, 1969

Bright, John *A History of Israel* SCM Press, London, UK, 1984; Warminster Press, Philadelphia, USA, 1972

Bruce, Frederick F. *New Testament History* Thomas Nelson, London, 1969; Doubleday, New York, 1971

Bruce, Frederick F. *Paul, Apostle of the Free Spirit* Paternoster, Exeter, UK, 1977

Cadbury, Henry J. *The Book of Acts in History* Adam & Charles Black, London, UK; Harper & Row, New York, USA, 1955

The Cambridge Ancient History (Vols I–III) Cambridge University Press, Cambridge, UK, 1971

Clayton, Peter A. *The Rediscovery of Ancient Egypt* Thames & Hudson, London, 1982

Comay, Joan *Who's Who in the Old Testament* Weidenfeld & Nicolson, London, UK; Holt, Rinehart & Winston, New York, USA, 1971

Contenau, Georges *Everyday Life in Babylon and Assyria* Edward Arnold, London, 1954

Cook, John M. *The Persian Empire* J.M. Dent & Son, London, 1983

Cook, Stanley A. *The Religion of Ancient Palestine in the Light of Archaeology* Oxford University Press, London, 1930

Cornell, Tim and Matthews, John *Atlas of the Roman World* Phaidon, Oxford, UK, 1982

Cornfeld, Gaalyah *Archaeology of the Bible; Book by Book* Harper & Row, New York, 1976

Corswant, W. *A Dictionary of Life in Bible Times* Hodder & Stoughton, UK, 1960

Cotterell, Arthur *The Encyclopedia of Ancient Civilizations* Windward, Leicester, UK; Mayflower, New York, 1980

Daiches, David *Moses, Man in the Wilderness* Weidenfeld & Nicolson, London, UK; Praeger, New York, USA, 1975

David, A. Rosalie *The Egyptian Kingdoms* Elsevier/Phaidon, Oxford, UK; E.P. Dutton, New York, USA, 1975

Davies, N. de G. *The Tomb of Rekhmire at Thebes* M.M.A.E.E., New York, 1943

Demus, Otto *Byzantine Mosaic Decoration* Routledge & Kegan Paul, London, 1953

de Vaux, Roland *Ancient Israel, Its Life and Institutions* Darton, Longman & Todd, London, UK; McGraw Hill, New York, USA, 1961

Dicks, Brian T.R. *The Ancient Persians* David & Charles, London, 1979

Dodd, C.H. *The Founder of Christianity* Collins, London, 1971

Dothan, Trude *The Philistines and their Material Culture* Yale University Press, New Haven and London, 1982

Doty, William G. *Letters in Primitive Christianity* Fortress Press, Philadelphia, 1973

Ferguson, J. *The Heritage of Hellenism* Thames & Hudson, London, 1973

Finegan, Jack *The Archeology of the New Testament: The Life of Jesus and the Beginning of the Early Church* Princeton University Press, New Jersey, 1969

Finegan, Jack *The Archeology of the New Testament: The Mediterranean World of the Early Christian Apostles* Westview Press, Colorado, 1981

Fox, Robin Lane *The Search for Alexander* Allen Lane, London, UK; Little Brown & Co, Maryland, USA, 1980

Frank, Harry T. *An Archaeological Companion to the Bible* SCM Press, London, 1972

Frankfort, Henri *The Art and Architecture of the Ancient Orient* Penguin Books, London, 1970

Freed, Rita E. *Egypt's Golden Age: The Art of Living in the New Kingdom 1558–1085 BC* Museum of Fine Arts, Boston

Gardner, Joseph L. (Ed) *Atlas of the Bible* Reader's Digest, UK and USA, 1983

Gordon, C. *The World of the Old Testament* Doubleday, New York, 1953

Gottwald, Norman K. *The Bible and Liberation* Orbis, New York, 1983

Gough, Michael *The Early Christians* Thames & Hudson, London, UK; Praeger, New York, USA, 1961

Grabar, André *Christian Iconography A Study of Its Origins* Routledge & Kegan Paul, London, 1969

Gray, John *The Canaanites* Thames & Hudson, London, 1964

Great People and How They Lived Reader's Digest, USA and UK, 1974

Grollenberg, L.H. *Atlas of the Bible* Thomas Nelson, London and New York, 1956

Hawkes, Jacquetta *Atlas of Ancient Archaeology* Heinemann, London, 1974

Hayes, John H. and Miller, J. Maxwell (Eds) *Israelite and Judaean History* SCM Press, London, 1977

Heaton, E.W. *Everyday Life in Old Testament Times* Batsford, London, UK; Charles Scribner, New York, USA, 1956

Hengel, Martin *Crucifixion* SCM Press, London, 1977

Hengel, Martin *Jews, Greeks and Barbarians* SCM Press, London, UK; Fortress Press, Philadelphia, USA, 1980

Hengel, Martin *Judaism and Hellenism (2 Vols)* Fortress Press, Philadelphia, 1974

Hengel, Martin *Poverty and Riches in the Early Church* SCM Press, London, 1974

Herodotus, The Histories Penguin Classics, Harmondsworth, UK, 1954

Herzog, Chaim and Gichon, Mordechai *Battles of the Bible* Weidenfeld & Nicolson, London, UK; Random House, New York, USA, 1978

Hicks, Jim *The Persians* Time Life International, Netherlands, 1975

Hock, Ronald *The Social Context of Paul's Ministry* Fortress Press, Philadelphia 1980

Hodges, Henry *Technology in the Ancient World* Allen Lane, London, 1970

Holmberg, Bengt *Paul and Power* Fortress Press, Philadelphia, 1978

Holroyd, Stuart *Mysteries of the Gods* Aldus, London, 1979

Hultgren, Arland J. *Paul's Gospel and Mission* Fortress Press, Philadelphia, 1985

Illustrated Bible Dictionary (Parts 1–3) Inter-Varsity Press, Leicester, UK; Tyndale House, Illinois, USA, 1980

Jacq, C. *Egyptian Magic* Aris & Phillips, Warminster, UK, 1985

James, T.G.H. *An Introduction to Ancient Egypt* British Museum, London, 1979

James, T.G.H. *Pharaoh's People* Bodley Head, London 1984

Jenkins, Nancy *The Boat Beneath the Pyramid* Thames & Hudson, London, 1980

Johnson, Paul *Civilizations of the Holy Land* Weidenfeld & Nicolson, London, 1979

Jones, A.H.M. *The Herods of Judaea* Clarendon Press, Oxford, UK, 1938

Josephus *The Jewish War, rev ed* Penguin Books, Harmondsworth UK; Viking Penguin, New York, USA, 1981

Judge, Edwin A. *The Social Patterns of Christians in the First Century* Tyndale House, Illinois, 1960

Käsemann, Ernst *New Testament Questions of Today* SCM Press, London, UK; Fortress Press, Philadelphia, USA, 1969

Kee, Howard C. and Young, Franklin W. *The Living World of the Old Testament* Darton, Longman & Todd, London, 1960; published in the USA under the title *Understanding the New Testament* Prentice-Hall, New Jersey, 1957

Keel, Othmar *The Symbolism of the Biblical World* SPCK, London, UK; Seabury Press New York, USA, 1978

Kees, H. *Ancient Egypt: A Cultural Topography* University of Chicago Press, Chicago, 1961

Kenyon, Kathleen M. *Archaeology in the Holy Land, 3rd ed* Ernest Benn, London, 1970

Kenyon, Kathleen M. *The Bible and Recent Archaeology* British Museum, London, UK; John Knox Press, Atlanta, USA, 1978

Kenyon, Kathleen M. *Jerusalem (Excavating 3000 Years of History)* Thames & Hudson, London, 1967

Kenyon, Kathleen M. *Royal Cities of the Old Testament* Barrie & Jenkins, London, UK; Schocken Books, New York, USA, 1971

King, Leonard W. *A History of Babylon* Chatto & Windus, London, 1915

Kitchen, K.A. *Pharaoh Triumphant, The Life and Times of Ramesses II, King of Egypt* Aris & Phillips, Warminster, UK, 1982

Koester, Helmut *Introduction to the New Testament (Vols 1–2)* Fortress Press, Philadelphia, 1982

Kubie, Nora *Road to Nineveh* Cassell, London, 1965

Landay, Jerry M. *The House of David* Weidenfeld & Nicolson, London, 1973

Landay, Jerry M. *Silent Cities, Sacred Stones* Weidenfeld & Nicolson, London, 1971

Levi, Peter *Atlas of the Greek World* Phaidon, Oxford, UK, 1980

Lichtheim, M. *Ancient Egyptian Literature (3 Vols)* University of California Press, Los Angeles, 1975

L'Orange, H.P. and Nordhagen, P.J. *Mosaics* Methuen, London, 1966

Lucas, Alfred and Harris, J.R. (Ed) *Ancient Egyptian Materials and Industries, 4th ed* Arnold, London, 1962

Magnusson, Magnus *BC The Archaeology of the Bible Lands* Bodley Head, London, 1977

Malherbe, Abraham J. *Social Aspects of Early Christianity* Fortress Press, Philadelphia, 1983

Mallowan, Max E.L. *Nimrud and its Remains (Vol. II)* Collins, London, 1966

Martin, E.L. *The Birth of Christ Recalculated* Foundation for Biblical Research, Pasadena, USA and Newcastle upon Tyne, UK, 1978

May, Herbert G. (Ed) *Oxford Bible Atlas* Oxford University Press, London and New York, 1974

Meeks, Wayne A. *The First Urban Christians* Yale University Press, New Haven and London, 1983

Millard, Alan R. *Treasures from Bible Times* Lion Publishing, Herts., UK, Michigan, USA, 1985

Montefiore, Hugh *Jesus Across the Centuries* SCM Press, London, 1983

Moorey, P.R.S. *Biblical Lands* Elsevier/Phaidon, London, 1975

Muggeridge, Malcolm and Vidler, Alec *Paul: Envoy Extraordinary* Collins, London, UK; Harper & Row, New York, USA, 1972

Munck, Johannes *Paul and the Salvation of Mankind* SCM Press, London, UK; John Knox Press, Richmond, USA, 1959

Naville, Edouard *The Stone-City of Pithom and the Route of Exodus* London, 1903

Negev, Avraham (Ed) *The Archaeological Encyclopedia of the Holy Land* Thomas Nelson, London, UK; 1986; SBS, New Jersey, USA, 1980

Oates, Joan *Babylon* Thames & Hudson, London, 1979

Parrot, André *Nineveh and Babylon* Thames & Hudson, London, 1961

Pearlman, Moshe *Digging up the Bible* Weidenfeld & Nicolson, London, UK; Morrow, New York, USA, 1980

Petersen, Norman R. *Rediscovering Paul* Fortress Press, Philadelphia, 1985

Porter, B. *Archives from Elephantine* University of California Press, Berkeley and Los Angeles, 1968

Pritchard, James B. (Ed) *The Ancient Near East, A New Anthology of Texts and Pictures (2 Vols)* Princeton University Press, New Jersey, 1975

Raphael, Chaim *A Feast of History* Weidenfeld & Nicolson, London, 1972

Rice, D. Talbot *The Beginnings of Christian Art* Hodder & Stoughton, London, 1957

Rivkin, Ellis *What Crucified Jesus?* SCM Press, London, 1984

Roetzel, Calvin *The World that Shaped the New Testament* John Knox Press, Atlanta, 1985

Rogerson, John *New Atlas of the Bible* Macdonald, London, UK; Facts on File, New York, USA, 1985

Rops, H.D. *Daily Life in the Time of Jesus* Mentor Books, New York, 1964

Rothenberg, Beno *Timna* Thames & Hudson, London, 1972

Rowland, Christopher *Christian Origins* SPCK, London, 1985

Sanders, Ed Parish *Jesus and Judaism* SCM Press, London, UK; Fortress Press, Philadelphia, USA, 1985

Sanders, Ed Parish *Paul and Palestinian Judaism* SCM Press, London, UK; Fortress Press, Philadelphia, USA, 1977

Shanks, Hershel *Judaism in Stone* Harper & Row, New York and London, 1979

Sherwin-White, Adrian N. *Roman Society and Roman Law in the New Testament* Oxford University Press, Oxford, UK, 1963

Smith, W. Stevenson *The Art and Architecture of Ancient Egypt* Penguin, Harmondsworth, UK, 1958

Soggin, James A. *A History of Israel* SCM Press, London, 1985

Stevenson, Kenneth E. and Habermas, Gary R. *Verdict on the Shroud* Robert Hale, London, UK, 1982; Servant, Michigan, USA, 1981

Theissen, Gerd *The First Followers of Jesus* SCM Press, London, 1978

Theissen, Gerd *The Social Setting of Pauline Christianity* Fortress Press, Philadelphia, 1982

Trigger, B.G., Kemp, B.J., O'Connor, D., Lloyd, A.B. *Ancient Egypt: A Social History* Cambridge University Press, Cambridge, UK, 1983

Vermes, Géza *The Dead Sea Scrolls, 2nd ed* Penguin, London, UK, 1975; Macmillan, New York, USA, 1974

Vermes, Géza *Jesus the Jew* SCM Press, London, 1975

Walbank, Frank W. *The Hellenistic World* Fontana, London, 1981

Waterfield, Gordon *Layard of Nineveh* John Murray, London, 1963

Wilkinson, John *Jerusalem as Jesus knew it* Thames & Hudson, London, 1982

Wilson, Ian *Jesus The Evidence* Weidenfeld & Nicolson, London, UK; Harper & Row, New York, USA, 1984

Wilson, Ian *The Mysterious Shroud* Doubleday, New York, 1986

Wiseman, Donald J. (Ed) *Peoples of Old Testament Times* Clarendon/ Oxford University Press, UK, 1973

World History of the Jewish People (Vols 1–7) Jewish History Publications, Israel, 1979

Yadin, Yigael *The Art of Warfare in Biblical Lands: In the Light of Archaeological Study* Weidenfeld & Nicolson, London, UK; McGraw-Hill, New York, USA, 1963

Yadin, Yigael *Hazor: The Rediscovery of a Great Citadel of the Bible* Weidenfeld & Nicolson, London, UK; Random House, New York, USA, 1975

Yadin, Yigael *Masada: Herod's Fortress and the Zealot's Last Stand* Weidenfeld & Nicolson, London, UK; Random House, New York, USA, 1966

Zohary, Michael *Plants of the Bible* Cambridge University Press, London and New York, 1982

Index

Ten Commandments **40–1**, 46
Terah, descendants of *27*
Tertullian *153*
tetradrachm coins *121*
Thaddaeus, apostle 141, 165
Thebes 30, 32, 71
Thermopylae 113
Thessalonica 172
Theudas 152
Thomas, apostle 141, 169
Thutmosis III 37
Tiamat 139
Tiberius *157*
Tiglath-Pileser III 98
    palace of *99*
Tigris, River 105, 118
Timna, copper serpent from *92*
Timnah 68
    valley of 32
Timnath-Serah 47
Timothy 172–3
Tirzah 43
titulus 163
Titus 157, 180, 182
Tjekker 67
Tobiads 122
toph 90
torah 8, 40, 116
Torrent of Kishon 62
Tower of Babel **16–17**
Transfiguration 141
Transjordan 25, 27
    climate of 10
    iron mines in 10
    Moses and 60
translations of Bible *8*
tribute money **156–7**
Triparadeisus 121
Troas 172, 176
Trojan War *23*
Trophimus 154
Tubal-Cain 12
Turin shroud *165*
Tushratta 28
Twenty-second Dynasty
    (Egypt) 94
Tychicus 173
Tyrannus, hall of 176
Tyre 87, 92, 140
    Alexander and 118

U

Ugarit 50
    buildings and excavations of
    51
Ur *14*, 16, 20
Urartu *102*
Ur-nammu 16, 42
Uruk *19*
Utnaphishtim 14

V

Valley of Hyenas 75
Valley of Kings 30
Valley of Mizpeh 59
Valley of Rephaim 84

Valley of Siddim 24
Vashti 112
Veronica 161
Vespasian 131, 143, 157, 180,
    182, *183*, 188
Via Maris 10, 95, 135
virgin-birth 132
Vitellius 180, 182

W

Wadi Arabah 127
Wadi Hammamat 38
Wadi Meghara 38
Wadi Suweinit 75–6
Warren, C. 74
Warren's Shaft *83*
Washukanni 18
Way of the Cross *161*
Way of the Philistines 36
Whit Sunday (Pentecost) *167*
wilderness, life in the **38–9**
Wilson, Ian 165
Woolley, Sir Leonard 14
women
    Jesus and 150
    marriage of 151
    religious teaching of 150
    role of in New Testament
        151
writing
    cuneiform *19, 23, 117*
    development of *19*
    equipment for *171*
    letters to the Churches
        174–5
    tablets for *19*

X

Xerxes I 112–4

Y

Yadin, Professor Yigael 184
Ya'osh *107*
Yemen 92

Z

Zadokites 186
Zagros mountains 115
Zalmonah 47
Zealot Party 156, 180, 184
Zebedee 140
Zeboum 24
Zebulun, tribe of 61, 64, 80
Zedekiah 73, 106
Zeus 115, 122, *123*
Zeus Ammon 119
ziggurats *16–17*
Ziklag 80–1, 84
Zion 107
Zoar 24
Zobah 84
Zorah 68
Zoroaster 115

Acknowledgements

The publishers and authors would like to thank the following people and organisations from whom they received invaluable help:

Alison Abel
Dr Leonie Archer
Dr John Bimson
Dr Rupert Chapman, Executive Secretary of the Palestine Exploration Fund
Egypt Exploration Society
Dr Martin Goodman
Heythrop College, London
Institute of Archaeology
David Rohl
Zilda Tandy

Additional artwork by
David Parker, Chris Forsey, Dennis Curram
John Hutchinson, Roy Flooks,
Angus McBride, Hayward and Martin

Computer maps by Creative Data Ltd

Index by Donald Binney

Picture Credits

l = left; *r* = right; *t* = top; *c* = centre; *b* = bottom

2 William Macquitty; 9 Bodleian Library, Oxford; 11 Popperfoto; 13 British Library; 14 British Museum; 15 Gascoigne/Robert Harding Picture Library; 19 British Museum; 20/21 Daily Telegraph Colour Library; 22 Picturepoint; 22/23 The Mansell Collection; 25 *t* Richard Nowitz, Black Star/Colorific; 25 *b* Peter Carmichael/Aspect Picture Library; 26 Picturepoint; 27 Erich Lessing, Magnum/John Hillelson Agency; 29 British Museum; 30 British Museum; 31 *b* Committee of the Egypt Exploration Society; 33 Roger Wood; 35 British Museum; 36/37 NASA/Bruce Coleman; 38/39 Committee of the Egypt Exploration Society; 39/40 David Harris/Zefa; 41 British Library; 43 *t* Michael Holford/British Museum; 43 *b* Biblical Archaeological Review; 46–47 Earth Satellite Corporation/Science Photo Library; 49 Daily Telegraph Colour Library; 52 Alistair Duncan/Palestine Archaeological Museum; 58 *t* Sonia Halliday & Laura Lushington; 58 *b* David Harris/Zefa; 70 Britain/Israel Public Affairs Committee; 72–73 Picturepoint; 73 Michael Holford; 79 *t* Michael Holford/British Museum; 79 *b* British Museum; 85 Bodleian Library, Oxford; 87 British Museum; 89 William Macquitty; 90 British Museum; 91 Oriental Institute, University of Chicago; 92 *t* British Library; 92 *b* Britain/Israel Public Affairs Committee; 93 BPCC/Aldus Archive; 95 Robert Harding Picture Library; 96 British Museum; 96–97 Reprinted by permission of Princeton University Press; 97/99 British Museum; 102–103 The Mansell Collection; 104 British Museum; 105 Bodleian Library, Oxford; 107 *t* British Library; 107 *b* British Museum; 110 British Museum; 111 Ed Mullis/Aspect Picture Library; 112/113 Ronald Sheridan; 114/115 Roger Wood; 117 *t* British Museum; 117 *b* Ashmolean Museum, Oxford; 119 *t* The Mansell Collection; 119 *b* British Museum; 120 C.M. Dixon; 120–121 C.M. Dixon; 121 British Museum; 122 Courtesy of Teheran Archaeological Museum & Malcolm College; 123 *t* BPCC/Aldus Archive/British Museum; 123 *b* Ashmolean Museum, Oxford; 126 The Mansell Collection; 127 Joan Wickes/Topham Picture Library; 129 Board of Trinity College, Dublin; 132 The Mansell Collection; 133 Sonia Halliday Photographs; 134 Sonia Halliday Photographs; 134/135 The Mansell Collection; 135 Britain/Israel Public Affairs Committee; 137 Sonia Halliday Photographs; 138 Robert Harding Picture Library; 138/139 Sonia Halliday Photographs; 139 Bridgeman Art Library; 140/141 Fred Mayer, Magnum/John Hillelson Agency; 142 The Mansell Collection; 143 *l* British Museum; 143 *r* Scala; 144 Ronald Sheridan; 145 *l* Sonia Halliday & Laura Lushington; 145 *r* British Museum; 147 *t* The Mansell Collection; 147 *b* From the archives of the Palestine Exploration Fund; 148 *t* Sonia Halliday Photographs; 148 *b* Sonia Halliday & Laura Lushington; 149 *tl* Sonia Halliday & Laura Lushington; 149 *tr* Sonia Halliday Photographs; 149 *bl* Sonia Halliday Photographs; 149 *br* BPCC/Aldus Archive; 150 Sonia Halliday Photographs; 151 The Mansell Collection; 153 The Fotomas Index; 157 *tl* Werner Forman Archive/British Museum; 157 *tc* Peter Clayton; 157 *tr* Picturepoint; 157 *bl* Sonia Halliday & Laura Lushington; 157 *br* Ronald Sheridan; 158 *t* L'Abbé Denis Grivot; 158 *b* Sonia Halliday Photographs; 159 *t* The Mansell Collection; 159 *b* British Library; 161 Aspect Picture Library; 163 The Mansell Collection; 164 Sonia Halliday Photographs; 164–165 Scala; 165 *t* The Mansell Collection; 165 *b* Sonia Halliday Photographs; 167 *l* British Library; 167 *r* Picturepoint; 168 Ronald Sheridan; 169 Sonia Halliday Photographs; 170 Phaidon Press Ltd; 171 *l* British Museum; 171 *r* William Macquitty; 172/173 George Philip & Son Ltd; 174 Anthony Bannister/NHPA; 176 Ronald Sheridan; 177 Pierre Putelat/Agence Top; 178/179 The Mansell Collection; 182–183 *t* The Mansell Collection; 183 *t* By courtesy of Lauros-Girandon Paris/Bridgeman Art Library; 183 *bl* Peter Clayton; 183 *br* The Mansell Collection; 186/187 *b* BPCC/Aldus Archive; 187 Milner, Sygma/John Hillelson Agency; 188 Pierre Putelat/Agence Top; 189 British Library; 191 Clive Hicks.